A Nazi Camp near Danzig

A Nazi Camp near Danzig

Perspectives on Shame and on the Holocaust from Stutthof

Ruth Schwertfeger

BLOOMSBURY ACADEMIC
LONDON · NEW YORK · OXFORD · NEW DELHI · SYDNEY

BLOOMSBURY ACADEMIC
Bloomsbury Publishing Plc
50 Bedford Square, London, WC1B 3DP, UK
1385 Broadway, New York, NY 10018, USA
29 Earlsfort Terrace, Dublin 2, Ireland

BLOOMSBURY, BLOOMSBURY ACADEMIC and the Diana logo
are trademarks of Bloomsbury Publishing Plc

First published in Great Britain 2022
Paperback first published 2023

Copyright © Ruth Schwertfeger, 2022

Ruth Schwertfeger has asserted their right under the Copyright, Designs
and Patents Act, 1988, to be identified as Author of this work.

Cover image: Stutthof guard tower behind locked gates and barbed wire fences,
shrouded in mist. (©Wieslaw Leszczynski/Stutthof Museum)

All rights reserved. No part of this publication may be reproduced or
transmitted in any form or by any means, electronic or mechanical, including
photocopying, recording, or any information storage or retrieval system,
without prior permission in writing from the publishers.

Bloomsbury Publishing Plc does not have any control over, or responsibility for,
any third-party websites referred to or in this book. All internet addresses given
in this book were correct at the time of going to press. The author and publisher
regret any inconvenience caused if addresses have changed or sites have
ceased to exist, but can accept no responsibility for any such changes.

Every effort has been made to trace the copyright holders and obtain permission
to reproduce the copyright material. Please do get in touch with any enquiries
or any information relating to such material or the rights holder. We would be
pleased to rectify any omissions in subsequent editions of this publication
should they be drawn to our attention.

A catalogue record for this book is available from the British Library.

Library of Congress Cataloging-in-Publication Data
Names: Schwertfeger, Ruth, author.
Title: A Nazi camp near Danzig : perspectives on shame and
on the Holocaust from Stutthof / Ruth Schwertfeger.
Other titles: Perspectives on shame and on the Holocaust from Stutthof
Description: London ; New York : Bloomsbury Academic, 2022. |
Includes bibliographical references and index.
Identifiers: LCCN 2021036366 (print) | LCCN 2021036367 (ebook) | ISBN 9781350274037
(hardback) | ISBN 9781350274051 (pdf) | ISBN 9781350274068 (ebook)
Subjects: LCSH: Stutthof (Concentration camp)–History. | Nazi concentration
camps–Poland–History. | Holocaust, Jewish (1939-1945)–Poland. | World War,
1939-1945–Prisoners and prisons, German. | World War, 1939-1945–Poland–Gdańsk. |
Gdańsk (Poland)–History–20th century. | Pomerelia (Poland)–History–20th century.
Classification: LCC D805.5.S78 S39 2022 (print) |
LCC D805.5.S78 (ebook) | DDC 940.53/1853822–dc23
LC record available at https://lccn.loc.gov/2021036366
LC ebook record available at https://lccn.loc.gov/2021036367

ISBN:	HB:	978-1-3502-7403-7
	PB:	978-1-3502-7404-4
	ePDF:	978-1-3502-7405-1
	eBook:	978-1-3502-7406-8

Typeset by Integra Software Services Pvt. Ltd.

To find out more about our authors and books visit www.bloomsbury.com
and sign up for our newsletters.

This book is lovingly dedicated to Alexandra Schwertfeger Solanki and Caroline Hambly Schwertfeger, the mothers of my grandchildren. May they pass on to these children the history of Stutthof, and especially the memory of Stutthof's mothers and children, in the spirit of Ecclesiastes 3: 15(b): "And God requires an account of what is past." (NIV)

Contents

List of Figures	viii
Acknowledgments	ix
Abbreviations and Key Terms	xi
Introduction	1
1 Promoting German-Consciousness in a Revamped Gau, 1930–9	13
2 Danzig-West Prussia and Stutthof: Implementing Germandom, September 1939–January 1942	47
3 Gaining the Next Tier of Germandom as a Nazi *Konzentrationslager*	79
4 Entering the "Final Solution," the Summer of 1944	109
5 The Collapse of Germandom—The Winter of 1945	143
Epilogue	171
Notes	183
Sources	210
Bibliography	213
Appendix	223
Index	252

Figures

1	A Grave and Its Gravestone Bear Witness	169
2	Tombstone at Będomin	170
3	Prisoner Data Collection Card	223
4	Prisoner list, with reasons for internment	223
5	Additional prisoner list	224
6	Registration with missing dates of death	224
7	Death Registry page for Jan Lesiński	225
8	List of Crimes for internment, including "stealing peas"	226
9	Death Registry entry for Alfons Mańkowski	227
10	Assignments for work duties	228
11	List of Names, Ranks, and Religious Affiliation of SS Guards with Danzig Connections	229
12	List of Guards with Danzig Connections	242
13	Local Guards who had served in the Regular German Army including service in the First World War	246
14	Sample Personnel Card	248
15	Map of Occupied Poland, including Danzig-West Prussia	249
16	Map of the Stutthof Camp, 1944	250
17	Map of Stutthof Subcamps	250
18	Evacuation routes from the camp, 1945	251

Acknowledgments

I first visited Stutthof eight years ago, accompanied by a local Methodist minister who, when he heard about my research on German Jewish literature, knew that the museum and archives of Stutthof would be of great interest to me. I left Stutthof that day with copies of documents mostly in German that became foundational to the research that I pursued during the years that followed. First of all, I want to acknowledge my gratitude to Piotr Tarnoski, the Director of the Stutthof Museum, for extending permission and the privileges of access to the archives from the start of this research project. The Head Archivist, Dr. Danuta Drywa, has given me unfailing support during each phase of the research and writing of the book. I have drawn extensively from her scholarship on Stutthof and her knowledge of Danzig/Gdańsk and surrounding areas. Aleksandra Gluba-Pieprz provided invaluable help as a research assistant in Poland. I want to thank her for her hard work and scholarly interest in the project.

In my home department of Foreign Languages and Literature at the University of Wisconsin-Milwaukee, I would like to thank Professor Michael Mikoś and Dr. Bożena Tieszen for their encouragement and support. Professor Mikoś read several versions of the manuscript and recommended secondary Polish sources. Dr. Tieszen translated all the Polish quotations used in the book into English and also helped me understand their context. Colleagues in the History Department at UW-Milwaukee made themselves available to me and answered my questions. I want to thank Professors Winson Chu and Neal Pease, both of them nationally recognized scholars in Polish History for their patience with someone outside their discipline. My colleagues at the Stahl Center for Jewish Studies could not have been more encouraging. I extend my thanks to Professor Joel Berkowitz, and to Dr. Rachel Baum who was always available to discuss my ideas for including Günter Grass in my project.

In 2019, I was invited to present my research at a workshop in Poland—"Recovering Forgotten History"—which exposed my work to the scrutiny of Polish colleagues engaged in comparable academic research. Three of these colleagues read the full manuscript and offered their commentary before the whole group of authors and press editors. They followed up with detailed written reviews which were extremely helpful and have greatly influenced the final version of the book. I also extend my thanks to Professor Marek Wierzbicki who also read the full manuscript and wrote a detailed commentary with information about Pomerania that enriched my understanding of its history. I would like to thank Richard Ratzlaff for recommending me to be a participant in the workshop. Anonymous readers—historians—on this continent and in the UK have been a vital source of correction, if not always of encouragement. I am grateful for and humbled by their expertise. I have secretly hoped that I get to review their work when they write about literature. I extend my thanks to the archivists at USHMM who were always courteous and patient with my requests for material. The digital age has certainly made research easier and accessible to all the archives that I have used, as far away as the Arolsen Archives, the Mauthausen Archives, and the Yad Vashem. I am grateful for the information and the documents that their archivists sent me.

I am deeply indebted to the contribution of Michael Zore whose technological and research skills have helped at every stage of preparing the manuscript. Others, like Professors Andrew Porter and Professor Emeritus Richard Monti from Classics and Professor Jonathan Wipplinger from German, have been there at crucial junctures when I simply needed to talk about my research plans. Their questions and comments always enriched and challenged my thinking. I am sad that two other people who used to fill that role are no longer with us—Dr. Alfred Bader and Father Michael Fountain. I miss the stimulating conversations.

I owe special gratitude to Rhodri Mogford, my editor at Bloomsbury Press, for his unstinting support for this project and his professional expertise as an editor. It has been a pleasure to work with him.

Family members and close friends have given me moral and spiritual support in the writing of this book and preparing it for publication. I single out for special thanks to my husband Fred who accompanied me on all my research trips and has supported me at every level. The home of my brother, Alex Crawford, in Northern Ireland has always been open to me as a retreat and a quiet place to write. I give special thanks to those who prayed for me, especially when a car accident laid me aside right in the middle of my research. Finally, I want to thank Rabbi Marc Berkson for many years of friendship. Before Marc's wife, Debbie, died she discovered that her mother, Edith Carter, had also survived Stutthof. We knew she had survived both Theresienstadt and Auschwitz but Stutthof? I also knew Debbie's mother and, in fact, dedicated my book on Theresienstadt to her and to the memory of my own mother. Surely it is not too late to acknowledge that my friend, Edith Carter, was also in Stutthof and that she kept her suffering silently to herself for all those years.

Abbreviations and Key Terms

AK
Armia Krajowa

Home Army

Amt D
Branch D
Office D

In 1942, the IKL became known simply as Amt D (Office D) of the consolidated main office of WVHA

Arbeitererziehungslager

A corrective labor camp

Arolsen Archives (ITS) Archives

The Arolsen Archives are an international center on Nazi persecution with the world's most comprehensive archive on the victims and survivors of National Socialism, with information on about 17.5 million people, and is part of UNESCO's Memory of the World

Aufseherin

Female guard

Block

Barrack. Sometimes used to refer to the prisoners in that barrack

Blockälterster

Block or Barrack Elder

Blockführer

The SS man in charge of one barrack or block

Bund Deutscher Mädel (BDM)

The "German Girls League" was the female branch of the Hitler Youth

DAW
Deutsche Ausrüstungswerke

German Equipment Works

DC
Deutsche Christen

German Christians

DESt
Deutsche Erd- und Steinwerke GmbH

German Brick and Tile Works, also known as the German Earth and Stone Works

DPA Deutsche Presse Agentur	German News Agency
die bekennende Kirche	Confessing Church
DVL die deutsche Volksliste	German National Registry or National Identity Registry
die zentrale Stelle der Landesjustizverwaltungen	The Central Office of the State Justice Administrations for the Investigation of National Socialist Crimes, established in 1958
Erziehungslager	A "re-education" camp where prisoners were indoctrinated through labor
Führerprinzip	The principle of absolute obedience to the Führer
Gau Gaue (plural)	Nazi Party administrative region
Gauleiter	Head of party regional administration
GDR	German Democratic Republic
Geheime(s) Staatspolizei. Gestapo, -a	The secret police
Generalgouvernement für die besetzten polnischen Gebiete	General Government
GKBZNwP Polska Główna Komisja Badania Zbrodni Hitlerowskich w Polsce	Central Commission for the Investigation of German Crimes in Poland
Gottgläubig	Belief in God
IKL Inspektion der Konzentrationslager	Inspectorate of the Concentration Camps
JVL	Jewish Virtual Library (online resource)
Kapo	The head or chief of a work unit. (Also written as *Capo*)

KL Konzentrationslager	Concentration Camp
Kommando	Work unit or detachment
KPD Kommunistiche Partei Deutschlands	German Communist Party
Krankenrevier	The camp hospital or infirmary
Kripo Kriminalpolizei	Criminal Police
Kristallnacht Also Reichskristallnacht	*Night of Broken Glass*, November 9–10, 1938 nationwide pogrom
Lagerkommandant	The officer in charge of the whole camp
Lagerführer or Schutzhaftlagerführer	The officer in charge of all the prisoners but not of the camp personnel
Lagerschreiber	Camp Secretary
Landrat	Head of state district administration (before 1939, *Bezirkamtsvorstand*)
LK Lagerkommandant(en)	Camp Commander
Muzeum Stutthof w Sztutowie	The Stutthof Museum and Archives
NARA	National Archives Record Administration, in Washington, DC
n.d.	(No date)
n.p.	(No page)
NKWD Naródnyy Komissariát Vnútrennikh Del Наро́дный комиссариа́т вну́тренних дел)	The Soviet Secret Police, otherwise known as the People's Commissariat for Internal Affairs

NSDAP Nationalsozialistsche Deutsche Arbeiterpartei	National Socialist German Workers Party
NSV Nationalsozialistische Volkswohlfahrt	A social welfare organization during the Third Reich
OT Organisation Todt	Todt Organization
Pfleger	Hospital nurse
POW	Prisoner of War
PZbWP Polski Związek Byłych Więźniów Politycznych	Polish Association of Former Political Prisoners of Nazi Prisons and Concentration Camps
Post(en)	Sentry/Guard(s)
Rapportführer	The adjutant or aide to the Lagerführer
Rasse und Siedlungshauptamt	Race and Settlement Office
RdI Reichsministerium des Innern	Reich Ministry of the Interior
Reichsarbeitsdienst	National Labor Service
Revier Krankenrevier	The camp hospital or infirmary
RFK Reichskommissar für die Festigung deutschen Volkstums	Reich's Commission for the Reinforcement (or Strengthening) of Germandom
RFSS Reichsführer SS	Leader of the SS for the Reich, Heinrich Himmler
RSHA Reichssicherheitshauptamt	Reich Security Head Office
SA Sturmabteilung	The political militia of the Nazi party in the 1930s, also known as the Brown Shirts

Scheisskommando	Work unit in charge of the latrines and the disposal of their contents
Schupo Schutzpolizei	The (municipal) security police
Schutzhaft	Protective custody. (Under the Nazis, it meant imprisoning anyone who opposed them.)
SD Sicherheitsdienst	Security Service, part of the SS
Selbstschutz	Self-defense unit
Sipo Sicherheitspolizei	Security Police Also applied to all the regular police force
SPD Sopade Sozialdemokratische Partei Deutschland	German Social Democratic Party
SS Schutzstaffel	Police and security organization under Himmler
Stapo Staatspolizei Gestapo	The State Police
Stubendienst	Service rendered to the Block elder
TWC	Trials of War Criminals Before the Nuremberg Military Tribunals
Umwandererzentralstelle	Central Agency for Relocation Central Emigration Office
USHMM	United States Holocaust Memorial Museum
Völkisch	Racial-nationalist
VoMi Volksdeutsche Mittelstelle	Ethnic German Liaison Office
Volksgemeinschaft	People's Community—Nazi concept of ethnically pure society free from division

VVN Vereinigung der Verfolgten des Naziregimes	Association of those Persecuted by the Nazi Regime
WP Wojsko Polskie	Polish Army
WVHA Wirtschaftsverwaltungshauptamt	Business Administration Head Office
YIVO	YIVO Institute for Jewish Research
YVA AYV	Archives of the Yad Vashem
ZBoWiD Związek Bojowników o Wolność i Demokrację	Union of Fighters for Freedom and Democracy
ZG PZbWP Zarząd Główny Polskiego Związku Byłych Więźniów Politycznych	Executive Board of the PZbWP
Zivilgefangene	Civilian prisoners

Introduction

Whether in the United States or Europe, many of us were taught in school that the Second World War began in Danzig (in Polish, *Gdańsk*) on September 1, 1939: the first shots were fired from the German battleship *Schleswig Holstein* that was anchored in the Danzig bay (with 250 men on board, I later learned) and unleashed a conflict that would last till the late spring of 1945. In all, around 60 million lives would be lost. That was our introduction to the war and the city where it all started. Later, I discovered Danzig in a different discipline—German literature—and this time in the novels of Günter Grass, especially in what was later called the *Danzig Trilogy*.[1] The stories by Danzig's native son transformed the dates we had memorized in history class and opened the gates to a city that was, during the 1930s, rowdy and vibrant, with an array of eccentric characters, including a drum-beating boy of arrested growth, all of them speaking German or Polish or Kashubian in a city that spilled over into other lively neighborhoods like Langfuhr/Wrzeszcz[2] that were never far from the Vistula River or the Baltic. We could imagine ourselves with one of these characters on the local narrow-gauge train all the way out to a village called Sztutowo that would soon give the Germanized name "Stutthof" to the camp nearby and confer on both an identity that is not well known beyond Poland. This book seeks to extend its identity beyond Poland.

But there was another association with Danzig that came up later in a research project on the fate of German Jews trapped in France during the so-called dark years—*les années noires*. It was the slogan "Mourir pour Dantzig?" that has been deployed in global discourse since its first usage to question any military intervention. The slogan was first used by Marcel Déat (who served in the Chamber of Deputies 1926–36) and was published in an article in the newspaper *L'Oeuvre* on May 4, 1939, that addressed the growing prospect of a war with Nazi Germany.[3] The implication was clear—was Danzig, a city declared a free city under the terms of the Versailles Treaty, worth dying for? Wasn't appeasement a better option? Why would France commit her military resources to defend Poland's right to have free access to the Baltic through Polish territory that the treaty makers designated, and was referred to as "the Polish Corridor"?[4]

This book will engage throughout with Danzig but will pursue a different set of questions that are related and connected to one another. The book's content is organized into five chapters and an Epilogue. In the first chapter, we will examine Danzig's significance for the Nazi regime, both emblematically, and as an incubator in the 1930s for Nazi ideology, specifically the development of *Deutschtum*/Germandom.

The role of Albert Forster, the Gauleiter of the district, will be central to my argument. The second chapter looks at the immediate repercussions in Danzig of the September attack on Poland, specifically on the identity of the first groups of local people—Danzigers—who were arrested and taken to Stutthof. The initiatives to "cleanse" the wider area are also examined. The next two chapters track how Stutthof developed and by January 1942 was designated as a concentration camp by Heinrich Himmler. Among the issues I address in these chapters are these: How did Stutthof's new status affect its relationship to Danzig and connect it to other concentration camps? Did the Nazi occupation beyond Poland and the course of the war affect its prisoner population and its personnel? In the final chapter I will look at Danzig as the exit point for thousands of refugees fleeing from the Soviet advance as the Nazi regime collapsed. The focus on Danzig and its connection to Stutthof some twenty-two miles away thus remains a fixed point of reference, whether as a free city in the 1930s, or as the supply center of goods and a workforce, and, finally, as the exit point for refugees. We return in the Epilogue to Gdańsk, with some final reflections drawn from contemporary Polish fiction on the city's former and current connections to Stutthof/Sztutowo.

"Dying for Danzig" is replaced with a different question—what does "Dying in or near Danzig" mean? Of Stutthof's estimated number of 110,000 prisoners, at least 65,000 died. As for the original question, it was posed by a man without political or moral credibility who initially supported Léon Blum's leftist government, and then became an ardent collaborationist with the Vichy regime, even working directly with Pierre Laval who engineered the deportation of French Jews and French Resistance members to the camps of the east, including Stutthof. Déat's question may have survived, but he himself received a death sentence *in absentia* from the postwar French government. He died in 1955, in hiding in Italy. We will meet others like him in the course of the history of Stutthof.

We also do not get enmeshed in the quarrel about where the Second World War really started. Historians like Niall Ferguson dispute the claim that it began in Danzig and argue that it was a global war that had begun earlier in Asia and involved other aggressors. To claim otherwise, Ferguson claims, is "an illusion caused by our own parochialism."[5] He was, of course, not the first historian to make that claim.[6] The context of this book is Danzig, parochialism notwithstanding, not as the launching pad of war but rather as a city that became the epicenter of the Nazi *Reichsgau* or district of Danzig-West Prussia. We begin with its prewar history and then examine its expanding connections to the camp where many local people from Danzig and surrounding areas were sent as its first prisoners. Thus Stutthof, at least initially, can also be viewed as a parochial undertaking because its prisoners were taken first from the local Danzig population, and then from regional communities in "the Corridor." In other words, Stutthof was all about being local, then regional before it entered the full orbit of the wider camp system.

German cities of that era can, of course, be forever associated with nearby camps—Munich with Dachau, Buchenwald with Goethe's classical Weimar. Nevertheless, Danzig's association with its nearby camp is very different, for the two cannot be uncoupled, and their connectedness is about more than proximity. In fact, the camp at Stutthof can be regarded as the predictable extension of a city that had become the breeding ground for an ideology that made the establishment of a camp possible in the first place. When we consider the long, multicultural history of Danzig/Gdańsk that can be traced back to the tenth century, the contrast with the cult of Germandom in the 1930s could not be more striking. In its early history Gdańsk's location on the estuary of the Vistula River connected it with major trade routes that brought merchants and tradesman with their crafts and skills to a city that had become an important hub on the Baltic. For well over a thousand years, Gdańsk was home to Germans and Poles and other Slavic groups like the Kashubians, as well as settlers from countries like Sweden and Scotland, and it became home after 1620 for a small community of Jewish merchants. Gdańsk was not spared major military conflicts, including a famous military campaign in 1308 when the town was captured by the Teutonic Knights, only to be returned to the Polish crown a century later. There were wars with Sweden, and prosperous times during the Polish-Lithuanian Commonwealth period in the sixteenth and seventeenth centuries when it became a thriving harbor town. Anna Cienciala calls the city during its pre-1772 history the emporium of the grain trade of East Central Europe, challenging the Western generalization of Gdańsk as a backward city.[7] In 1795, after the third partition of the Polish-Lithuanian Commonwealth, it was seized by Prussia and, in the next century after the Franco-Prussian War in 1870–1, it became part of a united Germany. The focus in this book is on the period that followed the establishment of the Second Republic of Poland in 1918 and specifically on the new status of Danzig/Gdańsk after it was declared a free city under the jurisdiction of the League of Nations according to the terms of the Versailles Treaty. Interestingly, the 1920 treaty was not the first time it had been named a free city. Earlier in its history, in 1807, Napoleon had declared Gdańsk to be a free city. Why are these events and dates relevant? The defeat of Germany in the First World War and the terms of the Versailles treaty provided enough fuel to ignite or reignite long-standing German/Polish tensions in Gdańsk/Danzig that made it easier for politicians to selectively mythologize the defeats and victories of the history described briefly above. There were other factors that will be considered in the first two chapters, but the consequences of the First World War and the subsequent peace treaty specifically on Danzig/Gdańsk were significant.

What then are the aims of the book? Beyond presenting a much-needed overview in English of Stutthof's five-and-a-half-year history, this book embraces a complex of interlocking goals that evolve in the telling of the camp's history. They can best be understood under the motif of "Germandom." By Germandom/*Deutschtum*, I draw on what Robert Koehl described as "the body of German people, or Germanness, the abstract or the essential qualities of the Germans."[8] At face value, the word *Deutschtum* may not look particularly threatening, but it was used in the context of other key words in the Nazi lexicon—"race" and "blood and soil," "living space," etc., and was enshrined in a particular agency that was given the mandate to implement its true meaning. Further, Germandom was specifically emotive and relevant in and around Danzig and grew in significance and repercussions. Thus, my first goal is to show how Nazi programs (and their proponents) used the seed of Germandom to indoctrinate the German community in Danzig during the 1930s. Although at this stage there was no official agency to "Germanize" the region, the soil to receive the dogma was well prepared. When Nazi Germany invaded Poland through the portal of the free city of Danzig, the first to be targeted were Jews and Poles, whose communities in and around Danzig were destroyed and dispossessed, the latter with shockingly high mortality rates that need to be understood as representing victims of Germandom and not primarily as the inevitable casualties of war. Interwoven in this aim is to show how Germandom had infected the whole area beyond Danzig. Stutthof was clearly a designated and carefully chosen center, but it operated in a wide area that had all sorts of camps—many of short duration—that functioned as transit camps, collection camps, camps exclusively for priests, etc. Yet these camps were not even formally recognized as "filial" camps of Stutthof.

My next goal is to show a paradigm that may not fit into the common image of camps in occupied Poland. The small community of local Jews was initially coupled with the much larger community of Poles, both groups already designated under the dogma of Germandom as "sub-human" and in Stutthof referred to as *Juden und Pfaffen*/Jews and priests. According to narratives written by Poles—especially priests—it was an unequal bracket, for the Jews were treated even more harshly. We track how the inequality of that bracket becomes more apparent after 1942 and how, from that point on, this secondary camp, with a strong local SS corps that had a high commitment to promoting Germandom, gradually gained its place in the wider camp system and used both the human and material resources of Danzig to contribute to the "war effort." The fate of European Jewry had now become central to the history of a camp designated in 1939 as a camp for political prisoners and has meanwhile grown in scope from parochial to global. The last two chapters share related goals and present the hideous, culminating consequences of Germandom and Stutthof's role in "the Final Solution." They present perspectives on the Holocaust from Stutthof that have been neglected in the history of the camps of the Third Reich. My last chapter examines the evacuation of the Stutthof camp system as a graphic representation of the collapse of Germandom.

How then can we effectively present the history of Stutthof, including the years that preceded the Second World War, in and around Danzig and argue for their connection to Stutthof? Historians generally expect a book that is based exclusively on archival evidence. Though I draw on archival data, this is not a micro-history of Stutthof, but rather a broader narrative that examines the impact of Germandom from different perspectives. I cite more extensively from memoirs than is customary in traditional histories and integrate the testimonies directly into the main body. What is most distinctive—and I hope will generate a more personal connection to the subject—is the judicious inclusion of the fiction and reflections of Danzig's most famous writer, the Nobel Prize winner Günter Grass. His voice is clearly heard in the first two chapters. Then, for good reasons, it recedes. Many readers will be familiar with Grass's fiction about Danzig, and possibly with his writings on German history. Yet, this book is not about Grass, or about his musings on German history: it is about the Stutthof camp system and its connections to Danzig. Grass's voice is present because he has something of value to say about Stutthof, and in fact, one of his characters is arrested and taken to Stutthof. More significantly, his depiction of the social and political realities of the predominantly German-speaking free city helps us understand why anyone from Danzig or "the Corridor" could have ended up in Stutthof in the first place. Grass's terrain is thus at the very heart of this monograph, entitled "A Nazi Camp near Danzig: Perspectives on Shame and on the Holocaust from Stutthof." The book has three strands that are reminiscent of leitmotifs in a traditional literary narrative: Danzig's pervasive presence, shame, and the suppression of memory, expressed at times by silence. In Grass's case, shame remains wrapped in silence until he confessed his guilt as an old man. These strands support the motif of Germandom, the organizing principle around which the book moves. Different from themes—and there will be an array of themes throughout—shame, silence, and Danzig are structural, are more discernible at crucial junctures than at other times when they simply evoke an unforced association with Germandom, its development, and demise.

In a general sense, shame will be forever associated with every camp that was part of the Nazi concentration camp system and Stutthof is no exception. Silence still hangs over many of the lesser known and smaller camps and Stutthof certainly belongs to that category. Yet Günter Grass, arguably the most recognizable name in German literature of the twentieth century, does not shrink from bringing the camp Stutthof into his fiction about Danzig. He is the one who brought up the subject. I think that Grass should not, and frankly cannot, be excluded from any discussion on Danzig and its nearby camp. One of his characters says he knew many victims died there; he was not sure how many. We know that the total population of the camp was at least 110,000, of whom 65,000 died. This may present the difference between fiction and fact, between a literary construct and archival data, but the difference is not a denial of data. The inclusion of literature does not imply a competition between modes of telling history. Archival data are the foundation of telling history but literary voices add a dimension that illumine and clarify the data. I offer another important dimension to consider that resonates with the title and is deeply relevant and specific to German history. It pertains to the deep sense of guilt and shame that Grass expressed about his personal experience fighting on the side of Nazi Germany. He was not the only German writer to feel shame. Contemporary writers like Uwe Timm are still grappling with its impact.[9] Grass wrote about this shame as a war veteran—a boy soldier, some might say—but old enough to voluntarily enlist as a seventeen-year-old with the Waffen SS. How he deals, I will argue, not only with Stutthof but with his identity as a wounded *Heimkehrer*, returning from war to a country in ruins and finding himself displaced from his native city, unlocks much larger postwar issues—homesickness, German guilt, shame, and suppression of memory, including his own. But there are other shapes to shame that are more relevant to this book. I refer to firsthand accounts by victims who were humiliated in Stutthof. Though Grass's fiction about Danzig may provide some keys in the first two chapters to help us understand the backdrop of Stutthof, it recedes as the history of Stutthof unfolds. Other voices take over—the voices of prisoners who were there. Prominent among them are two Lithuanians whose narrative skills elucidate the experiences of Stutthof prisoners in a way that merit greater recognition in the literature of the camps.

What then can we expect to learn from Grass about the city of Danzig and the camp at Stutthof? Günter Grass never forgot Danzig and though he could not return to it in 1945 he never left it.[10] His early fiction captured with uncanny accuracy the ethos that pervaded Danzig after Hitler came to power, even introducing by name the historical figures who shaped that ethos and bear some responsibility for the collapse of a community that once coexisted in an imperfect but relatively peaceful accord. Salman Rushdie writes of Grass's prose, "[w]hen Grass writes about literature he finds himself writing about politics, and when he discusses political issues, the quirky perspectives of literature have a habit of creeping in."[11] Readers do not need to have read Grass's stories about Danzig to appreciate how apt Rushdie's observation is. Nor do they need to have read Grass's stories to understand the trajectory of this book.

I am certainly not the first to identify Grass's narrative skills in depicting the history of Danzig. In a review of one of the earlier books in English about Danzig, Herbert Levine's *Hitler's Free City*, Richard M. Hunt applauds the many merits of the book yet ponders "what a different and more vivid picture of Hitler's free city comes through in Günter Grass's novels set in Danzig during the same fateful years. His fictional portrait opens up a new world of understanding about how it felt and what it meant to live through Danzig's historical travail."[12] Speaking about atrocities committed in the Third Reich, Ernestine Schlant has noted how literature is rarely consulted when the question is asked how "the Germans" look back at that past and how they came to terms with it.[13] Recent historiography has reversed that trend, and historians like Nicholas Stargardt have given readers the opportunity to know "how it felt" to live through those years, an achievement that does not compromise rigorous analysis of historical events.[14] We could, of course, produce a list of events in Danzig and the personages that engineered them—all backed by archival data—and still arrive at the camp of Stutthof. By drawing upon Grass at specific intersections in our narrative, we also seek to respect the lines of historical accuracy.

When the 1999 Nobel committee singled out *Die Blechtrommel/The Tin Drum* for special praise they referred to Grass's depiction of "the forgotten face of history." Stutthof is part of that forgotten history. Grass confronted the Nazi past in the *Danzig Trilogy* both effectively and selectively—his depictions of the prewar regional history of Danzig and Pomerania are specific and imbued with authentically regional flavor and vibrancy. But when it comes to Stutthof, he is selective, and he presents the camp in snapshot form, in metaphors, in brief anecdotes about minor characters or in rumors about shocking atrocities. While this oblique treatment of suffering underscores rather than obscures the camp's bleakness and cruelty, it also contributes to the silence that has lingered over Grass's relationship to local history, including the destruction of a community that he portrayed so effectively in his fiction. In the course of his long life, his responses to German history both in fictional works and in memoirs included his attempt in *Im Krebsgang/Crabwalk* (published in English in 2002) to write about *other* sufferings—like the anguish of displaced Germans in 1945.

One memoir, however, posed a major problem for Grass—and his readers. In an August 12, 2006, interview, the seventy-nine-year-old Grass revealed that he had served in his late teens, for a short period in 1944, in the Waffen SS.[15] He had, of course, never hidden the fact that as a young man he had been enamored with the Nazi movement and fervently hoped that Hitler would win. But this public admission was different and gave instant fuel to his detractors to deride the hypocrisy of a man who for years had made a name for himself as a defender of democratic values and had scolded those countries who had failed to do so.[16] Grass scholars have been divided on the impact of his confession. Stuart Taberner concluded that Grass's disclosure "will have little lasting or substantial impact on the way in which his work is read, or, indeed, on the way in which the author's lifetime of social, political intervention as a public intellectual is evaluated."[17] That may be true but, despite Grass's long silence, my engagement with his writings leads me in a different direction. I take very seriously Grass's response to the outpouring both of support and of condemnation, the former from international writers like Rushdie. Grass told the DPA (Deutsche Presse Agentur/German News Agency) that his service in the Waffen SS shamed him and that he had tried to lead an upstanding life ever since.[18] We do not need to dissect the probity of his life after 1945 to take his public confession of shame seriously. I do not view his confession as a casual, throw-away line but rather as a truth that has left a discernible mark on both his fiction and biographical writings, and particularly on *Dog Years*. Though there are few comments directly about Stutthof—and even these are veiled—one senses that Grass's discomfort with the subject hits too close to home.

Why did Grass not address the presence of Stutthof directly in the many interviews and statements that he made in the course of his long life? After all, he did have a lot to say about the Holocaust and specifically about Auschwitz. Is it possible that Grass used Auschwitz more as a symbol for the camps and the atrocities perpetrated in them and that, in fact, he camouflaged his engagement with Stutthof behind a camp that had become the metonym for everything that he was raging against? His engagement with Germany's Third Reich, his life-long emphasis on Auschwitz, and his support and tireless campaigning for the Social Democratic Party were all part of a life that dealt with the shame of the past, both personal and national, and his efforts to prevent it from happening again. Everything that Grass raged at and against is in full view in Stutthof—of course, not necessarily in German (there were as many as twenty-seven nationalities in the camp), and when it is in German (in memoirs, for example, by German-Jewish women) there are no literary conceits or attempts to obscure the identity of the narrator.

In *Peeling the Onion,* he writes that as a boy he followed the Führer's speeches and his military exploits, yet he was equally keen to immerse himself in other histories, like the Crusades:

> Blind to the injustices that were daily occurrences in the city's environs–between the Vistula and the Haff, only two villages away from the Nickelswald country house used by the Conradinum for school excursions, the Stutthof concentration camp was growing and growing ... Polish peasants and their families were being turned out of their farms in the West Prussian hinterland ... meanwhile I was a vassal of Frederick II.[19]

The trajectory of Grass's early life was typical of any young German boy of the era, beginning with joining at ten the *Jungvolk* that fed into the Hitler Youth. But he is also keen to explain something different that separates him from his peers. As a young boy he collected debts for his mother who owned a grocery shop in Langfuhr/Wrzeszcz, adding some detail that reminds us of the German-Polish community—he describes the local dialect as "Low German larded with Polish expletives."[20] Grass uses this debt-collecting experience to deal with other debts, pointing out that the two words "Schulden" and "Schuld"—debts and guilt, are closely related in the German language, adding, "I kept silent," and then rationalizing his silence with, "But because so many others kept silent, the temptation is great to discount one's own silence, or to compensate for it by invoking the general guilt, or to speak about oneself all but abstractly, in the third person."[21] In this way, Grass places himself beyond Danzig and identifies with a much wider German readership that has also lived under the long shadow of Auschwitz. In a public lecture given in February 1990, entitled "Schreiben nach Auschwitz"/"Writing after Auschwitz," he identified Auschwitz as the motivating force of his entire artistic career and political engagement. Schlant points out that he is including all the camps in what Grass called "a deep and irredeemable rupture in the history of civilization."[22] This may be true but, then again, he does not write about other camps. Katharina Hall has proposed that Grass's work foregrounds memory as a means of highlighting the involvement of "ordinary" Germans in implementing or supporting the Nazi regime, "arguably pre-empting the work of historians on the *Alltagsgeschichte* of the period (the 'history of everyday life') by over a decade."[23] In fact, several key passages in *Dog Years* are more than just references to the camp's existence but point at times to fairly detailed knowledge about how ordinary people became the victims of the internment practices of Stutthof. This book pays respect and homage to them— ordinary people who made up the majority of the camp's prisoners. Grass's depiction of "ordinary" men helps us understand and empathize with nameless prisoners who otherwise might remain as numbers and statistics on the roll call of the camp.

Why has Stutthof been neglected by historians? For a time after the war, all the documents were not in the same place and were widely dispersed; some were held privately and some were in the Soviet Union. There was no central depository until archivists began to assemble all the documents at the former campsite in the Stutthof Museum.[24] Early efforts to commemorate the victims of Stutthof were fraught with tensions between local agencies and branches of the PZbWP (*Polski Związek Byłych Więźniów Politycznych/Polish Association of former Political Prisoners of Nazi Prisons and Concentration Camps*) and the central office in Warsaw that governed such initiatives. In the spring of 1946, the Gdańsk office submitted a request and a statement to the Provincial Land Office, stating that it felt "obliged and compelled to take care of this cemetery, whose very existence is the best evidence of the policy to deprive the Slavic lands of their national identity. This policy, once used by the Teutonic Knights in their white habits, was latterly used by the Nazis in their swastika armbands."[25] They also attempted to persuade local authorities to use the camp as a site of recuperation for former inmates. The former prisoner Lech Duszyński, who chaired the executive board, was dismissed on the charge of mismanagement and arrested for profiteering.[26] He had asked for funding for the site of the old camp, but Warsaw countered that there were no plans to establish a museum at Stutthof. Debate among prisoners continued and questioned why Auschwitz and Majdanek were given such privilege and prominence. On September 1, 1947, Czesław Stanisławski replied in *Wolni Ludzie*: "Auschwitz was the first camp where defenseless victims of Nazi brutality were shot and murdered en masse; the first crematorium was built at Auschwitz." While not denying that prisoners had suffered in other camps, he continued,

Nevertheless, national organizations of former political prisoners have unanimously decided that it is precisely Auschwitz which should become the symbol of all Nazi concentration camps of the 1939–1945 period, and that is also why it has been decided that a museum for posterity shall be established at Auschwitz to illustrate all manifestations of Nazi savagery as well as the underground struggle within the camp against the violence of the SS.[27]

In July 1947, the *Act of Commemoration of the Martyrdom of the Polish Nation and Other Nations* in Auschwitz was passed. A year later, in April 1948, a monument to commemorate Jews who were exterminated in Auschwitz/Birkenau was erected and was replaced in 1966 by the International Monument to the Victims of Fascism.
There are other reasons for the neglect of Stutthof. In the immediate aftermath of the liberation, ideological differences hampered the processing of information about what had transpired during internment. The Soviet Secret Police—the NKWD (People's Commissariat for Internal Affairs)—interviewed former prisoners in 1945, and Polish suspicions were aroused at the time because they selected only those with a clear political bias—that is, pro-Soviet—and did not include all the Polish testimonies.[28] Krzysztof Dunin-Wąsowicz decided to write about Stutthof in the spring of 1945, basing his memoir on detailed observations and presumably notes he had taken. During the evacuation of Stutthof in 1945 he escaped and went into hiding for a few weeks in Gdynia, until the Red Army and the Polish Army liberated the area. When first arrested in 1944, he was a third-year student and member of the underground Warsaw University. While imprisoned in Stutthof (along with his brother, I later learned), he worked in the Central Registry where he had access to official documents and learned about the earlier history of the camp, including its structure and organization.[29] Dunin-Wąsowicz says that in 1946, everything was still very fresh in his memory—he remembered the names of the camp workers and prisoners with whom he had lived in the same barrack. He gained knowledge of the organization of the sub-camps, of executions, and of the story of the transports from Warsaw, including his own on May 24, 1944, to Stutthof.[30]
Atrocities that were perpetrated in the extermination camps in occupied Poland, by their sheer magnitude and scale, will continue to overshadow and dominate the story of Stutthof. Auschwitz, with its staggering statistics of victims and its elaborate complex of barracks, crematoria, and factories for slave labor will be forever associated with the Holocaust and the loss of European Jewry, along with Majdanek with its count of 360,000 victims, 18,000 of whom were killed as part of the grotesquely named *Erntefest*/Harvest festival on November 3, 1943. The Operation Reinhard Camps[31]— Bełżec, Majdanek, Sobibor, and Treblinka—belong to a category of unspeakable atrocity because they involved immediate and instant extermination. Jews deported from the General Government to these camps were deprived of all hope.[32] Beyond the parameters of the camps, the massacre of Polish officers in 1940 will be forever associated with the forests of Katyń. Although it took years to sort out the story, locate the sites of the massacres, and ascribe responsibility to the real perpetrators—the Soviets-Katyń will remain locked in public memory as a national Polish disaster.[33] The murder of the Polish intelligentsia, including priests—alongside the Jews of Danzig—

by cranial shootings in the woods near the Baltic is also a chapter of Polish history, though less known. This book will lift some of that silence though not its shame. And it will also show why Stutthof, as the first camp established outside the German borders of August 1939, needs to be recognized by a wider readership as a historical landmark in the history of the Third Reich, and indeed the Second World War.

Stutthof is surprisingly not as well-known as other camps in Jewish Studies. Thousands of Jews from all over Europe died in Stutthof or on "death marches" during its evacuation, yet their deaths do not command the same attention as do deaths in other camps, possibly because many of the victims had also been in other, better known camps. We talk about sites of memory and even about a surfeit of memory yet fail to acknowledge that a camp like Stutthof has been, even if unintentionally, assigned to the margins of history, where it is presumably well looked after by its Polish custodians. Including Stutthof in the history of Nazi camps is essential to expanding our understanding of the Holocaust. After all, 43 percent of the 65,000 victims of Stutthof were Jews. Between January 1944 and January 1945, around 80 percent of the victims were Jews.[34] Eighty years have passed since Stutthof was opened, and yet the camp is still off the beaten track for most readers beyond Poland; Danzig/Gdańsk may very well be still associated with a slogan that questions if it was worth dying for or commemorated as a site where the Second World War probably did not start. Dr. Roch Dunin-Wąsowicz, the grand-nephew of Krzysztof Dunin-Wąsowicz, argues for a broader approach to the concept of the Holocaust.[35] He draws specifically on the experiences of his grandfather Marek and his late great-uncle, both of whom had been interned in Stutthof as young men (twenty-one and seventeen, respectively) because of their activities in the Polish resistance which included saving Jews. Krzysztof and his mother Janina were awarded the honor "Righteous among the Gentiles" by the Yad Vashem in 1982. We do not need to disrupt the Holocaust as a historical category that pertains to the genocide of six million Jews to argue for a more comprehensive understanding of the racial hatred that was perpetrated in Stutthof on people like Dunin-Wąsowicz's grandfather and great-uncle, who not only suffered at the hands of the Nazis but were imprisoned, as he points out, for political reasons after their "liberation" by the Red Army.

Piotr Wróbel stated in an address given in September 1999 at the United States Holocaust Memorial Museum that most Westerners, even those who are well educated and well read, know next to nothing about the history of the Second World War in Poland.[36] I doubt that the charge of neglect is as valid today but Wróbel's warning about operating "with stereotypes and fragmented information taken out of context" is still worth noting.[37] Have these stereotypes hindered the pursuit of lesser-known segments of Polish history, like the history of Stutthof? It is beyond the scope of this book to integrate Stutthof's history adequately into those other histories that, relatively speaking, have received much more attention. Roch Dunin-Wąsowicz writes about the postwar politicization that happened in Poland when "public discourse on the Holocaust in Poland was for a time reduced to a national legacy of suffering that effectively downplayed anti-Semitism," adding that "Polish civilian complicity in pogroms on the side-line of German-orchestrated extermination of Jews has entered into the public sphere."[38] These are painful issues (including the assertion they were

"German-orchestrated") that historians of the postwar period have boldly addressed.[39] But so was the genocide that was perpetrated at Stutthof and its sub-camps. In the recent climate of anti-Polish sentiment that was exacerbated by the government's decision to penalize anyone who refers to the camps in Nazi-occupied Poland as "Polish camps," it is all the more imperative to present the story of this early camp that was the site of both anti-Polish and antisemitic persecution.[40]

A 2013 publication by a Polish journalist includes an interview with a woman who cleans the barracks of Stutthof.[41] She says that some people think it should not be cleaned at all and others think the place is too pretty for a concentration camp. Comments like these do not appear to have silenced the woman. "This place gives me more strength than it takes from me. When I think about people who were here, I pull myself together."[42] She wants to do the best job she can, and then she adds,

> You can learn a lot about yourself here. I realized that even though I can see, I am still blind, and even though I can hear, I am still deaf. When I look at the poems written by camp prisoners, when I study their drawings, I think that even in those tragic circumstances, they knew how to recognize surrounding beauty. Would you be able to name some of the birds that sing here? They heard them.[43]

This "ordinary" woman is expressing much more than gratitude for life and her willingness to keep the place clean. She is voicing empathy and solidarity with those who somehow were neither silenced nor blinded by their surroundings.

Among the diverse voices that will bear witness in this book about Stutthof are Polish priests, Jewish men and women (including a Czech ballet dancer), a Lithuanian priest, a noted Lithuanian writer and intellectual, a Finnish sailor, and a Polish boy scout. Most of them, like the survivors of all the camps, wrote their memoirs far from where they were born and had grown up. The notion of *Heimat* had become a distant memory. And there are many others who have spoken about Stutthof in video testimony. The personal affirmation for continuing with this research came to me one day while working at USHMM, watching a video from the Shoah collection. Paula (née Gerber) Borensztein was telling her story, which began in Vilna in 1925, as the youngest of three children. She cried often as she told her story, and she always cried when she spoke of her siblings, or when she described how old people fell when they were being pushed to move faster. Deported first to Riga where she lost three teeth in a beating, she recalls the horror of hearing hangings in the night. Yet it is the memory of the killing of children that elicits uncontrollable tears. She can speak only about the children. "All the children," she laments. In Stutthof, there was a gas chamber, and there were women on a truck that were headed there. She can no longer bear to see a factory chimney. The voice that had been choked by tears as she remembers, suddenly and unexpectedly becomes strong and decisive. She declares, "I promised that night, if I live, my life will be for my sisters."[44] I confess that I did not take note of the date of that night, but I know her appeal touched something deep within me, arousing in me a sense of urgency and a strength to keep on listening, reading, and writing. Paula and her sister were liberated in April 1945, and on May 14 they headed by train for Magdeburg. They met former French prisoners on the train who worked with them in a munitions' factory. They were all attempting to head home—as survivors and fellow-survivors of Stutthof and its sub-camps.

Grass writes about one of his characters in *Dog Years*: "They took him to Stutthof, and there he stayed–a dismal, complicated story, which deserves to be written, but by someone else, not by me."[45] By conceding that the story deserves to be written, though not by him, Grass is taking his leave and, I suggest, admitting the limitations of fiction in the face of facts. That distinction will be clear in the chapters that follow. But the more probable reason is that because of his guilt about his SS affiliation, though not disclosed when he wrote *Dog Years,* he had, at least in his mind, forfeited the right to tell the story of what happened in Stutthof. He will write about it indirectly and will even include characters with barely concealed ties to him, but these fictionalized characters will become adumbrations when we meet the real characters in the following chapters. Their experiences in Stutthof were significantly shaped by the actions of the organization that Grass joined in 1944 at age seventeen—the Waffen SS, specifically the 10th SS Panzer division Frundsberg. The shame of the SS haunted him. In his words:

> Yet for decades I refused to admit to the word, and to the double letters. What I had accepted with the stupid pride of youth, I wanted to conceal after the war out of a recurrent sense of shame. But the burden remained and no one could alleviate it … I will have to live with it the rest of my life.[46]

In his last work—a meditation on his life and on the debts that are still owed, Grass writes in the poem "Balancing the Books" about books being lined up, side by side, supported by a wooden shelf. In the final stanza he laments that, though he longer claims ownership of these books, yet they remain a burden. His final question is "Is something missing/that could add to the bottom line?"[47] I hear in these lines the pathos of debt and shame, as well as the desire for others to fill the bottom line, in case lives are lost in silence.

1

Promoting German-Consciousness in a Revamped Gau, 1930–9

The Call of Albert Forster to Danzig

Despite the presence of the SA (*Sturmabteilung*)[1] and the SS (*Schutzstaffel*) in Danzig in the 1920s, the Nazi Party was not a strong organization, a situation that was observed with some concern by Hermann Göring who visited the city in 1930 and noted that the party needed help. It was he who recommended an ardent Nazi supporter, a Bavarian by the name of Albert Forster, for the job of Gauleiter to unite the Nazi Party. Forster had already forged a good reputation as a Party loyalist in his hometown of Fürth where he had joined the SA in 1923, had met Hitler in person, and was reputed to emulate Hitler's rhetorical style, and had even memorized some of his speeches. He also was a personal friend and admirer of Julius Streicher, the editor of the *Völkischer Beobachter and Der Stürmer* whose rabid antisemitism had helped Forster become the regional director of the NSDAP in Franconia/Franken.[2] In Danzig, Göring contended that "only someone with a fanatical Führer-like personality will be able to affect change here."[3] It was an unintended compliment to Danzig, a city that at this time was seen as out of step with the Party in the Reich, though governed by a constitution that has been described as modeled on the Weimar Republic and the German city-state of Lübeck. "Politically, Danzig was a miniature version of Germany."[4] After Forster was appointed, he was encouraged to suggest plans to the Führer on how to bring about a new order in the Gau.[5] His zeal for the Nazi cause, along with natural gift as an orator, prepared him well for the job in Danzig but his unusually close relationship with Hitler was going to stand him in good stead during his long tenure, and he boldly drew upon it when other Party elites, like Himmler, attempted to discredit and undermine him.

Two factors stand out in the record of Forster's career in the 1930s—his constant and consistent message that Danzig must be restored to the Reich and the restraint he was forced to exercise in that endeavor. The first explains his appeal to a large segment of the local German population while the second factor is entwined in other decisions and events that were beyond Forster's control and were in the hands of the Führer himself. Forster knew all too well that the appeal to Germandom stirred deeply held patriotic emotions about the city that had been severed from the motherland as part of the Versailles Treaty, collectively seen as unjust, and he used that wedge effectively to keep the free city divided. His admiration for the antisemite Streicher certainly suggests he would do nothing as Gauleiter to protect the Jewish community in Danzig.

First and foremost, however, it was his relentless promotion of German consciousness that set the tone for his tenure, reminding the German majority that they needed to be restored to the German Reich. It was not a hard sell, even for those who were not—or not yet—Nazi party members. His *deutschbewusst* ("consciousness of being German") appeal excluded all who, at least at this stage, could not be considered German or in step with the new German Order. (More later on Forster's attempts to change that for eligible Poles.) The one group that would never be able to claim that "honor" were the Jews of Danzig, even those with Danzig citizenship who had fought for Germany in the First World War (there were around ninety-five). They considered themselves German by heritage, education, language, and culture and at a certain level were separated from Jews who had arrived in the 1920s from Eastern Europe and who were politically and religiously conservative, often with strong Zionist views that alienated them from their liberally minded fellow-Jews. Collectively, they were referred to with some derision as "Ostjuden." Yet as tensions grew, these same people found less to divide them and were united in the common aim—to leave Danzig as soon and as safely as possible.

Vulnerabilities and Protections

But Gauleiter Forster faced complex obstacles that obviated the goal of Danzig's return—at least immediate return—to the German fold. The Versailles Treaty included measures that protected the constitution of the free city and all its inhabitants—405,000 in 1929, of whom some 20,000 were Poles and 10,488 were Jews, all of them under the administration of the High Commissioner of the League of Nations. Citizens of the free city were referred to as "nationals."[6] This was particularly reassuring to Danzig's Jewish community, which had absorbed Jews from the east in the 1920s and had grown from 2,717 in 1910 to the number cited above.[7] To the road block of Danzig's constitution we can add Forster's frustrations working with the *Volkstag*—the local parliament or Popular Assembly, which was an elected body, with a Supreme Court and chose its executive branch and a president who was head of state. After its constitution was amended in 1930, the number of senators was reduced to ten, six of whom were unsalaried. But despite the personal animosities and jostling for power between Forster and his rivals, Danzig was being shaped into a Gau by a fanatical Nazi who was impatient to see its return to the Reich. He is uniformly described as enthusiastic to the point of childishness and as someone who had to be held in check and restrained by others—notably Hitler himself, with the need to exercise patience and restraint (*Zurückhaltung*).

"*Deutschbewusst*" and "*Zurückhaltung*" thus coexisted in an uneasy tension in the early 1930s in references to Forster. It was just a matter of time before Danzig would become reunited with the Reich. That desire was pervasive among the local German population, regardless of what party made it possible.[8] The question was how—and was Danzig going to become the cause or pretext of war? Meanwhile, would Poland stand by and allow her relationship to the free city be jeopardized? This was arguably the most complicated aspect of Danzig's situation in 1930. Poland was represented by a commissioner-general and although he does not appear to have as prominent a profile as the two League commissioners in the 1930s, he was responsible for a range of duties and activities that were both consular and cultural. Although Poland and the German Reich signed a Non-Aggression pact in January 1934, which provided some degree of protection from the threat of war between the two countries, it did not change the internal complexities in Danzig between the two main communities. In accordance with the Versailles Treaty, Danzig was part of the Polish customs area, and thus most of its customs revenue went to Poland, which, as Levine points out, also controlled "the formal conduct of Danzig's foreign affairs, owned the railways, operated its own harbor post office, and won the right to maintain a small munitions depot."[9] Citizenship of the free city was a coveted status that was conferred on its inhabitants, including, by virtue of the constitution, any Polish citizen, even those who were in the city on a temporary basis, and also on 3,000 Jews with Polish citizenship who had come to the city in the 1920s.[10] The city hired German bureaucrats from the old Reich who were well paid because the post was considered a hardship duty.[11] Levine tellingly points out that despite these complexities, "the everyday life of the city was surprisingly normal" and that the administrators of institutions like the railroads, namely Danzigers and Poles alike, "tended to leave the political wrangling to their chiefs while they got on with their more prosaic tasks."[12] Those prosaic tasks will be part of the narratives of Günter Grass's tableau of Danzig. Some of the people who performed them, however, will be among the first interned at Stutthof. Many Polish Jews from Danzig will perish. But for now, that fate seems remote. Few Danzigers may have even noticed that in October 1933 Germany withdrew from the League of Nations.

It is hardly surprising that Forster presented his promotion of German consciousness in terms of a struggle or battle, rhetoric that was mounting in fervor and certainly resonated well with Goebbels's propaganda speeches in the Reich, which were gaining attention among the growing numbers of Nazi supporters in Danzig. Among those supporters were Germans who were newcomers, just like the Eastern European Jews, though the Germans certainly would not have put themselves in the category of "newcomers." Some of them had arrived in Danzig after the Treaty as demobilized army officers and brought their own brand of patriotism to the free city. Clark claims that a large number of the new Danzig government officials had been German civil servants and although they now were citizens of Danzig, they retained their allegiance to Germany and Germandom.[13] Forster was adept at tapping into this patriotic pride, and for example, organized on October 29, 1930, a meeting in the Sports Arena for 2,500 people with the theme, "The struggle for the German soul in Danzig." In the November 16, 1930, elections, he saw a modest gain for the NSDAP with twelve new seats (of the seventy-two) for the Party in the *Volkstag*. But the failure of the Social Democrats to gain any ground in Danzig mirrored a similar result in the September Reichstag elections and did not bode well for their political appeal. The Danzig economy, which was never robust, saw an increase in the number of unemployed in December 1930 from 25,000 to 39,000 in 1932. An option for the unemployed (by 1933, well over 30,000) was to go to Germany where they received further political education.[14]

The appeal by the Nazis to vote for change in Danzig was falling on receptive ears. Tensions in the community were exacerbated by the growth of Gdynia's harbor, which by 1933 outstripped Danzig's shipment revenue. Levine frames the impasse in the following terms:

> To the Danzigers the new harbor was clear proof that the Poles, motivated by fanatical hatred of everything German and disappointed in their attempts to control Danzig politically, were determined to strangle it economically. To the Poles, Gdynia was the answer to Danzig's continued political, economic, and cultural dependence on Germany, as well as to the "treachery" of 1920.[15]

With his uncanny sense of timing, Forster reinforced the connection to the Reich and invited Propaganda Minister Goebbels to Danzig, who appears to have been somewhat amused by Forster, calling him "childish with boundless optimism."[16] It was, however, the declaration of Hitler in 1933 as *Reichskanzler* that elicited Forster's most ardent expression of German consciousness: "What we have longed for, what thousands of Germans have died for and have sacrificed for, has become reality."[17] Hitler personally congratulated him after the 1933 May elections brought in thirty-eight seats for the NSDAP—over 50 percent of the vote. Despite the best efforts of the opposition, the Nazi Party won forty-three seats in May 1935.[18] Yet, this result was not what the ambitious Forster hoped for and, in fact, was described in the *London News Chronicle* with the headlines: "Hitler Foiled in Danzig Election."[19] Ernst Sodeikat points out that the NSDAP was well funded from the Reich and was able to procure five weeks of radio propaganda right before the elections, whereas the opposition parties, notably the Social Democrats were not allowed to broadcast their views a single time. They were also threatened and attacked with tear gas and vilified by the press.[20] In Goebbels's congratulatory speech, he refers to Danzig as "this land" and reminds his audience, "This land will declare itself to be German. In this time of the greatest crises, it will not abandon its own homeland. It will affirm its German-ness—that is, declare itself for National Socialism, that is, for the Führer."[21] All that was German was now also assumed to be National Socialist. The concept of Germandom was taking root.

It is noteworthy that Forster aspired to be more than a native Bavarian from the Reich. In fact, he appears to have been keenly aware of his outsider status and wanted to be recognized as a Danziger. This ambition was affirmed early in his tenure when he was made an honorary citizen of Danzig in August of 1933, in the presence of his elderly father, in the Red Room of the City Hall.[22] In his speech, the president of the Danzig Senate, Hermann Rauschning referred to himself as having graduated from the same school as the new citizen and used the now-familiar military language. "In an unprecedented battle, you have brought Germandom to Danzig and we are proud to work under your leadership for the well-being of the people of Danzig."[23] He concluded by acknowledging their leader, "whom we all will follow with unswerving loyalty."[24] Forster further consolidated his connection to Danzig by marrying Gertrud Deetz, the daughter of a prominent and wealthy industrialist from Danzig. The wedding, held on May 9, 1934, in Berlin, was attended by Hitler, Rudolf Hess, Goebbels, and Göring. Two days later, there were further celebrations in Danzig, which were supposed to be kept secret (according to Forster), but the celebration became yet another occasion for demonstrating and celebrating National Socialism. The streets were decorated with swastika-emblazoned flags, and thousands marched in two parades. The guest list again included Rudolf Hess.[25]

Forster's influence went well beyond Danzig and his initiatives found approval with Germans who lived in predominantly Polish Pomerania where the number of Germans had fallen from 175,000 in the year 1921 to 112,000 in 1937. The first NSDAP groups that had been formed in Pomerania at the end of 1934 were growing in number, with the direct help of the German consulate in Thorn/Toruń,[26] and the school system in Pomerania was actively promoting Germandom by teaching national consciousness and a sense of German identity. Rossino claims that teachers went beyond promoting Germandom and instilled in their pupils the sense of Polish inferiority, also using textbooks that claimed that Poles were aggressively stealing territory from Germany and were now waiting to strike again.[27] The superiority of all things German is now openly contrasted with Polish inferiority.

Closer to Danzig, there were signs that the city was being brought into line with Nazi principles. For example, in June 1935, there were demonstrations, complete with banners organized by NS-Hago ("*Handwerks-Handels-Gewerbe Organisierung*"/ "the National Socialist Organization of Artisans and Tradesmen"). Public bathing beaches were targeted in Sopot/Zoppot by Nazis from Elbing/Elbląg. But what is striking about these demonstrations is that they did not enjoy great public support. Levine suggests it might possibly have been for fear it would harm tourism, since many tourists who came for the casino at Zoppot or for the Wagner festival were Jewish.[28] There may be a simpler explanation—it was not driven by the stereotype of financial gain but rather because local people were still not totally invested in Nazism, despite Forster's best efforts to make it so. That was going to change, but in the mid-1930s, local people—the majority of whom were artisans and solidly *kleinbürgerlich* were not yet committed Nazis. Besides, they were dealing with hardships closer to home—trying to put food on the table and to make a basic living. Grass captures this in *Peeling the Onion* when he remembers collecting debts for his mother:

> I learned by smelling, hearing, seeing, and by experiencing the poverty and anxieties of large working-class families, the arrogance and fury of civil servants who cursed in stilted High German and refused to pay their bills as a matter of principle ... tales of the proletariat and petite bourgeoisie, the former in Low German larded with Polish expletives, the latter in clipped bureaucratese.[29]

Does Grass's fiction yield other insights to help us understand the potential for Danzig to become politicized in the 1930s? Grass was clearly aware that his city's multiethnic history could be stirred up and exploited for political purposes. At the beginning of *Hundejahre/Dog Years*, the third and longest novel in his *Danzig Trilogy*, he asks, "What does a river like the Vistula carry away with it?"[30] He called it "a political novel," and in so doing, invites us to look at what exactly is political about this novel.[31] Unlike *Cat and Mouse*, where the Baltic is always within earshot, it is the river that has become the magnet for Grass in *Dog Years* and it is on the banks of the Vistula, as the opening sentence suggests, that he begins his journey. *Dog Years* has indeed several snapshots of "a boy with his dog" along the river, but this is not a charming, regional story, for the Vistula assumes a deeper, allegorical function in the novel and is depicted as swallowing up all sorts of everyday objects and forgotten histories and legends, all floating by together in its journey across the swampy estuary toward the Baltic:

> Everything that goes to pieces: wood, glass, pencils, pacts ... bones, sunsets too. What had long been forgotten rose to memory, floating on its back or stomach, with the help of the Vistula: Pomeranian princes, Adalbert came ... twelve headless knights and twelve headless nuns are dancing in the mill: the mill turns slow, the mill turns faster, it grinds the little souls to plaster ... Amazing how many things are becoming to the Vistula, how many things color a river like the Vistula; sunsets, blood, mud, and ashes.[32]

Yet even after the Nazi victory in 1933, "blood, mud and ashes" are not yet the political backdrop of the Danzig that Grass depicts, and unlike the Reich where a camp like Dachau was swiftly opened to receive opponents of the new regime, the possibility of an internment camp so close to Danzig does not appear to be a major threat, at least at this point in Grass's fictional world.[33] Of course, it was still a free city with a constitution protected by the League of Nations, and Seán Lester, the resident High Commissioner who constantly challenged infractions against the rights of resident Poles and Jews when the first rumblings of trouble came to his attention. That was, of course, his job and his assignment, and his brief did not include direct dealings with the German Reich. In fact, Lester was so diligent in defending grievances of Jews that he was accused on several occasions of being a Jew, and despicably depicted once with an elongated nose in a cartoon in *Der Stürmer*.[34] But even in the mid-1930s the Nuremberg Laws had not yet been introduced in Danzig, as the following conversation between a boy and his music teacher in *Dog Years* illustrates:

> The story is that although Mr. Lester still represented the League of Nations in a Danzig Free State and all racial laws were constrained to halt at the borders of the diminutive state, Amsel expressed misgivings: "But, sir, they say I'm a half Jew." The conductor's answer: "Nonsense, you're a soprano, I expect you to introduce the *Kyrie!*" This succinct reply proved to be long-lived and is said to have been cited with respect many years later in conservative resistance circles.[35]

Grass is drawing on the politics of the early years of Forster's tenure, a very specific period of history that is fundamentally regional (Danzig and environs); he then shapes these years into various patterns and transformations that converge with the history of the Third Reich that at times confuse—one suspects willfully—and at other times delight the reader with the sheer ingenuity of his storytelling. Grass's narrative skills, however, are not my focus, unlike John Reddick whose primary concern was to analyze the novel's aesthetic value. He concluded that it was marred by some fundamental weaknesses and fails in the end to carry conviction, which he attributes to the following: "So long as the fiction is detached in time, strongly localized (Schiewenhorst, Nickelswalde and the Vistula, and later Danzig) ... so long as this obtains, the novel carries conviction in a masterly way."[36] In an interview with Reddick in June 1971,

Grass said he was more attached to *Dog Years* than to any of his other prose works, and called it a work "that did not quite succeed," and was "the least rounded of his books."[37] Reddick identifies the break in the last two-fifths of the novel, which is set later in West Germany.[38] My focus is on the period before that break—in other words, on the local terrain that was the context for prewar Danzig and its aftermath. Why was he so attached to this novel and why did Grass consider it "the least rounded"? I think that his attachment was simply because it was about his home—his *Heimat*, including an awful stain on that *Heimat*, and on his own people—the German community. If this is true, then Grass's struggle was with the depiction of the escalating loss of basic liberties that evolved in Danzig in the 1930s and grew into such unspeakable acts of violence that Grass, seldom at a loss for words, is reduced to one line in *Dog Years* that conveys a stark reality—"You and I were never in Stutthof." His recognition and admission that Stutthof occupies a different space separate his fiction from the testimonies and memoirs of inmates who were there.

At what point in the 1930s can we see the changes that Grass evokes in his symbolic depiction of the Vistula? We need to consider some events in the Reich that inspired greater confidence in the Führer and the men he had chosen to implement his political and military agenda. He had clearly gained for himself greater power when the offices of the chancellery and the presidency were merged after Hindenburg's death in August 1934, and the plebiscite of August gave him unlimited authority. He had already taken care of his enemies that same summer in the SA Röhm Putsch, which he justified as "preventing greater bloodshed."[39] In the Saar plebiscite of 1935, 90 percent of the Saar population voted for reintegration with the Reich. Hitler also knew how to delegate authority without ever losing the aura of being *der Führer*, allowing his closest colleagues to develop far-reaching plans, like Göring's "Four Year Plan" or Himmler's ambitions for the SS. These factors happened far from the Vistula, but Nazi success stories infiltrated local politics and injected both confidence and arrogance into Danzig officials, especially Gauleiter Forster.

July 1936 is a good starting point to speak of change, when Seán Lester, the League of Nations Commissioner and Irish-born diplomat, resigned from his post—probably ousted. Gauleiter Forster accused him of working against the interests of Danzig.[40] Forster's antagonism toward him had become increasingly obvious, and his public statements include proposing that the Treaty be torn up, to the point that the Polish Foreign Minister Beck complained to von Moltke, the German ambassador in Warsaw.[41] With Lester gone, all Forster had to contend with were—ironically—fellow Nazis who basically shared his ideology but disliked him personally. The animosity escalated after Lester was replaced with the Swiss historian and diplomat Carl Burckhardt who, to Foster's chagrin, enjoyed a cordial relationship with his arch-rival, Arthur Greiser, the President of the Danzig Senate. This is how the new commissioner remembered his meeting with Forster:

> He was the type that comes from the Alps with thick curls over a low muscular forehead, and the dark eyes of a southerner set in a boyish, arrogant but friendly looking face … He stood in the middle of a room that was decorated in Viking style, observing me closely … Suddenly he smiled and said in a distinct Bavarian

dialect: "So you represent this Jewish-Masonic organization of gossip in Geneva! I recognize you, I saw your photo in a newspaper."[42]

Tensions became even more obvious when Arthur Greiser slowed down the enactment of the Nuremberg Laws in Danzig that were operating in 1935 in the Greater Reich, apparently more in opposition to Forster than for humane reasons. Later, in 1939 after Greiser was appointed as Gauleiter of the Warthegau (Levine describes him as "a brutal, uncontrolled Nazi despot"),[43] Forster was still not free of his influence, because Greiser continued to confront him from his new position.[44]

The year 1937 has been identified as the watershed year for *Gleichschaltung* (the standardization and coordination of daily life under Nazi rule), which took somewhat longer to be enacted in Danzig than in the main Reich.[45] It is possible that this reflects what Kershaw has identified as the turning point (in mid-1936) when Hitler himself began to believe that providence had placed him in this role, and he was convinced of his infallibility.[46] In Danzig, there had already been significant inroads into any semblance of democratic practice, especially with the dismantling of trade unions and the arrest of their leaders, the banning of the opposing political parties—beginning with the Communist Party in 1934, then the Social Democratic Party on October 14, 1936,[47] then on May 5, 1937, the banning of the *Deutschnationale Volkspartei*/The German Nationalist Party, which brought some of their members to the NSDAP.[48] But by far the most ominous signs that Danzig was being standardized within the Nazi regime were the measures taken to exclude Jews from the professional and social life of the city. For example, only two Jewish physicians were now allowed to practice medicine, and then only with Jewish patients. That Forster and his supporters were not totally successful in shutting down Jewish life can be explained by the privately funded support within the Jewish community—including, for example, the founding of a Jewish school. Levine writes, "Despite substantial restrictions on employment for Jews at every level, including cultural and educational, private organizations were able to offer employment and continued to lead an uncoordinated existence."[49] This also was the case for the Polish community, which set up its own schools and social organizations to compensate for the growing restrictions on their daily activities.

Journalist Marek Wąs summarizes the ways in which Forster implemented Nazi ideology in Danzig: He put a lot of effort into printed propaganda. The *Danziger Beobachter* was used throughout the 1930s as the main organ of communication and although it changed its name several times, its message was consistent, whether in a weekly magazine or later, after 1940 in the *Danziger Vorposten*, with the headline: "We want to come back to the Reich; we do not accept illicit treaties." He organized frequent demonstrations and parades and public gatherings of the NSDAP. There were special workshops led by people who were coached to speak, and six public events weekly, each with a special theme, like "Danzig under the Swastika Symbol," "Respect to the Fallen Ones," "Day of Brown Shirts." Eleven thousand guldens were invested in printing Nazi posters and in flags with swastikas that were to be seen everywhere in the city.[50] Mandates removed city councilors who were Jewish, and Nazi songs like the Horst Wessel song (with its blatant appeal to knives and blood) were sung at demonstrations.[51] Later, Forster used public money to finance a special SS unit that was responsible for killings, and for overseeing the building of Stutthof. Schenk claims that it was Forster's financial minister, Julius Hoppenrath, who made funds available to build Stutthof and also was involved in divesting local Jews of their wealth.[52] Forster's initiatives in closing down the social space of Jews included eviction from their apartments and houses, designating a separate area to sell their goods on market days, discouraging people from buying from Jewish merchants, and designating a separate time of day (Thursdays between three and eight) to use the beaches.[53] In short, the persecution of the Jews of Danzig was sanctioned on Forster's watch under the banner of Germandom.

In April 1937, Foster ordered that signboards of all shops and factories were to show the full names of their owners, thus assuring that Jewish owners would be identified. Everyday life for other Danzigers—German Danzigers, however, continued, like for the group who embarked on a *"Kraft durch Freude"*/"Strength through Joy" cruise to Madeira in October 1937. These state-subsidized vacation opportunities served to link Danzig and its people, at least its German population with the main Reich, even though it was still a free city. In May of the same year, Forster went on a promotion tour of major cities in the Reich to talk about German Danzig—"das deutsche Danzig."[54] His zeal for Germandom was now alarmingly matched by a growing agitation to bring "the Jewish issue" to the forefront, but even in this area he was restrained to exercise patience, not because Hitler disapproved but because he was engaged in promoting Germandom in other areas like the annexation of Austria.[55] When that happened the following spring, on March 12, 1938, it is no wonder that there was "deep despair on opponents on all potential victims."[56] Why was the impact so strong on a city on the Baltic that was miles away from Austria? The *Anschluss*/annexation was a blatant act of defiance against the same treaty that still offered some protection to all Danzigers and had explicitly forbidden Germany to unite with Austria. Two years earlier in 1936, Hitler had already shown total disregard for another stipulation of the treaty by reoccupying the demilitarized Rhineland, parading his new army of conscripts that had also been forbidden by the treaty. In view of these violations, it was logical to wonder if Danzig was next on Hitler's agenda. Anxieties among the opponents of the regime grew a matter of months later when Hitler marched into the Sudetenland, supposedly to free ethnic Germans from the yoke of the Czechs who turned to the French and the British for help. Kershaw attributes the confidence in Hitler's statesmanship to the success of bringing home the Sudeten Germans in 1938. He cites this as "a major factor in the relative composure of the popular mood during the Polish crisis of the following year, when the fears that it would lead to war were nowhere near so extensive as they had been in 1938."[57] At the conference that was convened in Munich in September, the delegates from France and Britain ceded the disputed turf to Germany, after which Britain's Neville Chamberlain returned home bringing "peace with honour."[58] What was even more relevant for the status of Danzig and alarming for many Danzigers happened within a matter of months, when German troops marched unopposed into Czechoslovakia, incorporated parts of it, and made the rest of it into a protectorate. Bergen refers to the substantial amount of territory Germany gained before 1939 and adds with pointed logic: "but Hitler was never satisfied. His ambitions went far beyond merely revising the terms of Versailles."[59]

In the 1930s, Danzig could not boast of producing spectacles like the Nuremberg rallies or gala events of huge national relevance. But there were attempts, unexceptional by comparison, to showcase local events and personages. For example, in the summer of 1938, Forster indulged in one of his favorite cultural activities—a full week devoted to *his* idea of German culture for the whole Gau (*Gaukulturwoche*) to which Goebbels, as Minister of Propaganda, was invited. Though a modest and parochial affair, it touched on themes near and dear to any ardent Nazi, especially Foster who had done enough homework to discover that Max Halbe, a local and deservedly minor dramatist espoused "blood and soil" teachings. He also hijacked the Danzig-born philosopher Arthur Schopenhauer (1788–860) on his 150th birthday celebration.[60] Goebbels was impressed and noted in his diary that his entrance to Danzig was triumphant.

> How truly German is the face of this city! … Forster spoke very enthusiastically. I gave a very a clear, basic speech. Loud applause. Ate in the delightful dining room of the city hall. Greiser spoke in a very friendly way. He told me about the economic upturn in Danzig. And that, of late, the Poles are getting very uppity again.[61]

Every word in this "clear, basic speech" as recorded in Goebbels's diary was an ominous portent to what lay ahead for Poles and Jews, many of whom would soon be denied any entrance to this "truly German Danzig." The political rhetoric of patriotic pamphlets heralding Germandom cut into the gains that had been made in the 1920s by moderate policies, referred to as *Verständigungspolitik*. In contrast, the Polish counterpart—*Polentum* used in the pamphlet *Wer kennt Danzig* was "treated as a threat, even a disease—a recent imposition, rather than an historical given."[62]

Kristallnacht (The Night of Broken Glass), the attack on Jewish property and synagogues on November 9–10 in the Reich was also carried out in Danzig and in nearby Zoppot, though several days later, between November 12 and the 15, 1938. The backdrop of this tragic event was as follows: In October, the Polish Ministry of the Interior had ordered Polish citizens living outside Poland to revalidate their passports in order to reenter Poland, an operation believed to be directed against Polish Jews. The order affected 14,000 Poles living in Germany. Germany took immediate advantage of this situation and escorted Poles to the border where many were refused entry and had to wait for weeks until Polish Jews promised to provide support for them. Among the expellees were the parents of a young seventeen-year-old Polish Jew who took vengeance on the maltreatment of his parents, went to the German embassy in Paris and shot one of the junior officials. The murder was enough to generate the fury of Propaganda Minister Goebbels who unleashed his storm troopers on Jewish synagogues and businesses, justifying the excess of force as warranted, in view of Jewish hatred of Germans and the Reich. Within days the pogrom reached Danzig, though the looting met with some local resistance from the local police. Gershon Bacon notes that storm troopers razed the synagogues in Langfuhr and Zoppot. A total of 1,500 Jews fled over the border—mostly Polish citizens—to Poland.[63] Erwin Lichtenstein, a prominent Jewish leader reported that the president of the Jewish community, a lawyer by the name of Bernard Rosenbaum phoned the police who promptly sent a patrol to the Great Synagogue, and the attackers fled when they saw the police. Thereafter, members of the Jewish community took turns to guard the synagogue.[64] By the end of 1938, the Nuremberg Laws (operative since 1935 in the Reich) had been introduced in violation of the Danzig constitution. Gradually the Jewish community was being extinguished. The German news agency, when announcing the law for the "Protection of German Blood and German Honor" that forbade sexual relations between Jews and those of German or related blood, was careful to explain that Poles were "Aryans" and thus protected.[65] At this stage, it was one of the rare distinctions that were made between the two groups. In the months that led up to the outbreak of war, the attempts to emigrate increased, especially in response to a clear message from Forster, who declared on March 4, 1939, that it was his duty to order Jews and Poles to emigrate from the territory. "It is the Germans' duty now to cleanse this land totally, first of all from rabble, marauding robbers, Poles and Jews."[66] Around 500 had been able to leave on March 3, with the hope of reaching Palestine via Romania.

The attack on the Jewish community in Danzig which had numbered over 11,000 in 1930 embodies many facets of Jewish communities in the main Reich in the 1930s[67] and converges with their fate—the loss of professional and social space, the attempts to emigrate and leave homes where many of them had lived for years, the reality of dealing with daily harassment and persecution, and for the Danziger Jews who had not found a way to emigrate by September 1939, internment and/or deportation.[68] As in the Reich, transports were organized in Danzig for children. On May 3, 1939, seventy-four children between the ages of seven and fifteen were allowed to leave on a *Kindertransport* for England, accompanied by six adults, led by Samuel Echt who had taught at the *Volksschule*. In early July, a second transport left with six children, again accompanied by Samuel Echt, and on July 10, a third one left with sixteen children under the care of Else Itzig, who led a further transport on August 23 with twenty-six children, among whom were seventeen who were admitted to an educational trainee program in England. The pathos of the brief sentence that follows this account captures the dark side of transports that rescued children: "Not all of these children were to see their parents again."[69] There were now around 1,700 Jews remaining in Danzig, and 500 of them managed to survive there until they left in a large transport in August 1940 for Palestine, but they were interned in Mauritius and did not reach Palestine till 1945.[70] Almost all the others were sent to concentration camps or deported to the General Government. The destruction of the Jewish community of Danzig was the direct outcome of Nazi propaganda and indoctrination that had first infiltrated and then smitten the free city under the direction of the chief flagbearer of Germandom— Gauleiter Albert Forster.

How much did the events leading up to and following Kristallnacht affect the wider local community, including the Polish community? Grass's fiction and later comments offer some sense of its impact. Sigismund Markus, a Jewish character in *The Tin Drum* and owner of the toyshop that supplied Oskar with his toy drums, recognizes the danger he faces and has resolved to leave Danzig. He implores Oskar's mother, Agnes with whom he is in love to leave with him for London. The problem is that she is having an affair with her cousin, the Polish/Kashubian Jan Bronski while married to the German grocer, Matzerath. Grass pulls major ethnic threads together in the three men and makes his female character decide where she belongs in the Danzig community—with her Polish/Kashubian lover who works in the Polish Post Office, her German husband who is not a Danziger but hails directly from the Reich or with the Danziger Jew who will provide for her and her little son in the safety of England? What is striking—and I submit also cynical—is that Grass presents the Danziger Jew as choosing the Germans to be the ultimate winners and as the second-best choice for her:[71]

> Don't do it no more with Bronski, seeing he's in the Polish post office. He's with the Poles, that's no good. Don't bet on the Poles; if you've gotta bet on somebody, bet on the Germans, they're coming up, maybe sooner maybe later. And suppose they're on top and Mrs. Matzerath is still betting on Bronski. All right if you want to bet on Matzerath, what you got him already. Or do me a favor, bet on Markus seeing he's just fresh baptized. We'll go to London, I got friends there and plenty stocks and bonds if you just decide to come, or all right if you won't come with Markus because you despise me, so despise me. But I beg you down on my knees, don't bet no more on Bronski that's meshuuge enough to stick by the Polish Post Office when the Poles are pretty soon all washed up when the Germans come.[72]

But it is too late, for on Kristallnacht, SA men vandalize his shop, defecate on the floor, and find Markus slumped, presumably dead, in his chair, "beyond being hurt or humiliated. Before him on the desk stood an empty water glass; the sound of his crashing shop window had made him thirsty no doubt."[73] Meanwhile, Matzerath has taken the day off to be a spectator of the despoiling of Jewish property.[74] Grass presents the characters in the Kristallnacht scene like they are characters in a fairy tale—"Once upon a time there was ... " In that way, he distances himself from the actual event that shattered Danzig a few days later than in the main Reich. He also inserts another layer of brutality, namely venomous cruelty to animals, which he uses to show the hypocrisy of the Nazis and their perverted views of bravery:

> There was once an SA man who did in four cats with a poker. But because the cats were not all the way dead, they gave him away and a watchmaker reported him. The case came up for trial and the SA man had to pay a fine. But the matter was also discussed in the SA and the SA man was expelled from the SA for conduct unbecoming a storm trooper. Even his conspicuous bravery on the night of November 8, which later became known as Crystal night, when he helped set fire to the Langfuhr synagogue in Michaelisweg, even his meritorious activity the following morning when a number of stores, carefully designated in advance, were closed down for the good of the nation, could not halt his expulsion from the mounted SA. For inhuman cruelty to animals he was stricken from the membership list. It was not until a year later that he gained admittance to the home guard, which was later incorporated in the Waffen SS.[75]

In an interview with Grass on May 30, 2010, Grass was asked if he had experienced any of the pogroms against the Jewish population. His guarded and unadorned responses suggest discomfort with the subject. It would seem that Grass's brilliance in satirizing political events and Nazi types like the SA became strangely muted when the issue came too close to home. He replied that he had not seen the destruction of the main synagogue in Danzig, but in his area of Langfuhr he had seen the destruction of the synagogue though he himself was not present when it happened.[76] Secondly, he was asked if he had been aware of the Polish minority in Danzig. He replies that he was aware of the building near where he lived in which the Polish minority had their offices. Polish young people had met there for meetings. The Hitler Youth organization had met in other parts of Danzig, and by 1937, Grass says, there were clashes between the two groups. He also mentions Polish institutions like the Post Office and the railway and the Polish harbor as landmarks of the city. When asked if there were Polish pupils in his school, one senses his reluctance to abandon the safety of inanimate buildings and talk about actual people. He cannot remember any. He points out that many names had Polish endings and that some families also had Kashubian backgrounds, people who had lived for generations in the city, like his own mother's family. He singles out the year 1939 as a demarcation line that separated people with mixed ethnic identities. He himself had an uncle who belonged to the Polish minority who was an official with the Polish Post Office and was shot in the attack on the Post Office. He goes on to say there had already been a certain distance between this man and his family and they no longer talked about him after his death in 1939. It was not until the last years of the war that his mother made contact again with her relatives who were Kashubians, and the family of this Post Office official whose name was Frank Krause.[77] In 2010, he can admit to family estrangement with a Polish relative but that is as far as the native Danziger can go.

The Tacit Response of Protestant Clerics

What about response in church communities in Danzig?[78] The story of Protestant resistance to National Socialism in Danzig (known as *die bekennende Kirche*/ the Confessing Church) is part of the broader history of what is known as *der Kirchenkampf*/the church struggle between the Confessing Church members and their opponents (known as *deutsche Christen*/German Christians) that was played out in every state of the Reich with varying degrees of visibility and consequences. There was a modest presence in Danzig of *die bekennende Kirche*/The Confessing Church that was claimed for the most part after the war. There is also enough evidence in Stutthof in the SS files of the Danzig-born Lutherans to suggest that the dominant allegiance of the local Protestant state churches was to the *German Christians*.[79] Doris Bergen's ground-breaking research on the role of the *Deutsche Christen* covers a wide area, but her findings in *Twisted Cross* are largely related to the main Reich. Her work on German Christians is at the same time a sobering reminder of the shortcomings of the opposition—*die bekennende Kirche*/Confessing Church, despite the well-known and heroic sacrifices of resisters like Dietrich Bonhoeffer. Bergen points out that even the highly politicized German Christians were never embraced by the Nazi Party, and that their efforts to coordinate their theology to fit the Nazis' political demands, including cleansing the Bible from all allusions to Jews, did not win them favor. Bergen does, however, briefly mention a memoir written by Gerhard Gülzow, the Lutheran minister of St. Marienkirche in Danzig in the 1930s. Gülzow's memoir has some nuggets of information about the Lutheran churches in Danzig in the 1930s that help us construct a general if limited sense of their role and influence. He also gives the names of seven local pastors who were part of the Confessing Church: These seven men challenged the authority of the "German Christians" group under the leadership of Bishop Johannes Beerman.[80] Gülzow complains about the early infiltration of the Nazi party into his church and gives an example. Just after he had been appointed, he had to face in 1934 a church elder and customs inspector by the name of Augustin who, in his brown uniform confronted him aggressively.[81] The tone of Gülzow's memoir is at times defensive, and he is especially sensitive to the criticism that Danzig's Youth ministry was absorbed in January 1935 in the Hitler Youth Movement. He says that this action weighed heavy on "*die kleine Danzig Landeskirche*." By making Danzig's state church "little," he is setting up a David-Goliath model that is hardly accurate, given the fact that there were, according to him, seventy clergy who were part of the "German Christians." He was accused by another Lutheran minister named Walter of sanctioning the hanging of the swastika in his church, a charge he strenuously denied. (An article in the *New York Times* of December 29, 1936, refers to the arrest of two Protestant ministers, one by the name of Walter (presumably the same minister) whom Gülzow had referred to in his list of clergymen in the Confessing Church.)[82]

There are significant omissions in this memoir, notably of the impact of Kristallnacht in November 1938. The most striking feature is the inclusion of the most recognizable personages of the 1930s in Danzig—namely Forster and Greiser. Their presence in the context of church activities underscores how ordinary life still could be in Danzig, at least for some people. One day, Forster turned up at the church. There he was, standing admiring a medieval altar piece, dressed in full SS uniform, along with an adjutant and several others in his retinue. After describing Forster as "a fanatical National Socialist," Gülzow comments on the Gauleiter's open and reasonable attitude to the minister's request—for less intrusion on his church activities—and makes this observation: "In his innermost being, the Catholic Forster had kept a secret respect for religion and for the church."[83] Considering that this memoir was published in 1968—that is, after the trial and execution of Forster for his war crimes—the irony of the positive image presented here is painfully obvious. He also narrates that Forster told him to keep his voice down as some of his retinue might be eavesdropping, adding—in all seriousness: "At this moment, it was clear to me that he too was spied upon and was a prisoner."[84] The other brief anecdote involves Greiser's daughter who offered an unacceptable poem for her confirmation "verse." When asked who had written this poem, Ingrid Greiser replied that her father had—"Proud in joy, hard as ebony in gloom." Gülzow writes that he thought of this when Greiser was condemned to death by the Poles, put in a cage, and driven to his execution. He further claims that when Greiser implored the Pope and the president of the USA for pardon, he was not as hard as ebony.[85] The dominant impression that this memoir conveys is the level of normalcy of everyday life in Danzig and the absence of allusion to the effects of the racial laws on the Danzig Jewish community. Later, the minister does visit some elderly Jews and baptizes them, without reference to what happened to the other Jews in the Danzig community. He does mention the weekly praise service for youth (over 200 present) in Langfuhr, the dismissal of a woman from a church office because she was married to a baptized Jew, and the sight of General Kurt von Falkowski kneeling at the altar in a suburban church to receive the sacraments.[86] All these incidents co-mingle without differentiation in their cultural or even religious significance. Germandom was successful in Danzig because there was little or no opposition to its tenets in the German community, including local protestant churches and because Forster, its chief interpreter, pursued a relentless path to establish it as a key dogma of National Socialism.

In the east of Pomerania, the contrast with Danzig is striking. Stories of resistance among Protestant noble families stand out, especially the resistance of the von Trieglaff family that includes one family member—Elizabeth von Thadden, founder of a Protestant boarding school for girls who was executed in 1944.[87] The chaplain who accompanied her to the door of the execution room on September 8, 1944, reported that she walked without fear and trembling, and recited aloud the words of the Pietist poet, Paul Gerhardt, "Put an end, O Lord, Put an end, to all our suffering."[88] The resistance of the Protestant nobleman, Ewald von Kleist-Schmenzin from Belgard, Pomerania is possibly better known. Courageously, he had warmed of the evils of National Socialism in the early 1930s. He wrote, "What separates us, and must always separate us, from National Socialism is our attitude toward religion. The cornerstone of our politics is that obedience towards God and faith in Him must always determine all public life."[89] Later, he had warned that Nazi slogans had "driven hundreds of thousands of decent Germans over to Hitler and prepared them for the poisoning of their souls."[90] He was beheaded on April 9, 1945, at Plötzensee.[91] Those same Nazi slogans were emblazoned on the banners that decorated the streets of Danzig in the 1930s when dignitaries visited the free city that became an outpost for proclaiming the cult of Germandom.

What about the response to the destruction of the Danzig Jewish community? There does not appear to be much difference in response between the Protestant and the German-speaking Catholic churches in Danzig to the escalating hostility toward the Jewish community. Noted scholar of church history, Ronald Modras writes that Catholic leaders in Poland criticized "the antisemitic brutality in Germany and Austria as barbarous and primitive." He continues, "But self-interest prevented them from criticizing too loudly. When that brutality came to Poland in September of 1939, it was too late to inaugurate a massive change of public opinion."[92] After all, the earlier signing of the Concordat with the Vatican in 1933 had helped silence doubt about the legitimacy of the new regime and, as Bergen pointed out, "dispelled any lingering notion that Nazi ideas were anti-Christian."[93] Modras's criticism goes beyond Poland when he points to the Vatican's silence in the aftermath of other major incidents in the Reich—the anti-Jewish boycotts, the Nuremberg race laws, and Kristallnacht.[94]

A muted response was also the case among the Free Churches in the Reich, many of whom joined the German Christians in 1933.[95] There was a mixed message earlier in 1933, in a statement published in the Prayer Week program condemning "the un-Protestant antisemitism" that was spreading across the country. But the next statement refers to "the arrogant nature of the Jews" as the prime cause of that antisemitism.[96] They also continued to believe that the Nazi regime gave them liberty to preach the gospel but fail to define what the gospel entailed. Bishop Melle of the Methodist

Church declared at the 1937 conference on "Church and State" in Oxford that the Free Churches in Germany were grateful. Why? "God in His providence has sent a Leader who had been able to banish the danger of bolshevism in Germany and to rescue a nation of sixty-seven million from the abyss of despair to which it had been led through the World War, the Versailles Treaty and its tragic consequences."[97] This statement touches on two resentments that must have resonated strongly with his congregants: an intense fear of communism that was often, though not directly stated in this case, associated with Jews—the Judeo-Bolshevism canard—and the reminder of the unfair terms of the Treaty of Versailles; the new leader was liberating them from both threats. At its heart was Hitler's "stabbed in the back" conspiracy theory—the Jews were responsible for the defeat of Germany in the First World War. Although the terms were not invented by Hitler, it was a view that was both widely propagated by Nazi leaders and the German public. And there was a further complication, expressed by a Free Church minister who reported that Bishop Melle was bothered by a statement of public sympathy for the afflictions of Roman Catholic clerics. He supposedly said that all the Catholic Church ever wanted and still wanted was power and influence over politics.[98] The *Kirchenkampf* is understood as both the struggle with the Nazi regime and the struggle between the two main Protestant groups, but it also was animated by the issue of uniting the 28 *Landeskirchen*—the state churches of the provinces. Division, strife, and confrontation also marked the Free Churches. These issues appear to have been more important than "un-Protestant antisemitism" or "the afflictions of Roman Catholic clerics." More importantly, these quarrels and silence about the suffering of Jews and Catholics help us understand how it was possible that so many Catholic priests from Danzig and "the Corridor" were about to be sent to Stutthof as its first prisoners. There was general indifference to their situation among both mainline and Free Church German Protestant ministers in the late 1930s, along with escalating hostility toward school and church activities that were conducted by Polish priests in the Polish language. Their use of Polish was viewed as an insult to the German language and German *Kultur*. These factors conspired to dull the conscience of the general public against the loss of basic rights for both Jews and Poles.

Grass's Depictions of Opposition by Ordinary People in Danzig

We turn again to Grass's fiction to gain some insights into the growing acceptance of National Socialism and its dogmas during the tenure of Gauleiter Forster. The Versailles Treaty and its consequences were clearly more than dates for Grass. After all, on this disputed turf, Grass had spent his formative years, living in a multiethnic community that embraced Germans, Poles, Polish Jews, Kashubians, liberal German-Jews steeped in German *Kultur*, and Yiddish-speaking, orthodox Jews from eastern Europe with Zionist sympathies who had flocked to the Free City in the 1930s. The Free City also included Danzig proper, Zoppot, and three rural areas—a total of 357,000 inhabitants.[99] The local people who populate Grass's novels were known as "*die Hiesigen*"/ "*tutejsi*" and they lived in little towns and villages that are never far from the Vistula, with names like Schiewenhorst, Nickelswalde, and Kokotzko. Within their ethnicities, Grass represents an array of religious persuasions, trades, and professions. What factors changed this multiethnic community?

Grass is not shy about calling out actual personages who are forever associated with Danzig in the 1930s—Albert Forster, the Gauleiter, members of the Reichstag/parliament, the League of Nations representatives—Seán Lester and his successor Carl Burckhardt. These prominent figures provide the narrative props and the political context for his fictional characters, people like Eduard Amsel—a boy with mixed parentage (Jewish and Lutheran) and his friend Walter Matern who is German with some Polish in his background. These two characters grew up together and were close friends, until political events and affiliations separated them. Matern joined the local SA, was dismissed from its ranks as a drunkard, was fired from his next job in a theater in Schwerin, and consumed with guilt, spends the rest of his time looking for his former friend, Amsel. Reddick attributes his heightened sense of guilt to Grass's fundamental humanist sense of morality and further claims that *Dog Years* is not concerned with political leaders and their acts, but with the mass of ordinary people.[100] I would frame it differently: Grass correctly understood that the power wielded by political leaders ultimately dispossessed and destroyed ordinary people—Poles and Jews.

We see these ordinary people in the minor characters of *Dog Years* who were arrested and sent to Stutthof when they fell afoul of the new order in Danzig, people like the high school teacher, Dr. Oswald Brunies who becomes an exemplar of the educated middle classes who were targeted for their humanistic and democratic views. The fact that Grass uses him also in *Cat and Mouse* underscores his significance as a political statement. In *Cat and Mouse,* he was sent to Stutthof for supposedly dipping into the Cebion tablets that were meant for his vitamin-deprived students. Parenthetically, we also learn in *Dog Years* that one of his crimes was his failure to fly the swastika on "his perpetually ungarnished flagpole." There is, however, an added version pertaining to Brunies's arrest in the earlier *Cat and Mouse* that makes the reader question which depiction is accurate. Alternatively, is Grass simply adding another layer to the characterization—another trumped-up charge for arresting the innocent that was possible in those days? In *Cat and Mouse,* we learn that Brunies, a devoted admirer of Joseph von Eichendorff (the nineteenth-century German Romantic poet whose poetic legacy contains poems celebrating Danzig), was arrested at school because he was a Freemason. In *Cat and Mouse,* it is the narrator—Pielenz—who expresses doubt about the source of his arrest: "Some of the students were questioned. I hope I didn't testify against him."[101] We have to wait until, in *Dog Years,* Grass explicitly points the finger at Tulla Pokriefke, a central character also in *Cat and Mouse* and one on whom he now unleashes merciless and sadistic character flaws that are reminiscent of the profiles presented in later trials of female guards of Stutthof.[102] Here, in *Cat and Mouse,* we meet her as an unpleasant, promiscuous teenager, depicted in images of various animals, and we last see her in wartime tellingly in uniform, even if it is only as a streetcar conductor. (As in the cities of the Reich, many women in Danzig took on such jobs when their men were at the front.) In Grass's fiction, Brunies died in Stutthof in 1943, but in earlier days, as narrated in *Dog Years* before the Nazi takeover, he led a pleasant enough life as a teacher and at home as the foster father of an orphaned girl called Jenny who was later rebuked for wearing black when her cherished father died. She, too, has undergone several transformations—from an overweight child who ate too many sweets into a ballet dancer in wartime Germany whose dancing feet were later injured in an allied bomb attack. In *Cat and Mouse*, Brunies appears again parenthetically in a reference to Stutthof, in the context of Mahlke's vain attempt to be pardoned for his theft of the Iron Cross from the visiting Lt. Commander years earlier. But the principles-driven school director, Dr. Klohse rejects the narrator Pielenz's fervent desire to find the right words to reach Klohse's hard heart: He laments: "Too bad they have taken Papa Brunies to Stutthof. He'd come out with his good old Eichendorff in his pocket and extend a helping hand."[103] It is as if Grass is endearingly playing with a literary icon associated with Danzig. Danzig is no Königsberg, with Kant's monumental presence towering over it, but in Grass's imagination, Danzig is represented by "good old Eichendorff" whose poems are taken by a kind-hearted schoolteacher to the camp at Stutthof.

Grass claims in *Peeling the Onion* that at least he had never turned anybody in to the Nazi block or ward leader. "But when our Latin teacher ... a priest as well ... was suddenly no longer there to test us on our vocabulary, when he suddenly disappeared, I again asked no questions even though the moment he was gone the word 'Stutthof' was on everyone's lips by way of warning."[104] Later in the mid-seventies, Grass brought up his silence during a visit to this same priest, now in advanced years. "We spoke about Danzig, when it was a picture postcard of towers and gables and when I brought up the topic of my silence during those years in school Monsignor Stachnik dismissed it with a smile and a wave of the hand. I thought I heard an *"Ego te absolve."*[105] (One wonders if Grass—the lapsed Catholic—possibly welcomed the absolution.) Grass also gives the example of Wolfgang Heinrichs, who was kept under observation until early summer of 1940, when the Gestapo arrested him. Grass refers indirectly to Stutthof when he writes that "he (Heinrichs) was sent to the concentration camp that was set up near the Frisches Haff just after Danzig was annexed to the Reich."[106] His son had played in school with the young Grass and had disappeared. "I had used my status as a child to play dumb and accepted his disappearance without a murmur, and once more dodged the word *why*, so that now, as I peel the onion, my silence pounds in my ear."[107] Grass pays belated homage to the Social Democrat and father of his school-friend, who had been taken to Stutthof. He visited the son on the island of Hiddensee and during the conversation the son described his father as "a true anti-Fascist, not one of your after-the-fact, self-proclaimed variety."[108] (At least, Grass was honest enough to include a designation that some might level at him.)

The presence of Stutthof grows in the last novel of the *Danzig Trilogy* in both direct and oblique references. Grass mentions it in the second novel of the Trilogy, not in a casual reference for he does not separate the fate of this aging, decent, liberal-minded teacher with a weakness for sweets who loved the Romantic poet, Joseph von Eichendorff—with the camp at Stutthof. His daughter was informed about the cause of death "of a heart ailment," the standard entry on death certificates at Stutthof. Grass then returns, as it were, in *Dog Years* to safer territory, to Danzig and to better times when political convictions did not send people to a camp and when characters like Brunies lived with his neighbors in the same communities—Catholics, Lutherans, Mennonites of different degrees of fervor, colorful, delightful characters, like the mill keeper, with uncanny abilities to measure with his flat ear the exact contents of floor sacks and predict when Hindenburg would die and that the Danzig gulden would be devalued in 1935. Though Germans were in the majority in Danzig, and German was the predominant language, there was a trove of local words that everybody used, words like "zellacken." One of the three narrators, Walter Matern is depicted in an earlier mode (that is, before he had joined the Danzig SA), standing on the dike, looking for the perfect stone—a "zellack," grinding his teeth like his old grandmother who had sat all day in an overhang room that her grandfather had built in 1815, shortly after the Russians and Prussians had taken Danzig.

But Grass is writing about "Dog Years" and the title alone is freighted, not only with the allusion to the heavy, humid days of late summer but also with reference to a specific curse of German history, one he never lets the reader—or himself—forget.[109] The title is also referring to Harras, the fictional German shepherd that supposedly sired Hitler's favorite dog, Prince. He belonged to the Pokriefke family, and the father proudly donated one of the pups to the Gauleiter, Albert Forster who in turn gave a signed photo of the Führer to Pokriefke, which prompted him to join the Party, along with several neighbors.[110] Pokriefke dresses up for the occasion to meet the Führer in the Grand Hotel in Zoppot, but the meeting does not take place due to higher duties of the Führer, and he receives a photograph instead.[111] Grass cleverly inserts commentary by Dr. Brunies who provides a brief overview of the famous paintings hanging in the Grand Hotel, and in this way Grass reminds the reader of the awful chasm between a photo of the Führer and the works of art by German painters—the juxtaposition of kitsch and *Kultur,* the intrusion of Germandom with its violent ideology on to the Baltic coast. Later in the novel, the dog is poisoned by Tulla Pokriefke who refuses to leave the kennel and assumes even more animal-like characteristics that reduce her in the end to the embodiment of evil.

In the nonlinear narration of *Dog Years*, Grass moves between past, present, and future tenses and in so doing confers greater significance and poignancy on the consequences of his characters' actions. Grass does not spare details—minute details— of the political events, including calamities that happened to *"die Hiesigen"/"tutejsi."* Though each of the three novels in the *Danzig Trilogy* has representatives of the German, Polish, Kashubian, and Jewish communities that populated the region, Grass's focus in *Dog Years* on ethnicity and race becomes central to the plot and to the representation of clashing ideologies. The two protagonists, Eddi Amsel and his childhood friend, Walter Matern, dominate the narrative. Inseparable as children, they attended the same school, traveling on the same local train with its terminus in Sztutowo, even exchanging clothing. But this is no paradise that is depicted here. Grass brings out the treacherous undercurrents that are close to the surface of their friendship, like a dreaded derogatory word for "Jew" (Amsel's father is eventually identified as Jewish). One day in the middle of a scuffle with other schoolboys who were attacking Amsel, his friend Matern abruptly changed sides, defended Amsel, and subsequently provided protection for his friend from further attacks. But his loyalty was not to last, for later after Matern joined the Danzig SA, and along with other SA friends, he attacked Amsel, after publicly denouncing him as part Jewish. In the attack, Amsel lost every tooth in his head and had them replaced with a mouthful of gold teeth that became his trademark thereafter. It was, however, not always like that, Grass reminds the reader: "But at the present point in our story, which is just the beginning, the laws are still mild, they do not punish Amsel's origins in any way."[112] More significantly, there were also no protests and no protections against such violence.

Grass clearly sets the stage early in the novel for the dramatic changes that the new regime will unleash on the status of Danzig's two main minority groups—the Poles and the Jews—and the communities that fell within its parameters. On this territory, the father of Eddi Amsel had lived and worked as a Jew, and his identity is finally revealed at the deathbed of Eddi's mother. Her last words were, "Ah, son, forgive your poor mother. Amsel, you never knew him, but he was your very own father, was one of the circumcised as they say. I only hope they don't catch you now the laws are so strict."[113] During his lifetime, people did refer to the prosperous merchant as a Jew, but his everyday life told a different story—after all, he sang in the Lutheran church choir and introduced the game of *schlagball*. Besides, his son Eddi has an extraordinary gift that is admired in the community, of constructing scarecrows that are initially used for innocent purposes, like protecting vegetable gardens from marauding birds, but he has to give up his lucrative hobby when his scarecrows become so grotesque and sinister that they frighten the locals. (He had used animal parts—pig bladders, etc.) These scarecrows loom over the work like a dark foreshadowing of the camp that will receive local people like Amsel himself, who fortunately was able to liquidate his family's assets and leave Danzig before it was too late. In fact, the scarecrow's precise location is mentioned in reference to Stutthof's proximity—the garden where the scarecrow stood "bordered the Stutthof highway."[114]

As the Nazi presence grew in Danzig, the threat of internment in a camp becomes increasingly feasible, even on ground that technically was still part of the Free City of Danzig. Grass's focus is again on local officials, including Forster and placing recognizable politicians in a fictional setting. In *The Tin Drum,* for example, he depicts a Nazi rally that is attended by local dignitaries. In one particular incident, Oskar is beating his drum behind the rostrum to the tempo of a waltz and thus disrupting the military beat:

> I looked out into the open through my knothole, I saw that the people were enjoying my waltz, they were hopping about merrily, they had it in their legs: already nine couples and yet another couple were dancing, brought together by the waltz King. Only Löbsack, who appeared on the meadow followed by a long brown train of party dignitaries, Forster, Greiser, Rauschning and others, whose passage to the rostrum was blocked by the crowd, stood there fuming and surprisingly disgruntled by my three-quarter time. He was used to being escorted to the rostrum by rectilinear March music.[115]

Oskar further claims that for several years until 1938, he and his drum successfully broke up rallies. These prominent members of the Danzig Senate are depicted by Grass in a solid display of solidarity in the mid-1930s though at least two of them, as was revealed later, were at the time at loggerheads, notably Greiser and Rauschning who fled from Danzig in 1938 and wrote in exile about his altercations with the Nazi Party.[116]

Grass's depiction is of a later date and is a fiction; Oskar's drumming did not disrupt Nazi fervor, and besides, it was played behind the scenes, in hiding under the rostrum.

What is clear, though, from the historical record is that Albert Forster's role in promoting German racial superiority in Danzig was well noted in the early 1930s. In a speech in Dublin in 1948, Lester had this to say of Forster's ego: "[M]ore corruptible than easily-acquired wealth was unbridled power in the absence of any control on the growth of a vast vanity. Provided he showed sufficient adulation to the Dictator, he could do as he pleased …. Forster was a great mob orator and fanatic, very impatient of legal obstacles to the institution of the Nazi dictatorship." Even the German Foreign Minister, von Neurath confirmed to Lester that he could not influence Foster—"only Hitler could."[117] Early in 1934, Danzig had a visit from Himmler, head of the SS and a parade took place of 12,000 uniformed men, infantry, cavalry, and motorcyclists. Lester adds,

> The situation as I find it on my arrival in Danzig is, therefore, that a minimum of 12,000, some estimate 20,000 men in the territory of the Free City are organized on what is no doubt semi-military bases and drilled and uniformed. They carry the same flag as in Germany; their officers have made the same declaration of loyalty to the Führer; they are occasionally inspected by superior officers from Germany itself.[118]

Appealing to a Regional Audience: Germanizing the "Polish Corridor"

Donald Steyer has pointed out that by appealing to its earlier Prussian roots Nazi propagandists invoked in Danzig "a history that was deemed more malleable to indoctrination than say in the Wartheland where the local Polish population was simply moved out."[119] The appeal certainly resonated well with the speeches that were being transmitted from the Greater Reich in broadsheets and booklets like "Der Führer spricht"/"The Führer speaks" with appeals like, "You are the living guarantors of Germany, you are the living Germany of the future, you are not an empty idea, you are not a pale pattern but you are blood of our blood, flesh of our flesh, spirit of our spirit—you are the survival of our people."[120] The appeal to an earlier and by implication, its true history was a ubiquitous plea, often expressed, as noted earlier, in battle and military terms, as in: "Let's approach Danzig not as a visit to a museum but to a battlefield on which the future of the northeast is being fought. It will be won back into the Reich with German-Prussian strength. It is not just German, it is Prussian."[121] Nazi propaganda never abated, and in fact, intensified, with more mass meetings, marches, parades. Berlin provided extra visual aids, as noted earlier, with frequent visits by German warships, like the *Admiral Scheer, Schlesien,* and the *Leipzig,* giving the citizens of Danzig yet more opportunities and pretexts for a parade or a demonstration.[122] In these ways, the image of Danzig was being shaped to transcend its geography and somewhat backwoods location as a city in the northeast. It had become a powerful symbol in the arsenal of Nazi propaganda, and the elite of the Nazi Party were by no means silent about it. In fact, they visited the city at critical junctures in the 1930s but, as we shall soon see, they reveled in its reclaimed identity after the invasion. German consciousness ("*Deutschbewusst*") was now pitched at a much higher level.

Germanization extended beyond Danzig and included targeting Germans in the "Polish Corridor." Germans from these areas were permitted to visit the city, by showing a border pass. They could meet with their friends, hear firsthand the rousing speeches, and observe the marches and demonstrations by the Nazi Party members. Local Party leaders cultivated every opportunity to reinforce German identity. Forster's role in these initiatives was intense and included personally naming county leaders in the Kashubian areas, which later, after the war began, became even more significant, in that Foster's deputies randomly decided about the fate of the people. For example, in the Berent/Kościerzyna region, the *Landrat* of *Kreis Berent*, Günther Modrow would put words "*tak*" (yes) "*nie*" (no) next to the name of the arrested person—signifying death or life.[123]

Voices from "the Corridor"

How successful were all these initiatives that essentially pitted local people—at one-time neighbors and possibly even friends—against one another? A 2013 publication draws on interviews pertaining to the relationship between Poles and Germans (and Kashubians) in "the Corridor" and suggests that the Germanization schemes in the 1930s were not always effective in turning Poles and Germans against one another. People who had shared their living space for many years still wanted a peaceful coexistence, and it was arguably a more powerful force than political ideology. The excerpts below pertain to the period before the war. They were recorded by Maria Krawczyk in Stara Kiszewa, one of many small towns in "the Polish Corridor," and published in 2013 with the title "Pogranicza, Stara Kiszewa" (Border Lands).[124] It contains recorded interviews of Poles, Germans, Kashubs, and Kociewie residents in Pomerania who describe themselves as locals ("tutejsi"/die Hiesigen).

Christa Burghardt: Nowe Podlaszki after 1933
After 1933, that is, after Hitler came to power, nothing had changed here, and we didn't even notice that something important had happened in the Reich. We hardly cared, for we were taking care of our own business. Father did not make any difference between Poles and Germans. He was a fair-minded man but most of all he had common sense. He stayed away from politics. He did not change his views like you would change shirts.[125]

Gerda Podehl: Nowe Podlaszki, after 1934
The time period right before the war was grim. Very seldom did we dare visit our cousins after dark. Landowners usually had more money, and they were mostly Germans. The Poles were laborers. We also had Polish citizenship and learned Polish in school. Poles on the other hand didn't study German in school, and knew German only from home, having learned it from their grandparents. Our relations

were generally very good until the time when friction between Poles and Germans begun. I suspect that it was all Hitler's fault.[126]

Stefan Brzozowski: Wilcze Błota after 1933
Poles and Germans lived together and understood one other—everything was going well. When Hitler took over, however, it was not long before Polish-German relations got worse and worse. The Germans started clubs and organized meetings. Even among us young people there were fewer social gatherings. It all began with those fiery Hitler speeches on the radio that changed their mentality so deeply that they greeted each other by raising their arm in salute: "Sieg heil, heil Hitler."[127]

Jadwiga Hintz: Nowe Polaszki, after 1933
How beautiful it had been here! When the Germans finished their school year they had *Kinderfest*. We all went together to a forest, made beautiful flower garlands, a band was playing. What a life it was! It was because of Hitler that everything turned into such turmoil. After he seized power, the local Germans got all uppity and organized meetings, and talks and sing-songs. They didn't acknowledge us Poles anymore. They let themselves become stupid. Church didn't count anymore, only Hitler. There was, however, a German called Oktan Bazowski, a religious man and he stuck by the Poles. The Chief of the Polish police used to tell us: "Never get involved in all this. Don't make enemies ... Let them do whatever they want." Still, those who were stupid got involved anyway.[128]

Franciszek Nierzwicki: Lipy
Poles and Germans lived peacefully here. But we could sense that war was near. Germans who were in the military knew that war was coming. In Maliki, where the German military man Neuman lived, military maneuvers were taking place, and the SA was there, too. These maneuvers were typically military with horseback riding, shooting. Poles were not surprised, though, that Germans were allowed to do that, for they were the "big shots," and nobody interfered in their business, nor commented on what they were doing.[129]

Adelajda Żywicka: Nowe Podlaszki
In our village, the Germans were good people. When we went to school, just like children do, we would sometimes call them names, and they called us names too. We called one another names, like children do, but we lived peaceably. We played ball together, and none of us would have hurt the other. The Schwonkis were our closest neighbors. One young woman was called Christel, the other Edith. Christel wasn't pretty but she had a strong character. She'd give you her last slice of an apple. The Lehrkis lived farther down. They were also very good people. They had a boy called Gerhard. I learned German from those kids.[130]

Jan Narloch: Bartoszylas
The Germans were rich. And the Poles had to work for them, but the Germans paid well. They always had the best soil because that's what they chose, and they knew

how to farm. They were good managers. They knew that war was approaching—they just sensed it was coming. It was at that point that they started having secret meetings, organized in such way that no one would know anything about them. That's when they began to avoid Poles. Nobody knew what was talked about at those meetings. Apparently, they were saying that Hitler was coming, and that they were glad that war was coming, and that the Poles were afraid. But yet, we were all still living in peace.[131]

Manfrid Baaske: Nowe Podlaszki-Gdańsk, April 10, 1938
Because our father was a Gdańsk citizen he was allowed to vote in the Gdańsk senate elections. I remember those elections. Germans from the Reich also participated in them. Hitler had added extra ballots, for example—"Do you believe that it was a right thing for Austria to be annexed into the Reich?" Voting took place on board the ship *Seedienst Ostpreussen* which was anchored in the bay close to Gdańsk. It was a big deal. Germans from the Reich voted 99 percent for Hitler. At that time, voting for Hitler was considered a matter of honor.[132]

Józef Gołuński: Stara Kiszewa, before Easter 1939
Sometime before Easter 1939, young hoodlums from the nationalist movement ganged up. There was such hatred, and they wanted to do harm to Germans. They broke their windows and painted the swastika on their houses. I saw it on my way to school, but I didn't know at the time what this sign meant. I remember I was in church with my mother on Maundy Thursday and our priest, Leon Kręcki came out after the mass, stood in front of the altar where communion was distributed and said: "War has not yet begun, but we want peace here. Please, do not do harm to any Germans, and don't break their windows, for those who are doing such things are simply hooligans. Those who want to fight better wait for the war to begin."[133]

What can we learn from these interviews? It seems feasible to conclude that the priorities and main burden of the day for both Poles and Germans were prosaic—namely, to make ends meet and provide for their families. Their recollections are certainly not of a lost paradise, but they do show a deep contrast with former days. Tensions have escalated due to the political rallies and meetings that drew the German neighbors into a political orbit that make the Poles feel like outsiders, nervously viewing the new developments. It had become harder for both communities to avoid the subject of politics, especially right before the outbreak of war. In a territory that had been predominantly Polish, the relationship between Poles and Germans does not appear to be equal. In fact, Germans who treat Poles as equals are described as exceptions. The other striking factor is the role and influence of the Polish priest who warns his congregation to avoid trouble with Germans. There is no mention or evidence that German priests or ministers made the same appeal. In general, these admittedly limited findings convey a level of commitment to coexistence, and are not far removed from the conclusions of historian Mieczysław Wojciechowski who claims that despite the initiatives of the National Socialists to indoctrinate Pomerania, hostile activities—espionage or direct attacks—were carried out by a minority of Germans and that such activities should not be assessed in the context of September "as the outbreak of war and the German invasion of Pomerania created a totally different social and political situation." He also cautions against dogmatic conclusions in the absence of data.[134] What we can conclude is that there were indeed vigorous efforts to promote Germandom—the language, the culture, and school education that included, for example, forcing the Kashubians to speak German and Polish families to speak German among one another for fear of being denounced by their neighbors.[135] Historian Andrzej Gąsiorowski places some of the blame on Polish officials, pointing out that they were irresolute in their policies regarding the German minority in Pomerania and were more concerned with not provoking the Third Reich, which led to conflicts and tensions.[136]

Military Preparations in Danzig and the Arrests of Local Jews and Poles

At what point does Stutthof begin to take shape as a potential place of internment? And at what point were there plans or military initiatives in place to arrest and intern prisoners? Heinrich Himmler, head of the SS, visited Danzig in July 1939 and just as Goebbels had ordered dramatic changes in 1930 to strengthen the Gau (notably in sending Forster). Himmler's visit resulted in strengthening even further the military presence in Danzig, especially the SS, which received a new unit called the SS *Heimwehr Danzig*. From this point onward, Himmler's role became stronger, specifically in his control and coordination of the paramilitary units. The Gestapo, Krimipolizei, and Sicherheitsdienst were merged under the umbrella of the RSHA in September 1939 and were under the command of the head of Police of Danzig, Richard Hildebrandt, whose authority included the *Gestapo, Kripo, Sicherheitsdienst,* and the *Schutzpolizei*. The units that were designated to carry out attacks on Jews and Poles belonged to a special defense unit, the SS-*Wachsturmbann* that was originally an auxiliary police battalion founded on July 3, 1939, under the command of SS-Brigadier General Schäfer. This unit was now charged with setting up places where selected Poles were to be kept, in the event of war. (Later, some of these SS men became part of the SS-personnel at Stutthof and worked as guards or in other capacities.) SS-*Wachsturmbann* had 500 people and was under SS-*Obersturmbannführer*/Lieutenant Colonel Kurt Eimann who worked alongside the police in Danzig during the military operation, which was code-named Operation Tannenberg, a name that conjured up other victories and defeats like the victory over the Teutonic Knights by the Poles and Lithuanians in 1410 and then in the First World War, when the German armies under Paul von Hindenburg defeated the Russians. The relative proximity of the Tannenberg monument to Danzig provided more fuel for commemoration that now included the presence of von Hindenburg's remains that had been reinterned there with great pomp and circumstance in 1934. The plan was to arrest local Jews and the local Polish intelligentsia, including members of the clergy and nobility, as well as all those deemed a threat to Nazi rule in Pomerania. Police Chief, Richard Hildebrandt provided them with weapons and other military supplies and was responsible for their training. Other duties included patrolling the streets and guarding strategically important buildings in Danzig. They also recruited actively. These prewar exercises were to connect Danzig with Stutthof—and with the fate of those who were interned there—right from the beginning of its history. All of the agencies of Danzig were thus working hand-in-glove and had already selected the man who would head up the camp—Max Pauly.

In July 1939, Pauly ordered a group of SS men and SS officers of *Wachsturmbann*, to prepare temporary prisons for Poles, and designated Victoria School and Neufahrwasser/Nowy Port as suitable venues. Pauly then initiated in August 1939 the building of a camp at Stutthof. Everything was in place at the end of August 1939, when two divisions of the *Wachsturmbann*, under his command, worked as SS guards in the three designated places for prisoners. The remaining three units, working with Danzig's police units and one unit of SS-*Heimwehr* were given the task of arresting Poles (whose names were compiled on special lists). Their other assignments were to take over Westerplatte and the Polish Post Office and to fight in Gdynia and Oksywie.

Annexation and the Declaration of War: Poland Is Invaded

At the beginning of September 1939, several strands of history—local, regional, and international—begin to overlap, intersect, and compete for attention. Beyond Danzig and Stutthof, a world war was brewing and threatening to involve the countries that as victors in the First World War were responsible for crafting the peace treaty that had made Danzig a free city in the first place. No single strand can be identified as the defining one in establishing a camp at Stutthof, but from March 1939 onward, the possibility of Nazi Germany going to war was becoming more likely, given the precedence and significance of events beyond Danzig. There were successes in spring that provided ample proof of the military capabilities of Nazi Germany on March 15, 1939, with the occupation of Prague and Czechoslovakia. Five days later, Germany demanded possession of the Memel/Klaipėda region, despite the 1924 Klaipėda Convention guaranteeing Lithuanian sovereignty over the area. When Britain and France followed a policy of appeasement, and Italy and Japan openly supported Nazi Germany, Lithuania accepted the ultimatum on March 22, 1939, the last prewar acquisition of territory before the outbreak of war.

There were reminders of international support to Poland on March 31, with the announcement by Prime Minister Neville Chamberlain that Britain and France would support Poland in the event of an invasion by Nazi Germany. However, given the absence of direct opposition about Memel/Klaipėda, Nazi Germany took this as an encouraging sign that they could achieve their central quest—namely, to reclaim Danzig and then to press eastward for what was called *Lebensraum*, establishing Nazi control over the whole area, and in the process eliminate Polish resistance.

Does the quest for more "living space"—*Lebensraum*—fit in this narrative about Danzig? Historian Epstein links Hitler's plans for *Lebensraum* to the summer of 1936 when he abandoned efforts to overcome the restrictions of the Versailles Treaty and instead began to forge alliances to help him acquire *Lebensraum*. For example, in 1936 he openly supported the Spanish Civil War by sending well-equipped volunteers, despite the Soviet Union's support for the Spanish Republicans. On November 5, 1937, he outlined his foreign-policy plans that were recorded in the Hossbach memorandum in terms of Germany's need for *Lebensraum,* even naming Austria and Czechoslovakia as his first targets because of their economic and manpower resources. Epstein adds that they also would be useful staging areas for eastward expansion.[137] Finding a justification for attacking Poland seems to have been more important and certainly more prominent in the initial rhetoric immediately after the invasion. In fact, Kershaw claims that although "*Lebensraum*" had been brewing in Hitler's thinking, he rarely used the term. Kershaw writes, "He was portrayed as a man of peace, seeking to attain his goals through political skill, not force of arms, and building up military might as a defensive not an aggressive weapon."[138] Bergen frames it succinctly—"Hitler's approach to foreign policy was talk peace, and plan for war."[139] The German invasion was rationalized on the false charge that the Poles had attacked a radio station in Gleiwitz/Gliwice in Upper Silesia. This was exposed after the war as organized by the German SS who dressed German convicts in Polish uniforms.[140] Elizabeth Morrow Clark, citing her mentor, the noted historian Professor Anna Cienciala points out that a popular view that the loss of German territories to Poland led straight to Poland's failure to recognize the "larger racial and territorial goals implicit in the principles of *Lebensraum.*"[141]

So, who was to blame for war, according to Hitler? Schenk proposes that Hitler liked to place the possibility of war on Poland and warned that her "unbearable provocations" might give him no other recourse than to declare war[142] (although von Ribbentrop laid the blame on Britain, as we will soon see). But meanwhile, there was every indication that Nazi Germany was prepared for military action before the first shots were fired on September 1. The German battleship Schleswig-Holstein was already in Danzig Bay on August 25, in preparation for an attack that was originally scheduled for the morning of August 26. The heroic Polish defense of the Westerplatte lasted for seven days when the Germans assaulted the Polish Transit depot, resulting in the deaths of several hundred Germans and between fifteen and twenty Poles. It took three weeks before the fighting in and around Danzig ended.[143] On September 2, 1939, the main Polish Post Office on Helveliusplatz was fired on by the SS-*Heimwehr* Danzig and three battalions of the SS-Wachsturm Eimann. After an attack that lasted fourteen hours, facing heavy artillery the thirty-eight Polish defenders capitulated. The building itself was set on fire. Eight were killed, six managed to escape—two of whom were later captured, and six others died as the result of their injuries. (They were buried in a mass grave but in 1992 their bodies were given a decent burial in Zaspa and commemorated by the then-President Lech Wałęsa.)[144] Foster sent a telegram to Hitler, announcing the successful return of Danzig to the Reich. The local prison in Danzig was ready and equipped to handle Polish resisters who were already known to the authorities.

The 1,500 people arrested on the first day of the war in this initial assault by the Danzig Gestapo had already been targeted and their names turned in to the local police and the SS. Several Jews were arrested, but most of the arrested were Poles who represented the main Polish institutions, the Post Office, railway workers, members of the General Commission of the Republic of Poland, Harbor and Customs workers, teachers, priests, and Trade Union members. After transporting them to the Victoria

School, they selected 150 for imprisonment, and then transported them by bus to Stutthof. Erwin Lichtenstein, former president of the Jewish Synagogue (1933–9), includes in his memoir of these years a report of September 2, pertaining to the experiences of Oskar Grau, who had moved earlier from Leipzig to Danzig: "He and numerous other Jews could thank *Polizeirat*/Police Councilman Heribert Kammer who intervened in the proceedings at Victoria School and was able to procure the release of a large number of Jews."[145] "Unfortunately, Kammer was removed from his post at the Police headquarters on September 9 and transferred to Gdynia."[146]

Kammer himself wrote a report about this incident. On hearing that something was going on at the school, he had gone there to check on the wellbeing of his Jewish acquaintances, and to his astonishment found around 300 people assembled—both local Jews and Poles from the Railroad office. He saw money stacked up high on a table in the courtyard. Kammer writes that he returned immediately to the Police Headquarters where he learned that the police were not aware of these measures, and they attributed them to the office of the Gauleiter. Kammer then instructed Zube, the Inspector of Police, to return the money that had been confiscated immediately to the owners and to release the men who had been unconstitutionally arrested. When the office of the Gauleiter objected, Kammer reminded them that the Danzig Constitution was still valid and had to be respected. Technically, the Constitution was still in effect until April of 1940, which provided a certain measure of protection to the remaining Jews, though all sorts of restrictive new ordinances were soon imported from the Reich and enacted, including the mandatory registration for Poles, and the restriction on valuable items (especially jewelry) from being included in their luggage when they left Danzig.[147] The ordinance that affected the remaining Jews the most significantly was the loss of their Danzig citizenship on November 25, 1939. People who had lived all their life in Danzig (one elderly man's grandfather was buried in Danzig) now had to report to the police by November 1 and apply for residence permission. Robert Sander was appointed to take charge of the immigration of Jews, and like Kammer, turned out to be a sympathetic and tireless advocate for the now small Jewish community. He describes them in the following report:

> The community that I came to know in the fall of 1939 included really old people, who were unable to come up with enough money to emigrate; but among them there were some old Danzigers who could not part from the site of their childhood. Those were the ones I talked about a lot to many people. They were still of the opinion that despite all the sadness that surrounded them in their old *Heimat*, people would continue to accept them because they would never get on the wrong side of the law.[148]

Sander concludes that these elderly people had no idea that Forster (and his helper, whom he calls "conscienceless Löbsack") had just one objective in mind—to present the Führer with Danzig as the first "Jew-free" city of the Reich. Wilhelm Löbsack's solution was to send the Jews of Danzig to Poland because he knew the Danzig constitution would still give them some protection. As fragile as this protection was, it certainly explains why any Jews survived in Danzig in the first weeks of the war.

Echt writes that a mass emigration in the first weeks of the war was unimaginable yet individuals and small groups continued to leave. In these early days, local German officials like Kammer and Sander clearly played a role in protecting (at least for a while) the rights and the wellbeing of Danzig's Jews. Their responses might be dismissed as rare exceptions in the German community, but they also could easily be overshadowed by the larger story of a man like Forster whose cruel, racist voice has dominated this chapter. The compassionate profiles of these men are given by a Jewish teacher, Samuel Echt. Echt includes Sander's report about his conversation with two elderly Jews who still love their native city—"Old Danzig." Sander's words are filled with compassion and solidarity with fellow Danzigers; they would never get on the wrong side of the law.[149] Grabowska-Chałka comments on the pressure that was exercised against Germans in Danzig and adds: "[I]t must be said that many Germans preserved their decency and didn't yield to Nazi pressure."[150]

The next steps for those on what had become "the right side of the law" were the so-called *Säuberungsaktionen*/Cleansing Initiatives, which allowed them to arrest "undesirables" in the Polish communities of the surrounding towns, before taking them to collection centers, and from there to Danzig. By the middle of September prisoners were being sent to outlying areas, like Grenzdorf/Graniczna-Wieś where they worked in a quarry, or to farms where they worked on the turnip or potato harvest. According to the archivists at Stutthof Museum, it is still hard to determine exact statistics for the number of Poles and Jews who were killed in the first days of September, when the Wehrmacht marched into Pomeranian towns and summarily executed prominent Polish citizens, along with local Jews.

"Traitors, Arsonists, Pillagers and Enemies of the State Are Interned" was the title of an article published on September 13, 1939, in the *Danziger Vorposten*. The writer proceeds *to* identify the imprisoned as belonging to Polish terrorist groups who were interned by the SS and by the police in the Victoria School in Danzig, thus preventing further bloodshed. The chaff, the author explains, was being separated from the wheat. "Some were able to be released while justice would take its course for the others." Further information is given on Stutthof, describing it as "a large internment camp under construction near the forester's lodge in the middle of the forest." The article continues, "When completed, around 2,000 from this mob will be able to be housed there. Right now, there are 480 civilian prisoners in the camp. Because all sorts of trades are represented, the construction of the camp is moving forward very quickly." The report then points proudly to the erection of a barbed wire fence topped with wired entanglements that surround the area. A huge barrack is almost complete, and tents have been set up for provisional housing for the prisoners. The tone of this article is reassuring: the prisoners at the Victoria School (referred to as *Gesindel*—rabble/riffraff) have been disinfected, deloused, so there is no possibility of bringing diseases to the camp. They will be sent to Stutthof—unless they deserve harsher treatment—and will be catalogued with a number.[151]

The pro-Nazi stance of this newspaper article is to be expected, given its support in the 1930s of the party in Danzig, but particular facets of the venom stand out—the notion of retribution for an earlier conflict, the prediction of a common fate for Jews and Poles—already reduced to a number, and the loss of identity in a camp that is being prepared to receive even greater numbers. The name-calling in its heading can be read as the distillation of over six years of Nazi indoctrination. All of these actions—and hostilities—were the backdrop for the celebration of the military victories of early September and the subsequent return of Danzig to the Reich. Civilian Germans celebrated in the streets of Danzig. The euphoria among German Danzigers was supported by the majority of German religious leaders in their communities, whether Catholic or Protestant. The Nazi invasion of Poland was endorsed and celebrated in a letter written by the Bishop of the Diocese of Danzig, Carl Maria Splett, who had been nominated to this post in 1938. In a letter, he prayed for

> the blessing and protection of Hitler and the Reich, that He would provide grace to our Führer, nation and motherland ... and protect our forces on the ground and sea, ships and planes ... Then might and prosperity will blossom in the Reich and will assure that our nation will hold an honorable place and power among other nations. Amen.[152]

Danzig's Return to the Reich Is Celebrated

Hitler did not linger in visiting the restored city and, along with Himmler, on September 19, 1939, "triumphantly entered the city, ... drove, as he had in Vienna, the Sudetenland and Memel in an open car through the streets where swastika flags practically covered the buildings, through masses of cheering people celebrating their return to the Reich with loud screams of Heil and often tears of joy."[153] The visit was followed in October by that of von Rippentrop, the Reich Minister for Foreign Affairs who made a rousing speech in Danzig on October 24, 1939.[154] He began by referring to the glorious entry of the Führer into the liberated city. "I shall never forget how our Fuehrer, [sic] coming straight from the scene of his victories in Poland, entered your beautiful city, and how he was greeted by Danzig's bright-eyed youth and by all of you with unending cheers and fervent enthusiasm. After more than twenty years of hardship and bitter oppression, Danzig is once more truly a free city."[155] Playing on the word "free," he appeals to the youth, to their vigor, to their pride in their native city, and to their passionate reception of the Führer. In soaring rhetoric, he invokes the past, calling their problems "among the worst and meanest injustices perpetrated at Versailles."[156] These problems in Danzig and the "Corridor" have now been resolved by the Führer. Von Ribbentrop also makes a very telling connection to the city by reminding his audience that they are also celebrating another anniversary that day—Albert Forster's arrival in Danzig in 1930. On that date, he claims, Forster provided the watchword "Back to the Reich" as the catalyst to confront the six and a half years of struggle against "the political pressure exercised by the Poles" and the burden of maintaining "tolerable relations with the Polish State." He also expresses gratitude for leaders who were exemplary fighters in the Führer's cause—(at this point he refers to himself as the minister most directly involved) for whom Danzig was "a child of sorrows."[157] This was not a new concept and resonated with the words of one of the most popular poets of the day—the East Prussian poet, Agnes Miegel who had joined the

NS-Frauenschaft/National Socialist Women's Organization in 1933 and the Nazi Party in 1940. To her, Hitler was the new Hindenburg and she celebrated the 1939 recovery of Danzig in the poem "To Germany's Youth, Autumn 1939." In another poem "To the Führer," she rejoiced that Hitler's hands "had wiped away her past troubles like tears from the face of a widow."[158]

Forster received the most lavish praise in von Ribbentrop's speech, because "his calm confidence and unfailing optimism imbued not only the Party but all Danzig and determined the level-headedness and excellent behavior and discipline of the population." By calling Danzig "a child of sorrows," von Ribbentrop pulls on the heart strings of every citizen of Danzig and conjures up the image of a lost child finally being wrapped up in the welcoming arms of the Fatherland. It is powerful rhetoric that echoes the maternal imagery of Miegel's grieving widow. It is interesting to note that later in the speech, von Ribbentrop lays the full blame for the war at the feet of England and not of Poland. In fact, he is somewhat restrained in his comments about Poland. British intransigence exemplified in Chamberlain led to the war, despite the patience and forbearing attitude of the Führer. At the core of his speech is the rationalization that war was never Hitler's idea, but nonetheless, it must be fought for the sake of the honor of the German people. Von Ribbentrop goes on to praise

> the courageous behavior of the SS. Home Defence [sic] units and the brave part they played on the attack on the Westerplatte and the Polish Post Office, as well as the frontier encounters in the neighborhood of Zoppot, in the storming of Dirschau and in many other engagements, are deeds of valor which from this time onward will be forever bound up with the history of the liberation of German soil from under the Polish yoke …. Danzig will never again be separated from the Reich![159]

Unsurprisingly, von Ribbentrop (who had negotiated the pact between Hitler and Stalin in August) holds the British responsible for the outbreak of war and complicit with the Polish government in rejecting "the Fuehrer's generous offer" toward Danzig and the "Corridor" in favor, he even claimed, of Polish interests. He was dumbfounded when the Polish Ambassador to the Reich said that the pursuit of Germany's plan for a political reunion of Danzig with the Reich would mean war with Poland.[160] The only explanation for this rejection was that Britain was behind it. He invokes the earlier offers of a settlement to Poland by Hitler and his "unparalleled long-suffering."[161] He further accuses Britain for failing to recognize the natural dynamic qualities of the German Reich, the vitality of the German people, and above all, the determination and creative force of the Fuehrer.[162] After having laid the full blame for the war on Britain and her leaders, notably Chamberlain, and after praising the alliance with their Soviet neighbors and even offering some modest praise to the United States, von Ribbentrop concluded his speech with a passionate appeal to the people of Danzig: "The German people, welded by National Socialism into a solid block of steel, stand united behind their Leader while in front of the Reich there stands today a glorious Army and Air Force, and a Navy which has gained for itself fresh laurels." He reminds his audience that Germany did everything in her power to avoid "this utterly senseless war," which was forced on her, but she will win. Victory is assured by "her own strength and by our faith in the man who is the embodiment of our highest ideals in the world—Our Fuehrer!"[163]

Von Ribbentrop's speech captures key aspects of what Kershaw has identified in the process behind the propaganda of the "Hitler myth," which Goebbels took credit for formulating and which he heralded as his greatest achievement.[164] Danzig was particularly vulnerable to the manipulative purpose behind the propaganda, especially regarding its status as the victim of the Treaty of Versailles. Forster had exploited this by constantly preaching German consciousness, and as the personal representative of the Führer himself, he was the consensus builder in Danzig, including among voters who were on the left of the political spectrum but who longed for Danzig to be restored to the Reich. Kershaw points out that the most notable factor in Hitler's appeal to wide sections of the population was his record of success as a statesman.[165] He cites as examples the withdrawal of Germany from the League of Nations in October 1933, the Saar plebiscite of 1935, the march into the Rhineland on March 7, 1936, the homecoming of the Sudeten Germans in 1938 as the result of the Munich Peace Settlement.[166] These key events in the Third Reich gave tangible proof to Danzig that Hitler was capable of doing the same for them—annulling the Treaty of Versailles, bringing home exiled Germans, as he did in Memel, and preparing them, as Kershaw proposes, for a war that no one had wanted earlier. He writes that the subsequent confidence in Hitler's statesmanship was "a major factor on the relative composure of the popular mood during the Polish crisis of the following year, when the fears that it would lead to war were nowhere near as extensive as they had been in 1938."[167] "Hitler stood for at least some things they admired," writes Kershaw.[168] For the Danzigers, what made the difference in their admiration of Hitler was his appeal to Germandom and the need to restore the territory they had lost after the First World War. Like the majority in the Old Reich, they were not looking for war, and in fact, wanted to avoid it, but his successes and military achievements since the mid-1930s confirmed the trustworthiness of his leadership and affirmed the correctness of preserving their German identity. German identity was thus much more than patriotism or even nationalism. It excluded all elements that were perceived as antithetical to that identity. Steps had already been taken to exclude Poles and Jews, but they were going to become increasingly more radical. Kershaw situates the shift in gear of Hitler's race policy to the Kristallnacht pogrom, pointing out that it was instigated by Goebbels (though approved by Hitler, as Goebbel's diaries later make clear). "Territorial expansion and removal of the Jews, the two central features of Hitler's *Weltanschauung,* had thus come together in 1938 into sharp focus in the foreground of the picture. The shift from 'utopian' vision to practical policy options was taking shape."[169] The treaty of nonaggression (Ribbentrop-Molotov Pact of August 23, 1939) gave both leaders assurance that, at least for now, they would not attack each other. On September 1, Nazi Germany attacked Poland and annexed its western provinces. The Red Army invaded western Poland on September 17 and annexed its eastern territories. The Second Republic of Poland was thus crushed between two superpowers and ceased to exist. Polish resistance to both Soviet and Nazi domination, however, did not cease. It was not a monolith on either side, but despite collaboration and coexistence in now occupied Poland, the Polish resistance persisted throughout the long years ahead, not just in its exiled government in London but on annexed territory like Danzig-West Prussia and especially in the camps where those who survived the first onslaught of "cleansing" were sent.

Twenty miles away from Danzig, Stutthof was already operating, if in primitive conditions, thanks to the skills and manual labor of the men who had been interned and now were constructing the barracks that they would be forced to live in for years, some until the camp's liberation. The local SS had, in fact, already identified those with carpentry and masonry skills. The young SS men from Danzig and the villages and towns of Pomerania who had been recruited earlier to Germanize Danzig and Pomerania, to perform ethnic cleansing, to fight on local terrain like the Westerplatte in the invasion of Poland, these same young men would soon become the backbone of the camp. Their role in the camp as representatives of "the new dynamic Reich" will be pivotal. Some who entered Stutthof in September 1939 will still be there in 1945, to lead half-starved prisoners on the long "death marches" toward the Baltic, fleeing from the Soviet forces, with whom they are—at this point—still allies.

Grass eventually brings the subject of Stutthof into full view, including the taboo subject of soap being made there, a claim that has found little or no support among historians, including the Stutthof archivists. Grass's focus, however, is on more indisputable realities—on earlier days:

> Stutthof: that little word took on more and more meaning. "Hey, you! You got a yen for Stutthof?"—"If you don't keep that trap of yours shut, you'll end up in Stutthof." A sinister word had moved into apartment houses, went upstairs and downstairs, sat at kitchen tables, was supposed to be a joke, and some actually laughed: "They're making soap in Stutthof now, it makes you want to stop washing." You and I were never in Stutthof …. In his (Brauxel's) day Stutthof was a rich village, larger than Schiewenhorst, Nickelswalde and smaller than Neuteich, the county seat. Stutthof had 2698 inhabitants. They made money when soon after the outbreak of the war a concentration camp was built near the village and had to be enlarged again and again. Railroad tracks were even laid in the camp. The tracks connected with the island narrow-gauge railway from Danzig-Niederstadt. Everybody knew that, and those who have forgotten may as well remember: Stutthof: Danzig Lowlands County, Reich Province of Danzig-West Prussia, judicial district of Danzig, known for its fine timber frame church, popular as a quiet seaside resort, and early German settlement … and between 1939 and 1945, in Stutthof Concentration Camp, Danzig Lowlands County, people died, I don't know how many.[170]

In the chapters that follow we will attempt to determine their number, their identity and more importantly, how that identity played out during their imprisonment. The article from the *Vorposten* cited earlier went on to reassure its readers:

> At that point there will no longer be a person with the name Salomon Totenkopf or a Bronislaw Franzkowiak but just a number. How long they will stay in this camp where they will have to work hard is not yet clear. But for now we don't have to worry about that. But one thing is clear: These prisoners behind barbed wire will

despite everything be treated too decently when you consider how our Germans were murdered and slaughtered in what was once Poland, how they were brutally assaulted and abused, how wounded German soldiers were treacherously killed, and their eyes poked out. But all these crimes and shameful acts will perhaps be ever so slowly expiated.[171]

The next chapter will show how that these alleged "crimes and shameful acts" were indeed expiated by Jews and Poles in Stutthof, though not "ever so slowly." Some victims were murdered right away and never saw Stutthof. Others were sent to "special" camps that we are still discovering. Those who did enter the camp, among them the remaining Jews of Danzig and a group of Polish priests—were mockingly coupled as "*Juden und Pfaffen.*" Together they bore the initial brunt of the cruelty leveled at them in the wake of the successful invasion of the free territory of Danzig and "the Corridor." The passages cited from Grass's fiction and the interviews from "the Corridor" give us some sense of the level of indoctrination that was aimed at making believers out of the most politically apathetic and conversely, making resisters out of the timid. Many in the latter group will end up in the camps of the annexed territories. As the history of Stutthof continues, the voice of Grass will recede. Has he been a valuable and credible witness thus far? If only for one reason, he deserves to be heard—he correctly understood that ordinary people bore the brunt of the suffering that the ideology of Germandom and its subsequent consequences inflicted on the annexed territory that was soon to be named Danzig-West Prussia.[172] Grass chose to depict a Danziger German (Brunies)—his former teacher—as a dissident, and one can argue, he is hardly representative of Stutthof's mostly Polish prison population. I suggest that the endearing traits that Grass has given Brunies remind us of the fundamental humanness of every single prisoner who entered Stutthof and were soon to be divested of any trace of external dignity. Indirectly, Grass's fiction also exposes a lacuna in his depiction of Stutthof. Where does he even mention Polish and Jewish prisoners? Among the prisoners in Stutthof there may well have been former Polish neighbors. Parishioners in the German-speaking Catholic church in Langfuhr, along with priests who had catechized these same people, must surely have known that the Polish neighbors on the other side of the street were among those arrested in September 1939 and transported on trucks or by narrow gauge railway to the camp in the woods—"Stutthof *Waldlager.*" And many read the article in the *Vorposten* that had satirized Danzig Jews as "dead heads" (Totenkopf) and "Franzkowiak." But now they were reduced to numbers and stripped of identity. Stutthof itself will become more and more isolated from public view, though as we know from Grass's fiction, rumors about it will reach Danzig. Between 1939 and 1945 around 50,000 to 60,000 Poles will be interned behind the barbed wire, with few traces of a former life.[173] The connection to Danzig, however, will become stronger, for there will be a greater need for transportation to and from the city as new prisoners arrive from farther afield. And there will be more opportunities for local people to join the workforce there, including the SS. They will work as guards in the camp and its growing sub-camps.

2

Danzig-West Prussia and Stutthof: Implementing Germandom, September 1939–January 1942

A Camp for Civilian Prisoners

After September 1, 1939, Stutthof/Sztutowo lost forever its former identity as a pleasant village near Danzig and the Baltic beaches, and its namesake camp began to receive first hundreds, then thousands of prisoners. These "civilian prisoners," as they were called, were local people from Danzig and Pomerania who were either representatives of the Polish intelligentsia—clerics, teachers, lawyers, doctors, and other professionals, or Jews from the Danzig community. All of them were arrested because they were seen through the one lens of "Germandom"—any deviation from the ideal meant treatment as an opponent and an enemy of the Third Reich. Not every prisoner who was arrested in these early September days was sent right away to Stutthof, but it was soon to become central in the camp system of Danzig-West Prussia. For many reasons, but especially its proximity to Danzig, it was ideal. Every publication and pamphlet on Stutthof points out that it had water on all sides—the Baltic to the north, a lagoon (das Frische Haff) to the south and east, as well as canals and marshes, and to the west, the Vistula River.[1] Stutthof was clearly an ideal spot for the purposes of internment. No one could easily escape from Stutthof, surrounded as it was by such forbidding terrain; few attempted in the course of the next five plus years. Besides, it was extensive enough in acreage to accommodate opponents of the regime beyond Danzig in Pomerania that was soon to be officially annexed to the Nazi Reich as Danzig-West Prussia. From approximately eleven acres, it grew to over 300 acres in size, accommodating initially around 250 prisoners. This is how Waclaw Lewandowski, one of the first to arrive on September 2, 1939, describes his reception:

> After getting us off the closed trucks and buses that brought us there, we were again brutally searched, with frequently raining fists and whips … We were immediately put to digging foundations for huts under construction, felling trees and clearing stumps. The tempo was murderous … Late in the evening we were issued some 500 grams of very watery, lukewarm turnip soup and about 100 grams of dark bread. Dead tired, we fell to our pallets in the tents without undressing or washing. Even the physically strongest broke down, weeping with pain, exhaustion and humiliation.[2]

Grabowska-Chałka describes Stutthof as striking "fear in the hearts of Polish inhabitants of Pomerania and synonymous with bestial cruelty, terror, murder and finally mass extermination."[3] It is a fair summary of what will follow.[4]

Not all arrived by truck or bus. We recognize the same narrow-gauge railway that transported the two schoolboys, Matern and Amsel in *Dog Years,* but now it has a different function and many more passengers. The last station on the line was Tiegenhof, which was connected to Danzig by ferry. It was at this point that the newly arrived prisoners were moved from big wagons to the small ones of the narrow-gauge trains.[5] This became the main means of transport for delivering prisoners to Stutthof. The local predominantly German community was warned about the arrival of "Polish bandits" (a common insult), thus ensuring isolation for the camp inmates and no possibility of their escape. Next to the camp's main entrance was a special track for the narrow-gauge goods and passenger railway, built at the end of the nineteenth and the beginning of the twentieth century.

The first prisoners were forced to sleep in army tents but, within days, these same men were already building the huts and barracks that would house them for whatever time they would be kept there. For some, it would be short, and not because they were released. If hard labor, malnutrition, and beatings did not kill them, typhus often did. Others would survive for a while, and some even lasted the long years of the war though not necessarily the evacuation of the camp. Between September 1939 and May 1940, ten barracks were erected, including Barrack Eight and Barrack A that were later used for inmates in quarantine after several outbreaks of typhus. The barracks were enclosed in double strands of barbwire and referred to as "the old camp." Early in 1940, they built special accommodation for the SS, and a short time later, administration buildings. Also in 1940, the SS guardhouse was erected, near the main entrance to the camp so that everyone entering and leaving the camp had to pass the guardhouse. In 1941, they also added horse stables, pig stalls, and rabbit hutches. Prisoners were utilized in every aspect of the building of these barracks. Although the SS did attempt to identify skilled workers, the physical abilities or current state of health of prisoners were of less interest. Right from the beginning, brutally hard labor was a leading cause of death.

Krzysztof Dunin-Wąsowicz has provided quite detailed information about this period of the camp's history, though he himself did not arrive in Stutthof until May 1944. He based his information on the notes that he began to record shortly after his arrival in May 1944, which he gleaned from either prisoners who had been there at the beginning or from camp files to which he had access. We learn that the first prisoners were taken by six buses to Stutthof, and among those who arrived on September 2, 1939, at the camp was Senator Antoni Lendzion who had been a representative of the Polish minority in the Free City Senate.[6] Dunin-Wąsowicz writes that Lendzion was forced to clean toilets in the Victoria School even before the bus left for Stutthof. When the local people saw the first group of prisoners arrive in Stutthof, they taunted them with pro-German jeers.[7] He also gives some information about the first commandant Max Pauly and how he ordered the execution of thirty-nine Poles who had defended the Polish Post Office in Danzig, adding that during Pauly's tenure the role of the Commandant was paramount, that he had the last word on all decisions and that everybody in the camp kept out of his way on Mondays when he was in a bad mood.[8]

Though this first labor unit of Poles and Jews was treated brutally, the Jews were assigned to even more primitive housing that had not enough space on the bare floor even to sit on.[9] They all had to store their bedding of straw against the wall during the day and sleep on it at night. In these early days of the camp, there were neither bunks nor bathhouses, which were built the following June. Two weeks after the declaration of war, the Danzig Gestapo made more arrests, this time of 250 Poles, and after a trial, they were found guilty and taken to Stutthof, guarded by members of the SS *Wachsturmbahn* Eimann that had been active since July. These first prisoners were joined a few days later by 450 Jews from Danzig and by 6,000 Polish soldiers, after their surrender at Gdynia. During the following months, they were joined by Poles from the Gestapo prisons in Toruń/Thorn, Bromberg/Bydgoszcz, Grudziądz/Graudenz, and Elbing/Elbląg and by Boy Scouts from Gotenhafen/Gdynia. Testimonies that describe the first days of the camp frequently refer to the overcrowding, the crude troughs where they had to wash and especially the harsh treatment meted out to Jews and priests, always referred to together as *"Juden und Pfaffen."* We will return to them later in this chapter.

Was there an official mandate in place for the arrests and incarceration of all these people? By order of Hitler on September 20, Danzig-West Prussia, along with the neighboring Gaue of Warthegau and East Upper Silesia were to be "cleansed" of Jews, Poles and the Roma/Sinti and were to be replaced by ethnic Germans from Eastern Europe. On October 7, 1939, Hitler appointed Himmler to be head of the "Reich Commission for the Strengthening of Germandom"/*Reichskommissariat für die Festigung des deutschen Volkstums*—RKFDV, thereby giving additional responsibility to Himmler as head of the police and more significantly, formalizing and enclosing his authority in an agency that spelled out and named its purpose without shame—to strengthen Germandom, and by extension to dilute and destroy what stood in the way of that goal. Its effectiveness was virtually assured by assigning the mandate to Reinhard Heydrich and the agency he led—"Reich Security Main Office"/*Reichssicherheitshauptamt,* known as the RSHA. (On September 22, 1939, the RSHA became one of twelve main offices under the SS.) But even these high-ranking Nazi elites could not have carried out Hitler's orders without the help and cooperation of local Nazi leaders, like Gauleiter Forster who spelled out Hitler's guidelines on November 27, 1939: "We have been sent to this country by the Führer as trustees of the German interest with a simple goal—to make this country German again."[10] Reichsgau Danzig-West Prussia now included the newly annexed Polish province of Pomorze, the northern segment of "the Corridor" that included Gdynia, with its 1.5 million inhabitants. The new Reichsgau also embraced areas in East Prussia that had never been separated from the Reich, and two new districts that once had been part of Russian Poland, and one—Kreis Bromberg/Bydgoszcz that had formerly been part of Provinz Posen.[11] The whole Gau was governed by district leaders hand-picked by Forster, who from October was enjoying the dual role of Gauleiter and State Governor/*Reichsstaathalter* with the authority to also make civilian appointments. Earlier, Forster had been humorously referred to as *"Gaukönig,"* the king of the Gau. Now, he really was. This chapter will track the actions and effectiveness of the commission that set out to strengthen Germandom.

The Annexation of Pomerania: Cleansing by Mass Deportations and Killings

In order to carry out the "cleansing" part of the task to strengthen Germandom, special camps had to be set up to receive and sort out those who needed to be "strengthened" and those who needed to be sent elsewhere. Between September 1939 and March 1940, there were sixty-five detention camps scattered throughout a wide area that interned mostly Poles but also Jews and Roma/Sinti. They were located over a wide area in around Bromberg/Bydgoszcz, Chełmno/Kulmhof, Mewe/Gniew, Graudenz/Grudziądz, Karthaus/Kartuzy, Pelplin/Pęplin, Putzig/Puck, Dirschau/Tczew, Schöneck/Skarszewy, Skurz/Skórcz, Stargard/Stargard, Schwetz/Świecie, Briesen/Brzeźno, Neustadt/Wejherowo, and Hochstüblau/Zblewo. From the beginning of 1940, there were an additional three camps labeled as "isolationist camps" exclusively for Catholic priests, and a camp in Koźliny where they interned Roma and Sinti groups. According to historian Donald Steyer, the fate of some of these people is still unknown though some of them ended up in Stutthof.[12] Steyer emphasizes that the camps that existed between September 1939 and March 1940 were the origin of Stutthof and although they were of short duration, more prisoners were murdered in them or died of illness or starvation than in Stutthof's whole history. In fact, he calls them "extermination camps for Polish prisoners" who constituted the majority of the 40,000 victims, along with the Jews and Roma/Sinti of Pomerania—the minority among the prisoners.[13]

Meanwhile in Stutthof, conditions for this first group of prisoners were made even worse during the winter of 1939–40, which was particularly severe, with bitterly low temperatures and heavy snow. Every single prisoner was battling the elements, which no doubt contributed to the rampant sickness and deaths among them. Temperatures inside the barracks were often as cold as it was outside, even though there was a small iron stove in each of the barracks or huts. Up to 200 people had to share this common space of 50 square meters. A former principal of the Polish Gymnasium describes the conditions:

> Puny huts, hurriedly constructed from thin slats with holes through which winds and chills sneaked in, were extremely crowded. People lay on bare straw, cleared for the day with two planks nailed together in a T-shape. Those planks were the sole equipment of the room that could be sat on somehow. After the straw was cleared there would appear a narrow passage through the middle of the hut. It was covered during the night, so that those sleeping on straw could stretch out.[14]

The Autumn of 1939

The net spread rapidly beyond Danzig and with the help of the paramilitary organization—the *Selbstschutz* identified the first targets of the "cleansing" operation—priests, who were killed in shockingly high numbers. In the dioceses of Danzig and of Chełmno, there were around 670 priests, of whom 450 were murdered, mostly in the fall of 1939.¹⁵ Sixteen canons in the Peplin Cathedral Chapter—District Stargard—were arrested on October 20, 1939, by the local SS and *Selbstschutz* members, with the intent of shooting them near Peplin but they were seen by witnesses, and were taken instead to Tczew/Dirschau, where they were killed.¹⁶ Priests and teachers in the Stargard district were targeted in October 1939. Of eight priests, five were shot instantly and the other three on Good Friday 1940 in Stutthof. The fate of the other Polish priests was to be sent to Dachau or to be shot in the woods of Piaśnica. Priests who were ethnically German and who resisted the Nazis met a similar fate, among them Johann Ältermann, Ernst Karbaum, and Robert Wohlfeil.¹⁷ Mass graves in Pomerania were found in the Piaśnica area forests, where from October 1939 until April 1940 12,000–14,000 people were executed under the direction of Rudolf Tröger, the Inspector of the Security Police and the SD. The place came to be known as "the Kashubian Golgotha."

According to postwar trials, Gauleiter Forster had called two meetings between September 10–15, 1939, to discuss these "purges" with his subordinates, including his Finance Director, Julius Hoppenrath and District Inspector Günther Modrow (of District Behrent). Modrow testified that Forster instructed all present at these meetings "to maintain the strictest silence." The order involved removing "all dangerous Poles, all Jews and Polish clerics" and its execution would be the responsibility of the Head of Police in Danzig, with help from the local police force. Only the very closest colleagues should be informed of the "cleansing" actions. At the end of the meeting, the Gauleiter reminded them that they were bound to professional discretion/"Schweigepflicht." The postwar investigation of these actions indicates that Forster's command went beyond maintaining confidentiality: this was about silencing witnesses, as is clear in the original German. Hoppenrath testified that he held Forster responsible for "the shootings at the beginning, as he wanted 'Polish blood to flow.'"¹⁸ Mass graves were first discovered and dug up by local German farmers, then by a group of forty prisoners from Neufahrwasser. In late spring, 1940, the Germans attempted to cover up the evidence by planting bushes and trees, but animals dug up the bones and human remains, leading to intervention on November 1—All Saints day—by the local people who clandestinely lit candles and laid flower wreaths on the burial area.¹⁹

Historians identify two stages in the attack on the Polish population of Pomerania—the first stage—the most instantly deadly—in the fall of 1939 and the second of longer duration during the years 1940 to 1945. Both phases are connected to Stutthof, if in different ways. The early phase exemplifies what Hitler had in mind when he referred to the annihilation of Poland's "living forces." Rossino puts it this way: "Although the Nazis regularly employed violence against their enemies, never before had Hitler charged his SS and security forces with so expansive and merciless a mission as the murder of Poland's leading and educated social-political classes."²⁰ The survivors of these attacks were deported to the General Government or sent to Stutthof or other camps, many of them either radicalized or deadened by the brutality they had experienced.

A key agency deployed in these attacks was the *Selbstschutz*, the paramilitary self-defense organization that had been placed under the SS control in October 1939 and attracted more than 17,000 volunteers in Danzig-West Prussia, men between the ages of seventeen and forty-five. Known for extreme brutality, its goal was to avenge crimes against ethnic Germans. One of its duties was to assist in the removal of 10,000 people to Stutthof. The group was terminated by year's end by Himmler. It is estimated that they were responsible for as many as 20,000 killings in the twelve months following the German invasion.[21] Three days after the invasion, the killings in Bromberg/Bydgoszcz (described by the Nazis as "Bromberg Bloody Sunday") of ethnic Germans by a retreating Polish military unit incurred several thousand fatalities.[22] The actual death toll was likely around 4,500, in contrast to the reported 1940 German Criminal Police toll of 5,437.[23] On September 19, Hitler referred to the event as a veritable carnage where women and children had received bestial treatment.[24] The *Selbstschutz* played a significant role in these early days by assisting the SS special task forces—the *Einsatzgruppen w*ho brutally murdered the enemies of the Nazi Reich and followed the military units as they moved eastward to occupy other territories. When the units were disbanded, the men were reassigned to other duties, including working as guards in Stutthof.[25] The Bromberg/Bydgoszcz killings sparked outrage in the Danzig community and were duly reported in the local papers. Günter Grass remembers the clear black-and-white picture that it created in him: "I had been properly appalled by the 'Bromberg Bloody Sunday' horror stories that were plastered all over the local Nazi daily, *Danziger Vorposten* which made all Poles out to be treacherous murderers, and I perceived every German deed as justifiable retribution."[26] A different perspective is given by a minister of the Confessing Church. The Bromberg/Bydgoszcz attack was later recalled by Helmut Grollwitzer, as part of the propaganda promoted throughout the war to justify the German treatment of the Poles.[27] Meanwhile, other aspects of "cleansing" were carried out—removing Poles from their homes and replacing them with ethic Germans. By the end of 1940, around 122,000 were evicted from Pomerania and 78,000 from Gdynia. Of these, more than 91,500 were sent to the General Government, the others to detention camps or labor camps where they were either killed or sent to Stutthof and its sub-camps.[28] Large groups of children were identified as suitably Germanic in appearance to be sent to special camps to be further Germanized and then dispatched to German families, either locally or in the Greater Reich.[29]

Stutthof was still a fledgling camp, but it could already boast in the success of strengthening Germandom, by interning targeted enemies, especially local Danzig Jews and Poles. Though some files from the early period of the camp were destroyed, or confiscated by the Soviets after liberation, or lost, extensive documentation remains for the most significant events that followed the first months of the camp's existence. Archivist and historian Danuta Drywa points out that the documentation of Jewish deaths, especially for the earlier period has proven to be the most difficult because some of their names could have been Polish or German. Thus, there is not an accurate final number.[30] The category *Zivilgefangene* covered Stutthof's function as a camp between September 1939 and the spring of 1941, when it was under the jurisdiction of "SS *Oberabschnitt* Weichsel"/Vistula region. Though several agencies were involved, the 6,500 camp inmates of Stutthof and its filial camps who were interned during that period were under the supervision of the Danzig Gestapo, which was in charge of both prisoner arrests and releases. The *Schutzpolizei* (Security Police) in Danzig was responsible for covering pay, food, equipment, arms, and ammunition of the camp crew, while the costs of camp management and the inmates were the responsibility of the SS, which received its revenues from local farmers, and companies who paid them for the labor provided by the inmates.[31] The day-to-day supervision was assigned to Commandant Max Pauly who oversaw a work crew of 200 men. The main problem regarding the registration of the first prisoners was that the camp and sub-camps did not have a central registry until late October 1939, when the camp's administration began working on one that covered all inmates. Information about the first months is thus incomplete. Until that time, the administrators of each sub-camp ran only provisional registries of their own inmates. The numbers issued at that time continued to be used until the end of Stutthof's existence, and beginning in December 1939, the entry in the book and the number reflected the chronology of arrivals in the camp. Initially, prisoners' identification numbers were not even written on their clothing. They simply received a five-by-five-centimeter cardboard square, along with a registration book and index cards that contained personal data—the date and general reason for their arrest and information on their transfers between various barracks and camps.

Establishing the Filial Camps of Stutthof

The immediate aftermath of the invasion brought new challenges for the occupiers. There was immediate cleanup work to be done around Danzig. Thus, not all who were arrested were taken right away to Stutthof. On September 8, a group of prisoners, who had been imprisoned in the Victoria School, was taken to Westerplatte where a sub-camp was officially opened on September 15, 1939, under the command of SS Second Lieutenant *Untersturmführer* Paul Ehle whose career will ultimately lead him to higher duties in Stutthof in 1945. The prisoners (400 to 500 of them) were mostly Jews and Polish priests who had to clear the rubble of Westerplatte, which was then loaded on to trucks and taken to Stutthof to be used to build the camp. They also had to work in the dangerous job of removing un-detonated bombs, in back-breaking labor that entailed hauling heavy materials and digging up buried cables. Orski documents an incident on the Westerplatte when sixteen exhausted men were given permission to cut panicles (a type of meadow grass). Staff Sergeant/*Oberscharführer* Binke had told them cynically that the fresh air would do them good, but his motives were very different. At twelve o'clock, shots were heard, and on the same spot where the prisoners had cut the grass lay sixteen bodies, and beside them stood SS man Peters and two other unnamed SS men.[32] They were under the charge of the SS from Danzig-Neufahrwasser/Nowy Port, as well as young men seventeen to eighteen years of age from the *Reichsarbeitsdienst* (the National Labor Service). Two names are mentioned by survivors—Corporal/*Rottenführer* Paul Rexin and Second Lieutenant/*Untersturmführer* Kurt Mathesius. According to SS files, both men were locally born in Danzig-Ohra, in 1906 and 1910, respectively. Rexin was a carpenter by trade and gives his religion as Protestant while Mathesius lists Protestant and adds *"gottgläubig."* (The significance of their denomination and of *gottgläubig* will be discussed in the next chapter.) Mathesius went on to earn a bronze medal and in 1944 was transferred to Buchenwald.[33] Prisoners mention his cruelty frequently. Many were already suffering from the effects of malnutrition and brutal treatment on a daily basis, but on September 18, they were given a few days of reprieve when Hitler and Göring visited Danzig and the Hel Peninsula. This sub-camp continued to function until June 1941, by which time the prisoners had cleared the whole area.[34]

There were other connections to Danzig in satellite camps like Grenzdorf/Granicza, a stone quarry four miles from Danzig that was used to meet the growing demand for building material and was one of the busiest sub-camps. Located on an estate named Wieś Graniczna, it had been owned by the aristocratic Trembecki family; this land had been seized in the Nazi takeover and "Germanized" to be known as Grenzdorf. Grenzdorf's history, in fact, predates the outbreak of war. The Danzig Senate had set up a labor camp there in July 1939 for "the notoriously lazy and for slackers as well as for criminals."[35] In its early days, Grenzdorf had two barracks made up of twenty-five rooms (*Stuben*) that were basically bare walls—with neither stoves to heat the rooms nor chairs nor beds. A washroom and toilets were in a nearby administrative building. The prisoners had to build a third barrack, which housed a workshop and living quarters for the SS. The first commandant of Grenzdorf, Major Herzer/SS *Sturmführer* and his second-in-command Sergeant Paul Anker/SS *Oberscharführer* are described in relatively positive terms regarding their treatment of the prisoners, but their circumstances changed in December when Lieutenant Richard Reddig/SS *Obersturmführer*/(his name will recur) was appointed as head of the camp, with SS *Rottenführer* Fritz Meier (a local Danziger) as his substitute. Corporal Meier is listed as spending two years in Stutthof, 1939–41 after which he was sent to front line duty. Many of the prisoners were either killed outright or died in this camp as the result of hard labor and maltreatment.[36] The first group of prisoners after the outbreak of war arrived on September 13, 1939. During work hours they were kicked and bullied, and when they did not complete the assigned quota, they had to work longer hours. One prisoner, Fr. Henryk Maria Malak, a priest who arrived at the Grenzdorf sub-camp in November 1939 wrote in his memoir: "The unpleasant dampness penetrates our tattered clothing. Many of us don't have shoes anymore. Our feet, wrapped in some rags that are soaked through and now freezing, feel wooden ... We finally come into camp after 8 o'clock in the evening. Seven hours of work until dinner and seven until evening. The 14 hour 'penalty' work-day in Grenzdorf is coming to an end." They stand in line for a small slice of bread and a cup of soup, before going to sleep on bare planks. They have no covers and become stiff with cold. They sleep for five hours and then the grueling day begins once more.[37]

It was a particularly dangerous work because they had to use dynamite, under the constant supervision of the SS. This is how Polish prisoner Bernard Ukrzewski describes the maltreatment of Jews:

> I've seen with my own eyes and not just once, SS man *Rottenführer* Pflicht/Private First Class give some rope to a Jew, ordering that same man to hang another Jew in a forest nearby and return with a report. Jews executed these orders. In this way, only two Jews were left, and in the end Pflicht told them to sit down by a tree in the forest and he shot them both through the backs of their heads ... Another time the prisoners would have heavy rocks tied to their backs and be told to climb trees,

while the guards were beating them with sticks. When the inmates had no more strength left they were drowned in a swamp in the forest. By mid-December 1940, most Jewish inmates of Grenzdorf were murdered in various ways.[38]

Another local destination for prisoners was Neufahrwasser/Nowy Port. The role of Neufahrwasser within the Stutthof camp system was important in that it initially supervised the central registry of civilian prisoners for Stutthof and Grenzdorf. New transports kept arriving and were dispatched to other camps. At the end of January 1940, there were now a total of 5,150 prisoners, 3,000 of them in Danzig, and a further 700 scattered throughout the Vistula Delta area of Werder/Ostrów, working in agriculture. It is reckoned that at least 10,000 passed through Danzig-Neufahrwasser. Preparations to close the camp began in February 1940 and were completed at the end of March when the barracks were turned over to the military.[39] In mid-January 1940, they began to transfer 4,500 inmates to Stutthof, leaving 1,000 behind in Neufahrwasser until the end of March when it ceased to function as a sub-camp. It is estimated that between September 1939 and the end of March 1940, 700 prisoners died.[40] Other sub-camps had shorter life spans, like the one in Pletzendorf/Płotnik, which lasted only a matter of weeks. Pletzendorf was an agricultural camp that was under a farmer by the name of Brauser and was in operation between March 4 and March 26 in 1941. Prisoners returned each day to the main camp after their day's labor.[41] Another camp of short duration was Kalthof II (Kaldowa) that operated from the end of April 1940 until May 17 with twenty prisoners who, after rigorous testing of their physique, were selected by the camp doctor in Stutthof. Their job was to construct a breakwater across the river Nogat. This involved constructing layers of stones and planting flowers along the road leading to the river. Conditions were much better than in the main camp, in that they received food from a local kitchen that was supplemented by food from local people.[42] This relatively positive camp experience was not the case for Kalthof I, which ran from September 28 until November 15, 1939. The difference was that Gustav Fiehgut, the owner of the farm was a committed Nazi and former member of the Danziger *Volkstag* who harassed the prisoners (there were over twenty of them who appear to have been mostly Polish), forcing them, for example, to run with heavy potato baskets across the fields. According to the report of former prisoner Jerzy Piotrowski, only one woman gave them extra food, and he also suggests that the adverse conditions probably led to the premature death of at least one prisoner, the Jewish manager of the Hotel Continental in Danzig, whom they buried at night in a nearby wood. After their time in the camp, they were sent to Neufahrwasser.[43] The timeframe for Graudenz/Grudziądz, which had been established in a school building, has not been determined: what is known is that twelve SS men were responsible for twenty to twenty-five Polish prisoners who were put to work resettling Germans in homes previously owned by Poles, who had been forcibly evicted.[44]

One of the Stutthof sub-camps was even closer to Danzig, in Langfuhr/Wrzeszcz. Its short history contains some key ingredients of Germandom and a surprising escape that could belong in fiction. Seventy prisoners worked here in a cement factory from June 28, 1940, until the beginning of January 1941 in the re-named Adolf Hitler Street, owned by an ardent Nazi supporter by the name of August Roszkowski who had his name changed to the German name Röskau. The prisoners lived near the residence of the owner in broken-down barracks. Successful escapes from any of these filial camps were very rare but in the case of this sub-camp, there is an exception. One Sunday, three prisoners were able to elude the SS guards, make their way to a room where the civilian workers hung up their coats, etc., and change from their prisoner garb into the "borrowed" items. Suitably attired, they were able to make their way out of Danzig and arrived safely in Warsaw. One of them was the son of a circus artist.[45] It is a rare and happy anecdote about an escape from Adolf Hitler Street, located right on Grass's home turf in Langfuhr. But it is not fictional.

By the middle of 1940, sub-camps were now producing their own filial system. Elbing spawned the sub-camp of Elbing-Tannenbergallee in March 1940, for example. From the autumn of 1939 until April 1940, 200 prisoners, mostly Poles but also Russians, Germans, and Czechs were transported across the Frisches Haff to the main camp in Elbing. The camp leadership changed six times during its two-year history (plus two months) with men like Sergeant Willi Redder/SS *Unterscharführer* in charge—according to the SS files, a former carpenter, born in 1909, *gottgläubig* and in Stutthof till 1943. Work consisted of hard labor in the shipyard, as well as construction work in the town, but conditions were somewhat better than in the main camp and they were able to exchange their dirty clothing for Austrian military uniforms of the First World War, which were disinfected once a month. The camp leader also ordered a general delousing on Sundays—their free day. Although acts of brutality were not as common as in the main camp, the camp commandant Erich Müller and the man under him, Max Michelsen were said to have been responsible for the murder of Dr. Franciszek Gabriel, a prisoner-doctor who had tried to improve prisoners' sanitary conditions by pointing to the effects on their health.[46] This sub-camp closed around February 1942, having housed around 700 prisoners.[47]

Farther afield, a sub-camp of Gotenhafen/Gdynia was established in Adlershorst/Moczysko in February 1941 and was closed in the middle of 1942. There is some suggestion that prisoners worked on quarters for Max Pauly—carpenters, masons, painters, and decorators. It is also suggested that this was a gift to Pauly from Albert Forster for good services and that its former occupant was a Bromberg lawyer. This small sub-camp was under the direction of Corporal/*Rottenführer* Johannes Wall, and in the court hearing against him in 1947, he was sentenced to five years of imprisonment and the loss of civic rights. Witnesses gave a mixed testimony—that he was decent to the prisoners but also that prisoners were beaten under his watch. Promoted to Sergeant, he was transferred to Dachau in September 1942 where he worked in sub-camps. He died in prison in 1948.[48] Wall is listed in the SS spreadsheet as a laborer from Praust/Pruszcz with a *Volksschule* education.

Why is information on these sub-camps of Stutthof important to its history? What emerges is the recognition that right from the beginning, Stutthof was conceived as the *Stammlager*—the central point from which to organize these *Außenlager*—sub-camps or filial camps.[49] Whether they were seen as temporary measures until Stutthof was expanded is not always clear, but it is certain that in these early days of the camp's development, we can see how important sub-camps were in providing a labor force in and around Danzig—in agriculture, in clearing rubble from the impact of the invasion, and in local industries. Prisoners, at this stage predominantly Poles and Jews, would go each day to the site, where they worked from early morning until the evening, and on Sundays till four in the afternoon. Camp medical files indicate that prisoners in the sub-camps continued to work despite being chronically ill. For example, an entry on May 4, 1941, describes the condition of two prisoners: Stodolkiewiez (# 4601) who had worked in Elbing since April 28 with pleurisy and Karawatzki (#2352) with the same condition, as well as kidney disease. Their medical report says they would be unfit to work for four to six weeks. Others at Elbing were not so fortunate and were sent right back to work, like Edmund Grzegorzewski who was declared fit to work despite the contusion on his lower leg. Several other prisoners listed in these files had to work though suffering from enteritis.[50] What is also clear is that the local population at some level—even if superficially must have seen these prisoners coming and going. In some cases, they slept at the sub-camps, but most of them returned each day to Stutthof. It is also feasible to suggest that priests who had worked in parishes in and around Danzig could have been recognized by former congregants.

The introduction of a Germanization policy on race—the German National Registry or National Identity Registry (*die deutsche Volksliste, DVL*) was an important tool in the ethnic cleansing arsenal that was used, especially in the first phase of the annihilation of Polish life in the annexed territories. The DVL was introduced on September 2, 1940, by Himmler for the General Government and on March 4, 1941, for the three areas that had been annexed into the Reich—Silesia, the Warthegau, and Danzig-West Prussia. Historian Koehl offers several reasons why Himmler was essential for the implementation of resettlement and population program. In the public mind, Himmler was associated with an uncompromising readiness to fight for "Germanness." The SS had a special division, founded by Richard Darré known as the "Race and Settlement Office"/*Rasse und Siedlungshauptamt* and was also closely aligned with Reinhard Heydrich's secret service (SD) as well as organized ethnic German groups in eastern Europe—the Ethnic German Liaison Office/*Volksdeutsche Mittelstelle* or *VoMi* which was headed by SS men. Darré had developed theories of "blood and soil" and though he fell out of favor, and was demoted to Minister of Agriculture, his ideas on race and especially of "lost German blood" still had currency.[51] Early in the first stage of resettlement of ethnic Germans, there was tension and protest from Gauleiter Forster. Fifty thousand Baltic Germans—*Deutschbalten* were transported on "Strength through Joy"/*Kraft durch Freude* cruise ships in November 1939.[52] Koehl gives additional details: the first arrivals came between October 20 and November 10, 1939—around 20,000, including nearly all of the Estonians, were directed "temporarily" to the Adlershorst suburb of Danzig and Gotenhafen/Gdynia) before Foster protested.[53]

There were four categories in the DVL: those who identified as Germans and who were politically active and those with German parentage could apply for the first two categories and could be considered worthy of German citizenship. Admission to Group Three was offered to those who were considered "Polonized Germans"—Silesians, Kashubians, and Masurians—and to Poles of German lineage or to those married to a German. Their acceptance was valid for ten years—with the underlying threat that it could be revoked. The fourth category of the list was the least desirable and was designated for those Poles who were still active in Polish organizations, despite their German lineage. Such received admission infrequently and were excluded from serving in the military. Refusal to apply for the DVL was considered the ultimate insult and often resulted in being sent to a camp.[54] Schenk adds to the third category that in mixed marriages the dominant partner had to be pro-German.[55] The list was yet another point of heated contention between Forster and Himmler, with Forster favoring a more pragmatic approach, engendered both by his zeal to present a "Pole-free Gau" and by his antagonistic relationship with Himmler who favored Forster's counterpart—Greiser—in the neighboring Warthegau.[56] Their views on race and Germandom also betray Forster's insecurity. Greiser was himself from Poznań/Posen, was loyal to Himmler, and enjoyed the advantage over Forster of speaking Polish. (This perceived advantage will come up again in Forster's postwar testimony.) Greiser was intent on a total purge of his district, which was considered a model of Germanization, whereas Forster was willing to be pragmatic and to consider reeducation as a tool to Germanize Poles—including a stint in one of the detention camps. Forster appears to have been obsessed with the desire to present to Hitler a "polenfrei" Gau. Ethnic identity was easy to decipher: if you were a Pole with some claim to German ancestry, you had to produce evidence. Those who could, but refused to do so, were sent to Stutthof. The others—sometimes there were compelling personal reasons—were sent to special camps to be educated in Germandom, or they were enlisted for compulsory service in the Wehrmacht and often sent to the Front. Some defected to the allies.[57]

The agency for shifting some segments of the population and deporting others was benignly called the "The Central Agency for Relocation"/*Umwandererzentralstelle* (*UWZ*) and had been set up by Reinhard Heydrich under the authority of the Sipo (*Sicherheitspolizei*) and the SD/*Sicherheitsdienst* in Danzig to organize the deportation of Poles from Pomerania. As already noted, the whole business of resettling ethnic Germans, of determining who could or could not be considered German, betrayed a lack of unity at the top between Himmler, Forster, and Arthur Greiser, and also brought Hildebrandt into the conflict. On a visit to Berlin on October 31, 1942, he expressed the fear that Poles who had become "germanized" on the basis of the third category and joined the German army might defect, pointing out that these people had signed the list to avoid being sent to a camp.[58] The tensions included another conflict, this time between Forster and Himmler concerning their views on the Kashubians. Himmler thought they should be allowed to stay where they were, but should be separated from the Polish population and be Germanized, while Forster was against any, even temporary support, of the Kashubians—they were inferior as a people and not worthy of any degree of sponsorship.[59] The same argument was used with the local Roma/Sinti population. For a short time, they were allowed to stay and were able to work for the Nazis, but this too would change.[60] A major impediment in implementing Germandom appears to have been the lack of unity among the key players who prided themselves in being the epitome of Germanness. Mazower describes Forster as a dissenter to Himmler's policy, who, operating under what one official termed "ducal authority" claims that far fewer Poles were ever deported from his Gau than from the Warthegau under his archrival Arthur Greiser and far fewer Germans were allowed to settle there. (In Gotenhafen/Gdynia, for example, only 17,000 Baltic Germans arrived to take the place of the town's original 130,000 inhabitants.)[61] By the beginning of 1944, around 2.75 million people out of a total population of 9.5 million had successfully passed through the DVL. Mazower adds, "For the racial purists, the results were disheartening."⁶² What were the results of this effort? Forster was not only more lenient than Greiser, but in fact compelled Poles to become German, and was inclined to accept any Polish citizen who spoke German moderately well. Nearly two-thirds of the former Polish population of Forster's Gau found a spot within the categories of the DVL.⁶³ Hitler apparently allowed Himmler and Forster to deal with "Germanness" in his own way.⁶⁴ The Poles had the most to lose, regardless of what category they either chose or were forced to choose.

Nazi Policy Regarding Slavic People

The failure among the Nazi elite to agree on who belonged on the list was not the only point of disagreement. There was also no unified policy or even agreement on the nature of Slavic ethnicity. In a seminal article, historian John Connelly pointed out that there were differing approaches by the Nazis toward Slavic people across occupied territories. Some approaches were dictated more by acquiring *Lebensraum*. In the Czech lands, for example, the occupiers closed universities, but in occupied Poland they also closed secondary schools. Connelly also finds little of substance in prewar sources regarding Nazi anti-Polonism; Hitler's treatment of the Poles, he argues, was "worse for Poles who lived in western areas attached directly to Germany."⁶⁵ But even in that case, there were contradictions. Hitler's views on Poland changed radically after Poland refused Nazi demands, among them the return of Danzig, the construction of a railroad and highway through "the Corridor" and Polish collaboration in the Anti-Comintern pact. In April 1934, Hitler renounced the pact of 1934 with Poland and, Connelly argues, began to plan Poland's destruction and subsequent seizure of land in Poland since he could not have—at least at this time—what he wanted in Russia.⁶⁶ Connelly's point is that by blocking Hitler's path the Poles became the sort of "Slavs" destined for destruction. Thus, it was not "longstanding Nazi plans to destroy the Poles which engendered Polish resistance in 1930 and thereafter, but rather Polish resistance to such plans. To make the point absolutely clear: this Polish defiance triggered Nazi violence, it did not produce it."⁶⁷ The other important observation that Connelly makes is that racial theorists before the war made a distinction between the Jews of Central Europe and Eastern Europe. After the Nazi takeover, race experts settled on a monolithic model.⁶⁸ That model was based on "blood,"⁶⁹ and was also used in the argument that one drop of German blood was worth considering for admission to the VL.⁷⁰

A key player in the destruction of life in occupied Poland was Heinrich Himmler whose influence will become even more deadly after January 1942, when Stutthof finally met his "high" standards for admission to the camp system. In his role as *Reichskommissar*, Himmler undertook the job of destroying Polish national identity. Allen points out that this blueprint for racial imperialism was part of "a plexus of ideologies that overlapped with SS ideals ... with each eager to take charge of occupation and settlement policy of Nazi-occupied Eastern Europe."⁷¹ The push eastward—*der Drang nach dem Osten*—was thus more than a quest for new areas to settle Germans—*Lebensraum*; it was also a *Kulturkampf* and its object was to identify a specific form of life that had to be either German and thus racially pure or else a life that valued everything that was German—its *Kultur,* its people and history and now its Führer. The Nazi "purification" and invasion of Poland went "far beyond mere military victory," as Pawlikowski puts it: "Because the Poles were regarded as sub humans, they were to be reduced to virtual slave status, accompanied by the total destruction of all cultural, political, and religious symbols that would provide them with any form of human identity."[72]

The DVL attempted to reshape and reduce Poles into categories that measured them in terms of their desirability and potential to be Germanized, or what they called "within range" or "liable to Germanization." From March 1941 through February 1942—that is, roughly until the camp received its new status—this form of aggression was practiced, and by December 1941 produced 31,472 who were admitted to one of the categories.[73] The alternative was to lose your job, home or farm, or be sent to compulsory labor in the Reich or to work for the Todt Organization.[74] Economic measures were also taken to undermine everyday life for Poles, whose wages were less than for Germans and if they dared quit, they faced a detention in Stutthof for several weeks to reform them.[75] As the war progressed, many were sent to Stutthof or were enlisted in the Wehrmacht and sent to fight at the Front. It is worth mentioning that Grass fictionalizes the drive to promote German ethnicity—and implied racial superiority—in a scene in *The Tin Drum*. Jan Bronski's widow, Hedwig later married a Baltic German who was a local peasant leader in Ramkau. Grass writes, "Jan's parents were Poles no longer and spoke Kashubian only in their dreams. German nationals, group 3, they were called. Hedwig's two children subsequently took the name of their step-father, Ehlers."[76] He also states without preamble that in 1940 many with Polish names petitioned to have their names Germanized: "The local parish priest Father Gusewski became Gusewing. The local butcher Olczewski became Ohlwein." Grass then directly intervenes to address the reader with, "but in these papers Father Gusewski will continue to be Gusewski for you."[77] Later, in *Peeling the Onion*, Grass recalls: "Shortly after the war broke out, as everyone—even I—knew, Polish peasants from the hinterlands of my native city, starting in the Kashubian region but reaching as far as the Tuchel Heath, had been turned out of their farms to make room for the Baltic trophy Germans. Their broad accent was easy to imitate, it was so close to our Low German; besides, for a short time, I had shared a bench with a boy from Riga … These people had been called *heim ins Reich* as a consequence of the nonaggression pact between Hitler and Stalin."[78]

A Closer Look at the Internment of Priests

We associate the persecution of Polish priests above all with Dachau and Auschwitz and to a lesser degree with Sachsenhausen. We know that many Polish priests died in these camps that had, in fact, designated special barracks for their internment—868 died in Dachau.[79] The maltreatment of Polish priests and their ignominious deaths in

Stutthof is much less known beyond Poland and has been folded into a general history of Nazi crimes against clerics. At the most basic level, the testimonies about or by priests are invaluable for the historical record of the early days of the camps. Take, for example, the testimony of Father Henryk Malak, briefly mentioned above. He spent in all six years in camps—four of them in Dachau. His life before Stutthof shares many aspects of other priests who were also imprisoned: born in Pomerania, ordained after his studies in seminary in Thorn in 1912 as a priest. He was arrested in November 1939 and sent to Grenzdorf where he worked in the quarry pits. Henryk Malak survived Stutthof, Sachsenhausen and Dachau. He was buried in 1987 far from home, in a grave in Lemont, Illinois.

Malak is one of the priests, who despite his maltreatment, frequently comments that the Jewish prisoners suffered even more and would not survive. These observations are particularly valuable to researchers in the absence of memoirs written in these early days by Jewish victims. The empathy is more than the recognition of a common fate of suffering. They had been bracketed together as *"Juden und Pfaffen"* to demean both groups, but because Nazi racial laws had segregated Jews to the lowest possible category, the inclusion with priests implied an even stronger insult to priests. As the excerpt below illustrates, the representation of Jewish maltreatment surpasses that of other prisoners. Malak was a member of a unit that worked in the forest all day in freezing rain. When they finally returned to the camp in evening, they often were deprived of their evening soup. This is how he describes it:

> It often happens that the SS man standing by the vat allows a prisoner to take food, but then gives the order "Bend over!" and beats him with a person's club! He beats and beats! Woe to the bent-over prisoner if he spills any of the liquid moving around in his tin. Then he has to pour the rest back into the vat and take another beating for "wasting" food. This happens most often to the group of Jews. There was not a day when they were not mistreated, especially during the distribution of food rations. Often they were driven away without any food. Unfortunate ones! … Much worse off than we, the priests, although the SS men usually persecute Juden und Pfaffen![80]

Malak also describes the infamous event that was callously chosen to take place on a sacred day in their calendar—Easter Friday when they were taken into the woods to dig graves for fellow-prisoners. On Good Friday, March 22, 1940, forty men were chosen and told to take shovels and to wait in front of the Commandant's building. They were then marched into the woods where they had to clear deep snow from the road. They worked for several hours. In the clearing in the distance they could see holes, which had already been dug. After clearing this area, they saw heavy covered vehicles driving up the road where they had cleared off snow. They were told to fall down in the snow and were warned that if anyone lifted his head, he would get a bullet in it. When they returned to the camp they were greeted with the whispers that an entire unit off the camp had been escorted to this clearing. It consisted of all the Polish intelligentsia from Gdańsk and among them were two priests. On Easter day, after hearing in secret the Mass of the Resurrection, the Polish priests together with the Jews were ordered to carry excrement out of the camp latrine. Malak writes: "They treated the poor Jews even worse than us. Crammed into the hole, standing up to the waist and excrement, the Jews hand us full buckets and, in doing so, spill the contents on themselves. We pour out the contents into vats, located on vehicles, which are moved outside the camp."[81]

Malak's memoir is also helpful in tracking events of the early days of 1940 when the net had spread beyond Danzig to arrest dozens of priests in Pomerania. His testimony provides a significant insight into an earlier German-Polish history that serves to accentuate the dramatic change since the Nazi takeover. It is an important memoir on several levels, but especially in its depiction of an image of Germany and of Germans that could easily have been erased in the history of the new regime. In the following anecdote, he describes his farewell from his father. At one of the venues where they are temporarily imprisoned before being transported to Stutthof, Malak's father has been given permission to visit him. His father reminisces about how it used to be: "'You see, my boy, I have the feeling that we may never see each other again in this life, and that's why it doesn't matter anymore.' He gestured with his hand in resignation ... 'I was born under the partition, attended a German school, had to serve in the Army, and where did I serve? Right in the Kaiser's guard near Berlin. But, my dear son, these' ... his brows motioned towards the guard. 'These are not the Germans from World War I.'"[82] The author writes about kissing the hand of his father when he took farewell from him:

> Bent over as if he carried a burden on his wide shoulders, he walks along the poplar-lined road which is covered by snow. He turns around at the bend. He stops for a moment, it seems that he's hesitating, that he intends to turn back. He takes control of himself. He waves his hand, turns around and continues to walk without glancing back again. Three years later, when news reaches me in Dachau about my father being tortured to death, I could still see his tall, broad-shouldered, bent figure walking on this snow-covered road.[83]

But that was a different era. Malak's memoir includes a group picture of young SS men from Danzig that illustrates the effects of indoctrination on Danzig:

> The SS men are all very young. They are the offspring of Gdańsk families. Most of them speak to us in Polish ... We drive into the streets of Gdańsk at dusk. The drivers don't know which way to go next. They stop and ask for directions. From their questions we gather that they are taking us to Nowy Port (Neufahrwasser.) They line the priests up against the wall and take from them their inventory, mostly religious items. SS elements, but none so aggressive, none so depraved, and none to the same degree so brutal and savage as these young SS men from Gdańsk. This is what Hitler's propaganda accomplished after years of indoctrinating them.[84]

In another anecdote, he describes a brief stop in Danzig that gives a chilling picture of local indifference and shows how closely aligned Danzig was with the local camp:

We pass streets, cross bridges; we are extremely surprised to see people everywhere, especially men. We had imagined that by now everyone would be in uniform, that everyone would have been taken into the military … Passersby, curious about the transport, pause on the sidewalks. We must present quite a spectacle! Dressed in rags, covered with muck and bits of straw, unshaven and dirty, we probably look like a group of savages. Two guards armed with submachine guns ready to fire remained standing on watch. The rest disappear inside … Through the huge windows one can see them sitting down at a table, with smiling waitresses coming toward them. Based on the relaxed attitude of both sides, one can conclude that this restaurant is an old stopover for SS men from Stutthof, also on other occasions. The fat restaurant owner goes up to the transport officer; they greet each other, slap each other on the back, gesture in our direction, laugh.[85]

The experiences of Polish priests either had to wait or else be told by others. The excerpts I have chosen belong in the latter category and are translated from Elżbieta Grot's book on the fate of local Polish priests.[86] We will begin with Polish priest Franciszek Rogaczewski whose parish was in Danzig where he was arrested the day that the war began, taken to Stutthof, tortured for four months before being shot to death on January 11, 1940.[87] He had already drawn the attention of the Germans in the 1930s, specifically after the papal blessing on four parishes designed for Poles living in Gdańsk. His efforts to connect with the Polish community of Danzig were met with growing antagonism inside the local Catholic Church, presumably also by fellow priests in the German community. His musical gifts and pilgrimages did not abate, and he was among the Polish priests—in this case with direct ties to Danzig—who was killed within months of his arrival.

The case of Marian Górecki (1903–40), a priest born in Posen/Poznań, exemplifies on many levels the fate of Polish priests. Before the war started, he was sent in 1939 to Danzig to work as a youth minister in the suburb of Nowy Port/Neufahrwasser among Polish families, many of whom were mail carriers. He was one of the first to be arrested at dawn on September 1, and along with 150 others, was in the first group to be taken to Stutthof where they were ordered to clear ground and put in windows in the barracks. At the end of September, he was accused by the Danzig Gestapo, along with other local priests, of hiding weapons in churches, a charge they all denied. For three days, they were tortured by beatings, and were specifically charged in December for inciting others to sing Polish Christmas carols while clearing snow. Sometime in early 1940, they were all transferred to Grenzdorf to work in the stone quarries, but he himself was brought back to Stutthof where in March they brutally interrogated him, before sending him on to the punishment commission where he was isolated, beaten, and tormented by the guards on the main square of the camp. On March 21, 1940, they partook clandestinely in communion and the next day—Good Friday—he, along with sixty-six others from Danzig and Pomeranian towns, was shot about a mile away from the camp. Their bodies were exhumed after the war and all were given a decent burial by 1947.[88] Twenty-two Polish activists were shot the next day in a wood near the camp.[89] On April 1, sixty-seven others were shot, and shortly afterwards the first deportation of 1,000 inmates left for Sachsenhausen, to be followed by a transport of 800 on April 19. Grot notes that prisoners were working all spring on the construction of the barracks—a sick bay, and workshops. During the month of May, five Jewish inmates committed suicide by hanging—"probably driven to it by guards," Grot adds.

Bronisław Komorowski was born in 1889 in Barłożno near Starogard and was among the first Polish priests in Danzig. He worked as senior pastor at Saint Stanislaus Church in Wrzeszcz/Langfuhr, which was built in 1934. In this capacity, he worked with Polish youth, organizing cultural events between 1934 and 1935, and as the only Pole in the Danzig City Council, played a significant role in establishing positive relations between Poles and Germans in Danzig. Komorowski was arrested on September 1 and brought to Victoria School. Witnesses saw him "walking with his head up, proud, not trying to avoid Germans' blows. Covered in blood, he reached our room."[90] Among the punishments inflicted on Polish priests was the confiscation of identity cards and whatever money they had in their possession. One witness, by the name of Wiesław, himself a prisoner, writes about seeing Komorowski, his lips beaten to a bloody pulp. He also adds that Hitler Youth members could be seen in the open windows, laughing at the treatment of people who were arrested, beaten, and kicked as they were awaiting the transport. "After the registration, our group was taken to the basement, and there I saw Father K. He was transported to Stutthof and worked in the '*Waldkolonne*'—the forest work unit." At the end of 1939, escorted by the SS, Komorowski and other Polish priests from Danzig (M. Górecki, F. Rogaczewski, B. Wiecki, and A. Muzalewski), he was brought to the Gestapo headquarters in Danzig to a meeting with Cardinal C. M. Splett; the issue at hand was the release of all Polish priests from Stutthof and the outcome was unsuccessful. Another witness, by the name of Roman Bellon testified that the Germans mocked Komorowski and wanted him to be a kapo in the latrine cleaning crew. Bellon writes that Komorowski was often beaten and tortured but his heart remained open and filled with love. He was always helping those who were weaker and shared his food portions with a smile. He would say, "I felt as if I were sharing a sermon and I wanted it to be a good one. I think those were my best sermons."[91] He participated in a secret mass on Good Thursday, March 21 and was killed the next day in a forest near Stutthof.

Władysław Demski was born in 1884 in Warmia/Ermland. During the First World War, he was drafted into the German Army and worked in the army hospital in Königsberg. On November 2, he and other priests were lured to a meeting with the Germans and arrested. He and thirty-four other Polish priests were taken to Górna Grupa, then Nowy Port/Neufahrwasser and then Stutthof. From there, they were transported in April to Sachsenhausen, where thirteen of the group survived.[92] Demski was a tall man, noted for his bravery. He spoke German very well, and for that reason, the Germans made him a kapo of a work detail of priests, whose task was to clean the camp's grounds of snow, crushing large rocks and performing general maintenance jobs. Demski is depicted as showing great empathy toward his fellow-priests. He died as the result of a severe beating in May 1940 in Sachsenhausen. Wincenty Frelichowski (1913–45) was born in Chełmża/Kulmsee, ordained to a parish in Thorn/Toruń, where he too was very active in youth ministry and boy scouts (*Harcerstwo*), and is described as very charismatic. On September 11, 1939, he and two other priests, Jan

Mykowski and Jan Manthey, were arrested and spent the night in Fort VII, Thorn. His fellow-priests were released the next day but Frelichowski remained in prison and when he was finally released, he was rearrested on October 18 and sent to Fort VII where he spent three months, before being sent on January 10, 1940, along with others, to Nowy Port where he remained for a month before being transported to Stutthof. He stayed until April 1940. One day he was punished for performing a burial service for a prisoner. Undeterred, he volunteered to remove bodies from the camp hospital, framing his reason to his fellow prisoners as, "This job befits us as priests. We have the opportunity to pray for our tortured brothers."[93]

Stanisław Kubista, who was born in 1898 in Kostuchno near Mikołajów (today's Diocese of Katowice), fought in the First World War, where he was trained as a radio and telegraph operator. In 1929, he became the editor of the "Little Missionary Post" and wrote a number of short stories. On October 27, 1939, his publishing office and printing press in Górna Grupa was demolished by the Gestapo, and he and sixty-four other clerics were arrested. The next day, along with other priests and monks, he was imprisoned until February 5, 1940, when all of them were transported to Neufahrwasser and from there to Stutthof. He became ill in Stutthof, and his condition worsened during the transport to Sachsenhausen on April 9, 1940. He died a brutal death on April 26, killed by a German kapo, one of the many criminal prisoners (*Berufsverbrecher*) who were used by the Nazis. "You shouldn't be alive anymore," he said, before crushing Kubista's throat with his boot.[94] Alojzy Liguda (Werbista) (1898–1942) was born in Winów/Winau in the Opole region. He lived and worked in the Monastery in Górna Grupa, before being arrested on February 5, 1940, and transported with other prisoners to Neufahrwasser. He, too, did not survive.

These third-person accounts of the imprisonment and deaths of priests from Danzig and Pomerania are characterized by a monotonous sameness that remain locked within horrific brutality. Humiliated, beaten, and forced to work despite starvation, many priests consciously sought to express the notion of redemption in their sufferings. Most of them did not write, for the simple reason that they did not live long enough; some were killed shortly after they arrived.

Other Civilian Prisoners

Testimonies consistently present primitive conditions that in some ways were worse than those we will meet later, after Stutthof was formally designated to be a concentration camp. The later difference lay in workforce organization rather than in more humane treatment of the inmates. During this period, when the camp was designated for civilian prisoners—*Zivilgefangene*—the most targeted group was the KOP—*Komenda Obrońców Polski* ("The Command of the Defenders of Poland").[95] Because it had a large following in Poland; it remained a target for the Nazis throughout the occupation. Already in November 1939, the regional commander of Pomerania was arrested in Warsaw, which led to the subsequent arrest of other underground resisters in Pomerania, in towns like Bromberg/Bydgoszcz. Those arrested were promptly brought to Stutthof, along with resisters from other smaller organizations, and some eighty of them arrived in Stutthof on March 10, 1941.[96] Malak's description of the Polish intelligentsia captures the fate of one segment of this group of resisters:

> The camp, which up to now has been quiet, suddenly comes to life—movement, running, shouts, cries! Suddenly from the dark line of woods surrounding the camp the blinding light of huge watchtower floodlights brightly illuminates barracks, streets and residents, who have lined up in columns. The block leaders "establish order" in their units. Clouds of steam pour out of open doors ... The block lining up across from us, on the other side of the street, consists almost entirely of half-naked people. Only some kind of tattered rags hang on these human skeletons. "That's our intelligentsia, arrested on the day the war broke out in Gdańsk." They are the remaining survivors. And these, too, will go soon. Not a day passes without them carrying out several dozen dead from their barracks. They are dying like flies. I bet not one will survive until spring![97]

Malak describes how the days passed in Stutthof: desperately warding off millions of lice, running like animals for a bowl of warm water with a large leaf of boiled cabbage in it, rushing to work from the dark of morning to the dark of evening.[98] These accounts corroborate the testimonies that are given by many others, for example, Wacław Mitura, incarcerated in 1941:

> We are led for supper through the kitchen, in groups. The kitchen is set up so that there's an entrance on one side, exit on the other, and the part with food in the middle. We line up at the entrance, somebody passes out dirty, dented bowls, the spoons are nonexistent here. Now we enter the kitchen, where at two parts two groups each pour three quarters of a liter of watery, fat-free soup. A kapo with a stake stands near and an SS man with a rawhide whip a bit further off. You have to be watchful when approaching the pots. If you absentmindedly present your bowl at the wrong pot, the kapo's stake will land on your head, and the SS man will lash with the whip and kick you a few times. Such an embattled inmate loses half his soup. You have to be watchful to avoid it. After receiving soup you have to streak out the exit door to the square, drink up the bowl's contents and pass the bowl on, as others are waiting.[99]

Given the degree of hard labor, the daily diet was totally inadequate: a small cup of dark, bitter, watery corn coffee, and a slice of bread, baked with bran and sawdust and other refuse, plus a piece of margarine and sometimes a slice of horse sausage. For dinner, there was a bowl of soup of half-rotten vegetables. Thirst was a serious problem, and if inmates drank the water from the faucet or local well, they risked dysentery and other diseases. Meals were eaten in bowls and rusty cans. Often, prisoners had to eat their so-called meal during a short break at work time. Many prisoners became very emaciated and were barely able to stand for the roll calls that took place twice each day, in the rain and cold where they stood for hours. Prisoners were punished severely for the slightest infraction, like stealing turnips in the fields, a camp transgression that could lead to death.[100]

Dunin-Wąsowicz's 1970 publication includes some anecdotes about cultural and religious activities in the camp during these early years, claiming that there were evening events, held clandestinely when the priests, under the leadership of Father Gajdus, discussed and often dismissed camp rumors. As early as November 1939, a group of prisoners went from one barrack to another, singing simple folk songs under the leadership of a Kashubian by the name of Lubowmir Szopiński who had been a choir conductor in Sopot/Zoppot.[101] It was common, Dunin-Wąsowicz writes, to compose songs with simple words and set them to well-known Polish melodies. He also comments on the absence of any cultural activities in the Jewish camp, ascribing the lack to a more basic need—to survive.[102]

Even before its inclusion in the concentration camp system, Stutthof was the destination for other prisoners who did not necessarily fit fixed categories. Such were the Russian sailors who were crew members onboard ships in Danzig harbor when Germany invaded Poland. At that point they were considered allies of the Germans, but on the day that Germany attacked the USSR on June 22, 1941, an undetermined number, possibly "dozens" were brought to Stutthof. Later in June 1941, thirty-eight Soviet sailors from the *Magnitogorsk*, including two women were sent to work at Grenzdorf. They were transferred in November 1941 to the prison in Witzburg castle in Bavaria.[103] Another group followed in August from ships anchored in the harbors of Danzig and Gotenhafen.[104] These sailors were to be joined by much larger groups of Russian prisoners who were among the thousands and then millions who were sent to POW camps, and then scattered among the camps to work for the German economy and especially for the war effort. (See Figure 3 for a data collection card for a Soviet sailor from the *Magnitogorsk*.)

A Camp for Women

The other group that arrived in Stutthof in June 1941 were women, so that by April 1942, there were 120 women prisoners, and by November 1943 there were 332. They lived in the Old Camp because there was only one barrack for women at this time. Most of the women during the earlier period were Polish and their guard was Kazimiera Jackowska, an older woman who wanted to be perceived, according to Dunin-Wąsowicz, as a mother figure to the other women. Dunin-Wąsowicz describes Jackowska as devious and promiscuous with the German guards. She was replaced by another Polish woman, Walentyna Narewska, a petite, attractive woman with blonde hair who, according to Dunin-Wąsowicz, exceeded her predecessor in her availability. He does not say what became of either woman.[105] He adds that these women were interned in Stutthof largely because of loose contacts with the underground movements and not because they themselves were activists. Some of them had been recruited to work in the Reich, had fled, and were brought to Stutthof as deserters from the German workforce. Such women were considered prime candidates for the correction program and were given the usual fifty-six days of punishment (or multiples thereof) to reeducate them to think and act as Germans, even if they were Poles. This group included women from the occupied territories and prostitutes from the Reich.[106] Every inmate was given a serial number that was printed on a rectangular strip of cloth. They had to memorize this number in German and if they mispronounced, they would be punished. One woman, Wanda Ruczkal, who was imprisoned in 1941, was not able to repeat her number 11,972 during her first roll call. She writes, "I received a terrible beating. When I fell, my friends helped me stand up in my spot. I was called out again and had to tell my number, and I couldn't. Another pummeling. Unconscious, I was thrown into the block."[107]

A Hard Labor Camp

The different phases of the camp, at least until it was recognized as a concentration camp, tend to be like the tides of the sea: they overlap and blend so that is hard to identify the lines of demarcation. Himmler formally designated it as a corrective labor camp—*Arbeitserziehungslager*—at the beginning of October 1941, and already in the spring of 1941 had ordered each region to have one such camp. This phase did not mean that there were no prisoners in this category in October 1941, nor that the first phase was a thing of the past. And, it certainly was always a place of hard labor; it simply now formally incorporated another level of torture and broadened its base of inclusion. Thus, Stutthof became the correctional center for the whole region of Danzig-West Prussia, though it was still under the former commandant who assigned an SS officer—Erich Niemann the task of making the camp profitable. There were now 1,224 inmates, including the 100 women who had arrived earlier on June 22, 1941.[108] The "hard labor" prisoners had transgressed wartime restrictions in all sorts of ways throughout the Reich and the occupied territories, be it attempted sabotage, black market trading, etc., and were sent to Stutthof for a month or so of hard labor. Fifteen percent of these prisoners did not survive.[109] In the prewar period, the target of this forced reeducation regime were often simply loafers or what the regime called the work-shy. The camps of the 1930s had interned all sorts of drifters, men, and women, most of them Germans, who did not fit the expectations of "Germandom" promoted by the new regime. Now, prostitutes and pimps were being sent from all over the Reich to Stutthof to be rehabilitated by hard labor. The fate of this group was either to be sent to another place of forced labor within the camp system, or to remain in Stutthof under an even higher standard, after the camp was formally recognized in January as a concentration camp. They also had to sign a statement upon release that they had been well treated in Stutthof. Even if they were released, they were kept under the scrutiny of the police unit in their local town until the end of the war.

In 1940, a special court presided over by Dr. Helmar Tanzmann of Danzig's Police Department and Max Pauly, the commandant of Stutthof, condemned some dozen Poles who were active in various Polish organizations to death. The condemned were not only officials of the Post Office and Harbor Commission but included professionals and clerics. They were separated into two groups, the first made up of twenty-two men who were taken to the woods less than a mile from the camp and shot. The second larger group of sixty-seven men met the same fate on March 22, 1940, near the first site of killing. The second site was discovered in late 1946, and the remains were buried in Zaspe. The first site was only discovered in May 1979. The remains of that group finally found a decent grave in the grounds of Stutthof.[110]

The Fate of the Remaining Jews of Danzig and Pomerania

The fact that any Jews could leave Danzig in the late 1930s does not infer leniency in the local Nazi party but rather the ability of individuals and of the Jewish community to finance (at substantial financial loss) their own exodus. Not all of Danzig Jews were sent in the first weeks of September to Stutthof, mostly because there was still not enough room to accommodate them in the makeshift quarters. Besides, other camps like Dachau and Sachsenhausen were already under the jurisdiction of the IKL (*Inspektion der Konzentrationslager*/Inspectorate of Concentration Camps) and were considered better equipped to receive them. There was also still some degree of protection from the Danzig constitution, though that was to change in October. It is also erroneous to assume that the low percentage of Jewish prisoners in these early days—compared to the high percentage of Poles—somehow suggests that Stutthof can be dissociated from the destruction of European Jewry. Drywa is unequivocal in her claim regarding the fate of local Jews in 1939: More than 95 percent of this "group of inmates was murdered ... Stutthof was the only camp in this part of Europe to implement the extermination of Jews from the first day of the war."[111] She also attributes its remote location and lack of transport routes to the main centers of the concentration of Polish Jews as a factor in the initially small Jewish presence in the camp—that is, until mid-1944. Jews died in Stutthof in these early days, though at this stage there was no official policy for their deaths beyond the general plan to "cleanse" the whole area of anything that stood in the way of Germandom.

Thus far, archivists at Stutthof have been able to identify the names of about 300 Jewish victims out of an estimated total of nearly 600 Jews who were murdered in Pomerania in the fall of 1939.[112] Most of these victims never even saw Stutthof. Among them were at least thirty-seven Jews from the Starogard district and fourteen Jews from Kartuzy/Karthaus who were executed in the nearby forests. A significant number of Jews in the northern parts of Pomerania were arrested shortly after the German army had entered the country and were placed in prisons. Approximately 100 Jews from Gotenhafen were placed in Neufahrwasser and then transferred to Stutthof. Forty-six Jews who had been kept in a prison in Tuchola/Tuchel were executed at the end of September 1939. On October 7 and 8, eighty-three people were murdered in a cemetery in Świecie/Schwertz (forty-four Jews, twenty-nine Poles, ten others identified), among them Jewish women and five children. The executions were supervised by soldiers from the Wehrmacht. Around forty Jews from the Wyrzyski district were murdered on November 24 in a monastery garden in Górka Klasztorna. Fourteen Jews from the Chełmno district were executed in the fall of 1939 in Klamry, a place of mass executions of the Polish population. From the middle of October to the end of November 1939, nearly 200 Jews from the Lipno and Rypin administrative units were executed.

Voices of Local Clerics on the Persecutions of *Juden und Pfaffen*

What about Danzig? Cardinal Splett protested on September 5, 1939, about the arrest of priests and made appeals to top government and military officials, as well as the German Red Cross but to no avail.[113] The subsequent trajectory of the cardinal's relationship to the German authorities reflects a pattern of accommodation that characterized in large measure most leaders in both the mainline religions and denominations classified as sects or as "free churches." By the spring of 1940, the silencing of the Polish language had been imposed even on the private expression of penitents. Splett issued a statement on May 25, 1940, that priests no longer could use the Polish language in the confessional.[114] Later, in 1955, Forster's finance director Hoppenrath wrote that Forster's fight with the Catholic Church abated in the course of time, but then adds the chilling detail, "because the Polish-Catholic clerics were completely eliminated."[115] After the collapse of the Nazi regime, Cardinal Splett had to experience a different political reality—retribution—exacted this time by the new Soviet-led regime in Poland and later, yet another one, but this time, the extension of redemption that was offered to him in West Germany.[116]

In the memoir by Lutheran minister Gerhard Güzlow already introduced in Chapter 1, he attests to various harassments that affected him in his ministry, including being observed by the Secret Police during his sermons and even funeral services. The Gestapo, he writes, also raided his office and took away hymnals and church literature.[117] One of his congregants, however, a pharmacist lived in the same building as Lieutenant Colonel Wolff, SS *Obersturmbahnführer* who kept the pharmacist informed about the minister being spied on. The authorities were especially vigilant about his work with youth groups, which was ultimately closed down.[118] By 1940, however, some of his colleagues were arrested, when he himself was out of town. He does not say where they were taken and for how long. Gülzow attributes his own protection from arrest to his congregants, for example, when he clandestinely baptized a Jewish man in the *Mausegasse* as well as a Jewish woman and her two children. Since this was forbidden, it was only due to his trustworthy parishioners that he was not reported.[119] It had come to the ears of the Secret Police that he had visited a large group of Jews living at the address—"im vierten Damm" who were living in a pathetic state, waiting to leave Danzig. He then refers to Stutthof, describing it as a place that was generating a lot of rumors and gossip and which will not admit any representatives from the church to visit—neither Datschewsky nor his successor Pautzkeever were admitted, he says. (He does not explain why these ministers should have been admitted.) Stutthof took care of its own death registries.[120] This memoir again reflects to some degree what went on around the evening meal as is depicted in Grass's stories—ordinary people knew about Stutthof, including pastors and their congregants. There was clearly some degree of intrusion into Lutheran church life but certainly nothing in the order of what was happening to Polish priests and their congregants in Danzig and "the Corridor." German nationality gave Lutheran congregants protection. On the other hand, opposition to Nazi racial laws put the lives of German priests, and ministers of the Protestant churches, as well as their congregants, instantly in jeopardy. Gülzow ends his memoir by acknowledging the high price that Catholic priests from Danzig paid at the hands of National Socialists. Referring to "our Catholic sister-church" he cites the statistic of eleven Danzig priests who gave their lives as victims in that era.[121]

The relationship between Jews and Polish priests has figured prominently in this chapter. How representative were their experiences in occupied Poland? While it is beyond the scope of a monograph on Stutthof to address adequately the complex history of Jews and the Polish Catholic Church, one can at least provide a brief comment to frame the *Juden/Pfaffen* bracket and direct the reader for more information to the leading scholars in Religious Studies and to historians in that particular field.[122] Dariusz Libionka points out that measures against Polish clerics were not consistent, but the territories that had been annexed into the Reich were the hardest hit by Nazi directives, and it was in those areas that there were mass arrests, and deportations to the General Government.[123] The atrocities perpetrated in the Danzig-West Prussia Gau certainly illustrate his point. Libionka reminds us that the dominant self-image of the Catholic Church that emerges from the era of occupation is heroic, but this image does not tell the whole story.[124] (The reference here is presumably to the rescue of Jews by Polish citizens and especially to Jewish children hidden in monasteries by nuns.) While Libionka does not doubt that priests and religious orders played a significantly positive role, he also does not downplay the fact many of these priests in the era before the war were antisemitic.[125] He ascribes no influence on the occupiers of this antisemitic stance and in fact cites the example of Ignacy Charszewski, a co-author of the antisemitic *Samoobrona Narodu* ("Self-defense of the People") and other pamphlets that included descriptions of ritual murder. He was arrested and imprisoned in Chełmno/Kulmhof, then in Stutthof and finally in Sachsenhausen, where he died in April 1940 as the result of maltreatment.[126]

Can we then conclude that there was a preexistent condition in the frame of the *Juden/Pfaffen* relationship in Stutthof that included for some (like the noted example above) a troubled and indeed antagonistic relationship to Jews and to Judaism? That may be so, but if we use the lens of the past too forcibly and exclusively, we run the risk of overlooking the immediacy of the Stutthof experience for *Juden und Pfaffen*. While it is indeed possible—even probable—that some Polish priests in Stutthof once held views that were embraced and acted upon by their Nazi captors, for now, they are imprisoned and tortured together with Jews. What did these Polish priests and Danzig Jews have in common with their guards? The only bond was of language; the local SS men spoke or at least understood Polish and most local priests spoke both Polish and German. Both Jews and Poles suffered—many to death—under the racial ideology of National Socialism that promoted Germandom to the exclusion of any other identity. The priests were arrested and persecuted first and foremost as Poles who dared to stand up for the right to teach and preach in their native language, and to promote its culture and its history. The military and paramilitary units who rounded them up as resisters of Germandom and enemies of the Reich hounded them into Stutthof where they were shown even less respect. Catholic priests were divested of clerical garb and reduced to rags, just like the Jewish prisoners. But they defied their captors and behaved like *Menschen* who were also priests—extending mercy and kindness to all, including priests who were not Polish and to Jews who were Poles. The memoirs from which we have drawn in this chapter provide compelling evidence that the taunt *had* substance—

Juden und Pfaffen really did belong together as *Mitmenschen*. Despite the bleak and complicated pre-history of Stutthof, they offer a paradigm of humanity that should be at least acknowledged and respected. What we see in Stutthof in full operation was the level and degree of cruelty that the Nazi conquest of Danzig-West Prussia inflicted on both Poles and Jews. Historians have shown what a brutal annexation it was. In Stutthof, we also see some shafts of light and arcs of faith that transcend that dark history and need to be coaxed out of the shame and silence.

Voices of protest from the Free Churches in Danzig-West Prussia are scarce both before and after the outbreak of war, including from Methodists, Baptists, and other smaller groups. For the most part, they were not considered a threat by the Nazi regime, and certainly much less dangerous that the Jehovah's Witnesses who were interned the most frequently, especially because their men refused to do military service. (There will be more about their presence in Stutthof in Chapter 3.) According to Christine King, the Free Churches managed to escape the attention of the Nazis because they were politically neutral yet "conservative, loyal and patriotic."[127] Since "internationalism" was considered particularly dangerous, contacts with the free church denominations abroad were deemed the worst aspect of their religious practice, even for groups like the "*Christliche Versammlung*"/Christian Assembly, which had a small presence in Danzig as well as Elbing. They were banned across the Reich on April 13, 1937, but were permitted to continue services after they joined the group approved by the Nazis—the "Association of Christians of the Free Churches"/*Bund freikirchlichen Christen*. King notes that some were imprisoned for defying the ban.[128] What is striking about these groups is that they were invited to take part in large conferences in England, for example, in Oxford in 1937, where they had every opportunity to voice both support and dissent to what was happening in the Third Reich. Instead, these meetings were marked by infighting and squabbling. During a reciprocal visit in 1937 to Germany, the bishop of Gloucester commented of German pastors that "he had never known them to do anything but fight with each other or with or with the Powers that be."[129] The silence on the fate of European Jews is striking.

Schenk has summarized the fate of the Jews of Danzig as follows: Between February 28, 1941, and July 27, 1943, the Danzig Gestapo carried out mandatory deportations to the Warsaw ghetto and to Auschwitz concentration camp and to Theresienstadt. A total of 575 Jews were affected by these eight deportations which often meant certain death. Several hundred old and sick remained in a former grain elevator. In March 1941, the majority of them were sent to Lublin or the Warsaw Ghetto.[130] Grass refers directly to one of these deportations to Theresienstadt: "I used a setting far from the sieges of the summer of forty-one and the deportation of the remaining Danzig Jews from the Mausegasse ghetto to Theresienstadt." In his words, he had "managed to transfer his book-learned sense of justice entirely to the Middle Ages."[131]

The memoir of Kazimierz Badziąg, translated into German (2012) from the 2009 version of the Polish (first published in 2002), is an important narrative on several levels, not least that he survived both Stutthof and the perilous evacuation of the camp in 1945. The title, which would benignly translate into English as "Memories of a Boy Scout from Pomerania," belies the gravity of membership in an organization that was viciously targeted by the invading army in the newly annexed territories, in this case in the town of Tczew/Dirschau, and in nearby Chojnice/Konitz. The author offers firsthand proof of the consequences of having been a member of the Boy Scout movement—"Die Graue Reihen"/The Grey Ranks. Badziąg formally joined the scout movement in February 1941. The organization was of interest to the Germans because it had a clear mandate and purpose, which were considered antithetical to Germandom. Patriotism and the commitment to uphold Polish education and culture were already a dominant feature of life in the 1920s in an area that was heavily shaped by earlier Prussian history, a history that was quickly invoked and reactivated by the German occupiers. But in those days, commitment to the values of the Boy Scout movement was not life-threating. Badziąg's description of the interwar years and his relationship with German-speaking neighbors are largely consistent with the findings presented in *Pogranicza*. He, too, claims that Nazi agitators infiltrated the communities, influencing local Germans to hold military style meetings under the guise of church functions. Older women, he writes, would sing hymns loudly while the men clandestinely practiced military drills, and all of them listened to Hitler's speeches.[132] After the invasion, life changed dramatically for all Poles in Chojnice/Konitz, including his own family. The presence of the *Selbstschutz* became more pervasive, and their family had to share their home, their jobs with *Reichsdeutsche* and even give up their church building for the use of German Protestants. The invasion of personal space rapidly became the physical assault on their lives that resulted, in the second half of October, in the killing of the most vulnerable among them—249 mentally ill from the local mental institution.[133] In this small community of Chojnice that had known relative harmony, 155 inhabitants were murdered (including fifteen Jews) between 1939 and 1945 and, in the adjoining precincts, a further 581 victims perished.[134] The author survived the next two years. His ability to live undetected as a patriotic Pole ironically was helped by his fluency in German, which allowed him and his friends, for example, to remove the P sign that was mandatory when they went to the local bar, and to function as Germans.[135] One evening, however, they were recognized and, from that point, retreated from such excursions. The threat that lingered over the Polish community was to be sent to Stutthof, especially if they had refused the "honor" of being inscribed in one of the categories of the *DVL*. The information given in this diary is consistent with historian Koehl's research. For example, Koehl refers to the confusion in the annexed territories where several hundred thousand settlers were waiting to be placed and there was no place to house them. The answer was to keep Poles at their place of work and force them to live with relatives. The other solution was to build camps around industrial complexes and to send older relatives and children to live in special villages. Others were able to work as farm laborers and lived in rural villages that became known as "Z" villages. Their job was to serve the German settlers.[136]

And there were other ways of resettling ethnic Germans that strengthened Germandom and dispossessed Poles in the process. One example is a camp on the outskirts of Thorn/Toruń, which had been a factory for packing and processing meats, including lard, hence its name Szmalcówka. This camp operated from November 10, 1940, until June 1943—for thirty-three months. One of many hundreds of small camps throughout occupied Poland, it started out as a *Sammellager*—a transit camp where Poles were assembled temporally for the purpose of sending them elsewhere—in other words, resettling them since their own homes and farms had been reassigned to appropriate owners—ethnic Germans. They stayed for three to five days at the beginning, but then were moved on to other camps or to the General Government. This falls right after the "cleansing operations" that had meanwhile decimated the intelligentsia of Pomerania, but the internees of Szmalcówka were primarily farmers and small merchants. Thus, every segment of Pomeranian society was affected by the "cleansing." Though it was never considered a sub-camp of Stutthof—over an hour away—Szmalcówka drew on Stutthof's resources, especially as its function evolved. Its primary connection was to the Central Emigration Office—*Umwandererzentralstelle*— which, as noted, had been established for the purpose of facilitating resettlement. Resettlement was, however, not a benign bureaucratic activity for it was aligned with the *DVL*, which categorized Poles by four descending criteria of expendability. Those assigned to the fourth category were sent to the Warthegau, the neighboring Gau for hard labor, or to the Reich, or to camps like Stutthof. Lieutenant Colonel/*Obersturmführer* Radke, second in command in Thorn was employed in the Political Department and was responsible for tracking down Polish resisters. Scharf Zelma, the Jewish co-owner of the factory must have considered himself under threat for he had escaped already in September 1939 from Thorn to Włocławek. From September 1941 to January 1942, the camp was under the direct management of Stutthof, along with other camps, but was not considered a sub-camp. Commandant Pauly was responsible for sending SS men to be guards in the camp, including Richard Reddig, frequently mentioned in Stutthof memoirs and documents. Before Stutthof's involvement, they were helped by the Auxiliary Police and by volunteers who received their training at Stutthof.[137] The mortality rate in this camp tells a distressing story. Among the 515 Poles who died there, 68 percent were children younger than eighteen and 16 percent were elderly.[138] Szmalcówka personnel, including the men who ran the camp and guarded it did not serve any prison sentence after the war. Paul Ehle died in 1965 in Neumünster. Richard Reddig went back to serve in Stutthof, where he stayed until it was liberated. He died on August 13, 1970, in Hannover at age seventy-four. Willy Ehlert died in April 1995 in Oldenburg.[139] General/*Gruppenführer* Ludolf von Alvensleben headed up the *Selbstschutz* in Pomerania in the fall of 1939 and was never brought to justice for his role in the murder of hundreds of Poles or for the suffering of many in camps like Szmalcówka. He found sanctuary in Argentine where he died in 1970. He had declared: "The goal of public administration is to destroy and make these lands Pole-free."[140] The testimony of one inmate of Szmalcówka includes memories of better days before the invasion and resonates with similar experiences expressed in the excerpts that follow. Tadeusz Pipowski lived in a small village in Małoc and together with his three brothers was a prisoner in Szmalcówka. He remembers that Poles and Germans lived peacefully in Pomerania before the war. Germans could choose to attend either a Polish or a German school. Pipowski's German friends generally chose a German school, and he remembers them as his best friends. They were treated well in Poland, and there were no problems.[141]

Local People Remember the Outbreak of War

What do the findings of Polish scholars in memory studies reveal about what it was like to live in Danzig and "the Polish Corridor" between 1939 and 1945? In the segment pertaining to the war period, there are references to Stutthof—in contrast to Grass's fiction where the camp is admittedly referred to as a sinister place but remains oblique and distant. However, at least one reference in these interviews includes the Nazi rationalization of camps as a British construct (thus, a distant concept) and as in Grass, not much is known about Stutthof until a relative is arrested and sent there. Yet, these interviews personalize a history that tends to be flattened by statistics—the number of Poles and Jews who were incarcerated, the number of Jews who fled, etc. While such figures are foundational and essential to research, (and sometimes are hard to harmonize) they tend to mute or even erase the human voices behind them. The statements in the interviews presented below add nuance to the year the war started and what it meant to live in "the Polish Corridor:"

Hubert Bartsch: Nowe Podlaszki, September 1–2, 1939
September First was a Friday. Nothing was happening here, absolutely nothing—not yet. And on Saturday, on the second of September, we were all at home when the Polish army—the cavalry—showed up. They deliberated in Polish about what to do next. Then they left and nobody came after that. No shots were fired here, not a single one. We saw one plane, and we did hear some shots in the distance, but here in Nowe Polaszki, there was no war. On Sunday, the third of September the German army arrived in Wilcze Błota. Then they left for Stara Kiszewa and from there probably went on to Starogard. A bridge on the main road from Kościerzyna to Stara Kiszewa was blown up and they couldn't move forward. They waited on the road. They didn't come to our house. I was sixteen at the time, and I can't say I associated any feelings of liberation or hopes for *Germandom* with the outbreak of the war.[142]

Jadwiga Hinz: Nowe Podlaszki
When the German army was about to enter these territories, many Poles fled. We didn't, we stayed with our neighbor Schwonki. "May it be what it's meant to be!" Hanne kept saying. "Where would you want to flee, Hedwig, and what for?" For a short period, there was no government, neither Polish nor German. Then the German army came to Nowe Podlaszki. I remember them marching and singing, "Keine Angst/ Have no fear."
  Have no fear, Rosemary dear,
  We'll catch Chamberlain in his night gear!
Such handsome boys. I thought to myself: my God, they are going to the slaughter. His daughter Hanne tried to convince me to go and greet German soldiers with flowers. I spoke German very well, so they treated me as a German. But my mother told me to go and hide in a barn. And Hanne went alone to greet the soldiers. During the war, none of my German girlfriends turned against me.[143]

This is how Kashubian Edmund Odya remembers the outbreak of war:

> I remember I was in the field when my older brother came running, "Come home, we are at war. War has broken out," he said. I took the cow that I was tending and went home. Planes were flying in the direction of Stara Kiszewa. They wanted to bomb the church, but bombs hit a clothing store instead. The store burned down. We hid in a ditch that our mother had dug. We were curious and observed the Schwabs.[144] All our German neighbors put on SS uniforms and armbands with the swastika, took out rifles and decorated the city gates in anticipation of greeting the German army. But yet, there was not a single German soldier to be seen. They were coming via Stara Kiszewa.[145]

Manfrid Baaske has this to say:

> We knew that there was a concentration camp in Stutthof, that some had been taken there. But apart from us, generally speaking, nobody in the village knew about it. My father knew more. Our uncle worked in the Telecommunication Office and he installed telephone cables in Stutthof, but he didn't want to say anything specific. My father learned more about the concentration camp Stutthof when he was arrested by the Gestapo. We didn't know that it was so bad there. According to Nazi propaganda, the English built concentration camps in South Africa, and the Church—the bad one—persecuted witches. The Stutthof estate belonged to the family of the great philosopher Schopenhauer. Goethe strolled once in Buchenwald. Concentration camps would be built in places like that? I didn't know anything about it, absolutely nothing. Whether Jews were persecuted? I also didn't see that. I remember that they were looked down upon, like when our school friend Hildegard Schadow disappeared. We all thought that she got lost. She was hidden by a teacher who used Nazi slogans over and over again on a daily basis. I noticed that right after opening his store, one Jew vanished, and in Kościerzyna, Mendelson vanished. We used to buy groceries in his store. I had not heard anything about organized killings of Jews.[146]

What is clear from these excerpts is the escalation of fear and the recognition, expressed by a Polish woman that German youth, now marching proudly through the local villages "are going to be slaughtered." German neighbors put on the swastika armband, and Jewish neighbors disappear. Stutthof is now part of the conversation. Admittedly not much is known about it but strikingly, it is called a "concentration camp"—over two years before it became one. An uncle worked there installing cables but did not talk about it. His silence thus becomes part of a narrative of vanishing Jews and the lack of knowledge about the camp. That is, until the Gestapo arrested you and took you there.

The Lament for a Lost Community

"Hell" is a recurring word in the depiction of all Nazi camps, and it is used with striking frequency about this first phase of Stutthof. It will not go away, and in fact by the end of 1944, there will be new permutations of the word. Whether in memoirs written by priests or by other survivors, it is consistently used, and at times in comparison with other camps. What made this early phase of Stutthof such a hell? Is it feasible to propose that the camp's connection to Danzig and Pomerania embodies the loss of a life that once was—for both Poles and Germans? We think of Malak's father bowed over in grief, taking his leave from his son, reminding him of "other Germans," and we go back to Grass's stories when "*die Hiesigen*" (locals) lived decently together. The cult of Germandom exploited and revived old Prussian loyalties, and targeted Germans who had once lived in relative harmony with Poles. The intent was to replace former notions of civility with an inflated, prideful identity as *Reichsdeutsche,* where even the Polish language was banned in schools. The other losses include the grief of local Jews who had been part of a small but vibrant community. For them, "old Danzig" was home. Now they had to find ways and means to leave it, and collectively they had to sell their priceless religious artifacts to fund their exodus. They also had to deal with the loss of a free city with legal protections. The Polish community had to live with the daily reminder of the superiority of the master race, which must have revived stories of the *Kulturkampf* of the previous century when Prussian superiority was foisted on Polish communities. I am not claiming that the post-Versailles Treaty years of comparative peace in Danzig and "the Corridor" had erased the deeply held sense of ethnic identity for Germans and Poles. Rather, the ideology of Germandom that was unleashed on Danzig and Pomerania in the 1930s stirred up old animosities and convictions that infected large sections of the community and incited citizens to turn their backs on one another.

Beginning in the autumn of 1939, every inhabitant of Danzig and Pomerania, whether German, Pole, Jew, Kashubian, Roma/Sinti experienced at some level the annexation of their territory by German troops and special commando units that followed the army. It is no wonder that Berendt Grzegorz referred to the first two months of the assault as "Pomerania's bloody autumn."[147] Various agencies operated in tandem to "cleanse" the whole area, headed up by military leaders and paramilitary groups like the *Selbstschutz*. Their common goal was to strengthen Germandom. Their most destructive tool was to destroy what stood in the way of that goal. Dwork and van Pelt commented aptly on Nazi claims of superiority over every aspect of Polish culture: "National Socialists transformed a legitimate chronicle of past achievement into a pernicious caricature of German-Polish relations. Ewald Liedecke, the chief planner of the new Gau of Danzig-West Prussia declared that every trace of culture within Poland was the result of German achievement."[148] Germandom took that notion of superiority to a new level, and projected it upon every aspect of life in the annexed territories—race, culture, politics, education, religion, social life—and placed its execution under a specific program with one aim, to strengthen every aspect of Germandom. This program operated on all occupied territory.

Our focus on Danzig-West Prussia has shown the disastrous consequences for local Jews of Danzig and for the Polish population of Danzig and Pomerania. In terms of the loss of human lives alone, the perpetrators of this program must have considered it successful. But they were also disappointed with the results in Danzig-West Prussia. There were weaknesses and failures of the program due to "human errors," like the inability of Nazi elites to agree. They were unable to come up with a consistent Slavic policy, even at the very top with Hitler. They faced major challenges in moving ethnic Germans and resettling them in the homes and farmsteads of Poles. The shift of priorities after the Soviet invasion in June 1941 brought new demands for armaments and human resources to make them. There was now an urgent need for more facilities in camps, including the labor camps. Germandom was more than about reclaiming a glorious Prussian history and teaching the Nazi youth to sing heartily "Heute gehört uns Deutschland, Morgen die ganze Welt." ("Today Germany belongs to us, Tomorrow the whole world.") They could celebrate that Danzig had been brought back into the fold but in the process the Jewish communities of Danzig and the small towns of Pomerania had been destroyed. The celebration of Germandom cannot be separated from its consequences—dispossessing Poles, silencing, and killing their Catholic priests and educated classes, shutting down the Polish language and culture, exploiting the uneducated for cheap labor, and corrupting those who collaborated with them with false promises and premises for which future generations of Poles would have to pay—and are still paying.

We know from the many photographs in Stutthof's archives that Himmler visited Stutthof in November 1941, presumably to give it the final inspection for promotion. During that visit, he also warned Forster not to be so rash in his assessment of who was German, emphasizing that no decision would be better than an incorrect one.[149] His comment reminds us again of the lack of a consistent policy on Polish identity among the Nazi leaders. Allen points out that in the same month of the visit, Himmler was planning to expand Auschwitz, Stutthof, and Majdanek. Stutthof, the smallest of the three, was to have a labor force of 25,000, "with whom we can then complete the buildup of settlements in the Gau Danzig-West Prussia."[150] A related plan was to use Soviet POWs for slave labor in these camps. By year's end, this plan was severely thwarted because most of the prisoners died *en route* to the camps from the consequences of maltreatment. Himmler acknowledged this new reality on January 26, 1942, in a message to Richard Glücks, head of the IKL (*Inspektion der Konzentrationslager*/ Inspectorate of Concentration Camps). Instead of Russian POWs, he would be sending Jewish men—100,000 and as many as 50,000 Jewish women. The new order specified the nature of the assignment: "In the next few weeks the concentration camps will be assigned great industrial tasks. SS Maj. Gen. Pohl will inform you of the details."[151]

The consequences of this turn of events and of priorities for Stutthof will generate a new set of questions posed in the next two chapters. Among them—what about Danzig? How will the events of the war change Stutthof? Will local guards retain their same status? Will Grass have much to say? The next chapter will provide information, commentary, analyses, and personal narratives on how these "great industrial tasks" were performed, who performed them, and who supervised the performance.

3

Gaining the Next Tier of Germandom as a Nazi *Konzentrationslager*

When Heinrich Himmler granted Stutthof the status of a concentration camp in January 1942, it was still a relatively small camp, with a fluctuating prisoner population—mostly Poles—that included both correctional inmates and political ones. Some of them had been sent there as escapees from forced labor camps, others were sent as punishment for lesser "crimes" like sabotage or simply accused of being slackers.[1] Once there, they were subjected to cruel and harsh treatment, and as many as 15 percent of them did not survive.[2] Since October 1941, when it was designated as a "labor camp," Stutthof and its filial camps had been under the authority of the Gestapo bureau in Danzig but even after its new status was granted in 1942, the ties to Danzig did not cease or slacken. What did change, however, was that the camp could now claim legal and financial ties to the main agencies of the Third Reich, notably the IKL and the WVHA (*Wirtschaftsverwaltungshauptamt*/Business and Administration Main Office) under Oswald Pohl. Pohl continued to focus on economic matters and left the other decisions to Glücks whose IKL agency now operated under the new name of *Amtsgruppe D*.[3] Stutthof's new status conferred on it the lofty mandate to be a camp for "the protection of the people and of the state."

What role did Himmler's office for "Strengthening Germandom" play in the new status of Stutthof and did it protect Germans? Now that the enemies of Germandom had either been killed or interned, it might seem that the office to strengthen Germandom had fulfilled its function. After the first wave of violent assaults on the annexed territories, the methods of strengthening Germandom took on different initiatives that focused more on the running of the camp and the demands of war efforts. Himmler had consolidated every branch of the police under the umbrella of the RSHA and placed it under Reinhard Heydrich, thereby aligning it with the powerful SS, an organization that had been growing steadily in influence since 1933, becoming over the years what has been aptly called "a favorite instrument of terror."[4] Himmler's role in Stutthof (though it still was not considered a major camp within the system) would be critical in shaping it into a camp where SS values would flourish and local men could do themselves proud as members of a master race, educating the wayward, and punishing those considered in the way of promoting Germandom.

Where does Stutthof fit in 1942 within the larger camp system? Given the high mortality rate in Stutthof right from the beginning in September 1939, it is hard to imagine that worse brutalities had already been perpetrated in the Warthegau, and farther afield, in the occupied territories of Eastern Europe. The Nazi invasion of the Soviet Union in June 1941 in Operation Barbarossa was a turning point in the course of a war that was rapidly changing direction. The Third Reich's defiance of its August 1939 accord with the Soviets added a new dimension to its military prowess against the powerful Red Army and also affirmed Germandom by helping resettle the scattered ethnic German communities. The counterpart of these endeavors was to attack what was considered subhuman people in brutal acts of revenge. The latter was enacted in September, when over 34,000 Jews were massacred within a few days in the ravines at Babi Yar on the outskirts of Kiev in occupied Ukraine. In the weeks that followed, a series of killings of local Jews by special German commando forces took place on the same killing sites. Thousands of captured Soviet prisoners who had originally been designed for slave labor in the camps died en route of starvation. Some in this cohort of prisoners would eventually arrive in Stutthof.

Yet Stutthof's initial function as a camp to intern civilian Poles (and later their family members) did not change fundamentally and remained so until the camp was dissolved in the spring of 1945 by the Soviet army. Polish prisoners constituted the majority of the camp population until mid-1944, though many other prisoners from multiple ethnic groups and political stripes joined them in the course of those years. The Polish prisoners were not necessarily the same ones who entered the camp in September 1939, since many in that group had already been killed or died, or had been sent to the General Government, or to the Old Reich for hard labor, or to one of the other camps; the dead and departed were quickly replaced by other Polish groups from the main resistance organizations in Pomerania and later from farther afield.

Closer to Stutthof, an extermination camp was already operating in December 1941 in Chełmno/Kulmhof in the Warthegau and was shamelessly designated "a single purpose" camp for mass murder. Under Arthur Greiser, Gauleiter and Governor of the Warthegau, 100,000 Jews were exterminated there.[5] Greiser was Forster's counterpart, and their rivalry and competitive spirit, which reached back into the 1930s in Danzig's Senate, were well known and still active. Of course, Danzig-West Prussia was a very different Gau than Greiser's Warthegau which was home to 400,000 Jews, most of them around Łódź, as well as in smaller communities. By mid-1940, rural ghettos had been established in the central part of the Warthegau.[6] Forster's Gau, by contrast, had roughly a tenth of the Jewish population. There were, however, trends in occupied Poland that did not portend well for the inmates of any camp, especially one that had just received the coveted status of concentration camp. By dint of this status alone, it is reasonable to assume that Stutthof's prisoners would not be spared at least some of the acts of carnage that were taking place elsewhere. Among the most troubling activities was the continuation of the so-called euthanasia program—*Aktion T4* killings that Hitler had halted when faced with protest from the Catholic Church, but the practice continued and was administered clandestinely by doctors and nurses using lethal injections. Over 70,000 disabled were killed between January 1940 and August 1941.[7] The key figure behind the Kulmhof camp was Herbert Lange who had been attached to Einsatzgruppe V1 which followed the German army into Poland and was engaged in the same "cleansing" actions that happened in the fall of 1939, when after the invasion perceived enemies of Germandom were also eliminated. Patrick Montague points out that the SS became increasingly involved in the Euthanasia program in the spring of 1941 when it launched the "Aktion 14f13" program which involved the killing of concentration camp inmates. It is also significant that other Gauleiter were interested in Lange's earlier "success" in killing the disabled. Erich Koch, Gauleiter in East Prussia invited Lange and his *Sonderkommando* to come with their gas van to Soldau/Działdowo where they killed 1,558 patients between May 21 and June 8, 1940. Himmler expressed his satisfaction with the operation and told Lange and his men to take a vacation.[8]

Stutthof was not an extermination camp like Chełmno/Kulmhof but by 1942 it was poised to extend its reach more effectively into the agenda to strengthen Germandom and promote the ideals of the Third Reich. The hardships and cruelties perpetrated in it thus far did not decline but simply took on different shapes that reflected the practices of other camps—the use of Zyklon B, the construction of a small but effective gas chamber and a crematorium to dispose of the bodies. It was now one of the four new camps—joining Auschwitz, Majdanek, and Natzweiler. Its new status did not diminish its connection to Danzig and above all to its local police force and to the local Gestapo. Nor did the zeal to subjugate Poles abate. For the next three years, the Danzig Gestapo remained active and to a large extent successful in combating the resistance movement in Danzig-West Prussia. Those who were arrested in the round-ups, mostly between 1942 and 1943 were brought to the camp as prisoners of the police and were kept in a separate block in the Old Camp—in Block Five—isolated from the other prisoners. The group included women, but neither men nor women were allowed to have any contact with the other inmates. Unlike the other prisoners, who wore triangles to indicate their primary identity, they were designated with numbers and did not receive a triangle until after they had been sentenced to a longer stay in the camp.[9] They also stayed within the jurisdiction of the Danzig Gestapo who came to the camp to hold hearings. Many of these prisoners were maltreated in the camp and tortured to death. Others died of starvation.[10] Stutthof was also becoming a destination for prisoners from a broader network of camps, including some of the ghettos that were liquidated in the summer of 1941 when special labor camps were set up by German firms that either employed Jewish workers or sent them to camps like Stutthof.[11]

This chapter will concentrate on two broad areas of inquiry: the composition of the camp's population between early 1942 and the fall of 1944—who the prisoners were, where they were housed, and their labor assignments in the camp. The second focus will be on the role of the SS but especially on local SS men in Stutthof and will include Heinrich Himmler's role in shaping it into his image. In what ways did they represent the agency to strengthen Germandom? At the local level, we will take a closer look at the files of men who were from Danzig and environs. What can we learn about the background of local men from their files? What kind of educational and work background did they have? For how long had they been associated with the Nazi Party and with the SS? Do they represent broader facets of what we typically associate with the SS?

The Prisoner Population

With reference to the prison population after January 1942, there was certainly no change in the policy of targeting local Polish dissidents, who continued to be arrested and dragged into the camp by the Gestapo and the *Ordnungspolizei*. In the spring of 1942, the criteria for the VL were fine-tuned by Himmler and were used in the occupied territories after the Nazi invasion of the Soviet Union in June 1941. In "the Corridor," however, the Nazis faced a major hurdle because ethnic Germans constituted a small minority of the population. In their zeal to stamp out all traces of resistance, the net grew wider and reached into the outlying towns and remote villages, as in June, when forty men from the underground were accused of sabotaging a railway line. By the end of 1943, they had brought several hundred to Stutthof, including the families of partisans, mothers and fathers, sisters and brothers who were designated as hostages.[12] The most prominent among this group were Poles who, in the second half of 1942 had refused to sign up on the VL (see Appendix). The fate of those who were coerced into signing was often prompt enlistment in the German army. Some of these men deserted at the first opportunity to go over to the other side. As reprisal, the Nazis then arrested the whole family and called them deserters. In the personnel files of September 1943, for example, there is an entry pertaining to a family from Neustadt, a man called Antoni Kuptz who was imprisoned along with his wife and his sixteen-year-old daughter. The entry reads, "Your son Bruno defected to the Russians." It was also claimed that in a search of their apartments, they had found three songs that expressed anti-German sentiment. This notice was sent by the head of the Gestapo in Bromberg/Bydgoszcz to the Commandant of Stutthof.[13] In order to Germanize the area as quickly as possible, the use of the Polish language was forbidden and was considered a punishable offense that could land you in the camp. A typical entry reads simply "spoke Polish." Between 1942 and 1943, there were many prisoners whose reason for internment in the camp ranged from spreading hostile propaganda, refusal to wear the designated P, which was obligatory for forced laborers, listening to the radio, sexual relations between Germans and Poles, or between Russians and Germans. No pretext was trivial.

The prison population also now included several thousand forced workers of different nationalities who were working in industry and agriculture in the sub-camps of the Danzig-West Prussia district.[14] Prisoners also began to arrive from as far as Stettin and Königsberg in February 1942. By April, there were also an increasing number of transports from other camps, for example, one with 114 prisoners from Buchenwald, and one on July 2 from Mauthausen with 122 prisoners. Among them were criminals who assumed positions of authority within the camp system (more on that subject later). The prisoner registration records (*Einlieferungsbuch*) indicate that between August 27, 1942, and January 8, 1943, 3,266 prisoners were registered. In a sample of 270 prisoners, 222 had been sent for "corrective labor," fifteen as career criminals, seven were asocials, twenty-four political prisoners, five Jehovah Witnesses, and one homosexual. There were 224 men and 50 women. The death rate for those in corrective labor appears to be the highest—fifty-five died within two months' time. The remaining ninety-five were held permanently, of whom fifty-three died within two months. The cause of death was generally listed as physical weakness, or often as "intestinal catarrh," or tuberculosis. Typhus was never listed, nor death by injection.[15] Between February 1943 and May 1944, there were at least twenty-three prisoner transports from Białystok who were for the most part Polish and Belorussian farmers accused of having helped the partisans. The mortality rate among this group was high—in some cases 70–80 percent.[16] After the ghetto in Białystok was liquidated in November 1943, a prisoner transport with around 300 Jews arrived in Stutthof. (The fate of Jews will be examined in greater detail in the next chapter.)

Organization of the Camp

After January 1942, Stutthof fell into line with the organizational practices of the other main camps. The revamped hierarchy reflected to some degree—but never perfectly—the rules that Theodor Eicke had put in place during his tenure as director of the camp system, beginning in Dachau where he served as Commandant. Recent research by Christopher Dillon on Dachau and the SS presents a systematic study of prewar Dachau and the ways in which the SS were trained in violence. Dillon calls Dachau "the academy of violence for a cohort of future SS murderers."[17] He refutes Daniel Jonah Goldhagen's arguments that ascribe proto-genocidal intent to German antisemitism and asks if his arguments might better apply to the SS.[18] In view of the later role of the *Totenkopf*/Death's head Division in the camps, his claim has merit. Richard Glücks replaced Eicke who in July 1942, as part of a general commandant shake-up in the camps, recommended Paul-Werner Hoppe as the replacement of Max Pauly for the job of running Stutthof.[19] Prior to that point, personnel had assumed multiple roles in running the camp. Now, the hierarchy was standardized and organized around six main departments that were frequently at odds with one another; from July 1942 all were under Commandant Hoppe, who was known and supported by his bosses in Berlin. A former *Totenkopfdivision* officer, Hoppe had been injured in combat and had spent a short period in Auschwitz. In other words, he fit the leadership criteria well and, though prisoners mention him infrequently in memoirs of this period (presumably because he was insulated from the more mundane aspects of everyday camp life), it was under his leadership that the camp gained recognition within the camp system with which Hoppe was already well acquainted. He was recommended to the post in a conversation on July 24, 1942, when Glücks praised his suitability for the job based on his intimate knowledge of the camp system. Four days later Pohl named him as the new Commandant of Stutthof. Pohl knew him from earlier days when, right before war broke out, the two of them had worked together in Danzig, setting up protection measures, for which Hoppe had been given the Danzig Cross. Hoppe had met Pohl again in the summer of 1942 when he was recuperating from his war wounds and at that time Eicke had told Pohl to consider him as suitable to run a concentration camp. He also mentioned that the camps should get into the armaments business.[20] Stutthof was coming into its own within the Reich camp system.

Forster issued another call to join the VL on February 22 with a deadline of March 31, 1942, and the threat of reprisals to be taken on those who did not confess to having German blood, considered as grave an insult as being among Germany's greatest enemies. Stutthof's incomplete files indicate that between 1942 and 1944, around 100 Polish men and women were arrested and sent to Stutthof for either failing to register or falsifying their records. Among these prisoners were also military deserters or those who had been caught providing shelter for them. Their families were also not spared from incarceration.[21] Because of the need between 1942 and 1945 for soldiers at the Front, there was in 1942 a deficit of 625,000 soldiers at the Front. Grot proposes that by sending Polish men to the Front, Forster saw a rapid way to handle the Germanisation program and also as a way of sparing German blood.[22] The expression "in die Wälder fliehen"/ "to flee to the forests" was used to indicate it was time to hide from the enemy and to join one of the partisan groups. What had changed by mid-1942, for the Poles, at least in Danzig-West Prussia was the process by which they applied for German ethnicity. Under Himmler's orders it was streamlined and now consisted of basic questions that asked, for example, what the applicants thought of Germany, if they approved of the war and if they shared the work ethic expected of Germans. The reasons given for Poles registering for the VL range from the fear of being sent to the Reich—or to the front lines—and especially the memory of 1939 when so many Poles were brutally murdered. Among the more basic fears was loss of "hearth and home." For those who refused and ended up in Stutthof, every effort was made to keep all resisters apart, but it was never foolproof, and there was some success in resisting the SS. For example, in the spring of 1943, a group of Polish political prisoners challenged the SS by infiltrating various workshops with the goal of dismantling SS power. They are described as young, competent in German and had joined forces with the old timers—the so-called *alte Nummern,* who had been in the camp a long time. As a result of this solidarity, camp conditions improved somewhat, especially because they had managed to run the central office where work duties were assigned. The outcome was that one prisoner was represented in each of the work units as a clandestine presence of the resistance movement. Some of these prisoners had come in transports from Warsaw and Lublin between 1943 and 1944 or were Soviet officers or juvenile prisoners.[23] Dunin-Wąsowicz reports that SS men Foth and Chemnitz executed prisoners who were suspected of sabotage in an ammunition factory in Danzig. These prisoners were separated from the others and put in a bunker. According to Wachsmann, Chemnitz modeled his work on his earlier experience as a block leader in Buchenwald during the 1941 murders of Soviet "commissars"—among the most hated prisoner group in the whole concentration camp system.[24]

Sociologist Wolfgang Sofsky's groundbreaking research into the internal operations of the concentration camp system has provided valuable keys to understanding how a camp like Stutthof ever developed the way it did, even though (unsurprisingly) Stutthof is not central to his analysis. Sofsky examines the functions of each of the five main departments within the camp administration, beginning with the Commandant's office, then Department Two which admitted and released prisoners— the Camp Gestapo, the Political Department that dealt with prisoner files, carried out interrogations, ordered executions and issued death certificates. Department Three was responsible for the protective custody issues and ran the operations that entailed labor deployment. Department Four was responsible for managing the material equipment and prisoner possessions—food supply, clothing, etc. Department Five was responsible for the medical services and the hospital/sick bay. Sofsky points out that each department guarded its turf. "The bureaucracy of the camp was anything but monolithic."[25] A sixth department in Stutthof was responsible for training the SS and providing them with further education and entertainment.

Sofsky essentially answers the question of how all these departments and people running them could possibly function. The answer, he argues, was not due to bureaucratic efficiency but rather to the "high degree of camaraderie, local autonomy, and personal initiative that pervaded its structures."[26] This resonates strongly with the narratives we will look at in this chapter. How much were the camp personnel in these six departments influenced by the ideology that shaped their lives in the 1930s? Sofsky emphasizes that the SS leadership valued propaganda greatly but warns that one should not overestimate the impact of SS ideology as a guide to action. "The content of instructional materials was thin and unsubstantial: expurgated German history coupled with glorification of 'Germanic' culture, sundry legends from the 'period of struggle' of the Nazi party, a few tenets of biological racism, and a lot of images of the enemy."[27] From the start, the Death's Head regiments were conceived as paramilitary formations and not merely guard units.[28] Theodor Eicke instilled in his men the notion of the "political soldier," that is, men with the same qualities as fighting men on the front. Wachsmann defines these as "brutality, racism, ruthlessness."[29] Sofsky places special emphasis on the role of camaraderie within the units. He writes: "They counted on the goodwill of their superiors ... As militarily as the camp SS were wont to present themselves, they tended more to resemble a band of conspirators who stuck close together when faced with external checks and controls, even by other SS authorities. Eicke was personally antagonistic towards the military spirit and soldiering, promoting camaraderie and 'du.'"[30]

Stutthof's structure fits in large measure the model described by Sofsky, certainly after January 1942. Within that structure the ethos of daily life was shaped by obligatory roll calls—the infamous *Appell* on the parade ground—the presence of vicious guard dogs in the canine unit, electric fences, guard turrets, etc. Prisoner Yla writes: "We lived in mortal fear of the police dogs. These animals followed every move we made; and if an SS man so much as pointed his finger at a prisoner, his dog went immediately for that prisoner's throat."[31] Within the main departments the roles were designated: camp elders, (*Lagerälteste*) and their deputies, some of whom were further aided by secretaries (*Schreiber*). There were also block elders, room or *Stube* trusties, kapos and their helpers, the former sometimes referred to with the name *Speckjäger* (bacon chasers) to reflect the benefits that came with the job. Nowhere does that combination of structure and ethos come together more clearly than in the memoirs written by camp prisoners. The more skilled writers, like Lithuanian Balys Sruoga, give the reader more detailed profiles of the prisoners, the kind of work they were forced to do and who supervised them. Their narratives underscore the claims made in the Introduction for the unique contribution of literary accounts.

Profiles of Inmates

Prisoners, including hardened criminals, taken directly from the cells of Danzig had initially been employed both to build Stutthof and to supervise the prisoners who were doing the work. Nothing changed in that regard; prisoners still provided the labor to build this camp throughout its history. Now, though, as throughout the rest of the camp system, dependence on prisoners with a criminal background increased. After 1942, *Berufsverbrecher*—professional criminals, both local ones and those from other camps known for violence toward prisoners—were used at the camp. This included those transferred from Mauthausen, (the first, arrived on July 2 1942), from Buchenwald, and ten criminals from Flossenbürg (March 23, 1943) who used whips on the prisoners working in the forest commando.[32] The rationalization was "because of their professional abilities." Camp authorities considered criminals to be particularly useful for gaining the upper hand over fellow prisoners, "to keep them working, to humiliate them and break their resistance." This argument was taken from the trial of Commandant Hoppe and SS man Otto Knott.[33] SS Teodor Meyer rationalized his use of criminals in his memoir as based on a language issue—they needed the German speakers.[34] Wachsmann questions the brutality that has been ascribed by historians to *Berufsverbrecher,* arguing that the claims are exaggerated and that most of them from the state prisons were not hardened criminals but rather small time offenders, if guilty at all.[35] Stutthof memoirs do not reflect this view.[36]

During the period from January 1942 till late summer 1944, a lot changed inside the camp parameters. In October 1940, it had been designated already as a *Sonderlager*—a camp for hard labor; this role had added yet another layer to its initial identity as a camp for civilian prisoners. These overlapping roles continued throughout the camp's history. By mid-1942, however, Stutthof's internal functions had begun to reflect the course of military actions in the east, particularly after the German attack in June 1941 on the Soviet Union that brought in its wake a new influx of prisoners from occupied territories who now constituted the second largest contingent in the camp—Russians, Belarusians, Ukrainians, Lithuanians, Latvians, and Estonians. Soviet POWs later joined these groups, directed to Stutthof because of their pro-communist activities in prisoner-of-war camps. These Soviet prisoners or "commissars" were put to work in the underground munitions factories in Brahnau, near Bromberg/Bydgoszcz, among them a group of officers and petty officers of the Soviet army.[37] The commissars had been targeted as "Jewish Bolsheviks" and were marked for extinction by Heinrich Müller, head of the Gestapo in July 1941.[38]

In 1943, other prisoners arrived including some prominent Latvians as well as Lithuanians who had resisted the Nazis and were, from the camp perspective, relatively protected. Himmler had designated them "honorary prisoners," a term that does not resonate in their memoirs. They arrived at the Danzig railway station in a group of 200 prisoners who were Belarusians and Poles from Białystok. Among the Lithuanians, two have contributed significantly to the history of the camp—Balys Sruoga, a prominent writer and former professor, and Stasys Yla, a priest—and we will draw from both memoirs.[39] Sruoga gives us a striking mixture of information and factual statements in narrative prose that draws from conventional strategies—irony, understatement, and hyperbole. The effect is twofold: he underscores the credibility of the information and renders the atrocities more shocking. Sruoga worked for a time in the Political Department of the camp where he had access to camp files, including personnel files, which he transposed into notes that provide detailed information pertaining to the years 1943 to 1945. The counterpart of this group was the cohort of young men who, following the defeat of the German army in Stalingrad in 1943, were mobilized by the SS and accepted into the SS corps on the basis of racial desirability—they looked Germanic, and though they may not have spoken any German, they were welcomed and replaced other ethnic Germans who were being sent to the front.

The other large group of prisoners in this period was the German group. The diversity, both politically and socially, found among German prisoners is arguably the most striking of all the groups. Their numbers included the groups already alluded to—professional criminals, as well as the so-called a-socials. There also were political dissidents who included communists, union members, Social Democrats, military deserters and spies. The following year will bring a different group—German aristocrats. Between 1942 and 1943, Stutthof's population fluctuated, rarely rising above 4,000 prisoners at any given time. Prisoners were transferred to other camps and were quickly replaced by those on incoming transports. Sruoga comments:

> At any given moment the SS could shoot the prisoners, hang them, stone them or club them to death, throwing them to the dogs, rob them, beat them, smear them with tar and so on and so on. A prisoner was unprotected by laws ... On the other hand, the SS could not run the camp without the help of the prisoners or even live in reasonable comfort without them.[40]

Career criminals were not in the same category as prisoners who provided a different sort of usefulness in running the camp.[41] In fact, the camp elites were very dependent on prisoners who had skills that they themselves frequently lacked. As noted earlier, among the prisoners who came in the early days of the camp were skilled laborers who were capable of organizing work units. These local Polish prisoners from Danzig had the advantage of speaking German, and thus were more likely to be appointed to head up work units. Provided they survived the first two years of the camp, they often assumed the jobs that had been held by German criminals who were routinely sent to other camps where they could be equally useful in meting out abuse. Among the Polish survivors, two are singled out by Sruoga for special praise in an otherwise bleak landscape of thugs. He describes the chief of the clerical department, a kapo called August Zagórski from Danzig who before the war had been the Polish postmaster-treasurer and had been sent to the camp "simply because he was a Pole and lived in Danzig." Sruoga continues, "He was a very just, honest and wise man ... For his orderliness and integrity, the authorities valued him highly—for a long time they kept him in one of the most important and influential camp positions. While he held this post, he was able to render aid to many—and he imparted it abundantly, saving many lives."[42] His assistant was a Pole called Bruno Rekajski who had been on the Polish general staff as an officer of the second division in Poznań. He had been in the camp for four years and held a very important position. Sruoga writes that he was accepted by these two men with open arms and they taught him the prisoner philosophy of work: don't hurry; work is not a wolf—it won't run away.[43] These two men helped the author gain some strength for the healing of his body. At the time of their arrest, both men were married but their wives went through the process of becoming Germanized while the husbands remained Polish. Consequently, they were forbidden to return to their wives because the Germans had prohibited Poles from having relations with German women. Sruoga worked in the office with these men till the end.[44] He adds that political prisoners came from a variety of countries and political persuasions; some had been activists, but others had never had anything to do with politics. He provides these statistics: "From 1942 to 1943, there were 3,500 to 4,000 prisoners in the camp. During that time, the prisoners' census changed three to four times per year. As prisoners died, others were herded in to replace them. In this way, the headcount remained the same: 3,500 to 4,000."[45] He adds that camp functionaries valued them enough to allow them to operate at higher levels in "important and influential camp positions."[46] They also were able to aid their fellow-prisoners in humane ways.

Prisoners who were skilled laborers were in a better position to survive than intellectuals—teachers, clergy, clerical workers, etc., who often ended up doing the hardest manual labor in work units like the dreaded Forest or the Construction Work Units. With few exceptions, they worked in jobs for which they were the least physically equipped. The only release from such a fate was to find employment in the various workshops or infirmaries or better still, in the administrative office. (This was the case for a brief period for Sruoga.) Most prisoners throughout Stutthof's long history, however, belonged to the lowest level of prisoners who, regardless of their previous social position, labored on the most back-breaking worksites both within the camp and in its sub-camps—felling trees, making bricks, working in the huge laundry, or even worse, in the crematoria. Their daily food intake consisted of a piece of bread, ersatz coffee, and watery turnip soup. All newcomers to the camp were initiated at this level by the professional criminals who, under the direct supervision of the SS, beat them mercilessly. If they remained at this level, the inevitable decline was to an even lower level of cripple or "*Muselmann.*" Even Sruoga was for a time in this rank. He arrived in an emaciated state to work for an SS man called Sergeant Bublitz. This is how he described himself and his boss:

> When I found myself working for him, I was a cripple, no question about it: emaciated as a church rat, with swollen feet, a rattling heart, quivering thighs. Bublitz didn't force me to work much. Better yet, he provided me with extra meals from the SS kitchens leftovers. He even organized a small mess tin for me so I could retrieve these meals. SS meals, compared to ours, were chefs d'oeuvre ... Leftovers from here—sometimes there was a vat full—were given to almost all the prisoners who worked in the red building. They were doled out with full knowledge of the authorities, secretly, nonetheless.[47]

An emaciated church rat with quivering thighs, eating a gourmet meal (relatively speaking) right under the eyes of the SS inserts a level of irony and subtle pathos that instantly engages the reader's mind and heart. We know that prisoners in Nazi camps were generally viewed as lower than vermin, but Sruoga projects on his rat recognizable heart symptoms that elevate the prisoner to a human status, yet he does not sentimentalize the subject. These conditions were temporary and could easily change in the next shift. We also know there were other buildings in Stutthof where this did not happen.

Bronisław Tuszkowski remembers the emaciated figures like this:

> Initially I didn't know that word's meaning, but when I became a crip myself I understood it was a man doomed to die now or on the next day. Strong and healthy men turned into crips quickly. ... They were dead but yet they had to work. Horrible things happened in their huts. Crips looked awful: filthy and swollen from hunger and beatings. People died there all the time. They were mostly Russians and Poles in those huts. Such a block had to attend roll calls along with the others. Those unable to stand were laid out by the huts to lie there in rain and cold for hours on end.[48]

This state of total emaciation was a common sight in all the camps. In October 1942, Dachau became a central collection point for prisoners who were too weak to work—in other words—*Muselmänner*. Among them were several hundred prisoners from Stutthof who arrived on November 19, 1942, on board cattle cars. They were already slated for extermination in Dachau, but many had died en route from Stutthof. One was trampled to death by an SS guard.[49] In December 1943, around 6,000 prisoners remained in Stutthof; the others either died or were deported to other camps.

The old camp that had housed the first prisoners in primitive huts had by now outlived its usefulness and besides, Stutthof had been identified as a camp that could potentially receive many more prisoners. The first buildings of the New Camp were set up during 1942, with the view of interning 10,000 inmates. Three rows with ten barracks to every row had been completed by January 1943, housing all the main DAW (*Deutsche Ausrüstungswerke*/German Armaments Works) workshops from carpentry to bicycle repair shops. The prisoner blocks were designated with Roman numerals up to XX. Construction of the main buildings was followed by laying a plumbing and sewage system and then street construction. To the west of the New Camp they—that is the prisoners—built a barrack for the guards. Officers and petty officers lived in relative comfort in the Commandant's building. Constructing new buildings was a constant activity in the camp and they were still building in 1944, when there was the need to provide room for the confiscated goods of incoming prisoners. A new kitchen and a washroom were also part of the plans.

The Sick and the Dying

If a kitchen and washroom suggest an easing in camp conditions, other plans point to a different and more sinister function. The new construction included plans to build a crematorium with eight double ovens and a morgue in the cellar that was to be connected with an elevator to the ovens. The estimated capacity was for 100 corpses in one hour. However, the plan did not materialize and instead, an oil-fired oven was delivered in the summer of 1942 with the more modest capacity of five to six corpses every forty-five minutes. The first cremation took place on September 1, 1942, according to a former prisoner, E. Kamiński who testified at the trial of Teodor Meyer and of others. He stated that he knew exactly when it had happened, and the first to be cremated was the pharmacist Stefan Kopczyński.[50] At the end of 1942, the Berlin firm Kori built two walled crematoria and a high chimney. The capacity was slightly higher than the previous one, but a wooden structure that had been built over the ovens caught fire in early December and the crematorium was out of action until December 1944, when a brick building replaced the wooden construction. In the meantime, bodies were burned in a crematorium in the woods over a pit. A gas chamber was built in the fall of 1943, not far from the one in the woods, under the command of SS Sergeant/*Unterscharführer* Paul that was fired by coal. In the roof was a pipe, into which Zyklon B canisters were thrown. The chamber was initially used to burn the clothing of prisoners.

Within the expansion of construction plans and the fluctuating population, all prisoners suffered various levels of maltreatment, depending on their status, nationality, and if they were Jewish—especially, as the next chapter will reveal, from mid-1944 until April of 1945. Some languished in isolated barracks, many who worked in various industries related to the war effort—both in Stutthof and its sub-camps—were starved to death, transported to other camps, killed by various means that included cranial shootings and gassing, or died of typhus—there were three major outbreaks between 1942 and 1945. The level of care to gravely ill prisoners varied during these two and a half years and depended on the presence of skilled physicians and their helpers, and the level of infection. From August 1942 until the end of the year, it is estimated that 30–40 percent of the prisoners died, mostly of typhus. Camp officials, however, did not disclose those numbers to the local Stutthof death registry or to other camps, giving instead the cause of death as heart attacks or other more "respectable" diseases.[51] According to the French prisoner, Jean Maitre, the second outbreak of typhus that began in April 1943 took 1,500 lives.[52]

Was there a euthanasia program in Stutthof? Given the widespread practice of euthanasia in the Nazi Reich until August 1941, and the infamous T-4 program (named after the street address of the Chancellery office, *Tiergartenstrasse* 4), it is not surprising to find in a 2015 publication by Danuta Drywa the assertion that euthanasia was practiced widely in Stutthof by SS doctors, including Dr. Heidl. Drawing on archival sources, Drywa cites the testimony of a Polish physician Juliana Węgrzynowicz, who claims that by 1943 the practice had intensified. On an average, seventeen patients were given phenol injections daily in 1942, and the victims were always patients in the general ward, and not in the typhus or tuberculosis wards where it might have been more easily justified. Dr. Heidl would always ask about the patient's prognosis, but the attending physicians and nurses had been instructed beforehand to give the correct response—namely that the deadly injection should be given. The doctor also claims that a group of German political prisoners—Communists—were trained in Stutthof to perform these tasks, presumably sparing the SS doctors like Heidl the abhorrent task. Patients were then carried or dragged into an adjoining washroom and were often dead from the effects of the phenol by the time they were laid out on the floor, sometimes stacked on top of one other.[53]

Dunin-Wąsowicz also comments on the significant role that SS doctors played in the camp and writes about the central role of Dr. Heidl.[54] He gives other examples of the use of lethal injections of phenol and drowning in bathtubs—by submerging the victims underwater until they drowned. The SS were helped in these activities by kapos, like Jan Czerwiński, a Pole from Strasburg/Brodnica whom he calls a "typ spod ciemnej gwiazdy"—("a real sinister type of guy") and even in the eyes of the commandant, he was considered too eager to kill. (He was sent later in September 1944 to Neuengamme.)[55] The infirmary could hold 200 and was not a desirable place for the sick. The supervisor was an SS man, but the doctors and orderlies were inmates. It was said that no German national would want to be under the care of the Poles. SS Sergeant Haupt was in charge, a former carpenter, and male nurse in an insane asylum. He was known to dispense shots of carbolic acid, which were deadly.[56]

Working for the War Effort

Stutthof was now functioning at an even higher level as a bona fide concentration camp of the Nazi regime, not least because it was contributing to the war effort. Many prisoners were employed—and exploited—by the DAW with a bare minimum of daily nutrition. Some food supplements were added for prisoners who were doing the hardest manual work, but it was not a consistent practice and was certainly never adequate. The atrocious conditions show the basic features it now shared with all the main camps, including extermination, if on a smaller scale. Stutthof's 65,000 victims of 110,000 prisoners also place it at a high level of mortality rate among the camps. Beyond the main camp in Stutthof, sub-camps were becoming a more prominent part of its orbit and proliferated around Danzig and Elbing. Since sub-camps will be examined in some detail in the next chapter, I want to simply introduce one of them— Hopehill-Riemannsfelde, to foreshadow a major feature of the Stutthof camp system. Situated near Elbing on the Frisches Haff, this camp was established on May 29, 1942, and functioned until January 1945—the longest in operation. Run by DESt (*Deutsche Erd- und Steinwerke*/German Brick and Tile Works), it was a profitable operation, not least because of its easy access to the sea, as well as its free labor—prisoners from the camp.[57] It has been described as one of the worst in Stutthof's network, not just because of the harsh climate of the area and the hard labor of producing brick and tile, but because of the cruelty inflicted on the prisoners. The original forty prisoners were joined by German criminals from Mauthausen and Flossenbürg, as well as Polish political prisoners who were to assume powerful roles in the kapo system. We will meet some of them later.

Local SS Men: Backbone of the Stutthof Camp System

We want to focus now on the role of local SS in Stutthof. Before approaching the local aspect of the SS, and in view of the camp's status as concentration camp, we first need to consider the organization with a wider lens. Even before the outbreak of war, the SS had become a significant presence in the Third Reich and had expanded into a massive organization that ultimately controlled the secret police force as well as the civilian police, both of which were funded by the Reich. It also had control of elite military battalions, medical institutes, schools, government ministries, and an industrial empire.[58] By the mid-1930s, Himmler had obtained permission from Hitler to fund SS guard troops. Who was the model SS man? As already discussed, Theodor Eicke might well fill that role because of his success in constructing the ideal SS man as "the political soldier," with a superb esprit de corps. Like most of the young SS men in Stutthof, he had come from a socially modest background, had worked his way up the military ladder and enjoyed a close relationship with his men. When he was killed in action on February 26, 1943, on the eastern front, his obituary was sub-headed—"Eicke, the political soldier" in the *Volkischer Beobacbter*.[59]

Like all the camps, Stutthof profited from the elevated status that the SS enjoyed before war broke out. It was an honor to be inducted into this elite group of men, and there was no problem finding recruits to join the ranks. SS files at Stutthof show that many joined the SS early in their careers. In addition, before the war began, the professional conduct of SS camp guards—the *Totenkopf*/Death's Head Division was a matter of formal discussion, and the use of force or brutality was institutionalized. Himmler stipulated in 1938, speaking to SS leaders, that only the camp commandant had permission to flog prisoners. Their model should be Dachau and they had to send a written application to the IKL for permission to flog. In Stutthof, they had a "Declaration of Honor Code," dated November 17, 1942, and they pledged to follow orders strictly. They vowed not to strike a prisoner—only the Commandant had that authority. They promised to report to the Commandant any infractions of that order. There was also a vow to silence—everything that happened in the course of one's duty was kept to oneself. By the late 1930s, formal rules regarding flogging were written down and forms had to be signed, thus conferring a level of protection on the camp SS. The Death's Head SS expanded fast during the second half of the early 1930s, growing to 5,371 men (January 1938).[60]

Despite the respectable formality of these written rules, there is a striking disconnect between them and the documentation of violence in the camp. In reality, violence was a crucial and ubiquitous facet of all camps. Stutthof was no exception, so it might appear from reading accounts of prisoners, that SS men, guards and kapos used violence randomly and capriciously. Even if they did, their actions were part of a culture of violence that was condoned and had been accepted before the outbreak of war, in the early camps of the 1930s. As many as 300 prisoners died in the camps at the hands of the SS between 1934 and 1937—some by suicide. In fact, acting tough and ruthlessly was rewarded by superior officers in a culture that equated brutality with the values of the "political soldier."[61] Prisoners document this violent behavior, and I will examine this later in the narratives of this chapter. Our focus will be on those who used it.

Agnieszka Czerna estimates that 344 of the SS men in Stutthof were citizens of the Free City of Danzig and constituted 17 percent of the SS Guard there.[62] Their role in the camp was crucial to its functioning, as the data from SS personnel files demonstrate.[63] A sample spreadsheet of 270 names prepared and transmitted to me by archivists of the Stutthof Museum presents a list of predominantly German names. (Some, of course, had been Germanized.) See Figure 9 in the Appendix for this list of names, rank, and religion. For a sample of a personnel card with photo, see Figure 12 in the Appendix.

Under "Religion," for line 49, the entry was blank—that is, 18 percent. Seventy-two men listed "Lutheran/Protestant"—that is, 27 percent, thirty-nine indicated they were Roman Catholic—18 percent, one identified as a Mennonite, and one as Pentecostal. The majority, however, (38 percent) listed no religious affiliation, but instead indicated that they were "gottgläubig"—believers in God. At some juncture they had apparently abandoned their affiliation and replaced it with something else that, at least initially, looks non-denominational. What did it mean to be "gottgläubig"?

We know that in the Third Reich the role of the Church—both the Catholic Church and the Protestant Church—was crucial in shaping the attitudes of the laity who overwhelmingly supported Hitler and his regime. The Protestant Church had largely embraced the new doctrine promulgated as "unity," which was based on ethnic uniformity. Doris Bergen puts it this way—"The German Christians marched under the banner of the people's church."[64] Thus, *Volksgemeinschaft* informed their thinking and practice.[65] Bergen identifies the paradoxes in their thinking—they wanted to have a people's church, but they rejected the basic doctrines that had historically shaped the church. She points out that they continued to meet in church buildings, drew upon selected symbols of Christianity but edited both the New and Old Testaments and their hymn books to comply with their views on race, erasing any references to Jews.[66] German Christians liked to think that their church was a strong church "eine männliche Kirche" (a manly church) unified by German ideals. Marsh writes:

> German Christians would pursue a fully assimilated national church—*Volkskirche*—based on common blood. In Germany, baptisms now routinely concluded with the prayer that "this child will grow up to be like Adolf Hitler and Heinrich Himmler." Pastors had sworn, "I swear that I will be faithful and obedient to Adolf Hitler, the Führer of the German Reich and people, that I will conscientiously observe the laws and carry out the duties of my office, so help me God."[67]

SS men entering service in Stutthof were unified in a common cause that they might not have even been able to fathom or articulate. Their disconnect from their earlier religious expectations exonerated them and released them from ethical restraints regardless of if they had been catechized as a Catholic or as a Lutheran Protestant. There were few distinctions between any of the denominations, and antisemitism united them. Marsh writes that

> when ministers of the Confessing Church met on June 11, 1938, for their final disputation on the Jewish question—the issue that had become a religious touchstone—Bonhoeffer was to learn that the majority of them had taken the oath of allegiance to Hitler: 60% in Rhineland, 70% in Brandenburg, 78% in Saxony, 80% in Pomerania, 82% in Silesia, 89% in Grenzmark ... The Confessing Church would remain hopelessly silent if not indifferent on Jewish suffering and persecution.[68]

When they signed into the camp in September (according to the spreadsheet of 270 SS men)—71 percent of these local men arrived on September 9, 1939, they were prepared on several levels. First of all, their role in running the camp was the extension of the work they were already doing before Poland was attacked. As proud Danzigers they represented Germandom, no longer as reluctant citizens of a free city but now enjoying their status as citizens of the Third Reich, with several years of military training either in the Danzig police units or in the local Gestapo, fully indoctrinated in their racial superiority over their fellow Jewish and Polish citizens. Personnel files of this cohort of local men from Danzig and environs provide statistics of their age, profession, year when they joined the Nazi Party, marital status, previous military experience, including their military honors, year when they joined the SS.[69] A sample list of these guards is included in Figure 10 in the Appendix.

Some worked in Stutthof and its sub-camps until the end, in or near their own hometowns. Names of local communities that feature in Grass's fiction now housed sub-camps, the names of which recur in prisoner testimonies: Elbing, Grenzdorf, Danzig-Matzkau, Thorn, Hopehill, Westerplatte, Proebbnau, and Zeyersniederkampen. Officers and those of lower rank held important administrative jobs and, in the early days of the camp's history, some of them performed more than one function. The average age of SS men working in the camps was twenty-four, the oldest was fifty-two, and the youngest ones were seventeen. Of the 38 percent of the local SS men who declared themselves *gottgläubig,* only a few attached this appellation to "Protestant" or "Catholic." It was not just the loss or even the lack of religious belief that shaped the everyday lives of these young men. (After all, there were many agnostic French resisters, and they worked side by side in mutual respect of ethical principles with devout Christians like the Darbyists in Le Chambon.) These men had a new religion, a replacement theology that substituted the Führer himself for the Trinity. In fact, the Holy Spirit was now considered an ethos, not a person and was often cited in the context of the German spirit. Obedience to the Führer offered them a basic principle of living that was unencumbered by traditional impediments such as mercy and guilt. Peter Longerich convincingly argues in his long (948 pages) biography on Himmler that in order to arm the troops for the forthcoming epochal conflict between "humans and subhumans," Himmler wanted to direct the SS to one task above all: it was to act as the vanguard in overcoming Christianity and restoring a "Germanic" way of living.[70] As Himmler understood it, this was the actual mission of his Schutzstaffel; "it was to this task that it owed its identity and the justification for its existence." Longerich continues: "Christianity seemed to him so dangerous because the principle of Christian mercy contradicted his demand for unwavering severity in dealing with 'subhumans.'" Replacing Christian principles with "Germanic" virtues was the precondition if they were to prevail against the "subhumans" and "secure the future."[71] By claiming that Himmler was primarily interested in confronting Christianity, Longerich does not minimize Himmler's anti-communism and antisemitism; rather, he emphasizes that Himmler was promoting the ideals of a lost Germanic world. Hitler was able to link Christianization with re-Germanization—with Germandom, and thus had provided the SS with the goal and purpose all its own.[72]

Freed from religious responsibility, these men were members of a superior race and were part of a community of like-minded devotees—a *Volksgemeinschaf* that buffered them from basic introspection, self-awareness and from questioning the practices of everyday life in the camp. Allen proposes that incompetence was a dimension to this mentality and was prevalent at the top level of Nazi leadership. Commitment to the Nazi cause was more important than competence. He cites as an example Oswald Pohl who, though energetic and competent himself, relied on a lazy and incompetent man like Hans Beier, based on Pohl's commitment to the Führer principle "which encouraged leaders to believe they embodied the 'will' of their subordinates."[73] In Stutthof, which was arguably still seen as a secondary enterprise in the grand scheme of the camp system, testimonies of former prisoners frequently attest to the incompetence that permeated the highest level of camp administration. But as long as the symbols of authority and the Führer principle flourished, the SS men could do their daily jobs without recourse to their individual conscience or to a higher power. That higher power was fluid enough to include "Waralda, the ancient, das Uralte," and occasionally Himmler invoked this higher power, as in a speech to senior naval officers in 1943, when he propounded the view that those who observed and understood the process of natural selection were believers in their innermost being, because they recognized that above us is an infinite wisdom.[74] This belief system was consistent with the Führer's own vague theology that had long since moved away from his Catholic background. It was also harmonious with the principles upheld by the SS and especially the *Totenkopf* Division that espoused the manly virtues preached by Theodor Eicke, who famously said that men who do not espouse these tough values belonged in a monastery and not in an SS unit. Everyday religious life had thus been institutionalized and assimilated into Nazi ideology and any attempt to thwart that assimilation—*Gleichschaltung* had already been addressed by banning, for example, church offerings, the printing of church bulletins, calendars of the Christian year, monthly newsletters, sermons, or reports from missionaries abroad.[75]

The political circumstances that had shaped Danzig's history in the 1930s may well have fostered the acceptance and growth of this dogma among local SS men. It is no wonder that so many abandoned their church ties and became simply "*gottgläubig.*" Though vague and devoid of doctrinal basis, it was a core belief. Two aspects of Himmler's persona and leadership are emphasized by Longerich which resonate in the Stutthof/Danzig connection. He had a great need for myths and accompanying rituals, and the SS cult became a kind of Holy Grail that substituted traditional religion and in Longerich's words "the restoration of a lost Germanic world and in particular the radical extirpation of the hated 'subhumans' as the prerequisite for the realization of this utopia."[76] What better place to realize this dream than in myth-saturated Danzig that had been restored to the German fold? He also saw himself as a father figure who was engaged in the private lives of his SS men and their families.[77] What better place to take care of these young SS men than a camp that conferred on them all the privileges of Germandom and deprived their Polish and Jewish neighbors of basic rights as *Menschen*? Dietrich Bonhoeffer had warned German Protestants about recasting the Christian narrative of guilt and salvation as the story of Germany's defeat and rebirth. He pointed out the danger of filling the void created by the shame of the Versailles Treaty with a promise of deliverance with Hitler as deliverer.[78] Danzig was emblematic of that history. One could, of course, argue that the existence of Stutthof cannot be separated from the rise of a totalitarian state under Hitler and the concomitant collapse of the key agencies of the Weimar Republic. But the fact remains that there was something uniquely parochial about Stutthof that aligned its initial mission—to intern Poles and Jews—with policies that fundamentally agreed that both groups were subhuman, a conclusion that was endorsed by many German-speaking clerics in Danzig and Pomerania (both Catholic and Protestant) before and after 1942.

Debórah Dwork and Robert Jan van Pelt have noted the responsibility of Catholic and Protestant churches to be agents of civilization and further note the difference between what the French call *la grande église* and *la petite église*.[79] There was virtually no distinction between big or small, between mainline or small churches whether they were free or affiliated, in and around Danzig, where there were no groups like the Darbyists in Le Chambon in occupied France who offered refuge to Jews. The Free Churches did not advocate for Polish priests. Kristallnacht was a watershed event in Danzig, but it did not spark outrage. As in the greater Reich, the response to the pogrom among civilians ranged in the words of Victoria Barnett "from horror to shocking equanimity."[80] She cites as an example a young pastor in the Confessing Church who made this statement:

> I frankly admit to you that sometimes you had to push yourself not to be a coward .... I had married in 1936, and then, perhaps, isn't that so—I'm speaking unguardedly here, but I'd rather say it that way than weigh every word on the scale. When you have a child, then you are not so courageous as the Catholic priests are, with their light baggage.[81]

At a certain level, one can appreciate the pastor's honesty; a father's love certainly shapes and motivates his moral and ethical choices, but his words also betray an erroneous message. The celibate state of priests or clergy who protested the Kristallnacht pogrom in Danzig was not the prime motivator for their actions and did not make them either more or less courageous. These men resisted because they knew it was morally wrong and against every religious principle they had preached. It was a courage that had nothing to do with "light baggage." Later, that same courage sustained them in camps like Dachau and Stutthof.

Did the local church continue to exist as the mostly silent witness that we saw in the previous chapter? Catholic priests who were Polish were treated first and foremost as political dissidents because they had dared to keep alive the Polish language and had encouraged their parishioners to retain their identity as Poles. They were not persecuted because of their religious beliefs, even though many, if not most of them, would have gladly died for those beliefs, and it is clear from other witnesses that their beliefs were detested. In fact, the greatest frustration to the SS guards that emerges from the memoirs of Polish priests is that they were sustained by their religious beliefs. Because the consciences of the Stutthof guards were seared and exonerated from guilt, they could more easily dismiss any pang of guilt and operate as spokesmen of a new order—specifically The New Order.[82]

Even with this moral isolation and insulation from consequences, in examining the camp SS files, one is struck by the tone of the correspondence between the guards and their superiors. Though not all their requests were granted, there is a level of civility and, in some cases, of humanity that is consistently absent in all other camp communication. For example, SS Staff Sergeant/*Scharführer* Richard Akolt had joined Danzig's police in July 1939 and now—on January 15, 1940, is requesting an extension of his vacation time. The response is that he is indispensable in his job at the Commandant's office. Furthermore, he is reminded to use his Germanized name—Akolt—rather than Adamitzki. In March 1941, Akolt's wife wrote to ask for an extra soap ration.[83] Requests for home leave were handled generously. They ranged from requests for a week to help with the harvest or leave to attend a funeral or help with a sick wife. On April 7, 1942, Else Gohl wrote to ask permission for a week's leave for her husband to help cultivate the fields. She writes that she has only two Polish hired hands, and a nineteen-year old—presumably not Polish—and a maid to help her. She adds "Heil Hitler." (On December 2, 1941, Oskar Gohl had requested a five-day leave to look after his wife who was in hospital in Bromberg.)[84] SS Alfred Albrecht was accused of maltreatment by his wife in February 1942. She received a stern rebuke on February 11 from the office of the Commandant who strenuously defended her husband and accused her of wasting his time. There would be consequences for her, he warned, if she pursued this worthless grievance. The husband's file suggests he had "proper" credentials: cranial size—54 cm, the ability to produce proof of his Aryan lineage, membership in the SS since July 1939 and is *gottgläubig*. Did this factor possibly protect him from the accusation of domestic abuse? It is not clear, but what is clear is that petitions from SS men of lower rank were handled like family requests. And that's exactly what they were living in—a family-like community that looked after their needs that were far removed from the indifference—at best—and the violence—at worst—that characterized their behavior in Stutthof. They had enough free time to enjoy in summer the nearby Baltic beaches. Feig writes: "To lie in the summer on one of the finest beaches in Europe after a long hard day at work in the smelly, diseased, and depressing camp was a welcome relief. Himmler had special seaside buildings constructed for the camp staff 'for recreational purposes.' Their survivors never mentioned the ocean beaches in their memoirs."[85] Of course, morale boosting was not unique to Stutthof. In other camps, like Groß Rosen, bonuses were given to the SS for bravery, and in Sachsenhausen, SS leaders held comradeship evenings to help them cope with mass shootings.[86] Browning writes that after a massacre of Jews in Simferopol in the Crimea in December 1941, Himmler encouraged his men to have "comradely get-togethers" to soothe the ragged nerves of his men who had taken part in massacres of Jews.[87] The Nazis promised the lower classes of ethnic Germans better opportunities for professional and social advancement.[88] When you look at the files of these local SS men—from Danzig and the small towns of Pomerania, most of them with minimal education—and trace their advancement, it is apparent that their rise through the ranks was meteoric relative to their former status.[89] (See Figure 10 in the Appendix for educational data.)

To what—or more aptly, to whom—can we ascribe the formation of a community with such strong family-like ties right in the middle of a place of torture and terror? Though their oath of loyalty was given to and in the name of the Führer, there was a mediator between them and Hitler in the person of Heinrich Himmler whose role at Stutthof as *pater familias* was not secondary. Stutthof elites had to work hard after September 1939 to get the camp recognized as worthy of its next step, and the SS played the key role. Admitting Stutthof into the camp network was more than simply conferring the title on another camp. In May 1940, Himmler warned his subordinates that many other camps were sometimes regarded as concentration camps. That was wrong; only the camps under the control of the SS could bear this name.[90] Wachsmann adds to this portrait of Himmler when he calls him "a mass murderer greatly concerned with decorum. He had long cultivated an image as a deeply principled man and during the Second World War he became a prominent preacher of a new kind of Nazi morality that saw mass killing as a sacred duty to protect the German people from its mortal enemies."[91] Yet, Himmler remained distant and, at every level, far from Stutthof, and was too busy and engaged elsewhere—especially in Auschwitz—to deign to visit it. It is also striking that Forster himself was only there twice. Was it because of their confidence in the SS to represent Germandom and propagate its values?

Memoirs written by survivors of Stutthof attest uniformly to the extremity of terror and torture that was inflicted on them by the SS guards during the first two years of the camp's existence. Though that did not change after the camp acquired its new status, inmates became more experienced, more solidified in their common fate and more adept in survival tactics to elude the blows of the guards. Prisoner tolerance of pain appears to have grown in direct proportion to SS indifference and frankly, sadism. SS personnel were known for their cruelty, especially the *Totenkopf* division who ran the camps. Dębski refers to a speech given by Himmler on March 16, 1942, in which he describes the duty and the qualities of the ideal SS man: "It was the task of the SS to give the German people, the Germanic people, that superior ruling class that knits together and holds together this Germanic people and Europe." In the same speech he enumerated the essential qualities of an SS man: "loyalty, obedience, courage, truthfulness, honesty, camaraderie, the joy of responsibility, industriousness and abstention from alcohol."[92] Given the frequent allusions in memoirs to the abuse of alcohol among the top brass of the SS in Stutthof, the appeal to abstention does not seem to have found many followers.

The Danzig-born SS members constituted the cornerstone of the camp personnel and held positions of privilege and influence. A few had served in the First World War,[93] but the majority were part of the so-called war generation. Orth writes, "This generation had not experienced the First World War itself, but grew up with its myth, which, for a section of male youth, endowed them with an identity."[94] Not all of these men were violent, but the majority must have condoned brutal behavior. They did not become violent overnight. Thoroughly indoctrinated in Nazi ideology, they were then socialized into a like-minded community, silent about the absence of religious belief or practice. Doris Bergen certainly sets to rest in *Twisted Cross* any notion that the German Christian movement (of at least 600,000 predominantly Protestants) was not of great national significance during and after the Third Reich. Though references to its role in West Prussia are scant, and Bergen's data derive largely from the Greater Reich, her findings on the "new" theology resonate with the data that is available on Stutthof and Danzig. Gerhard Gülzow claims in his memoir that the Confessing Church had an active presence in Danzig and though small in number, Lutheran ministers stood up to the German Christians and were able to oppose the coordination/*Gleichschaltung* measures imposed on the church from Munich which had greatly affected the church in

Posen/Poznań.[95] Yet, as noted earlier these ministers were not allowed to enter Stutthof, to give religious instruction or to hold funeral services, or even register deaths in the church records since the camp had its own registry. SS men from Danzig and "the Corridor" were thus insulated from any religious teaching that might have made them question their actions behind the barbed wire of the camp. Many of them embarked as former artisans and tradesmen on a career as soldiers of the Third Reich. A few of the older ones were veterans of the First World War. Whether these veterans were more animated by revenge than the younger soldiers would be hard to prove, but based on the testimonies of the interned, the pervasive impression is that many were uniformly cruel and even sadistic, without ever having served on the front lines or known battle fatigue. Rossino contends—I think correctly—that the escalation of violence against Germany's racial enemies did not occur because the war brutalized the SS and police personnel but rather was based on previous indoctrination and on their experience in death squads *(Einsatzgruppen)* and *Einsatzkommandos* (military task forces).[96] Several of these men stayed for the whole period in Stutthof. Their behavior is depicted in several memoirs as being the cruelest among all the guards—the same men who according to the personnel files, received favorable treatment from their superiors in the course of their work at Stutthof and its sub-camps. These two realities coexisted in the workplace—cruelty unleashed on prisoners by those who were being well treated.

Victims and Perpetrators: Conflicting Stories

The responsibility of depicting the suffering experienced by victims of the Nazi regime with sensitivity confronts every writer. While the data from the SS files give important personal history (date of birth, marital status, religion, education, year of joining the Nazi Party and the SS, former military experience, military awards, length of service in Stutthof and elsewhere, etc.) prisoner files are essentially devoid of personal history and are reduced to an office file card, and in the workplace to a triangle that indicated the nature of their "crime"—mostly political, or religious, or social. In other words, these prisoners were not treated as humans or social beings, which makes the job of turning numbers back into people, to quote Snyder, dependent on sources beyond the stark filing cabinets of the camp.[97] The primary responsibility is thus to find ways to present real people who transcend the tortures they endured, so that they will receive the respect they deserve as humans, as individuals, despite being pummeled into the very dust of Stutthof. We think of Yla's first impression of his fellow-prisoners—they looked "surprisingly alike, obviously standardized by hunger and the cudgel."[98]

Himmler claimed that SS men had special qualities and were thus able to guard villains and crooks. Wachsmann criticizes historians who have fallen for this idealized image of SS guards as a select force of fighters, pointing out that the prisoners describe these men as "a freak show of misfits and sadists."[99] There are certainly enough incidents recorded in Stutthof memoirs and narratives to confirm this, but there are also exceptions (some will come up in the next chapter) that display human decency against a backdrop of depravity. They do not change the darkness, but they stand out and need to be acknowledged. Prisoners may indeed have been "standardized by hunger" but the narrative skills of writers like Sruoga and Yla and their engagement with characters allow us to construct a more complete portrait of other prisoners and of their guards and help us get to know these people as individuals.[100] I think that Timothy Snyder recognized how easy it is to get in the way of the victims' stories and simply allowed attached narratives to speak for themselves. He has also accomplished the most important responsibility—the victims speak and are no longer simply numbers. Whether attached or presented—as I intend to—in juxtaposition with the files of the SS, or in one case with a memoir of an SS man, the responsibility shifts to the reader, whether in greater sympathy for the prisoners or in deeper understanding of the depth of depravity unleashed on them. Unapologetically, my aim is to humanize the victims since we already have a profile of their guards.

At the top of the list is a Captain in the SS, Teodor Meyer,[101] SS-*Hauptsturmführer—Schutzhaftlagerführer* who made a voluntary, formal statement in his prison cell on August 13, 1947, in what was to be less than two months before his execution on October 10, 1947. Imprisoned in Gdańsk after his capture by allied troops, Meyer did not know at this point what his fate would be. He hopes, however, that his story will persuade his prosecutors of his innocence. He became involved with the Nazi Party in Munich, along with his two older sisters, and was convinced that only a radical party could bring change into the political confusion of the years 1931–3 and create jobs and food. Trained as a mechanist, he found himself out of work and dependent for pocket money on his widower father. "I joined the Party and at the same time the SS," he adds. His first assignment was training in Dachau where he worked under the camp engineer. This was followed by a post in Neuengamme, then in Ravensbrück. He married in 1934 and describes his wife as coming from a good bourgeois family. "We led a happy, untroubled family life."[102]

This report might be dismissed as a typical "ordinary man" rationalization were it not for the mention in his statement of key locations of torture in the Third Reich, alongside expressions of *kleinbürgerlich* domesticity, apparently with no sense of discomfort.[103] It is a jarring juxtaposition when these two realities happily share the same space. The line-up alone of Dachau, Neuengamme, and Ravensbrück is code for a brutal training—all before he even entered the gates of Stutthof. But Meyer's testimony is devoid of irony and proceeds predictably to present himself as a good family man, doing his duty, looking forward to better times, suffering the hardships of a job that often separated him from his beloved family—"his all," interjecting in his testimony the inevitable question—"What was I supposed to do?" Now, after two years of prison he is hoping that his statement—"these lines," he calls them, will convince people that his guilt is not that great, and if he can do that, then he will have achieved his goal. Meyer claims that because of a dispute with Himmler during a visit of the latter to Ravensbrück, he had been transferred as punishment to Stutthof. He had meanwhile reached the rank of captain and was a Protective Custody Camp Leader. He makes this claim casually, without explanation and certainly with no attempt to present a dispute with Himmler in 1940 as a possible advantage in his postwar status as a prisoner of the allies. Nor is there any attempt to comment on how Stutthof must have been viewed by his superiors as a place of punishment in 1940. He also claims that his new rank of Captain was not the result of political dependability but rather of professional knowledge.[104] Meyer's focus is his domestic life—the simple, untroubled family life—far removed from the brutalities of the camp, where he is second in command.

Meyer's testimony and attempt to present his activities as benign are in sharp contrast to the depictions in Yla's *A Priest in Stutthof*. He describes a particular incident early in his internment that features Meyer in his role as Vice Commandant. At the center of the drama is the failure of one man to remove his cap in the presence of Meyer. The kapos that day appeared to be very nervous and were dealing out blows at the slightest provocation. Yla writes:

> Everything was more or less in order by this time—even the corpses of those who had died during the day had been lined up with stiff military precision. All eyes were focused expectantly on Meyer—with no results. He remained silent.
>
> We waited. After a while, rain began to fall. It soaked our uncovered heads, and trickled down our necks and our shoulders. But still no word from Meyer. He stood with arms akimbo, moving his head slowly from side to side as though he were contemplating something. There was a look of utter disgust on his face. Suddenly we became aware of what he was gazing at so attentively. Another corpse had apparently been resurrected, and had by this time managed to prop itself on its elbows. But horror of horrors! His cap was still perched on top of its head.
>
> Meyer had taken about as much as he was going to take. He let his arms fall to his sides and began to walk slowly toward the ranks of the dead. We noticed that his gait was unusually awkward: almost to the point of lameness, in fact. Still maintaining silence, he stopped right next to the prisoner and kicked him with all his might. Only then did the unfortunate man become aware of his negligence, and he had just enough time to cast aside the offending article before he rolled over and died. The cap itself was seized by a sudden gust of wind and carried out of sight.[105]

With consummate skill, Yla directs a scene that belongs to the genre of drama rather than prose narrative. The tension is so palpable that we forget for a brief moment that we are in Stutthof and are pulled into the last act of a tragedy. The setting is a military parade ground where obedience, discipline, and timing are clearly the expected order of the day. But there is a problem. The players in this theater piece are not soldier recruits but corpses in a concentration camp. Earlier in this chapter, we noted Sruoga's narrative skills in depicting a prisoner—himself—as an ailing church rat, under the somewhat benevolent eye of SS man Bublitz who breaks prison rules and allows the prisoners to eat the leftovers of the SS kitchen. In Yla's drama there is no such mercy, for these prisoners are lifeless and even lower than vermin. Yla places his characters under the direction of a silent sadist whose strong boot awakened one of the "corpses" just in time to take off his cap before him—the commanding officer. It was to be his last gesture, before rolling over to die. The depiction of his last moments is followed by a haunting detail that directs us to look up, above the ranks of the dead to where the prisoner's cap is carried by a gust of wind "out of sight." Yla's culminating short sentence captures the poignancy and tragedy of a death that is totally senseless and beyond the grasp of the rational mind. There is no *deus ex machina* in this drama, no mitigating factor as in the Sruoga narrative. This one segment of the Yla memoir could stand on its own as a hidden gem of Stutthof—its silence and its shame are perfectly captured for one brief moment. The cap may be "out of sight" but the anguish of the anonymous prisoner's death will live on in Yla's prose drama. The effectiveness of Yla and Sruoga as writers lies in their ability to connect both directly and indirectly the interned and their guards. Both these Lithuanians describe daily life in Stutthof, but they implicitly ask more from us as readers. Their literary strategies—irony, understatement juxtaposition—are not constrained by the camp setting, and the characters, whether self-portraits or a dying prisoner remain as written testimonies. It is not that they give better or more accurate information about the camp than the archival files or even other less skilled writers. Their testimonies are compositions that infuse ordinary words with new life despite the presence of death that threatens to quench them.

The kind of drill described above was a daily torture and it is frequently described as such by prisoners. Polish prisoner Lech Duszyński describes what newly arrived inmates were subjected to like this:

> On the call of 'Mützen,' (hats) the right hand had to be at the hat, as if saluting, and on 'ab' (down) the hand had to strike the inmate's thigh. All the inmates had to execute this simultaneously. Block trusty Zimmerman slapped the faces of the tardy ones. Others stood there, waiting for when he hit their faces or heads. They learned in an hour. A seventy year old Kashubian, ill with cerebral palsy was unfit for this drill. The Block trusty finished him off—the man was ready for the crematory.[106]

Block leader Johannes Mielenz, known as "The Bomb," is described by a woman called Maria Pitera-Zalewska. Her depiction presents a gendered facet of maltreatment that degraded and humiliated women prisoners. Similar to Yla's portrait of Meyer, it pits another sadist—SS Mielenz against helpless women who are forced to "perform" in their night attire—relegated men's shirts—just because one pair of work boots was placed too far under the bunk bed. This Kafkaesque world of perverse values is set on Christmas Eve and is far removed from a "silent night" setting:

> He rushed into their room on the night of Christmas Eve in 1942. The room trusty stood at attention in her night underwear reporting the room. Asked if all was in order she answered "yes sir" and was immediately slapped so hard she swayed. As it turned out, a pair of sabots was shoved 10 centimeters too deep under the bunk. This wasn't the end of it—the whole room had to fall to at a mad speed. You have to imagine the women standing for the roll call in so-called nightwear, consisting of a man's shirt, usually a very short one. Mielenz found it all hilarious and apparently wanted more fun, for he ordered "To the beds—march!" In the blink of an eye the women scattered, straightening out the shirts, climbing the three-tier bunks and hurriedly pulling the blankets over themselves. When they all were in beds he ordered them out, for another roll call, and we had to hurry down into the double ranks again. Such muster was repeated several times, and if one of the older less agile women was late in getting into her bed, hard whip blows would hurry her up.[107]

Who was Mielenz? There are two Mielenz entries in the SS files—one for Johannes and the other for Franz. Franz worked for a time in the Women's barracks, so can more feasibly be the one in question here. (They may not have been related as their place of birth in the files, though local, is different.) In July 1940, a local company in Elbing that built dikes and retaining walls sent a confidential complaint against SS Sergeant Franz Mielenz, who was the head of a sub-camp in Zeyersniederkampen. The complaint was about the way Mielenz treated the prisoners who were employed by the company. It was not based on humanitarian concerns but rather on profitability. The letter stated that Mielenz treated the prisoners so badly that it was affecting company profits; more and more prisoners were unable to work, and the company had been forced to cover the costs of bandages. The company requested that Mielenz pay for bandages and other materials for wound dressings. There was a hearing on July 20, attended by representatives of the dike company as well as SS men. Mielenz acknowledged that he had hit prisoners with a birch rod because they were too slow unloading materials that were brought to the sub-camp.[108] He received the proverbial slap on the wrist—not for cruelty but for affecting profits—and continued to serve at Stutthof.

Master Sergeant Otto Haupt's personnel file indicates that he joined the Nazi Party in 1931 and the SS the following year. Born in Nowy Dwór in 1896, he was a veteran of the First World War, having served between 1915 and 1917. His profession is listed as carpenter and nurse (or caregiver) which supposedly should have equipped him for the job in the camp infirmary, where we meet him in the Sruoga memoir. Haupt left Stutthof in the summer of 1944 for further duties in Neuengamme. Sruoga describes him as working for SS Doctor Heidl but since the latter "liked to go courting," Haupt functioned as the boss. Work conditions were one of the best in the camp—enough to eat, easy work and longer rest periods. Sruoga writes: "To tell the truth, the hospital didn't have a good reputation in camp. The old prisoners claimed that prisoners were actually poisoned there. In fact, by the time I went to work there, Haupt was still poisoning prisoners, but under specific orders."[109] Once more, Sruoga's understated, tongue-in-cheek description gives us essential information both about the SS officer Dr. Heidl and his "infirmary." Sruoga describes Dr. Heidl's nocturnal visits beyond camp in old-fashioned, genteel terms of "courting"—appropriate language for an officer and presumably a gentleman. And while he is gone, his assistant poisoned people. But Sruoga adds "under specific orders," indirectly alluding to the practice of "euthanasia" which was practiced in the camp and makes sense of the widespread fear among prisoners. No matter how sick they were, no one wanted to go to the infirmary.

The SS considered the camp its personal property and got furious when outsiders became involved in their affairs. The Political Division was led by a master sergeant by the name of Lüdtke, the son of a businessman from Danzig. Sruoga describes his head as resembling that of a garter snake; he goes on to say he was a sadist who thought that everyone sent to the camp was a criminal or an enemy of Germany. When newcomers arrived, he would make them leap like a frog and if the prisoner did not comply, he was given the impact of his cleated boot. Among his duties was to produce a list of hangings and shootings.[110] Lüdtke's official SS file is less colorful—a former salesman, *gottgläubig*, He was in Stutthof for the duration of the war and attained the rank of sergeant in 1942.

SS Lieutenant Maelstaedt was in charge of the Political Division (which was under the Gestapo) and worked there between 1943 and 1944. Around forty years of age, the Danzig-born Maelstaedt is described by Sruoga as a bit of a dandy—always wore clean leather gloves and polished shoes. (The contrast, of course, is with the calloused hands of prisoners and their ill-fitting clogs.) Maelstaedt received the list from the Gestapo with the names of incoming prisoners. His job was to sign the list and pass it on to other camp agencies, with whom he was known to quarrel. In the summer of 1944, he was demoted, and his new job was to guide prisoners from Danzig to Stutthof. Sruoga's portrait of Sergeant König has one redeeming feature—he typically only yelled at the prisoners when his superior was present but allowed them privileges, like cigarettes, when Lüdtke was not present. Sruoga writes: "His motto seemed to be, you never know how things will turn out it in the end."[111] Before the evacuation of the camp in January 1945, documents pertaining to the Political Division were burned. Between 1943 and 1944, the kapo of the division's labor detachment was a German prisoner by the name of Schreiter. Sruoga calls him "one of the most conscientious of the camp's swindlers" who had turned his gift for beating into a business.[112] Like Maelstaedt, he took good care of his appearance: "Young Schreiter became quite a well-to-do fellow. He pattered through the camp in patent leather slippers and little leather gloves, the last word in wartime elegance," adding that it really grated, given the indescribable poverty that reigned among the other prisoners. Then there was Ziehm, a tall, good-looking guy, who liked to lecture the prisoners that the SS was comprised of the most honorable men in all Germany, selected as the best of the best for Hitler's court elite. Ziehm, Sruoga concludes, was "relatively harmless but he was a pig." The author goes on to say that a young Russian who worked for Ziehm went berserk one day and hit Ziehm on the head with a hammer. Ziehm shed a little bit of blood but in two weeks he was fine again. However, the Russian was hanged for his crime. A short time before the hanging, three of the Russian's neighbors were also killed and Ziehm did not raise a finger.[113] The Danzig Gestapo, Sruoga writes, are "creatures of an entirely different species, who themselves don't seem sure if they are humans or just some two-legged malformations; certainly, they don't view the prisoners as humans, especially when they attempt to stuff them into trucks, and bludgeon them with clubs to slim them down."[114]

Richard Evans attributes deep roots to the subject of violence in the Third Reich. He refers to the "virtues of violence"—toughness, hardness, brutality, and the use of force—as having been inculcated into a generation of young Germans since 1933. He extends the terror inflicted on occupied people and on Jews to the millions who were affected to one degree or another.[115] While it is true that every segment of German society suffered at some level under National Socialism, the terror that was unleashed on the camps was of a different sort and at an incomparable level of violence. It reigned supreme: in extermination camps swift and absolute, in concentration camps like Stutthof it was a daily—indeed hourly—hard grind that was exacerbated and magnified by the presence of professional criminals, most of them Germans imported from German prisons. Formidable foes, they did the dirty work of the SS who stood by and watched. The violence that was perpetrated in Stutthof was also close to home—as close as Danzig-born SS or even some who came from the villages near the camp. Though local men did not hold a monopoly on violence, their behavior is frequently singled out. Block overseers and kapos came from all over the Greater Reich; men like the notorious Fabro from Austria and Esser who murdered his own mother, but memoirs consistently point to the cruelty and sadism of local men, like Selonke whose lifestyle in the camp Sruoga describes:

> He was a burglar and described as a specialist in second story work ... He even stole from food parcels and was treated with great respect, had his own fleet of servants who cooked for him and polished his shoes etc., cleaned his room. He had his own room. He was the chief executioner of the camp with a sidekick in a man called Merkel who was a capo, in fact chief capo, and the two of them were referred to as The Big Two until Merkel got into trouble and was replaced by a former pimp. The men's quarters began with Block Two and this is where all prisoners were initiated by Esser.[116]

We may forget that he stole food parcels but thanks to Sruoga, we will never forget that his specific area of expertise was the second floor of a house. Information like that is not found in camp files.

The Demand Grows for SS Recruits

Recruitment policies for the SS had been modified by 1938 in response to a growing need for more men, a change that also reflected Himmler's recognition that neither the level of education nor social status should affect their acceptance within the ranks.[117] He also drew recruits from satellite states to become concentration camp guards. Rumanians and Slovaks were the first to fill these positions and soon were joined by Croatians and Hungarians. Initially they favored the tall, good-looking recruits, and carefully checked their genealogies, even if they could not speak German. After the German invasion of the Soviet Union, when more soldiers were needed to fight in the east, standards were relaxed to include men from rural areas of Ukraine, Romania and Lithuania who had signed the DVL but could barely read Roman script. Their German-sounding names and good looks were criteria for acceptance.[118]

Among the SS men at Stutthof were fifty *Volksdeutsche* Slovaks who arrived at the camp in 1943. After eight weeks of training, most of them became camps guards. Some were dismissed as unfit for the job or sent to other camps.[119] One, by the name of Anton Bartosch committed suicide, was reported by the Commandant as suffering from "mental derangement." These men worked both in Stutthof and in Hopehill. One of them, Josef Wenhardt, was in the canine unity and worked as a *Hundefuhrer/* dog handler, an assignment that we know from prisoner testimonies caused terror and terrible injuries. In the postwar trials in 1947, Wenhardt received the maximum prison sentence in this category of eight to ten years. Five Slovaks (of the seven who remained in 1945) faced trial.[120] There were fewer in the contingent that came from the Sudetenland and they were in a different social bracket. The ten SS Sudetens were well-educated and had already been in several camps before Stutthof and had received medals for their service. Physician Willibold Jobst arrived from Auschwitz in March

1942, and already by July was transferred to a field hospital. Josef Stahl was appointed as the Commandant's adjutant in June 1944 and stayed until liberation in April 1945. He was sentenced to ten years in prison and an additional ten years of the loss of civil rights.[121]

How do we begin to understand the level of violence in a relatively small camp like Stutthof? And is it fair to attribute the degree of responsibility, as I have done, to local SS men? I submit there is enough evidence in the memoirs and statements already in this chapter—there will be more compelling data in the following chapters—to indict them even more. Right at the end of his long history of the camp system, Wachsmann notes that though the character of individual camps owed much to the initiative of the local SS, the camps were run by the principles and aims of the leaders of the Nazi regime.[122] The first part of this statement is particularly true of Stutthof for the following reasons: Stutthof was in operation for a long time, and in the course of its over five-year history employed local men—and women—from the communities in and around Danzig that conferred on the camp an imprimatur that connected it in very specific ways with Danzig. Stutthof drew its main resources from Danzig and was associated throughout its history with all its main agencies—its police force, Gestapo and military units. It used its harbor to send and receive goods—including human "slaves" to work in its sub-camps which, as we will see in the next chapter, grew to be the most prolific in the whole camp system, even if its contribution to the war effort was arguably less significant. Beyond the many material connections, Danzig was emblematic—as I have argued—of all things German. Stutthof doubtless played a significant part in the economy of Danzig, but the symbolic value of Danzig as an outpost of Germandom far outstripped any city in the Reich.

New Demands for the War Effort

What then were Stutthof's contributions to the Greater Reich and to the war effort? Did its armaments production and the various businesses inside the camp and in the sub-camps really make much of a contribution to the Reich and to the war effort? Compared to other camps like Flossenbürg, Dora, or Mauthausen, Stutthof did not have a central industry that defined it, like granite or stone works or underground facilities like Dora to produce rockets. (Dillon refers to "the murderous quarries of Mauthausen and Flossenbürg."[123]) Its contribution was ancillary to the war industries and as such, vulnerable to sabotage. Its primary contribution was local and regional and consequently was never treated as paramount to the war effort. Allen has argued that in the wider camp system, WVHA managers wanted their businesses to serve the goals of the Nazi community without regard for pecuniary gain, that the SS and the WVHA opposed capitalism because of the threat that it posed to a homogenous German culture. He calls this doctrine "productivism" which he defines as an ideology "that meant that companies should not so much do business and make products as make Germans and German-ness. It promised to make the factory floor into a system with which to stamp managers and workers alike with an indelible national harmony."[124] Furthermore, Eicke showed little interest in the exploitation of prisoners' skills; in fact, he told the Kommandanten not to pay heed to professional criteria. He conceived of labor as a tool with which to impose the might of National Socialism upon prisoners. Allen argues that the primary aim was "to seek to control industry in such a way as to preserve the sanctity of Germandom, a cause in which mere cost could not be allowed to set the ultimate bottom line ... As one SS lawyer later wrote in a manifesto, the state is not there for the economy, but the economy is there for the state."[125] In this system, Allen contends, the kapos wielded the most power and were chosen for their brutality and not because they were skilled supervisors.[126]

Whether these factors, as outlined by Allen, penetrated Stutthof to the same degree as other camps is unlikely. The primary camps illustrate his point more convincingly. The more mundane reality in Stutthof is of effective sabotage that was ubiquitous in the camp. After all, the camp had become home to a core group of prisoners who knew how to exploit every weakness in the camp's structure and organization, including even the presence of disaffected Wehrmacht soldiers, many of them injured, who had been put in charge of prisoners. But more importantly, the presence of a strong Polish resistance in the camp, despite efforts to keep them separated, was a definite factor throughout Stutthof's history, and in 1943 these "old timers" were still active. In mid-1943, the DAW workshops were expanded, creating a need for new workers and supervisors. The aim of Polish resisters, as already indicated, was to place their own men in the office that assigned work duties and thus to spare prisoners from the units that had to work outdoors, like the forest commando where the death rate was among the highest. The camp slogan "work with your eyes, work slowly and work badly" was certainly not conducive to economic growth but beyond that, these underground cells were composed of experienced and hardened Polish resisters, Russian officers and Norwegian prisoners, who worked on sabotage strategies despite the dangers of being caught. They took terrible risks and were sometimes caught in the act. For example, on June 1, 1944, twenty-six Poles and twenty-two Soviet officers were sent to Mauthausen where most of them died.[127] The most egregious acts of sabotage happened in the gunsmith workshop where prisoners inserted slightly damaged pins which were good enough to pass the initial test firing but broke soon afterwards. It is interesting to note that when Wehrmacht soldiers who were invalids were supervising these tests, it was easier to get off with the sabotage. In fact, prisoners admitted (presumably later) that the liberal attitude of the Wehrmacht supervisors made the sabotage possible.[128]

By mid-1944, the fate of European Jews had changed drastically, and though it may seem impossible, for the worse. The new challenge for the camp personnel was the quarter-mastering of thousands of the new arrivals, mostly Jewish women—the focus of the next chapter. The first step for the new arrivals was to qualify for Stutthof's work force and thus contribute to the war effort in the main camp or in the many filial camps that stretched all the way up the Baltic. But first, they had to be registered and dispose of any possessions they still might have. The room in which prisoners had to divest themselves of their belongings was the bath house, and it was here that they turned over their rings, their gold, their fine pens and all valuables. The prisoner was asked to sign a list of what he had surrendered. But most of what entered the basket disappeared forever. The clothes of Jews and Russians were thrown into one pile. All their belongings were appointed for use by the SS.[129]

Camp records indicate that veterans of the camp helped process the newcomers and in some cases falsified the date of birth of Jewish children, thus saving some from selection and certain deportation to Auschwitz. (Those unfit to work were all sent there.) When possible, the prisoner helpers also listed them by ethnic identity as Poles, Russians or Georgians, and not as Jews. For instance, twenty Jewish boys were sent to the sub-camp in Stolp/Słupsk where despite the hard labor, they had a better chance to survive because the older prisoners protected them.[130] Unlike the earlier prisoner registrations at the onset of the camp, there was no more parity between Poles and Jews—and *Juden und Pfaffen* was no longer a bracket. The small Jewish community of Danzig no longer existed. When war broke out those Jews who had somehow survived the initial arrests—mostly elderly and infirmed—lived in daily fear in Danzig, harassed and persecuted, barred from public transport, restricted by a daily curfew, barred from shops and beaches at certain times, etc., living in constant dread of transports to the Warsaw ghetto and Auschwitz. By 1943, there were very few left—in hiding. Richard Hildebrandt had been replaced by Fritz Katzmann as Chief of the Main Office of Race and Settlements in April 1943. His murderous reputation in Galicia—in Lvov, followed him to Danzig.[131]

To return, in summary, to the statistics of Stutthof: In his chapter on international prisoners in the camp, Marek Orski estimates that of the 110,000 prisoners in Stutthof, the greatest number was Jewish prisoners. In terms of nationality, the greatest number of prisoners were Polish prisoners, followed by Soviet citizens, then Hungarians and Germans.[132] According to Orski, and based on incomplete records, at least 1,076 Czechoslovakian prisoners were registered, the majority of whom were Jewish.[133] Until the middle of 1944, there were more men than women in the camp. Of the 110,000 inmates around 49,000 were women, of whom the majority came in the summer and fall of 1944 from Lithuania, Latvia, Estonia and the USSR. On January 24, 1945, there were 46,505 prisoners of whom 28,390 were women and 18,115 were men.[134] They were registered by age, children under fourteen, children between fourteen and eighteen, nineteen to seventy, and then those over seventy. Most of the prisoners were between the ages of twenty-five and thirty-five and the fewest were in the age group fifty to seventy. The oldest was a Polish priest who was born in 1855 and died on April 22, 1940, of malnutrition.[135]

Albert Forster had proudly declared before the war began that the task before them was to solve the Jewish question by the spring of 1939. He had obviously not been successful in eliminating Jewish life at that time, but now in 1944 nothing stood in the way of his earlier ambitions that had meanwhile meshed with the murderous goals of the Third Reich, implemented locally by willing and well-nourished SS men and women in a camp that offered modest but adequate facilities to dispose of the bodies of the unwanted. Dębski points out the difference in the fate of Jewish prisoners: "The greatest difference between the Jewish and the non-Jewish prisoners was that all the Jews were to be killed sooner or later, but other prisoners could hope that they would survive the camps. No matter how small the chance for survival, hope existed for them, but not for the Jews."[136] The next chapter will show just how true that statement is.

4

Entering the "Final Solution," the Summer of 1944

New Offensives

The arrival of the first mass deportations of Jews—mostly women—from Auschwitz in June 1944 was soon followed by thousands more in transports from the liquidated ghettos and camps of the east and signaled a new direction for Stutthof that has aligned its history with "the Final Solution" and thus with the Holocaust.[1] If January 1942 was a turning point for Stutthof when it was recognized by Himmler as a bona fide concentration camp, the new directives in 1944 from Amt D[2] brought it into line with the earlier and the most inhumane practices of the primary camps—transports consisting only of Jews, a dramatic increase in the number of slave laborers for the war effort, the murdering of those unfit to work, the violation of their bodies when gold fillings were ripped out of their mouths, gas chambers, crematoria to dispose of corpses, the total degradation of women, separation of mothers from their children—all this and more now characterized Stutthof. Christopher Browning has this to say about the earlier onslaught on Jews in Poland: "In short, the German attack on the Jews of Poland was not a gradual or incremental program stretched over a long period of time, but a veritable blitzkrieg, a massive offensive requiring the mobilization of large numbers of shock troops."[3] Stutthof enters the narrative of "the Final Solution" in a different paradigm—as the destination for those who have already experienced and been victimized by this "massive offensive." Most of the Jews who arrived in the summer of 1944 had survived other camps like Theresienstadt, Auschwitz, and the Baltic camps.

Its change of status and activities has been collated and documented. Drawing on Stutthof's extensive data base, Drywa presents facts and figures from the transport lists—the arrival dates, where they came from, how many were on each transport, their ethnicity and gender, where they were housed in the camp, what sub-camp they were sent to, their subsequent destination if they were transported from Stutthof to other camps, whether to hard labor or to extermination.[4] Along with these statistics, she gives evidence that the incoming transports, bearing literally thousands of enfeebled prisoners did not simply arrive in Stutthof because it was a camp of last resort, the proverbial "any old port in a storm." Stutthof was being discussed at the highest level of management as a vital cog in the wheel of "the Final Solution," and its personnel from the Commandant down to the lowest camp worker were as engaged, if in varying degrees, as their counterparts in the wider camp system, in targeting Jewish prisoners for either death through hard labor or extermination by various means that will be discussed in this chapter. While this does not mean that non-Jews in the camp were spared torture or death, there is overwhelming evidence in the camp files and in the testimonies of both Jews and non-Jews that in the scale of expendability, Jewish prisoners occupied the lowest level. They always had, but the influx of thousands of Jews tipped the scale toward mass extermination in a new way for Stutthof.

The evidence includes documentation of the initial exchange in July between Commandant Hoppe and the Amt D Chief—Richard Glücks in the WVHA office in Oranienburg concerning the so-called Jewish problem. "The Final Solution of the Jewish Question" was certainly not a new subject to Amt D, but according to Hoppe's postwar testimony it was now presented to him by Glücks as a likelihood for Stutthof. After a second visit a few weeks later, procedures were set in motion for using Zyklon B on inmates. Hoppe informed his second-in-command Teodor Meyer, as well as the chief medical officer, Dr. Otto Heidl of these developments, and their plans to kill inmates by this process were further implemented by Rudolf Höss who was charged by Glücks to go to Stutthof and instruct camp personnel in the new method. Höss's "expertise" in this area had already been clearly demonstrated on thousands of Hungarian Jews earlier in the spring of 1944 in Auschwitz-Birkenau. In the 2014 exhibition "Jews in the KL Stutthof," an order dated June 14 is displayed "concerning sending two members of the SS KL Stutthof unit to Oranienburg to collect the 50kg of Zyklon B supply."[5]

Meyer later claimed that Heidl was given the order to gas 300 to 400 Jewish women who were declared unfit to work. The Danish prisoner, Martin Nielsen described the process of selection as resembling that of a horse trader: Heidl walked up and down the rows of women, inspected their teeth and then lifted up their skirts to inspect their legs. If any of them had gold teeth or if they had edema, they were pulled out of the line.[6] The healthiest women were destined to work in the German munitions sector, while the next group was assigned to a block or barrack, presumably to wait for an assignment but the third group—those deemed unfit—were transported on a flatbed truck in groups of twenty-five to thirty to the gas chamber. This procedure is confirmed by others, including the Lithuanian priest Stasys Yla. He writes:

> At first the prisoners were gassed in small groups but gradually the numbers became larger and larger, and by the time the SS decided to do away with the Jewish women, they were crowding 100 or more of them together at once. These women rode to the gas chamber in carts—two carts which were hauled by four Russian prisoners. Since the carts were comparatively small, it took several trips back and forth before enough women could be gathered to make the thing "worthwhile." Then they were ordered to strip and they entered the chamber—ostensibly for bathing and disinfection. Immediately afterwards the doors were sealed shut; when they swung open again, 30 minutes later, most of the women were dead.[7]

At Hoppe's trial it emerged that this way of gassing was replaced by another one—using a car of the narrow-gauge railway that was equipped with a pipe for the gas and sealed airtight.[8] Yla speculates that the victims thought they were about to be transported by train out of the camp.⁹ By the end of October, gassing was no longer needed as typhus was now effectively increasing the death rate. The typhus outbreak will be discussed later.

Marc Buggeln locates the decision to use gas chambers in Stutthof as part of a wider plan by the Armaments Ministry that was linked to the impending loss of the gas chambers at Auschwitz.[10] He points out that three other main camps were also equipped at this time to use gas—Sachsenhausen, Ravensbrück and Mauthausen—yet another indication of Stutthof's standing within the network of main camps. The goal was to separate the fit to work from those who were unfit and to place the chronically unfit in separate blocks where they would be kept until they died.[11] Stutthof implemented the plan, beginning with the arrival of the Hungarian Jews from Auschwitz in June until October during which period 23,566 prisoners arrived—21,817 of them women. These new arrivals were joined by and essentially overlapped with 25,043 Jews from the Baltic states from mid-July onward.[12] Clearly, Stutthof was now functioning as a primary camp.[13]

Another factor that aligned it with other main camps was that it was neither the first nor final destination for most of the new arrivals. In its earlier history, prisoners arrived at the camp directly from areas within Danzig-West Prussia and Pomerania, and though they were maltreated from the day they entered the camp precincts, they had, at least initially, some resources of strength to draw upon, as well as the likelihood of food parcels from home. These prisoners in 1944 were already depleted by their experiences elsewhere—in Auschwitz, Kaiserwald, (Riga) Łódź, and Kovno. Some camps like Riga and Kovno had been opened in the spring of 1943 explicitly for the exploitation of Jewish slave labor.[14] As depleted as they were, the stronger ones were selected for hard labor in other destinations in the Greater Reich or for equally strenuous labor in the sub-camps that were growing around Stutthof and, in some cases, miles away from the main camp. In both cases, they faced even worse conditions, working long hours in the hot sun in agriculture or in DESt brick works or in the DAW factories that produced armaments for a war effort that was rapidly becoming more desperate. By this time, the Nazi regime and its Axis allies were losing military ground in every area that they had occupied. As Allied forces prevailed, the efforts to shore up Nazi resources intensified and the demand for laborers in the camp system increased, along with increased harshness to the prisoners.

The Assassination Attempt on Hitler and Its Impact on Stutthof

Before returning to the fate of Jews in Stutthof, I would like to identify two momentous events in mid-1944 that also directly impacted Stutthof. The first was the assassination attempt on the life of Hitler at the Eastern Front headquarters at *Wolfsschanze*/The Wolf's Lair near Rastenburg/Kętrzyn, East Prussia on July 20. After the unsuccessful attack, hundreds of men and women were dragged into the camps as part of Operation Thunderstorm. According to Peter Hoffmann, 600 people were arrested, of whom only 160–200 had been directly involved in the conspiracy.[15] In the months that followed, more than 5,000 people would eventually be arrested on charges related to conspiracy, whether connected directly or not to the July 20 plot. The Gestapo used the occasion to settle scores with many who were perceived as sympathizing with the opposition. Count von Moltke was in this category and later told the court that his decision to take part in the coup was a matter of conscience—based on his conviction that the German position in Poland was immoral. This is as clear a case of shame in the face of the consequences of Germandom as we can find. In his court testimony, Moltke expressed deep regret for his former attitude to Poland and his zeal in promoting the German heritage in Poland.[16] What kind of impact did this momentous event have on the German public? Kershaw refers to "shock, dismay, and anger—relief at the outcome" and despite polarized public opinion, there was a backlash of support for Hitler.[17] "Thank God the Führer is alive!" appears to have won the day. Kershaw also points out that "[a]fter the assassination attempt, there was a cloud of silence. Hitler was rarely seen or heard."[18]

It is also noteworthy that the leaders of the Baptist and Methodist churches sent a telegram to the Führer, expressing their relief on behalf of the Association of Free Churches that he had been saved from "such a heinous assassination attempt."[19] Did Grass have anything to say about the plot to kill the Führer? In July 1944, the young Günter Grass was being trained for further duties with the Reich Labor Service, and a news bulletin was released about the assassination attempt on Hitler. He writes: "Clipped pronouncements about shame and craven betrayal ... about the base and insidious plot of a coterie of well-born officers." Grass deflects the impact of the assassination attempt and instead focuses on the social status of the would-be assassinators. It is a tactic that reduces the need to take sides. Grass has one side to support—the working class. This is part of the silence he cultivated: he had never in his life, he writes, "not in school, let alone in my mother's grocery—met anyone who could be called well-born."[20]

The "kith and kin" of the dissenters were sent to several detention centers and camps, including Stutthof where they were housed in special quarters. Just because they were judged as deserving to be sent to a concentration camp did not erase racial distinctions. They were separated from the rest of the camp population. Though deemed pure in blood line (in fact, aristocratic blood), they were held politically culpable and joined some dozen Hungarians opposed to Hitler under the loose term of *Sippenhaft*; in other words they were held liable for the misdeeds of their relatives.[21] Among the Germans thus held were family members of Count Claus von Stauffenberg whose maternal grandmother was to die at the outset of the evacuation. There was also a group of 150 German officers referred to as "*Haudegen*" who were accused of collaborating with the Allies.

The testimony of Fey von Hassell gives us some insight into the privileged treatment received by the German family members of the would-be assassinators. When they arrived at the beginning of December, they had already been for a brief time in other detention centers and only learned from one of their guards the name of their new camp. She writes: "We were received by the camp commandant. He gave the impression of being brutal and capable of any kind of cruelty yet seemed to be the type that did not beat around the bush but called things the way he saw them; he didn't seem to belong to the dirty and deceitful SS types."[22] Von Hassell then lists the duties that the commandant gave them and the indignities that they would **not** suffer—no prison garb or numbers affixed to clothing, they could cook for themselves, borrow books from the SS library, walk in the campgrounds till nine in the evening, write home every two weeks, receive mail and above all enjoy one another's company. Their duties included chopping wood for their stove, darning prisoners' socks, and keeping their barrack clean for the daily morning inspection. They learned from another prisoner who delivered their firewood that Himmler was very concerned about keeping them in good health because they were, in fact, hostages and as such were only useful alive. All of them became ill, with either dysentery or typhus which was rampant at the time in the camp.[23] Von Hassell writes that at night they heard the ferocious barking of dogs unleashed on prisoners attempting to escape—"the most miserable of the miserable … One could only hear the piercing, fearful screams of the prisoners."[24] She writes too about the shriek of sirens alerting of air raids and of the SS being so concerned about the group's health that they sent two female Russian POWs to chop their wood and tend to their stove. From these women they learned (through Mika Stauffenberg and Anni Lerchenfeld who spoke Russian) about the gas chambers and that the Russians were treated the worst of all the prisoners—forty people were housed without mattresses or blankets in rooms that were adequate for sixteen people.[25]

Though her testimony is not devoid of compassion toward other prisoners and though she acknowledges their own relative privilege, it also, if unwittingly, underscores the racial divisions in the camp. Von Hassell does not depict her experiences of the camp as shaped by race or ideology or politics but writes from a perspective based on social class—the opposite model of Grass's "lower class" perspective. These aristocrats are firmly enclosed within their barrack where they undoubtedly suffered privations and ultimately the same diseases as other prisoners, but she makes clear that every effort was made to protect them from these diseases—by Himmler himself—and to preserve their strength by sending Russians to help them. She reports without commentary that the latter claimed to suffer the most and that it was they who told the Germans about the rumor of the gas chambers. She does not question the Russians' claim nor comment on the possible identity of the victims of the gas chambers. This group of Germans was the fewest in number but claimed the most privileges. In the later trials, where some of these prisoners testified, they gave a favorable account of the commandant, even calling him "a gentleman." There is no doubt that these family members of the would-be assassinators suffered deeply, including the separation from their children who were scattered throughout the Reich in Nazi homes.[26] More troubling is her assessment of the camp commandant who, though brutal and cruel, was straightforward and candid, and not in the same category as the "dirty and deceitful SS types." They were well-treated (relatively speaking) for one reason—they were Germans, and though they or their relatives were a disgrace to their social class and especially to Germandom, they needed to be separated from other prisoners—like Poles and Jews. Besides, they might be useful as bargaining chips if prisoner exchanges were made.

A letter written on June 24, 1974, by Franz Ludwig Graf von Stauffenberg, at that time a member of the Bundestag, refers to the consequences of his father's role in the assassination plot:

We children were sent to a NSV children's home in the Harz. Adults and young people over twelve were incarcerated and were dragged together from one place to another. At that time, they were also detained in Buchenwald and Stutthof, although isolated from the other prisoners. My grandmother, Anna, Baroness von Lerchenfeld, neé von Stachelberg, died during this time of internment in Stutthof around the turn of the year 1944–45. The survivors ended up in the spring of 1945 in the southern Tyrol in American custody and were taken from there to Capri from where in early summer they were able to return to their families.[27]

Fey von Hassell provides some missing details of von Lerchenfeld's death. She died during the evacuation in Matzkau, one of the makeshift camps near Danzig where they were finally given proper food. "The abundant food and improved conditions came too late for *Tante* Anni von Lerchenfeld who had caught pneumonia during the icy trip through the snow. By the time we arrived in Matzkau, she could no longer recognize anybody and after three days lost consciousness and died."[28]

Other examples of enforcing Germandom were already in place, or at least a Nordic version of it among the Scandinavians inmates. In October 1943, 150 Communist Danes were imprisoned and in December, 265 Norwegian policemen who had opposed Quisling joined them in the special barracks called the *Germanenlager*.[29] The Danes and Norwegians had the advantage of being considered racially "Germanic" and despite their political position as communist resisters were housed in the barracks for "*Germanen*." Their survival rate was high because they received food parcels from home. They were given the choicest jobs, like gardening and working on the estate at Werdershof. A group of Finnish merchant marine seamen—138 of them—joined this group in September 1944. A memoir written by one of this group aligns them with the other Scandinavians.[30] The background for the arrest of Finnish sailors is as follows: their ship, the *Wappu*, had arrived in Danzig with a cargo of timber when it was seized by the Germans. Finland had signed the Moscow Armistice with Russia, dissolving earlier ties with the Third Reich. The Finnish ship had docked in Danzig apparently unaware of these developments. The sailors subsequently spent the next six months as prisoners in Stutthof, enduring the same privations as other prisoners but housed, at least, in better quarters. They were quickly assigned work in the DAW as machinists or carpenters either on site or in nearby sub-camps. Though they were not spared the rigors of hard labor, they were given portions from the food parcels that the Norwegians generously shared with them.[31] Once more, the degree of suffering of the Jewish prisoners stands out in the memory of this survivor—though everyone suffered in the camp, no one suffered as keenly as they. The memoir also refers to the outbreak of typhus in November (over a thousand died in one month) and the measures taken to disinfect the Finns who were covered in lice. One day they were taken to the crematorium, stripped of their clothes—the same ones they had arrived in and had worn for the duration of the camp—which were then fumigated by a team of SS men. One sailor made the unfortunate comment that the lice were still on him and was pummeled to the ground by a guard.[32] These men were also part of the evacuation and the memoir will be referred to again in the next chapter.

The Warsaw Uprising Brings New Prisoners

The impact of the Warsaw Uprising on the camp was arguably more significant in its impact on Stutthof than the events mentioned above. On August 1, 1944, the AK (*Armia Krajowa,* the official Polish Resistance Army) attacked the Germans, and though less equipped expected to take back the city of Warsaw. After two months of intense fighting, German troops defeated the Polish resisters, while Stalin ignored their need for aid, and even prevented Allied forces from providing supplies and from using Soviet airfields. The attempt by the Soviet-sponsored PKWN (The Polish Committee of National Liberation/*Polski Komitet Wyzwolenia Narodowego*) troops to cross the Vistula in September also received little support and failed.[33] The large-scale execution of civilians, combined with street fighting, resulted in 200,000 casualties, and enabled the Germans to defeat the Polish resistance and demolish the city.

In the course of the summer of 1944, many Polish resisters from the Warsaw Uprising joined other Poles in Stutthof who were there because they were Polish resisters or deemed to be resisters.[34] Poles still made up the majority of the prison population until mid-1944. The incarceration of supporters of the Polish resistance both regionally—Pomerania—and beyond had never changed.[35] It is estimated that 6,000 supporters of various underground organizations were prisoners in Stutthof during the period 1939–45. Earlier in the summer, there had already been two main transports—on May 25, a transport of 859 political prisoners was sent from the Pawiak prison who were members of the Warsaw underground (mostly *Armia Krajowa*). They were joined by 110 inmates from Lublin castle who were considered part of the resistance movement.[36] The potential dangers of a strong and diverse resistance group in the camp did not elude Commandant Hoppe and his team. They separated prisoners of the same groups from one another by housing them in different barracks, dispatched them to different outlying sub-camps, and sent them on numerous transports to other camps. When the first contingent of prisoners (2,757 of them) arrived on August 24 from the Pruszków transit camp, there was a flurry of telegrams exchanged between Hoppe and the WVHA. The commandant was ordered to use them as laborers. A contingent of them was put to work on a construction site that was being built near Brusy/Bruss for an SS training ground. These prisoners—some 500 of them remained unregistered in the camp files—worked on that site and slept in huts until they were deported from Stutthof on August 30. They were replaced the next day by another incoming transport from Warsaw of over 2,000 men, 664 women, and 7 children. These prisoners were joined on September 29 by 1,252 men, 6 women, and 40 female soldiers.[37] Dunin-Wąsowicz claims that the way these women were treated was in total disregard for the terms of the capitulation that General von-Bach-Zelewski had vehemently promised to follow.[38]

The new prisoners came for the most part from the Polish intelligentsia or were students with strong ties to the underground movement and the Polish government in exile in London. They brought fresh news—and hope—to the prisoners who belonged to the Pomerania resistance that was not as well organized or as strong—some had been in the camp since 1939. Within the confines of the barracks, there was also opportunity to talk about the future of the Polish nation, and there were lectures by Professor Jan

Rostafiński on religion, astrology, and on the influence of leading scientists like Louis Pasteur.[39] His presence was a great comfort and source of encouragement to all, but especially to Polish prisoners. The group of forty women soldiers who arrived on September 19, members of the AK were treated as heroes. They wore military-style jackets and caps adorned with the Polish eagle. They were punished for the adulation they received by being transferred to the worst of all barracks—the Jewish block where they were stripped of their clothing, had to wear striped rags, work for hours in the kitchen and endure the abuse of a German *Aufseherin*. Once again, Jews and Poles belonged in the same bracket of maltreatment but this time they were identified as separate categories. Classified as Polish POWs—*"Polnische Kriegsgefangene"* (to distinguish them from the Jewish women) they had to sleep three to a bed and were not allowed to write home. (In other words, they received no food packages, a supplement that often meant the difference between starvation and survival.) Without the solidarity of other women—presumably in sharing food—these female soldiers would not have survived. It was, however, not enough to save a baby that was born to one of them. Thirty-six of them survived until the end.[40]

Testimonies from this group include a video testimony recorded in 1998 by Piotr Kwiatkowski from Calgary, Canada who states at the beginning, "I am Polish. I am not Jewish," leaving us to wonder why this was his first statement.[41] As his testimony proceeds, however, it becomes clear that his was not a disavowal of identity but rather a plain statement of fact. He was among those referred to above who were transferred from Pawiak to Stutthof by truck at four in the morning of May 24, 1944. As a member of one of the leftist parties, he states that he had many Jewish friends who visited one another in their homes; he repeats that he "was spared antisemitic feelings."[42] He also points to the growing antisemitism of the late 1920s in Poland when the numerus clausus had been introduced against Jews, and he expresses abhorrence toward Polish chauvinism and the prevailing Catholic antisemitism. With these convictions very clearly in view, Kwiatkowski proceeds to describe conditions he encountered in Stutthof: the role of the kapos "the first person after God for you"—the SS were there but the kapos did the beating. It was now the end of May and he was part of a work unit that was digging ditches for irrigation. There were many Jews from Kovno, from Czechoslovakia and from Germany, but they were separated from them by barbed wire. He says some of the Germans were political prisoners but most of them were criminals—he calls them "bandits," the same term he uses to describe Polish kapos. The only decent Germans, he claims, were Jehovah's Witnesses. Kwiatkowski identifies the primary extermination tool of the camp as "planned killing by hunger and starvation." It was a matter of time before you were unable to work because of malnutrition. He places the Jews on the lowest level of work—only Jews cleaned the latrines. Other prisoners could see them through the barbed wire, and they saw them being selected to life or death—elderly people to death. At this point in his testimony there is a visible look of pain in his eyes as he recounts the suffering of Jews. Toward the end of his testimony, he recounts an incident that he and fellow prisoners witnessed, from the safety of the camp hospital where he had spent ten days under the care of a Russian doctor who had befriended him. One day he saw a cart being pulled by prisoners on which were twenty Jewish women—only Jews were selected, he explains. He saw a kapo with "crematorium" on his badge who was in charge, as the women undressed in an empty room, lay down on a table, were injected, and finally probed with a stethoscope in the heart area by an SS man dressed in white. Afterwards, personnel took the corpse by the hands and legs out of the area. Some prisoners watched these proceedings until an angry SS man caught them on, closed the curtains, and threatened them that they would have the same fate if they did not stop watching.[43]

By August, Stutthof was no longer functioning as a regional camp with some autonomy but had become the epicenter of the Baltic camps that were being threatened by the advance of the Soviet army. Prisoners came from liquidated camps in Erde, Vaivar, Klooga in Estonia, Kaiserwald-Salaspils in Latvia, Kozłowa, Ruda, Fort 1X in Kaunas, Promieniaszki near Kaunas and Vilnius in Lithuania.[44] Camp personnel were faced with the challenge of absorbing thousands of newcomers into an infrastructure that had inadequate facilities to accommodate them. They had been shunted from other Baltic camps or from the main camps, some of them arriving by barges and boats in Danzig, desperately ill from seasickness and sheer exhaustion. Some had been in other camps along the way. Kovno had already been liquidated in October 1943, and 10,458 people had been sent to Stutthof but not immediately. One deportation arrived on July 19, 1944. In August 1944, the Germans began the liquidation of the Kaiserwald camp near Riga. On August 9, 1944, the first transport from that camp arrived with 6,832 Jews who were sent by ship. There were six transports to the camp. Between August and October 1944, a total of 14,585 Jews arrived in the camp. At the end of June 1944, there were 37,600 registered. In the second half of 1944, 49,000 Jews were transported to Stutthof.[45]

Adolescents were also included in these transports of 1944, from every nationality. Based on camp records, it is estimated that there were 3,000 of this age category during the five-year history of the camp. Janina Grabowska-Chałka puts it very simply: "Their fate was very hard."[46] This is how Chana Borochowitz, a teenager at the time, later described it:

We arrived in camp Stutthof near the town Danzig … the gestapo hob-nailed boot soldiers began to shout and their shouts mixed with the barking of savage dogs. The people were weak and starved, and the soldiers shouted schnell (quickly). They beat those who were not quick enough. I thought: "we have come to the hell-gate." And really, camp Stutthof was a hell on earth. They turned us out of the train with bawls and curses. A human beast in the shape of an SS officer barked an order: men to the right, women to the left and so, we were separated from our father.[47]

These adolescents experienced the same privations as adults—hard labor, hunger, illness, maltreatment. It is no wonder that the mortality rate for the group was higher than 38 percent.[48] In June 1944, a group of young Poles from the Białystok transport was gassed, including an eleven-year-old boy, and in the winter, two Russian boys roughly ten years of age were publicly executed.[49] The preferred mode of disposal, however, was simply to select them for a transport out of the camp, as happened on June 19 when 239 boys were sent to Mauthausen.[50]

The fate of children younger than ten makes for even more distressing reading. Sruoga writes about the heart-wrenching scene when mothers were forcibly separated from their little children and tried to hide wherever they could—even under their skirts but all to no avail. After a few days, these children were transported to Auschwitz-Birkenau where they were exterminated. On July 26, 1944, a transport left Stutthof with 524 women, 416 girls, and 483 boys, followed on September 10, by 575 Jewish women with their children, as well as eight other non-Jewish mothers with eight children and nine pregnant women, all of whom perished in Birkenau.[51] In rare cases, babies born to Polish or Russian prisoners in the camp were able to survive, thanks to the support of other women. A Jewish mother, however, had absolutely no chance of keeping a child. "They belonged to a people that the Nazis had categorically designated for extermination."[52] Hörder claims that in August 1944, Glücks ordered that all Jewish prisoners who were unfit to work be deported to Auschwitz. As for other prisoners, he left that decision to the camp commandants in consultation with the WVHA.[53]

The majority of these prisoners were survivors—if barely—of Nazi wrath against Jews that had engulfed the occupied territories between 1942 and 1944. They had already suffered indescribable hardships for at least two years, not to mention previous harassments before they were deported. If they survived this new level of imprisonment and if they wrote about it or spoke about it in video testimony, everything they had to say about Stutthof was shaped and prefaced by previous suffering. By November 5, 1944, there were 57,056 prisoners in Stutthof—20,680 men and 36,376 women. These figures are staggeringly high in view of the camp's infrastructure that until this point had never housed more than several thousand prisoners at one time. Around 33,000 were living in the camp proper and the others were scattered throughout the region in the sub-camps.[54]

"Dying Zones" and Killing Sites

By November 1944, Stutthof had become a place where the SS had resorted to direct killings on a large scale, along with Mauthausen, Ravensbrück and Sachsenhausen. Conditions in the camp had deteriorated and now resembled conditions in other camps like Neuengamme and Bergen-Belsen where sick quarters were designated as "dying zones" and were segregated from the rest of the camp.[55] This also happened in Stutthof. But there were other effective killing methods that had been used earlier—the notorious *Genickschussanlage* in which a prisoner was shot in the back of the neck with a special device. Drywa proposes that this cranial device was the method used by Höss and had been passed on to Meyer by order of the SS-WVHA.[56] Prisoners—mostly older Jewish women—were duped into believing they were about to have a physical examination. They were seated at a table to answer family history questions, in a room that resembled a doctor's office, compete with file cabinets, etc. Chemnitz and Foth were in charge, the latter standing at the ready in an adjoining room. The victim was escorted to be measured, right in front of a small window which was abruptly opened. The fatal shot was delivered through the neck and the victim crumbled to the floor.

Four men then carted the limp body to a heap of other, still-warm bodies. "This room was so sound-proofed that no sound could escape to the outside."[57]

Between August and October 1944, numerous deaths also took place by phenol injections, called "needling" by the inmates. Archivists do not give a precise count for these deaths since directives for such "special killings" by injection, referred to as a special treatment—*Sonderbehandlung*—like the murders above, were not documented, but were rather ordered orally, and if the deaths were registered, they were generally attributed to heart-related issues.[58] These lethal injections of phenol were used throughout the camp system and had been applied as early as 1940 in Stutthof to invalids and those deemed insane. For those who lost their mind because of the terror they experienced, there is no registry. Their deaths therefore are ascribed to all sorts of heart-related illnesses that clearly do not recognize the broken-hearted as a category, as is apparent from the testimony of a woman from Leningrad called Taissa. She describes what happened to a fellow inmate:

> One day she suddenly started to break tables, smash plates, she threw off her dress and ran out naked from the *Stube*. In this state she climbed up on the wire fence and started screaming curses at the SS men. They caught her, manacled her and threw her naked into the bunker. In the morning they took her to the *Revier* and gave her a lethal injection.[59]

The closest estimate for the deaths of Jews during this three-month period is 430 women and 46 men, a figure that does not include deaths in the infirmary or in the sub-camps.

The other major cause of death in these months was typhus which was so severe that in November Hoppe ordered the immunization of the SS and key workers (242 were vaccinated).[60] In December, he issued a special order, prohibiting anyone from leaving the camp except for those who were critical to the running of the camp and even these people had to have special permission—the food commando, sanitation crew, and the work units that removed corpses. Sick prisoners in the Jewish Camp were not given medicines, along with those prisoners who were considered too ill. Jewish doctors were powerless to help beyond diagnosing the disease, despite the efforts of prisoner-doctors like Professor Finkelstein from Kaunas and the Polish doctor Alfons Wojewski, who was promised and received from Dr. Heidl (the lead SS doctor) a separate room to treat Jewish patients. Many of these doctors also died. When the wagons were sent to take the patients there, they headed in a different destination—the crematorium—where they perished.[61] Drywa gives the mortality rate in November as 1,680, and in December as 3,480. By January 1945, 9,400 Jews had died in Stutthof and its sub-camps.[62] Dunin-Wąsowicz gives more detail about the typhus epidemic that raged in the camp in December. Jewish women had to walk a mile and a half away from the camp to a special disinfectant area that had been set up for this purpose. They had to take a hot shower without the benefit of drying off with towels, then wait outside for the others, before returning half-naked to the camp. Dunin-Wąsowicz cites the testimony of Professor Rostafiński who described the bare-footed, ill-clad women, standing in the cold, waiting for the others. These same women lost a further 30 kilos in weight on a diet of watery soup with cabbage leaves. Many died of pneumonia in Barracks 28, 29, and 30.[63]

One group that was also the target of extreme maltreatment in Stutthof was the cohort of Soviet prisoners. There is not an abundance of testimonies by Russian POWs relating to their camp experiences, although there are many direct and indirect references to their treatment in memoirs. It is clear that the general stigma levelled by the Nazis at Soviet prisoners associated them with Jewishness and reflects Nazi obsession with the Russian commissars as the personification of "Jewish Bolshevism."[64] In a two-month period in Sachsenhausen, SS men executed around 9,000 Soviet prisoners.[65] Many of the Russian prisoners in Stutthof had been in POW camps before being sent to the camp.[66] One such representative was Gregori Semenjake who arrived from a prisoner of war camp in January 1944, along with eighty-five other Russian prisoners. He describes the circumstances and conditions in Stutthof as much harsher and stricter than in the POW camps where military discipline required that a German soldier obeyed basic military customs—like acknowledging a greeting from a POW. In Stutthof, however, the prisoner was forced to take off his hat or cap before a member of the SS and he could expect random beatings and even to be shot. They got very little to eat, became very thin and yet were assigned to hard manual labor. He then compares their treatment to the maltreatment of Jews in the camp and comes right to the point—they were going to be annihilated. Jews, he writes, were taken into the bath house, having believed the lie that they were about to take a hot shower but instead they were gassed with Zyklon gas.[67] By now, the ovens were functioning 24 hours a day to cope with so many corpses. He tells about a fellow-prisoner, also Russian who went insane and ran away, only to be dragged back again. He punched out a pane of glass from the window and ran toward the entrance but was shot by a guard in the tower.[68]

Russians were also the victims of numerous executions. On March 1, 1944, five Russians were sent to the camp from Königsberg for participating in resistance activities, and two weeks later six Russian officers, including a woman, were also shot. Another inmate, the Polish Dr. Lech Duszyński watched it from the hospital window. He describes how the Commandant, along with Meyer and Dr. Heidl brought the men into the room, searched their mouths for dentures, looking for gold. Then each of them stood with their back to Meyer who shot them in the back of the head. The woman was brought in last. She walked calmly, perhaps unaware of her fate. Many of the Soviet POWs were executed without being entered into the camp registers.[69]

Though the animosity toward Jews and Poles, especially clerics never changed, a layer of hatred was directed toward all Soviet prisoners who fell into the category of Russian, including, but not limited to, the Russian POWs. Anyone who could be loosely termed "Russian" was included. Prisoners arrested right after the Nazi invasion in June 1941 were the first targets, but the shift becomes more apparent in 1944. Jews and Russians were often forced to share the same space as a reminder of the repugnance in which both groups are held, often reduced to one group—Jewish Bolsheviks. A large group of Russian women died in February 1944 of malnutrition, largely because they were not allowed to receive food packages from home and also because they were assigned the most demanding manual labor.[70] Sruoga illustrates this fluid notion of national identity and its treatment very effectively: he writes about the day that a block leader by the name of Gerwiński was interviewing a Ukrainian—in Sruoga's presence—in the hospital office. When asked his nationality he innocently replied Ukrainian, upon which the enraged block leader attacked him physically. The victim then tried to answer with his religion—Orthodox—which further enraged Gerwiński. After losing a tooth in the course of the questioning, the Ukrainian finally got it right and answered, "Little Russia" which produced a mini-lecture on the nonexistence of Ukraine. Sruoga then gives the reader his own sardonic history lesson:

> Nationality and citizenship were often confused in the camp's official documents; the same was entered for one and the other. U.S.S.R citizens were all called Russians. Ukrainians, Belorussians, Kirghizes, Tartars, Mordvins, Georgians—"Russian" was written for all of them. Ukrainians, mobilized into the SS, the government referred to as Ukrainians. Here even true Russians carried the name of Ukrainians. Meanwhile the Ukrainian prisoners were always called Russians. When a prisoner answers Ukrainian, it was written: Russian.[71]

Tensions between the prisoners who were thus categorized frequently did not make for solidarity in their common suffering. There was not a lot of love lost between the different ethnic groups. Those who wore "R" (classified as Russian) covered many groups from the Soviet Union who were not necessarily supporters of Stalin. Ukrainians saw the Russian POWs as "henchmen" of the regime that had killed Ukrainians through its policy of forced collectivization.[72]

Stutthof's Sub-Camps

Sub-camps were a part of the Stutthof system from the very beginning of its history, but it was not until mid-1944 that they proliferated, stretching from Stolp/Słupsk all the way to Königsberg. The whole camp system began to change from the autumn of 1943 and became less centralized. By late 1944, filial camps became more crucial to the war effort. Their numbers grew as the demand for labor intensified. By this time, most of the inmates were working in them. In fact, Stutthof heads up the list as having the most sub-camps with 210. Auschwitz had 47 and Gross-Rosen, with a comparable history to Stutthof, had 100. Buggeln attributes this to the economic importance of the individual complexes but Stutthof is not in the same category, as most of its impact was largely local. He writes: "[T]he largest subcamp system (Stutthof) was comparatively unimportant from an economic point of view because the majority of the facilities were small camps where inmates manufactured products that were of only marginal importance to the war effort."[73] He contrasts it to camps in the south like Dachau and Mauthausen that were the most important economically.[74]

There are not many secondary sources on the sub-camps of the concentration camp system, a neglect noted by Buggeln. What we do know is that overpopulation of the main camps was a factor in the proliferation of sub-camps. Sub-camps were under the direct orders of Oswald Pohl who delegated further responsibilities to individual camps that in turn shared the duties between the three agencies that ran the camp—its administrative office, the branch that was responsible for food and clothing services and the medical department. Each sub-camp had its own commandant who was chosen from the main camp. Guards at the sub-camps were hired directly by the group or company in charge—for example, airfields were guarded by Luftwaffe members, shipyards by marine troops, etc. Those in charge of hiring workers were responsible for their food and lodgings.[75] This would account for a certain level of disparity regarding prisoner treatment that is expressed in both oral and written testimonies. Some prisoners were better treated than others, especially in agricultural work where there was at least adequate food provided by some farmers. The behavior of female SS guards toward women prisoners was a factor. Female guards were in high demand in the autumn of 1944 to cope with the growing number of female detainees.[76]

One common complaint sent to SS Willy Knott who was responsible for the Clothing Division was the lack of warm clothing and footwear. Jews were mostly employed in either transportation or unskilled jobs in industry—six sub-camps were on Luftwaffe airfields, with headquarters in Königsberg. Three others were organized around the state rail system in Stolp/Słupsk, Bromberg/Bydgoszcz, and in Rusocin/Russoschin near Praust. Two sub-camps became notorious for their maltreatment of prisoners—both of them under the Todt Organization that was building fortifications in Thorn and Elbing. The inmates of another camp—in Brusy/Bruss—worked on a training ground for the SS. Twenty-three new sub-camps were opened in the second half of 1944 that housed 30,000 inmates. Among these new camps were the following: Pölitz, opened in June with 2,800 male prisoners, and Praust-Kochstedt in July with 800 women working on a military installation.[77] The arrival of the latter group in Stutthof is described by Stasys Yla:

> The large barracks to the north were occupied in June 1944, when more than 3,000 Jewish women were brought in from Auschwitz. Most of them were of Hungarian or Greek extraction. Their heads cropped, their bodies wrapped in rags, these haggard and utterly exhausted silhouettes filed past the windows of our barracks in a seemingly-endless process. Never before had we seen so much misery all at once. We noticed, too, that the majority were young—many just barely out of their teens. Really old women were few and far between: they had apparently been unable to survive the rigors of Auschwitz.[78]

Several camps opened in August: Bromberg/Bydgoszcz in August with 1,000 women working in a dynamite factory, Königshagen with 5,500 women working on fortifications from Elbing to Strasburg, Königsberg with 500 male prisoners working on railway cars, Brusy/Bruss with 500 female prisoners working on an SS military site, Botten with 5,000 women working on fortifications from Thorn to Strasburg, Stolp/Słupsk with 650 men and women working on railway car repairs, and Danzig shipyards with 805 men building submarines. In September, another workplace was established in the Danzig shipyards in Schichau. Half of the prisoners were Poles, the other half were Germans, Russians, Lithuanians, Latvians, and Estonians. There was also a group of fifteen to twenty former Latvian policemen who had been interned in Stutthof as deserters from the SS and as criminals.[79] The first two camp directors were from Danzig—Willy Redder and Friedrich Walter. According to the SS files, Redder was a former carpenter, was *gottgläubig*, while Friedrich Walter—the second camp director of Schichau—was a member of the Death's Head, is listed as *Reichsdeutsch*, and as having worked at Lebensborn.[80] He, too, was *gottgläubig*.

In September, 300 men were sent to Bromberg/Bydgoszcz to work on the unloading dock at Bromberg-East Station. On the same day—September 13—300 women were sent to Rusocin/Russoschin to repair railway tracks as well as 2,000 men to Elbing. In addition to these camps, there was another complex of five camps that opened up around Königsberg in late September, with 6,000 prisoners both men and women.[81] There were also sub-camps in East Prussia—at Libau with 330 women working on fortifications and in other camps near Königsberg—Seerappen with 1,200 prisoners who worked at the Luftwaffe military airfield, and in Jesau where 1,350 prisoners were working for the same industry.[82] In the next chapter we will see that these far-flung sub-camps all had to be evacuated as the Soviet army approached.

A group of 500 Hungarian women from one of the first transports from Auschwitz was initially sent to the Praust-Kochstedt airfield to do construction and clean-up work. They were replaced a month later with different women who in turn were replaced by a third group in August that was fewer in number—300. The last group that was sent there was made up of mostly German or at least German-speaking women, among them Helen Lewis from Czechoslovakia whose memoir we will draw from later in the chapter. When the harsh weather replaced intense summer heat, the need for warmer clothing and clogs became the most urgent request to the home camp—600 pairs of clogs, for example, were dispatched with other items of clothing on November 15.[83] Until the end of the year, women were moved around from one sub-camp to another.

The Todt Organization worked closely with the camp authorities, drawing upon the human resources that were needed in construction and fortification projects, for example, in the sub-camp at Gurske which was under the supervision of Labor Unit Weichsel. It was in operation for a brief period at the end of 1944 until the turn of the year, employing Jewish women to build fortifications. For four months, beginning in September, the Todt Organization was in charge of similar construction work in the sub-camp at Guttau, a village west of Strasburg-Brodnika where 1,000 to 1,200 Jewish women worked on fortifications along the river Drwęca. These women—from many different countries—were housed initially in tents, then in unheated wooden barracks where they slept on straw on the floor. One such building was set aside for women with typhus where, in the absence of medical intervention, they were left to die. Food consisted of warm water for breakfast, a slice of bread for lunch and soup made from unpeeled potatoes for supper. Orski provides the names of the SS men whose treatment of the women he describes simply as "extremely brutal." In the four-month period around 170 to 200 prisoners died, including 5 to 6 infants who were born in the camp. They were buried in a meadow near the camp.[84]

Written Testimonies

Jeanette Wolff's memoir provides firsthand information about the differences that existed between the main camp and the filial camps and the degree to which treatment depended on the guards and commandant. She writes about setting off from the main camp under the supervision of seventy-two Lithuanian SS men and an SS Sergeant/*Oberscharführer*. They went by train to Marienburg in reasonable comfort—each one had seat—and then by foot to a tent camp in the woods where women were lodged sixty to a tent. A kitchen was set up outdoors with a huge cauldron where the women were able to make soup. Wolff describes their time there as tolerable, even though the Lithuanian guard told them he had waded up to his hips in Jewish blood in Kovno and they had better be on their guard with him.[85] She also writes that German Wehrmacht soldiers came to this camp and conversed freely with the women, scolded the Lithuanian guards for their maltreatment of the women and expressed disgust when they learned about what the women had endured; the German population certainly knew nothing about this, they said. Their next stop, after a ten-hour march was a camp called Schlüsselmühle, which once was used exclusively as a Russian prisoner of war camp but now shared its space with the Stutthof prisoners, separated by barbed wire. German Wehrmacht soldiers also came here to recuperate. Two days later, they set off again, this time for a camp in the woods called Korben, near Thorn. There were 1,700 women prisoners and only 2 functioning pumps to provide water for the field kitchen and the private housing of the commandant. With sixty women to each tent, they somehow managed to keep themselves clean with cold water and were able to dig a latrine 200 meters from the tents. In this way, they were able to keep lice at bay. Wolff claims that this camp had the highest rate of working women among the sub-camps. Yet, they were going to work with dysentery and all sorts of serious physical illnesses that were exacerbated by the onset of winter and greater hardships—frozen potatoes and raw vegetables. There were 1,700 women, of whom 1,500 were Hungarian. The others were from Poland, Lithuania and only thirty-six from Germany. The Hungarians were in the worst physical condition, were covered with lice and after weeks of dysentery, some forty women died. Despite the arrival of warm clothes from Stutthof, the death rate did not abate (four or five died daily) and the victims were buried in the camp naked, because the home office refused to allow them a covering.[86] Wolff's memoir stands out from others in its predominantly positive representation of Germans, particularly the members of the Wehrmacht who spoke freely and with civility to her as a German Jew. She paints a very negative picture of both the Lithuanian SS guards and the Lithuanian female prisoners, accusing them of receiving preferential treatment in food and implying that they slept with the guards. As in the testimonies by other survivors, she mentions drunkenness as causing additional hardship. She writes about the guards, including the commandant, returning to the camp at four in the morning after a night out with other SS men and causing havoc in the camp.

Jeanette Wolff's memoir, published in the early eighties in Germany, recounts the journey by sea from Kaiserwald to Danzig in the summer of 1944, in sealed barges that were normally used to transport cement or stones or coal. Despite the suffocating heat suffered by the women, the German women on board derived some hope when they first caught sight of the orderly, clean houses in and around Danzig; perhaps this was signaling a good omen for the camp where they were now heading. They reasoned that they were in Germany again and surely no atrocities would be allowed in a camp that was so near a German population. The reality that awaited them in Block 18 and 18a told a different story, one that is repeated in testimonies about Stutthof: 900

Jewish women were shoved into barracks designed for 250. Even if four shared one mattress, there would never have been enough room. So, most of them were lying on the bare ground, trodden on, screamed at by three block overseers, who disliked the German women, whipped by a German prisoner called Max Mosulf, especially when it was roll call and they all had to push their way to the open square at four in the morning.[87] Wolff's story exemplifies the anguish already endured before 1944 at the hands of the Nazis—the loss of two children in the camps, one in Ravensbrück and one in Kaiserwald. On the second day, Wolff volunteered for night duty, having deduced that it was impossible to sleep anyway. She was one of several Socialist women who had already formed close bonds and if she survived, she vowed to herself that she would see as much as she could in order to tell the world about "the brutality and bestiality that ruled in Nazi Germany."[88] Wolff's memoir also adds to the findings of scholars like Rochelle Saidel and Sonja Hedgepeth on sexual exploitation and maltreatment of women in the camps.[89] She gives specific examples, including names of SS men who made nocturnal visits to the women's barracks and threatened both the women they visited and the guards on duty. The threats were given by a guard nicknamed "the Hangman of Stutthof"—Max M (presumably Max Mosulf).

The experiences of Erna Valk in Stutthof and a sub-camp near Elbing are narrated (in German) in her memoir "Riga Ghetto and Stutthof Concentration Camp." She and her husband arrived in August 1944 from Riga, where the commandant told them that they would look back at Riga as a paradise once they experienced Stutthof. Her memoir does not contradict his bleak assessment. After a three-day journey on a troop ship, they arrived in Danzig where they were herded together onto barges and sent to Stutthof which she introduces with the by-now familiar words—"Es was die Hölle"—"It was hell."[90] What follows illustrates how hellish it was. For five weeks, they received minimal portions of inedible food, endured roll calls from dawn to dusk, and slept in groups of four in a lice-infested bed. To that list she adds typhus, dysentery, gaping wounds, and the growing daily death rate among the women, who were beaten to a pulp by the SS women.[91] Valk's experiences at the next level of her imprisonment include working on railway lines in Bromberg/Bydgoszcz, loading and unloading basalt onto train cars, all under the eye of guards equipped with leather belts and revolvers. On Sundays they built trenches. "It was torturous." Yet she compares it favorably to the treatment received in Bromberg East by the railway Inspector Ballhorn (presumably a civilian) who beat them to the point of *revierfähig* (suitable for hospitalization).[92]

During Valk's time in the sub-camp, two Polish women gave birth—in one case, she does not say what became of the mother and baby, but she does inform us of the fate of the other woman—she was sent back to Stutthof to be gassed. Each evening the prisoners returned to the main camp, hungry, exhausted and, if it rained, they slept in their wet clothes which were still damp when they set off again the next morning. And, if it snowed during the night, they had to get up and shovel snow from the rail tracks in the camp. Valk had the good fortune to be put in charge of the hut where the SS and soldiers retreated to warm themselves. She received extra bread and a warm place to work, away from the brutally cold train tracks. She writes that if soldiers threw bread to the prisoners, the SS women were swift to steal it, or trample it. She adds that they also whipped them. The SS guard, Gerda Hesper told them each day: "You will have to work till you croak."[93] Though Valk does not mention the role that her German identity played in her relatively good fortune, brief as it was, it is indeed feasible to conclude that the ability to speak German was an advantage in the camps. We will return to her story of the evacuation of the sub-camps in the next chapter.

Helen Lewis, née Katz, was born in Czechoslovakia, married in 1938, and in 1942, together with her husband Paul was deported to Theresienstadt and then to Auschwitz where they were separated. She composed her memoir *A Time to Speak* in Belfast, Northern Ireland in 1992.[94] She writes:

> At first sight, Stutthof looked to be an improvement on Auschwitz. The nearby Baltic Sea freshened the air, and lent a strange transparency that softened the outlines of the ugly buildings. We had enough room to stretch out at night, but there were no bunks and very few blankets. Accustomed as we were to SS guards everywhere, we were bewildered that they were only to be seen at roll calls. We were, in fact, left more or less to ourselves, with a minimum of food and water, appalling sanitation, and no idea of what was to happen to us. We sat and lay around all day, waiting, not knowing for what, becoming more and more depressed: we had survived Auschwitz, and now in this place we were doomed to die, lost and forgotten, of sheer neglect.[95]

It was August 1944 and that was her first impression of the new camp. Shortly thereafter, Lewis and other prisoners were marched out, pushed onto a train, and sent to the satellite camp of Stutthof called Kochstedt. At the first roll call the next day, Emma, the female SS head guard told them what they were dealing with. She boasted that she had been instrumental in the extermination of the Jewish children from the Riga ghetto. There were 300 newcomers who had previously been in Theresienstadt before they were sent to the so-called family camp in Birkenau. They were from Czechoslovakia, Germany, and Austria and shared a relatively similar background and outlook. The 500 prisoners had arrived some weeks earlier and came from Poland, the Baltic States, as well as Hungary and Romania. They all spoke their native languages but preferred to talk to each other in Yiddish, a language which many in the group didn't understand. These women resented the lack of religious ardor among the other Jewish women, who had kept their hair and did not have the shaved skulls like the others. They referred to them as the ones with hair—"*die Haarigen*"—and it was a long time before these women would call the newcomers by their names.[96]

Lewis provides a detailed account of their workday that was very much shaped by the guard in attendance, whether male or female. Some guards ignored them as they leaned on their spades or furtively grabbed a turnip to eat.

> On good days our guard would leave us more or less alone, so long as we carried out the day's basic assignment. We were allowed to talk, and sometimes could even stop and lean on our spades for a moment's rest. The guard himself might chat to the civilian foreman, smoke a cigarette or even glance at a newspaper, and pretend not to see if one of us dashed into the next field to grab a turnip.

Others denied them any respite and "[a]t the end of these days we returned to the camp limping from exhaustion." The third category she describes as "committed sadists" who stole the numbers on their clothing and then threatened them with a beating at the camp or the gas chamber.[97]

She writes about what happened one day when

> a very young girl broke down suddenly and leaning on her spade, cried helplessly. A German army officer, who was just riding past on his bicycle, stopped and asked why she was crying so bitterly. She said something; he replied, and we noticed with surprise, from the corners of our eyes, that some kind of conversation was developing. Carefully we drew nearer, while our SS guard glared at the scene from a distance. We heard the girl telling the officer that she had lost all her family, that she was alone in the world and that she would soon die here, far away from her home, which was in Romania.[98]

The officer comforted her and told her that she should not despair because soon she would be on the way up in the wheel of life. He turned up in other places, ignored the SS guard, and spoke for a while to the prisoners in simple words that were meant to give them courage and raise their hopes. It turned out that this man was from a small village in Bohemia at the foot of the mountains, in a place called Trautenau.

There was also another prisoner in the camp who came from there and he expressed the desire to meet her. Lewis writes: "That was the last time anybody ever saw him. He disappeared as mysteriously as he had arrived, but I shall always remember the voice of humanity that reached out to us, from, of all places, Trautenau-Trutnov."[99]

Lewis herself was helped by a young guard, a woman from Danzig who had expected to get an office job but instead was sent to a training center run by the SS to be indoctrinated for her future job as a concentration camp guard. She was very afraid of Emma and of the men who were making passes at her and threatening her when she did not respond. One day she slipped a little bottle into Lewis's hand and whispered, "'This is against dysentery. I told the doctor I needed it for myself.' For a moment our eyes met and she smiled."[100] Lewis also relates about an SS man, a German who had been a teacher before the war who kept part of his evening meal to give it next day to some starving prisoner, making sure that someone different received it each time. "He always made sure it went to somebody different each day and always dispatched it through the air, as if to say, it is not from me, it is from up there. He did not like to be thanked, the gratitude in our eyes was enough."[101]

Lewis had been trained as a ballet dancer in Prague and to her great amazement was able to help with the Christmas program that was being rehearsed with music, singing, and dancing, to be performed for the whole camp. They were performing Copélia and Lewis choreographed the performance and danced herself, though exhausted and near collapse from sleep deprivation. With swollen feet, she danced in front of Emma herself—the *Aufseherin*—and SS men from nearby sub-camps. Even the prisoners were allowed to come, although they were not offered the tasty goulash that was given to the dancers. She writes: "But the marvellous taste and smell were spoiled when I saw the hungry, begging eyes of the 'non-artists', who silently watched us eating."[102]

Like Lewis, some of the other Jewish prisoners belonged to the intelligentsia of Western Europe and of the great cities of Eastern Europe. Dębski points out that

> Often they had only a little contact with other Jews, did not know the Jewish traditions and more often than not were nonbelievers. They considered themselves primarily French, Italians and so on. They find their Jewish identity when they realized that in the eyes of the Nazis, they were Jews and only Jews, and when they saw the suffering of the Jewish people.[103]

Some groups of Jews had a negative opinion of other groups. Sara Nomberg-Prztyk, a Jewish woman from Poland, describes the German Jews with some bitterness:

> The Jewish women from Germany behaved in such a way as to keep themselves separated from the rest of the prisoners. "How did we get here with this rabble from the East?" said their offended expressions. "After all, we are from Germany." Their heads were shaven, just like ours, and they were dressed like clowns, the same as we were, but they still imagined that the Germans would eventually remove them from the Jewish block and that the theory of Herrenvolk would serve to elevate them above the Jews from other countries ... They probably subscribed to the German theory, "Germany above everything."[104]

Aldo Coradello was the Italian Vice-Consul in Danzig from 1937 to 1943 when he was dismissed from his post for his anti-Fascist resistance and sent to Stutthof. His testimony at the postwar trials about his time in Stutthof from July 12, 1944, until January 25, 1945, was presented in written form. Part of this narrative includes an account of the gassing of Jewish women from Block Two who were unfit to work. (Around 14,000 belonged in this category.) Herding them to the gas chamber in groups of sixty to seventy, the SS men told the women that they were heading for a school building near the camp that was being used as a hospital where they would recover. Strengthened by the illusion of hope, the women left the inner portion of the camp. Their destination was the gas chamber where, Coradello writes, there was sometimes not enough gas to kill them immediately and the German *Berufsverbrecher*, under the influence of alcohol provided by their protector Chemnitz, killed them with an ax. Gassings, he adds, took the lives of more than 400 women and stopped abruptly in November.[105]

Coradello's testimony includes this description of Russian POWs. One day in August 1944, he saw a group of fifty to sixty standing in front of the delousing station. Most of them were missing a limb—an arm or a leg or were blind. But one thing they had in common—all were emaciated from hunger and all were in rags and were shoeless. They looked even worse than the so-called camp cripples. Prisoners who were old-timers in the camp informed Coradello that most of these prisoners had come from the POW camps in Hammerstein. It had been a three-day journey during which they had slept outdoors and lived on leftovers from other prisoners. During the eight-hour registration period in sweltering heat, Coradello overheard Commandant Hoppe, Meyer, and Chemnitz discuss what to do with these men and how to get rid of them—"Russian rubbish," Chemnitz called them, looking toward the crematorium. In the afternoon, Chemnitz and Lüdtke approached the Russians and informed them that they were going to a convalescence home where they would certainly feel better. They responded positively—they finally were being treated humanely as was appropriate for POWs who were also invalids. "They tried to wash themselves in order to look decent with what was left of the water." Coradello then shares this unbearably poignant memory:

> I shall never forget how one of them tried with a shard of glass to shave another man who had lost his hands. They had neither soap nor brush nor shaving blade. I watched them prepare themselves to go to the convalescence home, distressed and agitated. They indeed were transported but not through the main gate ... For us who were veteran prisoners it was clear that those who had been transported would be cruelly murdered in a few hours.[106]

Oral Histories

Among the thousands of oral histories recorded by the Shoah Foundation—over 52,000—Stutthof is well represented, no doubt because the camp had become in mid-1944 a kind of transit camp for many prisoners.[107] If they survived Stutthof and subsequent transports to hard labor in the Greater Reich and if they survived the main evacuation of the camp in January 1945—that will be dealt with in the next chapter—then their story of survival will include the time, no matter how brief, they spent in Stutthof. Thousands of Jewish men and women have chosen to speak of it on video testimony in declarative, factual statements that rarely contradict other such statements and conspire to paint a collective story of unremitting misery, whether their starting point was in Poland, Russia, Latvia, or other Baltic states. Their statements are often punctuated by "before the Germans came." Our focus will remain on their experiences in 1944.

Rachel Abramowitz's testimony resonates with the memoir of Lewis at certain junctures.[108] She had been sent to the sub-camp Praust-Kochstedt. (Praust was, in fact, the first camp exclusively for Jewish women and was opened on July 7 under the command of SS man Otto Berger and initially seven men from the Wehrmacht who had been wounded in service.) In September, 300 Jewish women prisoners joined them from Auschwitz who had been deported from the so-called Theresienstadt "family camp."[109] The end was in sight, a fact, she claims, that changed the behavior of the female guard who began to show some pity. But what she remembers most of all was the half-hour walk to work, the meager portions of food, the presence of French political prisoners who received food packages, the three-tiered bunks, the beatings- including her own—with the buckle end of a belt, the danger of declaring oneself too sick to work. Those who did so were never seen again. She recalls how dangerous it was to steal, citing the example of a girl who was shot for stealing a potato. In this unmitigated picture of cruelty, she inserts the memory of a German guard who gave her a sandwich every day. The identity of this guard was never disclosed but he probably is the same man described in Lewis's memoir. The anonymous figure deserves to be acknowledged, and such figures make unexpected and welcome appearances in Holocaust memoirs. Neither he nor any other lone messenger of mercy do not change a landscape that is overwhelmingly brutal and bleak.

Maja Abramowitch's pre-Stutthof experiences suggest a life in Dvinsk, Latvia of social privilege, cultural refinements, loving parents who were both educated in France and Germany respectively. Her childhood included music and ballet lessons, the comfort of a loving nanny and a summer home on a lake. Abramowitch identifies the day in 1940 when this life of comfort and luxury abruptly ended, when "within an hour the city was occupied and the Russian army established nationalization."[110] Her testimony includes the abrupt shift in the war, when on June 22, 1941, a third of their town (which was near the Russian border) was burned when the Germans occupied it. From that point on, her testimony is about loss, beginning with her father who was shot, along with many others. She adds that local Latvians helped the Germans round them up and put them in a fortress—she claims there were approximately 32,000 of them—where they stayed till the adjoining ghetto of Duagavils was liquidated. Their next destination before being shipped to Stutthof was Kaiserwald where they were guarded by *Berufsverbrecher*. Her brief description of Stutthof is captured in "a terrible place ... Dante's inferno ... not a blade of grass."[111] She remembers too the mounds of shoes, and spectacles, prisoners hanging around in a weakened state waiting on the parade ground for the next roll call—the notorious *Appell*—three sharing an upper or lower bunk, prisoners committing suicide on the electric fence. But one anecdote stands out in this testimony. It was the day when they examined the women for a work detail that would take them to one of the sub-camps and presumably was seen as a lifesaver by the women. A table had been set up in an empty hall for the SS who examined the naked women. She and her mother had separated for safety's sake, but in the selection process the daughter was rejected. Somehow, she managed to hide under a bunk in the adjoining room and was safely reunited with her mother. Together they ended up in Brusy/Bruss, working on an airstrip, sleeping at night alongside fourteen others. She states in the same monotone voice, "It was summer and still very hot ... You didn't feel. Nobody cared."

Paula Borensztein's testimony shares some of the tender family memories noted above but not the social privileges.[112] She was born the youngest of three children in Vilna where they spoke Yiddish and occasionally her father spoke Russian—he came from Odessa. What marks this oral testimony is the open expression of emotion. Several events are narrated through her tears and in the end, she makes an impassioned appeal, to which I have referred in the Introduction as a motivating factor in my research. The word "naked" recurs when she describes Kaiserwald where she lost three teeth in a beating. Her testimony embodies the worst practices of the camps—naked women being shaved, beatings, children exterminated, hangings in the night, SS men with cigars dangling from their lips. She remembers the transport that took them by truck to Magdeburg away from Stutthof after being selected. Her testimony is not only a compelling entreaty to survivors but to those of us who are facilitating the telling.

Among the oral testimonies are those of Jehovah's Witness prisoners in Stutthof. Their presence was numerically not as strong as in other camps like Dachau or

Sachsenhausen, and those who were incarcerated tended to be from local communities in Pomerania.[113] Cornelia Gawior fits this profile though she was, in fact, born in France and her testimony is marked by a discernible French accent.[114] Her mother left France in 1939 with her children for Pomerania, where they worked on the farm of their paternal grandparents and attended German school, until they were sent to Stutthof (the date is not given) where they stayed until liberation. The information she provides adds some firsthand details of the religious practices of this group in the camp. They appear to have actively proselytized (corroborated by the narrative of Sruoga[115]) and according to Gawior, made some converts among the Latvians. They were permitted to hold religious services but without communion emblems. Gawior makes no claims that they were persecuted and in fact says they were treated better than other prisoners. In a similar way to Piotr K, she also speaks openly about the maltreatment of other prisoners by the SS—prisoners were stripped, then enclosed in one of the rooms in the crematorium where they were shut in and the Zyklon gas was inserted through a hole. She speaks of the SS guards pushing corpses through the gates where there were already ashes and bones.[116]

It is impossible to read the narratives and listen to the testimonies of survivors of the larger Stutthof complex without wondering about the response of local people. After all, these groups of prisoners were being driven by guards with whips in full view, across an area that spread to the east and west of Danzig, as well as within the city itself, including its shipyards. No other camp had such a widely spread network of satellite sites. When asked how much they were aware of the presence of prisoners, many Germans after the war replied they knew little or nothing. My point is not to question the veracity of the response of the greater population (of what was to become West Germany) but rather to show that, because of the proliferation of Stutthof sub-camps, it would have been impossible for those around Danzig to be unaware of the presence of Stutthof prisoners. If it is true, as Buggeln asserts, that their contribution to the German war was insignificant then one can conclude that prisoners were working for the exclusive economic benefit of Danzig and its surrounding area.

What Did Local People Know?

The German writer Walter Kempowski posed this question and presented his findings with minimal commentary in *Haben Sie davon gewußt?*[117] "Did you know about it?" (The "it" in question is, of course, the presence of the camps and their inmates.) In the chapter that focuses on 1944 entitled "Als wir das sahen, glaubten wir nicht mehr an den Endsieg" ("When we saw that, we no longer believed in the final victory"), Kempowski includes the observation of a woman born in 1928, who describes herself as a housewife and lived in Thorn in 1944. Indeed, yes, concentration camps were known to her as a child. She refers to the prisoners simply as "they." They lived in tents and in miserable huts, all cramped together. And she recalls the threat of being sent to the camp if they didn't belong to the BDM/*Bund Deutscher Mädel*—the League of German Girls.[118] They were guarded by what she calls "a little peasant woman with a gun around her neck." Then she recalls that as children (at sixteen, she could hardly be called a child) they would ask their parents why "they" didn't run away. She provides her own answer: "The Poles were so antisemitic that the people would never have received any food or shelter if they had fled."[119] While this may have been true, she does not offer any suggestion of what local Germans—her own family, for example, might have done, and if they harbored antisemitic feelings. Most of those interviewed by Kempowski lived at the time (1944) in the greater Reich but he does include one other interview that relates to Danzig in 1944.

The interviewee in this case is simply called "Woman" and her answer to the same question is somewhat fuller than the one from the woman in Thorn:

> I have only one recollection and actually just one. I was in Danzig, working in the office of a construction company in the summer of 1944. In the morning, when I came through the gate of the building, I would see women from Stutthof or Struthof[120] being driven—in the truest sense of the word—to work. (It was a dockyard or something like that.) They were walking three to a row, maybe a hundred or a hundred and fifty of them, accompanied by SS women in blue uniforms and boots, with a whip in their hand. And they were driving these pitiful women forward. They didn't use their whips. The women were so beaten down they didn't need to use them. You thought to yourself—that's the leftovers from the occupied lands. And we, too, had to work. Apart from sympathy, we didn't feel anything more than that. I was 23 years of age at the time.[121]

This is how Tighe describes similar groups:

> Prisoners from Stutthof in unmistakable camp garb—blue and white striped pajamas—and wooden clogs was by 1944 a sight that the population of Danzig could not ignore. These groups were made up of 70 to 1600 and they worked in the shipyards and in the brick factory at Langfuhr. In 1944 to '45 there were at any time over 2,400 Stutthof prisoners working on details within the city; there were 25,000 other Stutthof prisoners located at sixty sub camps and work sites around Danzig and Pomerania, and by that time the security services did very little to hide or disguise them.[122]

Wachsmann refers to the numbed response to such sights as "forced collectivism."[123] He also cites from Kempowski the encounter described above, but does not comment on the reference to Germans also having to work. This is too important to ignore since it was clearly not a casual, offhand comment but expresses what became a critical part of the postwar discourse in the Federal Republic, namely that "we Germans" also suffered which is essentially the message that Grass presents in *Crabwalk*. Among the prisoners working in the shipyards in Danzig-Schichau on building submarines was Joseph Katz, born in Lübeck in 1918. He arrived in Stutthof from Riga in October 1944 and was evacuated in January 1945. He describes being marched through the streets of Danzig. His depiction presents a nuanced view of the reactions of local Danzigers:

Our route takes us by old patrician houses and stately churches to the Danzig railway station. People look at us in astonishment, some even with sympathy but not a bad word is heard, unlike what we had heard before in Germany. I have the sense that people became very serious when they saw us, that they stopped for a moment in their tracks, shook their heads and walked on, recognizing that nothing good was going on.[124]

Katz writes too about the unspoken agreement among all the prisoners—he cites Latvians, Russians, French, Poles, Ukrainians and Serbians, and the Jews—to do as little work as possible.[125]

Ethnic Germans Join the Local Guards

Within the camp system, thousands of new guards were needed in 1944 as many of the former guards were sent to the frontlines.[126] As is apparent in Lewis's memoir, the new guards in Stutthof included men and women who occasionally showed some compassion, but these acts of humanity are presented as exceptions and at times with reference to the motives behind them—that they themselves might soon need mercy from the liberators. The participation of female guards in the camps is a subject that is of more recent research. Barbara Distel's overview of the role of women in the camps provides detailed analysis of their job description and their indoctrination, particularly in treating the prisoners with brutality, implemented with whips, sticks and a gun. In fact, brutal behavior was rewarded and used as an incentive for promotion. In the final months, educational courses were offered in Flossenbürg, Stutthof, and Groß-Rosen for female guards.[127]

The postwar trials of Latvian SS men provide some information about their recruitment. Interrogated by the Soviets in a military tribunal March 14–15, 1945, Alexandr Kruklis, when asked about his service, stated that he had been enlisted in the German army on June 25, 1944, and was sent to Stutthof on January 25, 1945, with the rank of Sergeant/*Unterscharführer*. He was given a pistol parabellum as a weapon and was responsible for supervising the prisoners—presumably as a kapo. He also claims to have been a mounted guard.[128] He lists the ethnicities of other SS men—Romanians, Czechs, Russians, and Ukrainians. The Latvians lived in a separate barrack and like the others just mentioned, called their unit "*rota*"—a military formation. All of these guards had received special training at the SS training facility at Trawniki.[129] He names a fellow-Latvian, Arkady Andreyev from Vilianski who, he claims, served as a guard in Stutthof from 1943 till October 1944. Given that Trawniki was liberated by the Soviets in July 1944, it is unlikely that Kruklis himself was trained there, though he does show knowledge of how recruits were trained. Although the ultimate defeat of the Nazis was becoming more likely, particularly as the advance of the Soviets within East Prussia confirmed its imminent arrival, many of the personnel at Stutthof did not believe they were already doomed and remained unshaken in their Führer and the ideology that had inspired them thus far. We will see this even when the camp was evacuated. Some of the local SS men introduced in the previous chapter were still functioning as human instruments of terror and in fact, their zeal had grown, fueled as much by alcohol (which seems to have increased) as by belief in the rightness of their cause. Teodor Meyer, according to Dunin-Wąsowicz, was an alcoholic who rode his motorcycle when drunk and crashed on one occasion into a tree, causing him to limp. When sober, he pretended to be a just and fair man who allowed the prisoners to speak their mind, but he still beat them after these statements of fairness.[130] The man directly under Meyer, Ernst Sette is portrayed by Dunin-Wąsowicz as stupid and naive but not as cruel as Meyer who, he claims, detested him. Sette liked to point out to the prisoners how easy their life was—a roof over their heads, food and clothing, etc. At times, he showed pity toward new arrivals who were mothers with small children and assigned to them better quarters. The main difference in the composition of the camp guards in 1944 is that they were joined by many more ethnic Germans from lands subjugated by the Nazis and many of them outdid the local SS in their cruelty and violence toward the prisoners.

The ethnic Germans were often used as sentries to protect the camp day and night. They patrolled the camp precincts, escorted prisoners to and from work outside the camp, and were watchmen on the towers during the night. Several of the SS men listed by Dunin-Wąsowicz had been in the camp from the beginning and convey in their attitudes and behavior the swagger and confidence of old timers—men like Willi Knoth who is described by Dunin-Wąsowicz as "a brute, primitive and cruel."[131] In the Stutthof trials of 1946–47, the names of several kapos who were accused of extreme maltreatment of the prisoners in Stutthof are listed with their respective verdicts. Wacław Kozłowski was tried in the first group and was executed on July 4, 1946. What is striking is that several of the kapos whose names recur in sources like *Forest of the Gods* are not on that final list. Yet the depiction of their cruelty and sadism is as prominent in several memoirs as for those who were executed. Grabowska-Chałka names them with the following brief but damning commentary:

> Among those most bestial towards the inmates were SS-men Erich Gust, Otto Neubauer, Kurt Mathesius, Franz Mielenz, Teodor Meyer, Franz Christoffel, Otto Haupt, Paul Schwitkowski-Lutz, Fritz Peters, Alfred Driemel, Ewald Foth, and Bernard Lüdtke; female supervisor Anna Kopp; trusties Fritz Selonke, Josef Pabst, Wacław Kozłowski, Arno Lehmann, Karl Kliefoth, Max Musolf, Alfred Hoelzer, Emil Bilkowski and many others. Block trusty Kazimiera Jackowska and her deputy Walentyna Narewska were infamous in the Women's Camp.[132]

A survivor of Anna Kopp's brutality later testified: "[Kopp] beat me over the head something terrible. I got a nervous attack then. … Through that great fear I regained consciousness and slowly returned to health. But when I returned home, for a long time, I would jump up in my sleep and scream 'Herr Doktor ich bin gesund' (Doctor, I am healthy)."[133]

Tech. Sergeant/*Oberscharführer* Ewald Foth was executed after the second trial in October 28, 1948, for his crimes in Stutthof as head of the Jewish camp. A local farmer before Stutthof, he rose through the ranks in Stutthof, having led the Forest

Unit earlier, before being named head of the Jewish camp. His file indicates he had a wife named Lucia, an intermediate education and was a Lutheran. Dunin-Wąsowicz calls him "a blood-stained sadist and murderer."[134] Eugenia Kocówna describes the conditions in the block that he was responsible for:

> In Block 23 there were about 1,200 people. There were no beds. In the middle there were two boards that designated a passage. During the day we were seated in rows, five of us in each row, close to one another. After evening roll-call, straw mattresses were rolled out on to the floor. Four women slept on each mattress, with one blanket per mattress. Nights were especially exhausting because of constant fights for sleeping space. Everyone waited anxiously for morning to come.[135]

Their greater fight was to survive Stutthof but according to Dunin-Wąsowicz, it was Foth who decided who was going to live or die and no appeal was permitted after his decision was made. The examples that Dunin-Wąsowicz gives of Foth's sadism are the roll calls that lasted for many hours, his selection of the ill and weak to die, a decision based on the condition of their legs. His worst act of sadism (mentioned in several memoirs) was to fool selected women into thinking they were leaving the camp by train for a sub-camp when they were, in fact, in the compartment of a train that was going to be hooked up to the gas chamber and filled with Zyklon B gas.

> Groups of 60–70 women, mostly Jewish got into the wagons; the train took them one or two stations from Stutthof and then brought them straight to the crematorium. During the trip wagons were filled with gas, and by the time the "train" arrived at the crematorium all the women were dead. The train made these trips twice a day. All of this was witnessed by men prisoners in their camp who stood watching helplessly.[136]

Foth's accomplice in these matters was Corporal/*Oberscharführer* Arno Chemnitz, member of the Party since 1923 who instilled great fear in the prisoners because of his sadism. His opinion was valued even by the Commandant. His death in the spring of 1945 as the result of typhus has not been verified.[137] Sruoga describes Chemnitz as the second most important figure in the camp who supervised all the camp's activities. A hotel porter in civilian life, he is described by Sruoga as a "morose and stubborn bandit" who beat prisoners with a whip of wires covered with rubber, or a bludgeon, and substituted for Meyer in the cranial shootings. He was known in the camp for his visits to local Stutthof widows whom he supplied with substantial gifts. "For him, camp supplies were inexhaustible."[138] The behavior of SS men like Chemnitz and Meyer, veterans of the camp, was not modified by the possibility of an allied victory. Sruoga tells of an encounter between a Polish prisoner and Chemnitz in which he asked the prisoner if the English [sic] were going to win the war. The initial response on Chemnitz's part was his usual taciturn silence, but suddenly he leapt up and in Sruoga's words, "blasted the Pole across his cheek with his fist."[139]

Postwar Fate of Stutthof's Guards and Other Personnel

Meyer's prison memoir denies any maltreatment of the thousands of Jewish women who arrived in the summer of 1944. They had warned "the gentlemen in Berlin" that the camp was filled to capacity—the commandant had even gone in person to Berlin to convey his dismay to the same gentlemen. The answer was to send the women to work in local industries, and a representative arrived to set that up. "Yet, transports kept rolling in day and night," he laments, "and because the barracks were segregated, they had to separate husbands and wives and adolescents from their mothers." Taking money from Jews, he explains, "was a direct order from Berlin." He is aware that two or three years later, the prisoners might indeed reproach him. "But can good also be acknowledged?" He doubts that and posits that "the bad" always sticks in the memory and keeps being refreshed. Not that he blames the prisoners when they sometimes condemn, but he feels they should also acknowledge the good. Regrettably—for Meyer—no surviving prisoner of Stutthof could dredge up a single memory of the good that he had done. And the memories of the bad, just like he predicted, had not only stuck but had become more painfully fresh with the passage of time. Major/*Hauptsturmführer* Teodor Meyer was found guilty in the second of six war crimes tribunals that took place in Poland. He was executed in Gdańsk on October 28, 1948.

Marek Orski is considered among the most productive Stutthof historians and has provided a wealth of information on several ethnic groups in the camp.[141] Orski, like Dunin-Wąsowicz, names notorious block leaders and kapos, some of whom are on the list of those executed after the war, people like Jan Brajt, called "*Totenschläger*," a man known to kill a prisoner with one blow, and one of the most brutal criminals.[142] Some of these men had been imprisoned for their political activism before the war, men like Piotr Przewała, originally from Silesia, who lived in Danzig before the war where he was active in Polish organizations. He was known to be decent to the prisoners at first but then committed what Orski calls "horrible acts of cruelty against them."[143] The postwar fate of other prisoners who were former Polish resisters and dissidents is presented by Orski factually and with little commentary. It is clear that they had become as cruel and brutal as the guards who had maltreated them before they had become kapos. He makes no attempt to soften their profile.

Marian Ziełkowski, born in 1895 in Wyrzysko, was imprisoned in Stutthof in 1939 and rose in the ranks to be a camp supervisor. During his trial in Gdańsk, he testified, "It was my task to make sure that there was order in the camp and that all regulations and orders given by German authorities were followed." To ensure that these regulations were properly followed, he used a wooden bat and a rubber baton or his fist. He acknowledged that he beat prisoners and sometimes these beatings could have resulted in the death of a victim. Because of his function in the camp, he got larger food rations and better treatment by the SS. He acknowledged that he beat the prisoners on orders from above but also "for pleasure."[144] Former prisoner Jan Kostrzewa testified that Ziełkowski had access to every part of the camp. He drove prisoners all over the camp and beat them with whatever he happened to find handy. He was described as the worst killer in the camp and very eager to strictly follow orders.[145] During his trial, witnesses corroborated the charges. He died of a heart attack on August 25, 1945, while in prison. Franciszek Szopiński, a kapo in Grenzdorf, along with Jozef Reiter, Waclaw Kozlowski and Tadeusz Kopczyński, were described as the most degenerate persons and were executed July 4, 1946.[146] Kazimierz Kowalski was sentenced to three year's imprisonment for his time as a kapo, Jan Preiss was found not guilty for his activities in the Crematorium Work Unit in 1943, and later as a kapo in the sub-camp at Neufahrwasser where he worked in the sanitation division.[147] In his book on the French in Stutthof, Orski includes the testimony of French resister Jean Le Maître who was interned from July 1943 until liberated by Soviet troops on March 9, 1945. He writes of Jan Brajt, the head kapo in the infirmary as demonstrating "une cruauté révoltante"—a revolting cruelty.[148] He held Brajt responsible for the death of another Frenchman whom he refused to admit to the infirmary and who consequently died. He adds: "How many Poles and Russians didn't he kill?" He further accuses Brajt of kicking another Frenchman in the stomach who was no longer able to drag himself along. He gives two further examples of maltreatment of Frenchmen—Robert Fortin who was turned away from the infirmary and forced to go to work with an abscess on his foot and another one who was denied treatment for a broken arm.[149] Stasys Yla also writes about the maltreatment of a group of Frenchmen who in 1944—for undisclosed reasons had been sent to Stutthof—about a hundred French S.S. legionnaires. He adds, "Perhaps they had finally enough of Germany's war." They shared the fate of a group of German sailors who had mutinied and were forced to march singing sea chanties, both patriotic and obscene. Classified as serious offenders and subjected to hard labor and floggings, the majority of them, like the French legionnaires, died.[150]

At his trial in Bochum, Hoppe ascribed responsibility for the gassings to his superiors, especially to Glücks who had warned him about Hitler's order regarding "the final solution" of the Jewish question. He insisted that there had been directives to Glücks from Himmler, reminding him that Hitler's command was, if the Jewish question is not settled now, that the Jews will later kill the German people. This sentence, he claimed, had stuck in his mind and was the main reason he had carried out the command for what he called "the action of gassing" in the camp. He also pointed out that he had been put on his oath not to speak about it and that all Jewish prisoners were to be killed by December 31, 1944.[151]

Ascribing blame to superiors was a standard response in the postwar trials, and in the case of Hoppe may have contributed to a verdict that helped spare his life. Sruoga's narrative skill rises to new heights in his characterization of Hoppe. His depiction is initially factual—Hoppe was petty and obsessed with his own grandeur, but then he adds that he was only seen in the camp for solemn events like "public hangings or formal floggings performed to fulfill a punishment ordered by Berlin … From time to time he came to watch the prisoners' dress parade in the morning, when the prisoners hobbled off to work. The commandant would diligently watch all the prisoners tramp past, metamorphosed into samovars."[152] He compares Hoppe favorably to his predecessor, Max Pauly who, according to the older camp prisoners, surpassed all the other SS men in "sadism and zest for execution."[153] The women prisoners who worked in his palatial home reported that he was a normal person at home with his wife and children. Sruoga writes: "In the summer of 1944, when her husband wasn't home, the commandant's wife would give the women prisoners anything she could lay her hands on." She lamented that the prisoners would soon be free but what would become of her family?[154]

What emerges from this depiction of Hoppe (that is corroborated in other testimonials) is the portrait of a pathetically conceited man, a man with a seared conscience and devoid of self-awareness, a coward who hid behind the uniform of his superiors to justify the heinous cruelties that were the daily events of the camp he directed. Sruoga's prose—in translation—captures the pathos of the prisoners who had to "hobble off to work" under his superior gaze as they "tramped past" looking like "samovars."[155] As an SS man, however, Hoppe remained obdurately tied to the past and to the nature of the times in which he served.[156] "Everything was so different," was his argument, even to his son who tried, unsuccessfully to get him to talk about his past and assume responsibility for it. He was sentenced to nine years in prison for accessory to murder, released in 1962 and died in 1974.[157] This was the verdict despite testimonies that he had been present when prisoners were tortured with jets of hot and cold water and were injected with gasoline.[158] Karin Orth points to later letters of Hoppe that to some degree suggest that he acknowledged remorse "for the shocking fate that the Nazi state had inflicted on innocent people, and its contempt for the ethical tenets of humanity." He also disassociated himself from those who had tried to justify their actions and writes: "I also know that I have heaped upon myself heavy guilt."[159] Orth points out that he was the only commandant who at least admitted guilt. Her point is clearly not to exonerate Hoppe—she describes his earlier attempts to justify his actions as having been drawn from "the usual arsenal of apology strategies" but the fact remains that Hoppe enjoyed some years on the run with a different identity before he was arrested and brought to justice. And even then, he was released early and was able to spend his last years with his family. Based on an interview with Hoppe's son, Segev includes the depiction of Hoppe's last days when his past appeared to haunt him. He was dying at age sixty-four in a hospital in Bochum and in his delirium thought that the doctors and nurses were secret Communist agents who were going to extradite him to Poland. Just before he died, he thought his son Jörg was a secret agent of Israel and that he had come to arrest him and take him to Jerusalem to be hanged—just like Eichmann.[160] Prisoners apparently were not the only ones for whom memories became stronger.

Before we continue, what does this say about Stutthof? It is clear that the events of 1944 catapulted Stutthof into the full orbit of the concentration camps system and brought to its gates human reminders of "the Final Solution," men and especially women whose fate was sanctioned by "the gentlemen" of Berlin. These newcomers were either worked to death to kindle the rapidly dying flames of the German war effort or killed off by the method *de jour*—be it cranial shootings, phenol injections, or the gas chamber. Typhus, by contrast, may have been a more merciful death. Stutthof in 1944 was internationalized. Every catalogue refers to the many nationalities represented in the camp—as many as twenty-seven. But this was no badge of cosmopolitan honor. It is no wonder that so many survivors describe Stutthof in their memoirs as "hell"— women like Marga Griesbach who was there for seven weeks and calls those weeks "eternity." "We lived like animals and were treated worse than animals. If we had the slightest sense of self-worth when we arrived in Stutthof, we were thoroughly dehumanized when we left it."[161] Stutthof was initially considered a backwoods camp by the Nazis—good enough, of course, for unwanted local Jews and Poles—but by 1944 it had become a site for any group considered enemies of the Reich, and by the summer a place for the most unwanted group of all—Jewish women. Stutthof has now come as far as is conceivable from the fictional ground of Günter Grass.

What about Danzig?

Danzig in 1944 was still a popular destination though certainly not quiet. Cultural and social life went on with few restrictions in an atmosphere of light-heartedness. There were regattas in Danzig Bay, people still flocked to the beaches, trains were running, those who could afford it went to the Zoppot/Sopot Casino and to the Grand Hotel, and the local theater—the Danziger *Stadtstheater* and the Zoppot Civic theater were still offering plays, including *Faust* in August 1944.[162] There was an exhibition of 300 painters from Danzig-West Prussia in the Danzig Museum. Danzig was considered a safer city than most places in the Greater Reich and as noted earlier, refugees were sent there from bombarded cities. Meanwhile, Danzig continued to flourish, still enjoying its new status and according to some reports, there were no shortages or rations and very few reminders of war. In fact, Marek Wąs calls Danzig in the chapters "1939-1944, an Oasis of Peace." Gertrud Rodischewski, a Danzig citizen, whose husband was serving in the Luftwaffe remembered the war like this:

> In Gdańsk we didn't feel effects of war. We heard on the radio that we had lost some territory and that the Allies had reclaimed some territory. We lived in peace until 1944,[163] and even though there were alarms there were no bombs. Gdańsk was bombarded and destroyed in 1945. We didn't have any problems with food, we still had everything that was lacking in the Reich–butter, cream etc. We could buy everything with ration cards; and we could buy produce which was not rationed on the market. Everything was inexpensive. ... Market days were twice a week ... I remember, though, that towards the end of 1944 we'd go to the farmers in villages around Gdańsk to pick up potatoes.[164]

Rodischewski's memories are also typical of middle-class citizens of Danzig, who claim that they didn't know anything about the killings—Stutthof, they said, was just a labor camp.

Danzig at the End of the Summer of 1944

By summer's end, a warning note was being sounded in the *Danziger Vorposten*, and a new slogan was inserted—"Danger is threatening the Homeland." Thousands of German refugees were arriving in Danzig from as far away as Riga in August.[165] More and more obituaries of fallen soldiers appeared in the *Vorposten*. Previously, death notices included a rationale for their deaths—"for the Führer, the nation, the Fatherland." By fall, this formula had disappeared and though propaganda for the Nazi cause was still active, it began to take on a different tone that reflected a new reality. The August 14 edition of the *Vorposten* warned that the time for window displays was over, with the implication that the local people were living in denial. By November 1944, there were new travel restrictions, and the feeling of euphoria was disappearing as Danzig prepared for a different phase of a war that the citizens had expected to win. A short trip from downtown, there were barracks enclosed by barbed wire. Shabbily dressed prisoners crossed the city on their way to work. They were part of a prison population of several thousands, housed in fifteen labor camps, six prisons, eight smaller sub-camps, and included three and a half thousand POWs from France.[166] This prison population does not appear to include the Stutthof inmates who came each day to work in various sites of labor in Danzig, including the docklands.

Nazi ideology had glorified the German mother for her role in producing more racially pure children for the Reich. By the end of 1944, her primary place in the home as mother had shifted to that of service-provider. As more and more men were drafted into military service, their places were taken by women, especially in public transport. Danzig was no exception; in fact, Wąs claims that it was now known as "The City of Women." Thousands of children were sent to outlying villages to be cared for. All women from seventeen to fifty years of age who were childless had to work for the Reich.[167] It is no wonder that Grass placed his character Tulla Pokriefke as a conductor on the streetcar in Danzig.

Last Impressions of 1944

Balys Sruoga has given vibrant pen portraits of both prisoners and their guards that allow the reader to enter the life of the camp beyond the statistics of the filing cabinets and the orders from Oranienburg.[168] The image of prisoners hobbling off to work under Hoppe's cruel eye is a powerful evocation of the helpless under the tyranny of the powerful. Other images of 1944, poignant and discordant, remain: Helen Lewis dancing on swollen feet in the presence of her cruel guard, not permitted to share the coveted stew with fellow prisoners, Alexander von Stauffenberg reading poetry to Fey von Hassell as she lay deathly sick with typhus, Nina Weilova accidently dropping a knife into the threshing machine on a sub-camp farm and being sent back to Stutthof to face the charge of sabotage,[169] the Russian prisoner attempting to shave with a shard of glass his fellow-prisoner who had lost both arms. Yet, as vividly as these individual portraits stand out, they are at best tentative images of humanity on the dominant backdrop of 1944: rows and rows of Jewish women on a relentlessly bleak landscape of misery, staggering along to and from work, yelled at from the time they were dragged out of sleep at 4 a.m. for roll call until they fell onto a straw mattress with other skeletal women. And they were considered the fortunate ones who had been selected for work and not for death.

Writing about Holocaust denial, Dwork and van Pelt refer to the language of denial used by the Nazis while carrying out their murderous deeds. They cite as an example the speech made by Himmler in Posen in October 1943, when he wished to address "a really grave matter which was surrounded by a 'tactful silence.'" He continued, "I am referring to the evacuation of the Jews, the annihilation of the Jewish people. In our history, this is an unwritten and never-to-be-written page of glory." What he said next is essentially the justification for living out Germandom with impunity: "We have carried out this heaviest of our tasks in a spirt of love for our people. And our inward being, our soul, our character has not suffered injury from it."[170]

The excerpts from memoirs and testimonies of Jewish men and women in this chapter have shown that there is no way to be tactful or silent about their treatment by guards, or by kapos, all sanctioned by a commandant who received nine years for this maltreatment. I have chosen to include the testimonies of other prisoners, not to show that "we too suffered," but to present Stutthof as all prisoners experienced it, whether they were Polish resisters, Finnish sailors or Lithuanian intellectuals. We are not able to tell all their stories, but we have tried to tell some of them. They all experienced the camp's brutal conditions, but Jews were already marked for death in a way that other prisoners were not. Himmler referred to the "evacuation" of the Jews. That is certainly true. They were torn away from the cities and villages of Europe, and the shtetls of the very province he was speaking in—with the shameful purpose of annihilating them. Clearly, he meant "murder" when he talked about Jewish evacuation. But didn't the word "evacuation" remind him of what the Poles had suffered: disrupted lives, dispossession of homes, divestment of national identity, and death? That story is also one that must never yield to "tactful silence."

5

The Collapse of Germandom—The Winter of 1945

The Plan: "Fall Eva"

Preparations to evacuate Danzig-West Prussia were already being made in September 1944 by Gauleiter Albert Forster and code-named "Fall Eva," an initiative that was precipitated by the Soviet advance across the Bug river in July and the arrival of a stream of refugees from East Prussia. Even in the face of these realities, Forster's rival, Gauleiter Erich Koch resisted the possibility of a Russian takeover of his region—East Prussia. Other Gauleiter, notably Franz Schwede in Pomerania, had a similar response of denial. At this stage Forster, unlike Koch and Schwede may have accepted the inevitability of the Russian advance, but he did not predict how swift it would be. Evacuation plans for Danzig involved all forced laborers and those working in agriculture and thus brought Stutthof and its sub-camps into the "Fall Eva." All were to be moved as far as possible from the advancing army. There were conflicting opinions, however, at the highest level of command about what should be done with the Stutthof system inmates. Two plans were discussed—to use the training school at Lauenburg/Lębork—a plan that was rejected in Berlin and secondly, to send the inmates by ship from Danzig and Gotenhafen to Germany, either to Lübeck or to the Neuengamme camp. In the end, both routes were used. In Hoppe's later testimony, he stated that the business of evacuating Stutthof had not been clearly agreed upon, even in January 1945. It is no wonder that confusion ensued.[1]

Daily Life Deteriorates in Stutthof

Meanwhile, daily life in the camp had become even worse for its inmates, and the mortality rate grew so high—450 a day—that bodies had to be burned outside the camp. The number of inmates in the camp and sub-camps was now around 50,000—half of them in Stutthof. Beyond the daily stress-producing hardships, tension in the camp was also fueled by rumors that the SS would kill off the inmates and burn the camp to the ground, a fear that was not unjustified when the SS and camp personnel began to burn camp records belonging to the Political Department and to the camp infirmary. Another sign of an imminent departure was that in the DAW workshops they were now producing boxes to transport goods and camp items that were considered valuable.[2] At a higher level, there was a change of command after the Soviet troops reached Elbing and Marienburg on January 23 and 24, when the camp became subordinate to the local

SS and Police Commander Fritz Katzmann in Danzig. Stutthof's ties to Danzig still remained central in its evacuation.

Because the Soviet advance was so swift, there was not enough time to assemble all the inmates from the outlying sub-camps, with the result that only those inmates closest to Stutthof were able to get there by January 25, the planned departure date. Some of these filial camps were as far away as Gerdauen near Königsberg, where 1,000 prisoners had been sent from Stutthof on September 22, 1944. Guarded by forty-six men from the Luftwaffe, six regular guards, and two women guards, the prisoners were made up of 500 Jewish women from the Litzmannstadt/Łódź ghetto who worked on the airstrip. The reason that their evacuation was earlier was because the airfield where they were working lay close to the Front. Only twenty-four prisoners had to be left behind, but there were casualties in the course of their march to Stutthof and many of them were to lose their lives during the evacuation from Stutthof.[3]

Heading for Lauenburg

The first phase of the evacuation quickly showed how ill-prepared the camp personnel at every level were for an event of such massive proportions.[4] When the day finally arrived, prisoners were ordered to proceed by foot to Lauenburg/Lębork on what was to be a seven-day march, planned in such a way that each of the 11 columns would have 1,000 inmates, separated by gender, with the women escorted by 15 SS men and female SS supervisors and the men by 40 SS men carrying guns and rifles. SS Captain/*Hauptsturmführer* Reddig was in charge of the SS men. Groups of SS men with dogs also were present. The SS were told to "ruthlessly break all the escape or rebellion attempts by using firearms."[5] Only the ill and those units charged with closing the camp were to stay behind. Dr. Heinrich Plaza was in charge of health concerns, helped by SS nurses. The prisoners were given food for two days and were to be resupplied at Burggraben some twelve kilometers away. There was also some confusion as to how sick you had to be in order to stay, with the result that many unfit people departed for fear they would be killed if they stayed. Grot writes that in the three-month period after the initial evacuation on January 25 and 26, the expectation of the remaining prisoners was that the remaining SS personnel would abandon the camp and that the Soviet army would liberate them. This was not, however, the SS plan, and when the front surrounded the area of the Großer Werder, the camp administrators decided to evacuate by water. Grot provides the following statistics: 4,508 inmates and thirty infants. Of these 1,976 were women: 1,424 of them Jewish, 19 from Scandinavia and 532 from other nationalities. Among the 2,532 men there were 250 Jews, 329 Scandinavians, 12 special prisoners, and 1,941 of different nationalities.[6] At least ten Jewish women were shot by the SS before they left. All inmates had congregated at 4 a.m. in the camp square for their marching orders, with Meyer in charge who, as noted, was now under the direct command of the SS and police chief in Danzig (and thereafter the commander in Stettin). The so-called privileged prisoners and the relatives of famous ones—"*Haudegen*" and the "*Sippen*"—were not included in the first phase of the march but left the following day, along with other groups, including 1,600

Jewish women of different nationalities.[7] Instead of following the original plans for the same number in each column, the camp was evacuated by block numbers. In all, 11,500 inmates left—almost half of the camp's population.[8] Many set off who were too feeble to walk, and the meager rations that they had been given—bread, margarine and a cheese spread—were eaten right away. Besides, many were already infected with typhus which was subsequently spread to others along the way. Added to this misery were other major factors—harsh winter weather with deep snow drifts and sub-zero temperatures, the unpredictability of the behavior of guards and the presence of evacuated East Prussian civilians who, also needy and desperate to escape from the Soviets, now clogged the roads, with the result that camp inmates were rerouted along back roads that were at times impassable.

For the first three days, there were no added provisions and all contact with local people was forbidden. They were locked up at night in barns and stables or in churches in various villages.[9] Danish survivor Martin Nielsen writes in his memoir about fighting for straw to lie on the dirt floor. There were, he writes, nine corpses the next morning.[10] Stragglers were shot and left at the side of the road. He continues: "Our dead comrades from previous columns lay along the road. The sight was always the same: the striped jacket, striped pants, thin naked palms and a bullet hole in the neck, sometimes so high that the top of the skull was torn away."[11] Others corroborate the shootings along the route, like Jan Jazebowski: "A column was marching a kilometer ahead. We could see it clearly, as the terrain was hilly. We saw the last ranks climbing up with difficulty, and the silhouettes dropping right after gunshots. After a few minutes we would pass by those fresh corpses."[12] No one ever reached Lauenburg as planned in the evacuation orders, and meanwhile Lauenburg had been requisitioned as a field hospital for the Wehrmacht. Desperate people who needed food, shelter, and medical assistance competed for help along evacuation routes that lead westward: Wounded German soldiers, famished camp prisoners and their SS guards, fleeing East Prussians, all had to share, if not equally, the chances of surviving these long treks in bitter cold.

In his postwar memoir, Meyer wrote about the terrible dilemma he faced, with thousands of inmates and nowhere to send them. "Everywhere the answer was the same: shoot your prisoners—we have thousands of our own refugees to place somewhere."[13] He also ascribes the heavy losses of human life to "unfavorable weather." His "terrible dilemma" is thus presented as a choice between providing for Germans—"our people"—that is, valuable people, while the deaths of prisoners in blizzards and freezing temperatures are ascribed simply to "unfavorable weather." Other smaller facilities were allocated to house the Stutthof prisoners who were now reduced in number to around 7,000. Of the missing 4,000, half had managed to escape, but the other 2,000 had died.[14] In the "new" facilities there was neither heating nor plumbing, and water could only be brought in from the nearest lake.

The First Evacuation Camps

An example of the conditions in these evacuation camps is Gans/Gęś, located to the north of Lauenburg where Columns 1 and 1V had been sent from Stutthof on January

25, with 840 and 630 prisoners, respectively. In the course of the march, 222 had already been murdered by the guards or had fled. Prisoners received two slices of bread weekly and a half liter of soup made of horse meat and potatoes or turnips. Prisoners ate the stinking refuse from garbage pails at night despite the risk of being shot. In the middle of February, 600 of the now 1,600 prisoners were ordered by the Wehrmacht to work—loading goods and inventory for the camp from freight trains in Lauenburg. By the time the prisoners were liberated by the Soviets, half of them had died of malnutrition and intestinal diseases, and of typhus. Meanwhile, survivors were liberated in Putzig/Puck and Neustadt. Teodor Meyer visited this camp on several occasions, having placed it under the leadership of SS Sergeant Bratke.[15] Yla tells about the month that he and fellow prisoners spent in Gans/Gęś and about the death on February 21, 1945, of Konstantin Čakste, Professor of Law and son of Latvia's first president. Yla writes: "We got permission to bury him separately on a small hill instead of the common grave. But we couldn't obtain a casket, so we placed his body on a wooden plank and covered it with roofing felt." Yla, the Lithuanian Catholic priest was asked to perform the burial ceremony for the Lutheran Latvian. He writes: "I blessed the grave and started to say a few words but could hardly get them out. We placed a cross made from two small branches of birch on his grave."[16] Again, Yla captures incongruity. This funeral takes place on what became known as a "death march," but yet presents a religious and respectful burial scene. It does not take place in a graveyard, but on a little hill in East Prussia, far from the home of the deceased Konstantin Čakste. The officiating minister is a Lithuanian Catholic priest and the departed is a Latvian Lutheran. There is no coffin but a wooden plank. Obviously, planks do not have lids. But his fellow-prisoners somehow found roofing felt to cover the departed, just like they persuaded the guards to allow them to rescue him from a common grave. This deeply moving scene is a still life that adds to the portrait gallery of Stutthof. It defies conventional notions of funerals and insists on a dignified burial for a prisoner. We have to think it illustrates the German poet Rainer Maria Rilke's notion of "der grosse Tod"/"the great death." (It is certainly not a small death.) Yla inserts himself briefly; it was hard for him to find words at the makeshift grave. We leave this graveside scene with no illusions, and silently commemorate the others—dozens of other prisoners who lie in a common grave.

Here is a summary of the make-shift camps: "The camps were filthy, lice-ridden and there was no food supply. The commandants only supplied for the crew, buying or requisitioning foodstuffs from local farmers. Inmates were left with scraps, mostly meat from old horses or horse offal. They recall only receiving a slice of bread per week."[17] Frostbite and diarrhea were common, along with typhus that was spread by the infestation of lice. One of the French prisoners wrote that of the 1,600 in his division, only 500 of them were able to get on their feet to work, despite the fact that they lost their bread ration for the day—the incentive to work used by the SS. One prisoner—Alfons Grelewicz wrote in his diary on February 23, "Until now we were decimated by hunger and diseases. Since today there's also the ditch-digging. And here we are, so weak we can barely get up from the pallets."[18] He was to die in the camp in Rybno a few days later. It is estimated that at least 4,500 victims died during these land marches, including those who died immediately after the liberation.[19]

Evacuating the Sub-Camps

What about the prisoners in the widely spread sub-camps that covered such a broad area? Their fate is harder to access because of the large number of sub-camps, but what we do know is there were 22,521 inmates in the sub-system that stretched from Königsberg in the north all the way west to Stettin and to Thorn in the south. The inmates of these camps may not have been able to reach Stutthof in time for the official camp exodus, but after January 20 many had set off independently. Presumably, some of these columns merged with the main marches. The hardest hit were the sub-camps located around Königsberg, camps like Heiligenbeil and Gerdauen which were under the jurisdiction of Gauleiter Erich Koch who had ordered all prisoners to be killed. This segment includes the infamous massacre at Palmnicken, some 50 kilometers from Königsberg where a column of around 3,000 of the 7,000 who had set off were led to a vacant amber works on January 26. They were kept in a workshop adjoining the mine with minimal food for several days. They were massacred on the evening of January 29 during their attempt to flee, many of them on the beach. There were only fifteen survivors, and some of them found shelter among local Germans.[20] The SS led the rear columns out on to the ice (near the aptly named Sorgenau—"meadow of cares") and machine-gunned them.[21] Survivor Fryda Gabrylewicz describes her column of forty prisoners. She and her friend were able to hide under corpses, but then a bullet ripped through her friend.

> After a minute I was hit in the leg .... My friend moaned "Oh Fryda" and dies. I lay in horrible pain and waited for death ... Silence fell all around. I heard a cracking noise but did not know what it was. It was the ice cracking. I raise my head and see the ice breaking and corpses sliding into the sea.[22]

This dreadful event has at least one redeeming, if tragic figure: the caretaker of the mineshaft, a German *Volkssturm* officer by the name of Feyerabend who defied the SS order and attempted to protect the lives of the mostly Jewish prisoners. (He took his life on January 30.) The rest of the story is equally gruesome and has also entered the history of the death marches as among the worst of the atrocities that happened to the survivors of the camps.[23]

Two of the largest sub-camps for women were Gutowo/Guttendorf (in the Elbing/Elbląg area) and Grodno/Garten (near Thorn/Torun), where prisoners had worked on fortifications along the riverbanks. The mortality rates for these complexes reflect what we have already seen—selections prior to evacuation on January 16 decimated their numbers by 30–50 percent.[24] Soviet troops entered the Gutowo/Guttendorf camp on January 21 where they found "163 extremely exhausted women, with frost bitten legs, some wounded." They noted that some of the women had boils on their hands from injections of poisonous fluids that had been given by SS Lieutenant/*Sturmführer* Engel and others. They had also found canvas tents in the area that had female corpses—some 120 bodies.[25] Women from the sub-camp at Grodno/Garten experienced a similar fate. The evacuation of 1,200–1,500 inmates began on January 19–21. Selections were made based on a forced foot race after roll call. Those unable to run fast enough were loaded onto a horse and cart and taken to a peninsula on a lake where they were drowned.[26] The route for those who survived these attacks headed northwest. The extant information is based on the testimonies of survivors and on the evidence produced by mass exhumations. One destination that appears to have taken two weeks was Praust-Kochstedt where 800 and 289 women, respectively, had worked on the airstrip.[27] Some joined the inmates of Burgsdorf. What is known is that around 1,000 evacuees from Thorn and Elbing occupied the vacated huts until their liberation on March 24. Each day a sled left the camp with bodies for an unknown burial ground.

Another destination, or at least direction—for survivors of sub-camp selections was around Bromberg/Bydgoszcz. This was the case for the sub-camp Chorab near Thorn from where 1,400 women were evacuated on January 19. There appeared to have been a real massacre at the end of the trip, but local people pulled twenty-eight survivors from the mass of bodies and moved them to a local hospital. The victims' bodies were exhumed in 1950 and reburied in Toruń cemetery. At the sub-camp in the Brusy/Bruss SS training ground, 82 women of 493 were selected and shot nearby. The SS doused their remains with tar and burned them. The survivors were liberated on March 10 in Chinow along with other evacuees. The remains of those who were killed were later buried in Chojnice cemetery.[28]

There were eight evacuation camps in the second half of February, along with another five camps that were used to house prisoners who had been evacuated from sub-camps. A report of February 13 gives the number of Stutthof inmates en route to Lauenburg as 12,046. "However, due to the high mortality rate and successful escapes not mentioned in reports, the number was in fact much lower, ca. 8,000."[29] Depictions of these camps in prisoner testimonies indicate that the term "camp" was an inflated term. They were simply barns and abandoned buildings without basic facilities that housed desperately ill and dying people who had dysentery and typhus. Many in that category were killed by injection during the three to five-week period. Half of them died—mostly Jews. As the front approached on March 9–10, they had to move camp again, this time toward Puck/Putzig, resulting in more deaths. Sub-camps located farther away from Danzig were liberated later, sometimes in large numbers, like Pöhlitz, near Stettin with 2,190 inmates. Its evacuation did not begin until April 17 and appears to have been in stages. Many of the evacuees were liberated during the march to Rostock. Others were sent to Bergen-Belsen. Some were too ill and were left behind at Pöhlitz. The files that survived indicate the following: around 33,000 inmates of Stutthof were slated for evacuation on land. Many of these were selected to die before they began the evacuation march. The number of victims in the latter group is estimated as 12,000 in the sub-camps and 4,500 in Stutthof. They were killed by those in charge of the marches.[30]

The Spring Offensive Begins: Liberation for Some

The Soviet army began its attack on Danzig and Gotenhafen in early March which placed the Stutthof prisoners closer to the front line.[31] Consequently, the Germans ordered the evacuation of these make-shift camps to prevent their liberation by the

Soviets. Because just over half of the prisoners were fit to walk, the others were left behind, to die or to be murdered. On their way to Puck or Gotenhafen, the prisoners were liberated. One of the worst incidents during the marches happened in Puck on March 10, when a column of around 500 from the camp at Rieben was placed in a large bunker. During the night, the SS took dozens of inmates out into the fields and shot them. They were buried in Puck, along with other prisoners who also had been killed or died on the marches. In all, 234 inmates were buried in Puck.[32] The sub-camp of Puck—located northeast of Danzig—had been set up for prisoners who had been evacuated in the second stage of the evacuation, involving between 276 and 500 prisoners who had been originally directed to a gathering point in Piaśnitz. Details of this evacuation are given by a former prisoner, Roman Kulbicki: "The SS men drove us across paths in the fields. They were raging in anger, like rabid animals caught in a trap who were powerless to escape. Unfortunately, we were their prey. Along the way, we came upon the abandoned bodies of female prisoners from Stutthof. They were mostly Jewish women, shockingly emaciated human skeletons."[33]

Throughout the area, however, the Stutthof prisoners were being liberated—women in Gnewin/Gniewino and Burgsdorf/Toliszczek on March 10, and in Tauenzin around 200 men, including 121 Norwegians and Finns. Those who had not arrived in time to be liberated were escorted back across the same ground they had traveled, returning to Danzig where groups of them were housed in a shipyard filial camp until March 23, when they returned to Stutthof. The sub-camp in Gotenhafen. was not evacuated until March 25 so that around 700 workers—many of them skilled workers—were forced to work as long as possible for the German war effort before the Russian troops arrived on March 28. Around 700 of them, under the supervision of SS Sergeant/*Oberscharführer* Joseph Bock were taken to the harbor, where over 600 were put on two small ships of the German merchant navy and sent to Hamburg where they arrived after four days at sea.[34] The survivors of this journey—239—were sent to Neuengamme where they worked on clearing rubble and unexploded bombs in the city, before being evacuated again to Sandbostel where survivors were liberated on April 28, 1945.[35]

Grot provides more detail and precise numbers about the evacuation described above. As indicated above, prisoners were finally evacuated on March 25, after two abortive attempts earlier in March, under Soviet air attacks. The 618 prisoners and their SS guards were put on board two ships (fourteen SS men on the first one and around thirty on the second one); their cargo holds were already filled with army trucks and German troops. Panic among the escorts on the way to the harbor made it possible for a number of prisoners to escape. The first convoy (*Elbing*) headed for Hamburg by way of the Kiel Canal. Conditions on board were miserable, though at least they received some drinking water and portions of margarine to be shared among them. As emaciated by illness as they were, these prisoners were put to work in their new camp—Neuengamme in Hamburg before joining other camp survivors in Sandbostel where they were liberated by British troops. In all, 3,600 were liberated by British troops (some were also rescued by the Swedish Red Cross), but despite their efforts, many died who had sailed on the *Elbing*. The fate of those 355 prisoners on the other ship—the *Zephyr* included the following incident: Right before they set sail, a group of men from the Gestapo and SS boarded the ship and stole their provisions. The ship was damaged at sea and they had to wait for it to be repaired. When they finally arrived on April 2 in Nordmark in Kiel-Hasse, they were put to work removing debris from the bombed streets. A number of the prisoners were transferred to Neuengamme which was evacuated to Lübeck between April 21 and May 1.[36]

The more detailed accounts of the journey of survivors, especially from the Gotenhafen sub-camp, show just how many nationalities were placed together as "prisoners of Stutthof"—Russians, Latvians, Lithuanians, French, Germans, Poles, and Austrians. And along with that blending there was another fusion—with prisoners and inmates from other camps, especially from Neuengamme. The barracks at Stutthof had categorized and segregated the prisoners along ethnic and racial lines, but now they were all just "prisoners of Stutthof." The British had issued the warning that if German ships did not proceed into the nearest harbor and hoist the white flag, then they would bomb them. When bombs subsequently fell on Lübeck harbor and on the ships *Cap Arcona* and *Thielbeck*, there were no white flags and, as a result, the 4,600 and 2,800 prisoners on each of these two ships were among the many victims. Prominent names from the Polish resistance in Pomerania were among the dead: Bogusław Adamczak, Witold Nicki, and Stanisław Sułkowski.[37] Some had spent years in Stutthof, only to be killed so close to liberation.[38] Orski includes the story of a Czech prisoner, the poet and writer Jan Týml, described by a fellow prisoner as a man "who instilled in us hope and faith that we would be freed." He survived five years of internment, the evacuation by land and sea, and died in quarantine in Lund, Sweden, "at the threshold of freedom."[39]

The Second Phase of the Evacuation from Stutthof

The thousands of prisoners (11,000) who were forced to be part of these marches between January and March by no means emptied the main camp of inmates. There were still 11,863 in Stutthof—the majority of them (6,922) women in the Jewish camp. The evacuation had severely affected the functioning of the camp and in fact, for a brief time, there were no roll calls or new admissions. On January 30, the roll call indicated that there were now 33,948 inmates, a statistic that includes inmates of the sub-camps who had finally arrived in Stutthof.[40] (Presumably this number also includes German refugees from East Prussia.) The dominant impression of the camp is of indecision and constant tension, generated above all by the possibility of being evacuated at any time or hour of the day. Prisoners were ordered to form columns that did not go anywhere. Yet some did, for example, between February 15 and February 17, several hundred left for Burggraben. Then, on March 9, another group of 300 left to build fortifications around Danzig.[41] But others took their place in the vacated barracks, including German civilians fleeing from the Soviet troops, as well as prisoners from the liquidated camps in East Prussia who were neither registered nor fed and simply roamed around as scavengers, desperately looking for food. All in the camp were vulnerable to typhus which was raging in the Jewish camp that was strictly isolated or more accurately, simply abandoned. Between the forced marches and the hundreds dying daily, the number of inmates fell to around 4,000 by late March. As already noted, prisoners evacuated earlier returned to Stutthof from camps like Tauenzin, inflating for a brief time the numbers. SS men who had accompanied them, like Meyer and Fritz Peters, were also now back in Stutthof. They put the prisoners right to work, digging underground air raid shelters around the camp which was under bombardment from the Soviet air force. In other words, prisoners were digging shelters to protect the SS and Wehrmacht units that were stationed nearby. Casualties from these air raids were suffered by both the inmates and by the civilians who were now housed in the camp.

There is little doubt that for both groups—those already on evacuation marches and those who stayed—the last months of Stutthof were the worst in its long history. It is hard to imagine that prisoners still alive in March 1945 could possibly have to face worse, but they did. Stutthof was the last camp liberated by the Allies, but the consequences of that delay were catastrophic, for it resulted in atrocities that in turn spawned even worse ones that kept heaping up, one upon the other and did not end after the surviving prisoners had reached the Bay of Lübeck. The Soviets had initially bypassed Stutthof primarily because it was not on the main arc of their sweep westward. There may have been other factors, but its location played a part. Stutthof had been chosen initially as a desirable location, conveniently near Danzig yet off the beaten track, surrounded on all sides by water that would instill fear in anyone attempting escape. In the spring of 1945, its location was still working against the inmates of Stutthof. There are harrowing descriptions of attempting to go by barges across lagoons, of being shot for failure to board barges quickly enough, of falling through ice in the Baltic while fleeing. This puts the Stutthof marches in a different realm of danger than other death marches, where prisoners also had to contend with harsh winter weather and equally brutal guards, but the naturally bleak winter landscape of these marches stands out. Whereas the January evacuation chaos can be ascribed to several factors—miscommunication from Berlin, disagreement between the Gauleiter in East Prussia and Danzig-West Prussia, the failure to estimate the imminence of the Soviet front's arrival, the liberation of Stutthof as the last camp to be freed by the Allies can still be ascribed to its out-of-the-way location and arguably to a lingering perception within the camp system of its secondary status. There was only one way to exit the area since it was surrounded on all sides by Soviet troops: by water. The inmates were therefore either marched or taken by narrow-gauge rail to Nickelswalde or Schiewenhorst (by now barely recognizable as key locations in Grass stories) and from there to the Hel Peninsula where the plan was to send them by boat to a port like Flensburg. To all these factors one can add the presence of thousands of German refugees who were competing for survival, and as miserable as it was for these refugees there was little doubt about who had priority. From February until April, the camp housed between 20,000 and 40,000—among them East Prussian refugees, prisoners of war from various nations as well as German troops, who were now housed in both the old and new barracks of the camp. Around half of them were evacuated, while the other half remained there until the liberation by Soviet troops.[42]

Commandant Hoppe claimed in his memoir that he informed the IKL on April 15 that he was handing over the camp with its remaining inmates to the Russians. (He had already left on April 4 with other SS men for Schleswig-Holstein, embarking from the Hel Peninsula.) The camp was now under the supervision of SS Captain/ *Hauptsturmführer* Paul Ehle and his deputy Corporal/*Rottenführer* Paul Kuklau. Ehle was a five-year veteran of Stutthof, a local man and former farmer, listed in the SS files as "gottgläubig," a long-time Nazi party member and SS man since 1938. By SS standards, Hoppe had placed the camp in good hands. The last report indicated there were now 4,508 inmates in the camp—1,976 women and the 2,532 men. The order to liquidate the camp and evacuate by sea is generally ascribed to Himmler's radio broadcast on April 14—"Surrender is out of the question. No inmate can be captured alive by the enemy."[43] The execution of this general order lay with Fritz Katzmann— commander of the SS and the Police in Danzig. (Both he and Gauleiter Forster were themselves poised to evacuate on the Hel Peninsula.)

One of the women evacuated on April 25 was Jehudith Kremer who had come to Stutthof from Vilna by way of the camps in Estonia at Vivikonia and Erede. After falling ill with typhus, she had spent a month in the camp infirmary which was destroyed in a bombardment a short time later. She writes that two of three sisters were killed instantly by bombs and the third sister was wounded.[44] She continues, "We succeeded in learning that Danzig was occupied by the Russians." Kremer then describes the three barges that were to transport the prisoners—two decks or levels, the upper one filled with women, all decks stuffed with people who were unable to stand upright and had to kneel the whole time. She remembers that there were four or five Germans on board the tugboat that was pulling them. They stopped twice during the eight-day journey, so that the Germans could get provisions and make contact with the officials in charge. They were all so weak no one thought of escaping. During their second stop, the Germans threw provisions up to their deck—cheese and *Knäckebrot*—and got drunk on brandy before disappearing and abandoning the barge. She notes too that the quarantine barge was nowhere in sight and speculates that it had been sunk. Kremer is unable to identify their rescuers, but the first sign of rescue was when blankets were thrown up on to the barge which they used as sails to propel them toward the shore. She is now aware that there were male prisoners on the lower deck. They were lowered from the barge, ten to twelve at a time. Some swam to shore while others were taken to land in boats by men who were speaking Norwegian. A woman emerged from a house and told them they would be rescued by the English within three hours, but while she was talking, a group of Germans in black uniform appeared, acted astonished to see them and retreated back into a wood, only to reappear with the guards who had abandoned ship. She writes:

> Shootings and beatings began as they took us through a forest to Neustadt. We arrived at a square where there were thousands of people and many Germans. This was in the harbor of Neustadt. I saw canon guns of the army directed at the sea and in the distance a large ship. We were told that we were going to be accommodated on this ship. But the ship was bombarded, just as it was beginning to pour with rain. We lay down on the ground. The Germans did the same. When the ship was set on fire I saw people leaping into the sea. At the same time, small armored jeeps came from the direction of the town to the harbor. They were English. When they pulled up in the harbor they left their jeeps. The Germans surrendered and were disarmed. We, on the other hand, received permission to take what we wanted in the course of the next 48 hours from the harbor camps.

We only wanted one thing—food. And then, we were off. We cut our hands trying to open up canned goods, but nobody paid any attention. Finally, we were allowed to eat as much as we wanted. As promised, civilians with armbands came after 48 hours to impose order. We were assembled in the hangars of the harbor, received a bath, were deloused and got fresh clothes. And that's how I was rescued on the third of May, 1945.[45]

Though Kremer and her sister survived, they lost their father and younger sister in Klooga.

Olga Barnitsch who conducted the interview of Kerner in November 1961 makes this comment: "The witness reports laconically but factually, in truncated sentences, and always strains at recall in order to concentrate. In the same way, she says briefly but tellingly, 'There was a kapo by the name of Maruka, a Ukrainian and after that a Jewish woman called Tania. These two women harmed people more than the Germans.'"[46] This testimony disrupts stereotypical expectations, and challenges the notion that a Jewish kapo could not possibly inflict harm on Jewish fellow-prisoners or that a female Ukrainian kapo could be worse than a German counterpart.

Grot gives more details about this portion of the April 25 evacuation that is depicted so sparsely above. She writes that the SS men simply wanted to be rid of the prisoners on the night of May 2–3 when they headed with the tugboat to Neustadt, leaving the prisoners to their own resources. This behavior understandably caused the prisoners to assume the worst and to believe the rumors that the barge was going to be detonated. It was the Norwegians who took it upon themselves to get the barge to land, using oars, planks, rags, and blankets for sails. Grot adds that three prisoners of the *Wolfgang* successfully escaped and headed for Oldenburg. We learn too that there were thirty SS men in charge of these barges and according to the reports of the Norwegians, they had returned to the shore from a night of heavy drinking. Initially they were going to proceed to Flensburg with the prisoners, but in the end, they headed for Neustadt because of leaks in the barges. Before sailing, however, they disposed of those who were too sick to abandon the barge the night before. Some were thrown into the sea and drowned. Norwegian prisoner Andersen witnessed how an SS man shot a woman who was clinging for her life to the barge. Another witness on the shore, Hans Fröhlich testified that after this carnage the SS men drove the surviving prisoners toward Neustadt. On the shore, there were around 200 bodies.[47] The British military tribunal held SS Sergeant/*Scharführer* Mathiä responsible.

Back in Stutthof: The April Evacuation

For prisoners who were still left in April in Stutthof, tensions mounted. Reports of the two days that followed the camp's evacuation of around 3,300 inmates (half of them Jewish) on April 25 are filled with verbs like "waiting," "herding," and "drowning." One barge was designated with a yellow flag as a quarantine vessel for 500 Jewish women who had typhus. When the others reached Hel, they were sent inland to a forest where they were kept without food or drink in a barbed-wire enclosure. Above them, allied planes were dropping bombs on a German military installment that also killed and wounded "many inmates."[48] On April 27, an additional 1,060 prisoners were evacuated from Stutthof, half of them gravely ill. When they reached Nickelswalde, the SS selected seventy of them, among them twenty-one Jewish women, herded them into a bomb shelter and shot them through the back of the head. Grot names the SS men responsible: Wensierski, Holz, Wippermann, and Mäder—a *Berufsverbrecher*—a professional criminal. Wanton sadism continued, when in the evening the SS ordered some men to walk across a narrow plank and then attacked them, causing the men to fall into the hold, some to their deaths, others to bear the scars on their bodies thereafter. Survivor Maria Witt has this to say:

> We traveled on for ten days between shipwrecks, threatened by mines and U boats. We experienced the air attack on Kiel. There was no drinking water on board the bark, and nothing to eat. Typhus was rampant among the prisoners. SS men threw the dead and the dying overboard. ... In Flensburg, I peered into the holds. A frightful and unforgettable sight met my eyes. I saw human bodies covered in skin that had turned black, lying in layers one on top of the other. They were the corpses of people who had died of typhus in the course of recent days and among them were human skeletons that were still decaying. SS men ordered some healthy people to take the corpses away and bury them, and then the infected ones died.[49]

Grot writes that mortality rates on the barge were higher among women than men. Of the 1,060 who set off on April 27 from Stutthof, only 700 arrived safely in Sweden. It is no wonder that they later called the vessels they sailed on "barges of death."[50]

The fate of the survivors of Stutthof from April 27 onwards depended on factors beyond their individual feeble physical state: the sea-worthiness of the respective barges that conveyed them westward, and the weather—for example, a storm on April 29 (with 600 on board) separated them from the other barges, and they landed in Rügen, with dire consequences for some (twelve were summarily shot when a mêlée broke out over food that had been provided by the islanders). Others fled inland on the island, but the remaining 345 prisoners ended up being saved on May 5 by the Red Cross. Twenty-one died despite the medical intervention. In all, 100 perished from that one barge. The other two barges finally entered Neustadt harbor on May 2, alongside ships that held thousands of prisoners from Neuengamme and hundreds from the subcamp in Gdynia/Gotenhafen.

Commandant Hoppe appeared in his last official role, to announce that the Stutthof inmates were to proceed to Flensburg where they would be received by the Swedish Red Cross who would take over. The Royal Air Force continued their bombing missions over Lübeck Bay which resulted in 7,000 being killed in the air raid. Of the 2,000 who boarded at Hel around 900 perished.[51] It was harder for archivists to assemble an accurate count for the "quarantine" barge. They know it was anchored in Lübeck at the beginning of May, when it came under an air attack and caught fire. It is not known how many died in that attack. Survivors did reach Bremen in a different vessel where they were liberated and cared for by British troops. Another barge—abandoned by its escorts—drifted west of Kiel and ran aground on the beach. They were rescued the following day, and forty were placed in local hospitals, of whom twenty-two died. The total casualities from that barge were 300.⁵²

The Last Days of Stutthof

In the end, was it better for those who remained in Stutthof? The particularly harsh weather conditions during the first two months of 1945 (even by Baltic standards) clearly contributed directly to the many deaths, but the spring evacuations, though in better weather conditions, brought unspeakable hardships at sea. The last roll call took place on April 27, 1945, for around 1,000 prisoners who had remained in the camp infirmary. The last transport of Stutthof inmates took place on the barge *Ruth*, arriving in Flensburg on May 4. They joined other camp survivors on a ship that had been requisitioned for this purpose by the Swedish Red Cross. After spending several days on board, they were transferred to another ship that took them to Sweden where many of them were cared for in Swedish hospitals. Seven hundred of this last transport survived, while 300 perished.

The final ignominious act of the SS in Stutthof was to set the barracks of the Jewish camp on fire, killing the dying and others who had hidden in the attics. They blew up the crematorium on April 29. All that was left to do for SS-man Ehle, his deputy, and the remaining SS men was to flee. It was, however, not until May 8 that the Wehrmacht surrendered, having fought to the end against the Soviet troops, including destroying drainage systems in order to cause flooding in the immediate area and thus impede the Soviet advance. It was to no avail and, at dawn, troops from the 48th Soviet Army entered Stutthof where they found around 100 inmates, as well as thousands of civilians who had been evacuated from East Prussia and Pomerania. A commission was set up right away by the commander of the 48th Army to investigate the crimes that had been committed. In less than a four-month period, 25,000 died either in the camp or during its evacuation. In other words, 30 percent of the victims of the camp died in the last months of the war.⁵³

Survivors Speak

The memoirs of survivors of Stutthof's death marches reflect the degree and type of danger experienced by every single prisoner at every juncture of their journey. Their stories are therefore diverse but present, with some variations, the basic facts and figures already cited and repeated. Depictions, for example, of marching through a desolate landscape in the heart of winter differ from the later experiences at sea. Some sub-camps were liberated earlier than others, depending on their location, so the duration of their sufferings was weeks rather than months. All prisoners suffered, but those who experienced both the marches on land and the unspeakable conditions on board overcrowded, unseaworthy vessels were the hardest hit—for some quite literally when they came under the fire of air raids by the Soviets and the RAF so close to liberation. Every testimony of the January evacuation tells about leaving Stutthof in a famished state, of walking through deep snow in frigid temperatures with minimal clothing, of being aware that falling behind meant instant death. For some the journey by foot was longer than for others, since some columns used back roads to avoid overcrowded main roads that were teeming with refugees. It took them longer because the snow had not been cleared. If the pace was not maintained, no prisoner was spared the threat of being shot, whether a Jewish woman, a French resister, a Finnish sailor or a Danish policeman. Many who started off on January 25 were still marching six weeks later, at that point in a more pitiable and deteriorated state. Many simply succumbed to the cold "and were left lying on the ground where they had fallen to sleep, never to awaken" according to Joseph Katz, who was suffering from typhus and was left in a delirious state at the side of the road and gladly would have succumbed to death.[54] One of the guards, in fact, declared him dead, and threw his bread bag on top of him. Katz remembers a stirring within him. He writes: "Then, like a bolt from the blue I thought—maybe I am not going to die. Maybe I'll live ... It was like everything else had been a bad dream. I began to move my limbs again. The guard lifted his bread bag back again, and turning to his companion said laconically, 'This one is alive after all.'"[55] Katz was liberated on March 8, 1945, in a camp near Rieben/Rybno by soldiers of the Red Army.

Some prisoners escaped during the night. Their fate is largely unknown. Of the 821 prisoners who had set off from Stutthof for the evacuation camp at Tauenzin in January, only 421 arrived.[56] This diminished column of prisoners was immediately put to work, surviving hard labor on watery soup until March 9 when the front line moved closer and they were forced to head for Gdynia/Gotenhafen and evacuation by sea. After weeks of misery, many of the original group found themselves back in Stutthof. Some of the Scandinavians hid out in Danzig, only to be arrested again and brought back to the camp where they were evacuated one more time on April 25, just as in January, though this time there were 3,300 prisoners, 2,000 of whom had survived to sail by barge. 900 of them would survive the sea journey from the Hel Peninsula. The three freighters already mentioned actually looked more like river barges, according to Finish sailor, Aarne Kovale. Telling his story to his daughter later in life, he remembered that the closer they got to them, the more dilapidated they looked. The passage of time had not diminished his recall, including details. Hundreds of prisoners were jammed into these barges that were towed out to sea by tugboats. Every account of these barges describes the deplorable conditions on board—no food or water, the stench from vomit, feces, bodies stripped of their clothing and cast overboard. They arrived after several days at sea in Neustadt where other larger vessels were anchored in the bay—the *Thielbeck* and the passenger liner *Cap Arcona* on which were prisoners from Neuengamme and from the Gdynia/Gotenhafen sub-camp. In the case of the Finns, they decided to jump overboard when it was apparent that the SS guards had absconded. Crowds of prisoners were on the shore. The massacre that followed the abandonment by the SS of the *Wolfgang* took at least 200 lives. Those left on board had attempted to abandon the barge, only to be gunned down from the shoreline by SS men and naval cadets from the nearby submarine school.[57] The journey for the survivors of this massacre was not yet over. They were ordered by no less an authority than Commandant Hoppe to embark for Flensburg. What followed the carnage on land was an aerial attack (already alluded to) on the two liners that were filled with camp survivors, including those from Stutthof.

Daniel Blatman's extensive research on this final phase of Nazi genocide (he calls it "murderously vicious") helps those of us working on an individual camp to situate its specific evacuation within a broader context. He offers the following statistics: in January 1945 there were 714,000 prisoners in the camp system and when the war ended there were 250,000. "Confidently, one can assume higher numbers."[58] Blatman contends that one reason the death marches have been neglected is that they have been subsumed in the overall account of the apocalyptic collapse of the Third Reich.[59] He argues that they were not, as Goldhagen had held, the extension of the earlier atrocities, including the forced migrations in eastern Poland to Russia. This was not murder by evacuation. Blatman is surely right to address the neglect of the death marches in the larger history of the concentration camps, but the wanton murder of the Jews of Stutthof as they marched toward liberation certainly warrants asking if they were not specifically targeted as Jews. Others were also gunned down indiscriminately, but memoirs and observations by prisoners who were not Jewish tend to emphasize the particular venom directed at Jews. The Stutthof evacuations may be among the most horrific of the marches because of their particular geography—the challenges of contending with water evacuations, the harsh Baltic conditions weather and the sheer numbers that had to be conveyed in these conditions. Above all, they had to share the roads with thousands of refugees, especially from East Prussia who were privileged in the struggle for basic necessities. This is particularly striking, as we will later see, when it came to evacuating Danzig. Blatman is right when he claims that the most salient factor in survival on these death marches was the role of the SS and the guards who accompanied the prisoners. Life and death lay in their hands. The overwhelming impression is that anyone who fell behind was a target, regardless of race, gender, or age. The guards walking alongside the prisoners were the ones who had the power to decide who should live or die, and their decision was not a spontaneous act but calculated from several factors, including utility and local conditions. The extermination process, Blatman argues, had become completely decentralized.[60]

In the chapter of his memoir on the death marches, Yla tells of one incident where a Kashubian prisoner begged the guard to shoot him, a plea that the guard ignored. Later, he found out that only members of the *Strafkommando*—the punishment unit—were allowed to kill.[61] While the existence of such units is certainly feasible, there is little evidence in other memoirs and documents that prisoners were spared during the marches for any reason. The core group of the Stutthof-trained SS were local men, and some of them were familiar with the terrain of "the Corridor" through which these marches took place. There is no evidence that the SS men and their helpers had been sensitized by the sufferings of those they tended. They still saw them as enemies of the Reich, whether they were political activists or racially inferior and thus disposable. Besides, even at this late date in the war, with Allied troops already around the next bend, they still believed victory was possible. Above all, the pride in the Reich and its Führer and their commitment as SS men never seemed to abate. These SS men were well-fed and, though they covered long distances, they always seem to have found somewhere warm to sleep and enough to eat.

Oral Testimonies of Survivors

When survivors of these evacuations give oral testimonies of their experiences, their language is pared down to absolute basic statements. Lilo Fern survived the death marches, after having been sent from Stutthof to Stolp/Słupsk to work on railway lines and repair brakes, along with other Jewish women. The treatment there, she recalls in video testimony, was not as cruel as it had been in Stutthof. They were housed in one large room, existing from one day to the next, without any contact with the local civilian population. Some died there and others simply disappeared, but after a few months they were brought back to Stutthof because the Russian front was moving closer. She recalls the terrible toll that typhus had taken and remembers walking over corpses. The long journey in a barge (she calls it a coal freighter) is recounted swiftly—no toilets, seasickness, drinking sea water. The SS wanted to kill them, but the Swedes intervened. They reached Neustadt and were given soup, but her system could not handle the food. She remembers the approach of huge tanks that turned out to be manned by British troops. She burst into tears, but the ecstatic man beside her collapsed and died. Lilo Fern was slowly nursed back to stable health—she had both typhus and jaundice—by "a kind German lady doctor." It took six months. How did she survive? Fern answers that she always believed in God. But her relatives did not want to hear her story, so she kept it bottled up within her, hiding her pain even from her own children. But the nightmares she experienced kept it alive—running from the SS, the feelings of suffocation.[62]

I suggest that the evacuation segment of her testimony reflects a pervasive facet of survival statements—the sheer fatigue of survivors who have already expended their energy on narrating earlier events—typically beginning with expulsion from their homes, ghettoization, loss of loved ones, the sufferings in camps, and then at the end, the long marches. It is no wonder that their fatigue permeates the narrative. Maja Abromovitch remembers some details of their liberation—the sky was red, walking on the snow-covered roads was like walking on stilts. Liberation came suddenly, or at least she describes it that way. They had been eating snow. All day they had seen covered wagons carrying retreating Germans. In a barn in a little village, where they had gone through a forest, she remembers the arrival of the Russians and adds that some of the prisoners "went mad."[63] Maurice Benadon from Salonika (who appears to have been arrested for his activities in the French Resistance) records his release on February 15 as bringing a ray of hope, though surrounded by the dead. He had been sustained during his months in Stutthof by the hope of seeing his wife and child and Salonika again, but had also contemplated taking his life. He remembers the blows from the SS, his enfeebled state, but he can't remember if there was work or not. He remembers the trek to Vaihingen very succinctly—suffering from constant dysentery, thousands of lice swarming on him and no medication.[64]

Whether in English, German or French, the oral testimonies that I have listened to are marked by the same terse style. Trude Friedrich's testimony (in German) contains abrupt statements that summarize large chunks of history, such as Hitler's desire, as she states, to annihilate the Jews: "Der Hitler wollte die Juden ausrotten," she explains. Raised in a happy home and environment in the Rhineland, she and several of her family were deported to Riga from Düsseldorf on a four-day journey. She remembers how cold it was in the camp at Kaiserwald, from where they were transported to Stutthof which she calls "a proper camp," followed by the simple description—quite bad. "Das war ganz schlimm." She found her sister there and singles out her sister's shaved hair—she calls it "hairless" before adding, it was terrible—"furchtbar." Together, the two sisters were sent to a sub-camp in East Prussia where there were 500 women. She describes her time there in the same truncated style that is often reduced to one or two words—criminal, always cold, always hungry, standing in line for soup. They spoke of how much better their dogs and hens had it at home. She introduces the evacuation march with the simple explanation that is singular in number—"Der Russe was schon in der Nähe/ The Russian was already near." Then she adds a detail that is striking in its directness and in its insight into human behavior under such circumstances—"We were all aggressive from misery." When the Russians liberated them, she and her sister clung together, thinking they were about to be shot. They then went to the houses that had been abandoned by fleeing Germans. She adds that many women were raped by their liberators.[65] The effect is unbearably poignant.

Stutthof inmates, attempting to survive during evacuation, were not all treated alike, and arguably the most favored of them all were the Jehovah's Witnesses. As noted earlier, the Jehovah's Witness, Cornelia Gawior, was candid about her experience in the camp, how much worse others were treated. In her video testimony, nowhere is their privileged position—relatively speaking—more apparent than in the portion of her testimony that pertains to the evacuation. The Jehovah's Witness group was brought along with the other prisoners to Danzig to be transported by ship. They were on the beach waiting to embark on the barges when the plans were changed, and they were herded into a room—she says there were twenty Jehovah's Witness prisoners –and they were sent back to Stutthof where they stayed until the end of April. Gawior talks about their second attempt to be evacuated from the harbor in the Hel Peninsula. A tugboat pulled their barge out to sea. She says there were twenty soldiers and six SS men on board during the eight-day journey. Gawior's testimony contains language that is rarely found in other statements, particularly those that depict the death marches. While other prisoners were dying of thirst and casually thrown overboard, the Jehovah's Witness group was offered a different barge that would take them to safety. In fact, the captain pled with them to leave the barge—"I don't want you on my conscience." She says he had tears in his eyes as he begged them to think of their own safety. Even after the Russians arrived to liberate them, they again found favor when Gawior told them they were Jehovah's Witnesses, refugees from a concentration camp. The Russian soldiers ordered the owners of a house to provide lodging for them. They were cared for in that home for the next two weeks.[66]

A Written Testimony

The contrast between oral and written testimonies reveals a broader recall of events in the latter genre and in the case of German-speaking prisoners, offers some additional information on the role of local Germans. Though German Jews had some advantage in possibly finding shelter with Germans, it is clear that if their identity as Jews were discovered, their reception would have instantly changed. This is particularly apparent in the memoir by Marga Griesbach. She was sent to Bromberg/Bydgoszcz to work on train tracks and was housed in barracks with the other women in groups of fifty to sixty. There were two main barracks that were made up of six rooms and supervised by female kapos from Czechoslovakia, one of whom was a medical doctor, all of them under the command of an older SS man who berated them; they were lower than animals and did not deserve to be alive.[67] She writes about working outside on train tracks on harsh December days and finding food—potatoes, beets, and turnips, deliberately left for them by Polish farmhands. "I am sure that the beets kept life in us and gave us the little bit of strength that we had."[68] Griesbach fell ill with typhus, but was protected by the Czech doctor from being sent back to Stutthof—to certain death. Her "death march" led her to a women's camp where she stayed along with 1,000 women for two nights, without food. Her narrative entails all-too-familiar stories of trudging through snow, eating it to slack thirst, sleeping on the bare floor in barns while their guards found shelter in farmhouses that had been abandoned by their owners. Some prisoners slipped away from the main march, especially when Russian armed vehicles appeared. "We could hardly believe that we were free."[69] Gradually, she writes, the Latvian and Polish women disappeared. But the liberation still had not come and their group had shrunk to forty women, reduced to "skin and bones, hungry and unbearably exhausted" and 400 Russian POWs.[70] Fighting persisted, and their SS guards were now joined by older men from the *Volkssturm*.[71] "No matter who they were, they shot anybody and they shot to kill."[72] One day, in her famished state, she approached a bucket full of food for pigs in front of a farm. When the farmer caught her, he struck her with the bucket, giving her a bloody lip.[73] At one point in their march, a goods train appeared with open flatbeds on which they were able to proceed through the night, though seated on one another's legs. Griesbach subsequently was unable to move her limbs, at which point another woman intervened and told her not to cry or she would be shot by the guards. Her mother and the woman supported her on either side for the next hours. Her name was Erna Valk and she came from Goch in Westphalia.[74] At their next stop, a man provided fresh milk which, though well-intended, caused diarrhea.

The situation for German-Jewish inmates on these marches was different, at least in one gendered aspect: as women, they did not have the marks of circumcision, and thus could pass as German refugees. Griesbach and her teenage daughter posed as German refugees for a brief period but, even though they were able to fit in among the other refugees who had taken shelter in German homes along the way, the mother decided one morning to announce her true identity and her intent to inform the local police. Her plans were thwarted, however, as much by intense hunger as by her failure to find the police station. Though they received food to eat, the effect was the same. Their digestive system was unable to process the food they so desperately craved and needed. The story they now presented was that they were victims of a bomb attack on Bromberg/Bydgoszcz which elicited suspicion at their next stop, where the son was in SS uniform, causing them to beat a hasty retreat at the first opportunity. The subsequent days were spent begging for food and for clothing which replaced the striped prison garb they had been wearing. A common malady of the marches was frostbite, in the case of Griesbach's mother so severe that by the time they reached the town of Wangerin, her toes had become blackened and gangrene had set in. Thanks to the intervention of a local doctor, they were able to secure transport to a military hospital where twenty other patients were also waiting for amputation. These desperate women were also dealing with lice that had become part of their clothing, and when their German "hosts" became aware of lice, the women were promptly ejected from the home. Griesbach writes about the fiction she created to cover and protect her mother and herself: on the refugee form she had to fill in all the details of their previous life. With one stroke of the pen, they became Protestants, *Volksdeutsche* from Bromberg/Bydgoszcz. Her father was a German soldier from Witzenhausen, her mother's maiden name was "Katzen" and she was from a farm in a community called Wichmannshausen. She writes that Katzenstein sounded too Jewish. Griesbach found work in Sternberg as a maid with a pharmacist (who was a high-ranking SA man) and his wife whom she describes as "a fanatical National Socialist."[75] The woman prodded Griesbach with questions—how the Poles had treated her as a German, if she had ever known any Polish Jews, berating her as "deceived" when she said the one Polish-Jewish couple in her acquaintance had been nice and friendly. She had also given her *The Protocols of the Elders of Zion* to read.[76]

Other perils of the marches included running into people who might recognize them as former prisoners of Stutthof or its sub-camps. Bromberg/Bydgoszcz was one of the larger ones, and one day Griesbach was introduced as a refugee from Bromberg/Bydgoszcz to the former stationmaster of nearby Thorn/Toruń where Griesbach had, in fact, worked for a while on the rail lines. The brief encounter and his strange look that suggested recognition caused her inner panic. Once more, she beat a hasty retreat. At the end of April, the hospital was evacuated and Griesbach was allowed by the pharmacist's wife to bring her mother to the home. The woman had earlier declared her ability to sniff out the particular smell of a Jew, a skill that in this case let her down. In fact, she described the mother as "a refined lady," having expected a peasant woman. Besides, the family had other jobs to attend to, in face of the imminent arrival of the Soviets—they set about burying their Nazi uniforms, a bust of Hitler and *The Protocols* in the barn and covered the hole with soil. The author uses the first-person plural to describe the activity, conferring on her narrative a note of profound irony that adds depth and dimension to an otherwise relentlessly stressful tale of danger—a seventeen-year-old Jewish girl helped bury icons of the Nazi regime. In fact, the German language that had given her entrance to a German identity helped during the next stage of their journey which she spent on an open truck with German soldiers, fleeing to the west, along with French, Belgian, and Dutch prisoners who had worked for the Todt Organization. The vehicle was running on wood alcohol (methylated spirits) which the soldiers began to imbibe, causing them to become both inebriated and sick. In their drunkenness, they began to sing the Nazi song, "Today, Germany belongs to us and tomorrow the whole world." Griesbach writes: "It was so funny that I turned around and smiled at them."[77] She writes that among the German soldiers there was some discussion of turning themselves in to the Americans who, they reasoned, would welcome them now as allies; together they would push back the Russians. Griesbach describes the chaos on the roads that were clogged with armored tanks, refugees, soldiers, SS men, camp prisoners, animals, etc. She writes that some soldiers were attempting to divest themselves of their uniforms and their weapons, but were stopped by SS men who called them betrayers of their country and shot them—"prosecutors, judges and executioners had become one."[78]

This memoir also includes anecdotes about American liberators who were Jewish, some of them German-born. When she first approached an American soldier to ask about getting in touch with her aunt in the USA, he informed her they could not fraternize with Germans, upon which she declared herself to be Jewish. "I am too," he told her and gave her chocolate. She then approached a man in prisoner uniform and asked if there were Jews among the prisoners gathered in the street. He explained he was Jewish. It was from him that Griesbach learned that terrible things had happened to the Jews, especially German Jews. Yet, she was not able to identify herself as a Jew when he asked her if she was Jewish. "I still was afraid to admit that to a German-speaking person and I answered, 'No, but I had some Jewish relatives.'"[79] The next day, however, offered another opportunity, again with an American Jewish officer, by the name of Sternberg who was able to find help for her and her mother as camp survivors. He also told her that four million Jews had perished, a number that later she had to correct. Because Griesbach and her mother were posing as German refugees when they were liberated, their story was questioned. Lieutenant Sternberg brought a survivor of Auschwitz and Sachsenhausen to her mother's hospital bed to verify their identity and because the other patients did not know they were Jews, she had to speak to him outside the hospital room and explained to him their story. Upon accepting the veracity of her story, the Americans sent them with fifty other survivors to Lübeck where they came under the protection of the British. They spent two and a half years there, before immigrating to the USA. They later learned that her fifty-eight-year-old father had died on November 21, 1944, in a sub-camp of Stutthof. Her brother was deported on September 10, 1944, from Stutthof to Auschwitz where he too perished.

The Collapse of Towns near Danzig

What about other towns, like Elbing, that have been part of this book, especially as centers for sub-camps? The inhabitants of Elbing also joined the long treks to the west after it had fallen into Soviet hands. Foster was still the loyal Gauleiter and remained adamant that the town had to be defended, and ordered that he would have every official in Elbing shot who did not remain at his post.[80] On the dawning of January 24, it was still possible to evacuate the hospitals and the prison and move them to Danzig, but as the day progressed all order was lost: "Unwanted items discarded by the refugees—suitcases, boxes, bedding, typewriters, small items of furniture, items of clothing—were strewn across the streets. It was a dismal train of old, totally exhausted people, crying children, young women with screaming babies."[81] According to Kieser, there were about 20,000 refugees and homeless persons in the cellars of Elbing.[82] About 4,200 made their way to Danzig where they encountered a life full of activity like they had known in Elbing before January 23: "The trains were running, people were strolling along the Langgasse and shopping. The cinemas were showing the same film as in Elbing, *Opfergang,* and the refugees were blocking the streets to the harbor."[83] In the treks that made their way to the west were also prisoners of war—French, Russians— and whether they were prisoners of war or forced laborers, they, too, were sent to labor camps of the east.[84] Kieser claims that the Soviets believed that these people had already been infected with fascist ideology and had to be isolated, and that already in 1941, Stalin had ordered that all prisoners of war had to be treated as traitors.[85] There were thousands of French and Belgian prisoners of war who had been employed in the gardens of the Prussian gentry, like the Frenchman who worked for Count Eulenberg and was now driving him to the west.[86] By the end of January, the Soviets had the southern coast of the lagoon between Elbing and Frauenburg in their hands.[87]

Prussian Apocalypse is focused on the plight of Germans attempting to leave East Prussia in 1945, but in presenting their misery it also provides a context that underscores an even greater one—the predicament of camp prisoners who were not part of these treks but who were caught up in them—as participants and victims.[88] On some roads, these treks stretched for sixteen kilometers. On January 26, refugees from Heiligenbeil had blocked Ice Road One when the Fourth Army designated it as a supply route—there were five such roads. In the six weeks from January 26 to March 4, hundreds of thousands of the 2.3 million people resident in East Prussia were allowed to use that route to safety.[89] By the first days of March, only a few were able to cross because the ice was already deep under the water. It vanished on March 4, taking everything with it "shot-up wagons, dead horses and the many thrown-away pieces of baggage."[90]

Prisoners Move through the Former "Corridor," and Locals See Them

The exhibition *Jews in Stutthof* offered the following segment about the response of locals toward the marches as the inmates of Stutthof made their way through largely Kashubian territory in "the Corridor." This is how Shoshana Rabinowicz described it:

> Local people shouted "Stutthof goes." People looked at this march of skeletons, march of shadows with interest. They gathered along the route and waited for hours in cold and snow to see us. Some came from far away and stood there in silence despite the shouts and scolding of armed soldiers that guarded the column. But at that time, most people weren't afraid of them anymore. They stood, like grey stones along the road in the cemetery of Europe; full of anger, accusing without words. That evening local people brought big buckets full of hot, thick soup to the church where we were put for the night. It was bean soup, with meat, with pork fat. We ate it without spoons, straight from plates or cans. We drank this hot soup, burning our lips. Our lips, burst from frost and snow which we ate while marching, were infected because we slept on dirty straw and we were exposed to dirt everywhere. Most of the women had swollen lips with painful, festering wounds.[91]

The evacuation and aftermath of the Stutthof camp complex are also included in the interviews with family members that we have included in the preceding chapters. How was the relationship between Germans and Poles affected after the war? It is also clear that reference to the maltreatment of Jews recurs in several interviews. Edwin Knut (referring to Chwarzno, 1944) makes a distinction between local Germans and East Prussians. He says that in 1944, local Germans became religious, giving as an example a man called Schneider on their farm who started to read the Bible. Germans from East Prussia, on the other hand, were afraid, even before the Russians came, and began to flee. They were coming through the area with all the belongings they could carry—with wagons and horses. They were broken people who did not expect to lose the war. He distinguishes them from local Germans—whom he calls "our" Germans. (Presumably these are the same group referred to earlier as "die hiesigen.") When local Germans fled, they didn't take anything, only wagons and horses. In two or three weeks, the front moved, and the Germans came back. Some even stayed and died there, years later. Apparently, there were at least some who did not see themselves as Prussians—if, in fact, they ever had.

Janina Dąbrowska gives personal and regional details about the marches from the perspective of a Kashubian family living in the former "Corridor." Without giving dates, apart from "At the end of the war," she refers to the kindness shown to the prisoners, a welcome detail after such grueling accounts. "The Germans brought prisoners from Stutthof to Bytów. They stopped here for the night. They slept in barns, each SS-man had two or more prisoners who pulled a wagon with his belongings."[92] Her mother gave two pieces of bread to the prisoners. One of these prisoners turned out to be a local man who reappeared after the war as a policeman. Janina's father had advised him to flee through the forest which he did. Six months later he returned to the neighborhood for the funeral of a friend and made his way to the Dąbrowska home.

Zofia Lichy's recollection reminds us that these marches did not take place in a vacuum. Local people saw the prisoners as they dragged themselves through the snow. What she saw was unmistakable abuse of Jews. She says, referring to January 1945:

> I was on my way to Kiszewa to get rationed butter and milk. I saw Jews moving down the road. I heard screams and shots being fired. It was January, terribly cold, no snow. I stood near the house at the road. I saw SS-men in black uniforms on bicycles. They told me to get off the road and turn around facing the wall of the house and put my hands up ... They rushed a group of Jews along the road. They did not look like humans, barefoot, wrapped in dark blue blankets, beaten up, half-frozen. Eyes and faces were not human anymore. I can still see those faces before my eyes ... As I walked down Kiszewa Hill, I saw, on both sides of the roads, people who were shot and were not yet dead. I saw bodies wrapped in blankets, with bare feet.[93]

Franciszek Słomiński places his memory toward the end of the war. He, too, remembers the maltreatment of Jews:

> I saw Germans driving Jews through Kiszewa. It was a noise like wild geese passing by, those Jews were groaning so much. It was a large group of around 50 people,

and there were bicycles with guns on the ready, aimed to hit Jews who had to keep up. If anyone lagged behind, they were shot right away. Every few meters there was a corpse. The corpses and those barely alive were left while the rest walked on. Nobody stopped. When we learned that they were going through Kiszewa and that they were very hungry, we prepared slices of bread, potatoes and we threw them from a distance in the direction of the Jews, otherwise the Germans would have beaten us up or shot us. They caught food in the air, and if people bent down they risked being violently hit with a rifle. It was a horrible, terrible experience, and I will never forget their agony as long as I live. Corpses were strewn, massacred, half-naked. Later, the villagers collected the bodies and buried them in the cemetery.[94]

Stanisława Dysarz's worst memory is of Jews being led by Ukrainians (presumably guards) into Kiszewski Manor. "They beat them terribly, like animals. When Jews spotted a pot with fodder for pigs, they ate it all. If some of them couldn't walk anymore, they were shot on the spot. In Kiszewski Manor two Jews were killed. They were driven, terribly hungry, and cold, and their legs were frostbitten."[95]

Destination Danzig: The Fall of a Former Free City

The destination for all refugees was Danzig where preparations had already begun in October to evacuate the city, in contrast to the chaotic preparations and conflicting orders that were in Stutthof. The contrast in the depiction of prisoners on marches and the evacuation of civilians, whether from Danzig and environs or East Prussia, could not illustrate more vividly what it meant to be German and what it meant to be a prisoner of the German Reich in 1945. Wąs's chapter on "Danzig during and after the War" points to the difference. On October 25, 1944 mobilization was directed at all men between sixteen and sixty.[96] They were ordered to assemble on Heumarkt (today's Długa Street and Plac Sienny). Right after the pledge of allegiance, they were given shovels and directed to dig trenches around the city. Mobilization also included refugees from the East. Wąs points out that the early fall 1944 evacuation from East Prussia was still quite orderly. Horses pulled wagons loaded with belongings and food supplies—lard, back fat, and salted meat. They also arrived by train, and in the town of Saspe/Zaspa (where Stutthof's dead used to be buried) a refugee camp had been set up where refugees could rest and prepare a hot meal. By the end of the year, however, the situation had changed dramatically and was heading for chaos. A Pole originally from Gdańsk, sent from Stutthof in November to build trenches comments, "On the platforms of Gdańsk's train station I saw pyramids of luggage. These were the belongings of East Prussians who were waiting with their owners to be sent to the West."[97] Danzig would not have been able to cope with the evacuations of refugees, without the high level of organization for the refugees in the west. Preparations to evacuate archives, valuable collections and antiques were already in place before the *Deutschland* set sail in January 1945 with 500 cargo containers that held the most sophisticated and most valuable laboratory equipment from the Politechnika Gdańska, along with 300 faculty members and their families. The ship set sail to Kiln and from there they traveled to Schmalkalden in Thuringia where they intended to set up the Polytechnic.[98]

It is also clear that there was preferential treatment, as happened to the group described above. Many high-ranking members of the SS and Gestapo had left by February. Only the first wave of refugees was allowed to take along their valuables, mainly furs and jewelry, but furniture was not allowed, unless someone had special connections with railroad workers. In depicting the human misery of refugees, streaming into Gdańsk, Wąs emphasizes the dramatic difference between their sufferings, as real as they were, and the wretched condition of the prisoners from Stutthof. He writes that the misery experienced by local people does not even approach what the evacuated prisoners from Stutthof experienced—forced, as they were, to cover 140 kilometers in seven days—through Pruszcz Gdański, Kolbudy, Żukowo to Lębork. He adds starkly: "They never made it."[99] One of the evacuees from Stutthof— Maria Chodakowska relates, "There were a lot of bodies on the snow, shot because they couldn't walk anymore. I saw one SS-man kicking a prisoner to death. It was a beautiful winter day, on a hill, and the SS man kicked this man so long that he died."[100]

Taking Responsibility

Who was responsible for this last phase of Stutthof and its sub-camps? Wąs places the primary blame on Commandant Paul-Werner Hoppe, the man who introduced the gas chamber to the camp and on whose watch some 47,000 Jews, mostly women and children (Wąs adds), died. He also notes that when Hoppe was tried in Bochum in 1955, he was charged only for organizing a "death march" from Stutthof. In his court testimony, Hoppe blamed Fritz Katzmann, claiming that he informed Katzmann and the Amt D in Oranienburg that they needed to look at other options for the evacuation.[101] He also claimed that Katzmann had set him a later directive, saying that even the sick had to be evacuated. Among those who stayed were prisoners deemed to be "economically essential and those who worked in the workshops or in administration."[102]

The initial verdict on Hoppe was five years of imprisonment, and after an appeal, nine years. Hoppe was a free man in 1960 and died in 1974. Charles Sydnor points out that during Hoppe's trial he was especially criticized for the brutalities inflicted on the inmates in January 1945, so that they would not fall into the hands of the Russians alive. Sydnor also castigates the allies and the West Germans for their ineptitude, citing the fact that while in custody, having been arrested by the British in Holstein in April 1946 and while waiting to be extradited to Poland, Hoppe escaped and went into hiding. For the next seven years, he remained free under various aliases in Switzerland and West Germany. He was finally arrested by German authorities in April 1953 and after a lengthy, protracted court case of four years, was sentenced in Bochum to nine years in prison as an accessory to several hundred murders while Commandant of Stutthof.[103] Segev gives more details about Hoppe's life after his release from prison. He worked in an insurance agency in Bochum, estranged from his son for most of the time that was left to him before his death at age sixty-four in a hospital in Bochum. In an interview with Segev, Hoppe's son spoke openly about his father's agonizing deathbed experience.[104] Jörg Hoppe had visited Stutthof and was shocked by the impact that photographs of his father in uniform had on him. He saw firsthand evidence of the gas chamber and on his return, visited his father to let him know he had gone to Stutthof, bringing back Polish guidebooks as proof. His father's response was: "All this never happened. It's all lies. Communist brainwashing." He further claimed that the Poles had brought instruments of torture and murder to Stutthof which had existed only at Auschwitz. He assured his son that he was going to write a book and set it all straight. He had done his duty.[105]

Blatman's contribution to our understanding of the death marches is particularly valuable when it comes to the fate of the prisoners from the filial camps. Wąs also refers to the smaller "death marches" that involved 22,500 prisoners, mainly Jewish women. In the death marches that left Stutthof and its sub camps, 16,500 lives perished.[106] Blatman says that Hoppe's January 25 directive made no mention of the plans for any of the sub-camps, including ones in Silesia.[107] He cites the case of a small sub-camp called Szerokpas where 500–600 Jewish women had been sent to work in August. It was evacuated on January 13 with 150 of the women who had survived it. Thirty remained behind with one guard who killed all of them by lethal injections.[108] This policy of liquidation (before they even started off) occurred in several camps, for example, in Gutowo/Guttendorf where 1,000 of the 1,200–1,500 prisoners survived. He draws from testimonies of survivors of these sub-camps, like Nowa Mito, where they murdered the women with injections of kerosene, strychnine or Lysol. At Hopehill, fifty women were shot before the evacuation which Blatman places in a larger camp context, attributing their deaths by murder in part to being Jewish. In larger camps like Auschwitz and Groß-Rosen the sick and dying were simply left to their own devices.[109]

Some were fortunate, in that the Soviets caught up with the convoys and could liberate the prisoners, like the 500 Jewish women in Sophienwalde/Dziemiany which was evacuated at the end of February by the Soviets. Others escaped into the forests and survived there until the Red Army arrived on March 10–12 and liberated them.[110] Esra Juerman was also one of the more fortunate. This is how he remembers his liberation early in February. He was in a sub-camp in Danzig, working in the kitchen unit and along with others in "special units" had to stay behind when the others were evacuated. After a few days, they were taken to the sub-camp at Treil where he hid under boots and covers (presumably from German soldiers) and ended up in Burggraben which already had been liberated. Sick with typhus, he was taken to a Russian hospital where he was nursed back to health. He was sixteen, and in his words, "sincerely believed that anyone who wasn't German could not be antisemitic."[111]

Archival data, the scholarship by historians, and the testimonies and memoirs presented in this chapter essentially support Blatman's thesis that the evacuations of the camps of the Third Reich were not a footnote to their previous history and constitute a separate narrative that, though linked to what preceded, needs to be read as a separate phase of terror. The death marches were not the last segment of "the final solution," with the exclusive aim of killing the remaining Jews of Europe. Many Jews were indeed killed or died during the evacuation from the Stutthof camp system, but not as part of a separate, predetermined plan to kill them. There were several factors involved but as in other evacuations throughout the occupied territories, their immediate fate lay in the hands of SS guards, which could not have bode well, given their previous brutal treatment of prisoners at Stutthof and its sub-camps. Besides, the presence of thousands of refugees fleeing from East Prussia reminded them that the advance of the Soviet army was imminent and was a juggernaut that irresistibly and mercilessly threatened all in its path.

R.M. Douglas's book on the expulsions of Germans from East Prussia at the end of the war has filled a huge gap in the history of this neglected period of the war. He refers to the later reception in the Federal Republic of refugees from East Prussia, saying that their flight was:

> memorialized and mythologized, becoming one of the founding tropes of the Federal Republic in 1949: a new democratic Germany, born in victimhood and suffering, standing as a beacon of hope and a haven for those seeking refuge from the Bolshevik hordes. Unquestionably, for the millions who fled the Soviet offensive, and the millions more who, after days or weeks on the roads of East Prussia and German Silesia in subfreezing temperatures, were overwhelmed by the Red Army's shockingly rapid advance, the withdrawal was a grim ordeal. Large numbers did reach relative safety, thanks in part to the greatest seaborne evacuation in history in which more than two million refugees were transported from the collapsing northeastern provinces by the German Navy.[112]

But was it, as he also claims, one of the few events "not to be disfigured by a lengthy list of Nazi atrocities?"[113] Relatively speaking, this is a reasonable claim, but it is hard to accept it fully in view of what the victims of the Baltic camps suffered. The absence of references to other people who also were part of these long marches and treks in East Prussia is not deliberate, but it is nonetheless an omission, namely of the human remains of the liquidated camps of Stutthof. They are likewise barely present in the popular history—*Prussian Apocalypse*. What Kieser writes about is the morale of German soldiers in April, right before the fall of the Nazi regime, and how officers of Artillery Regiment 1/551 had celebrated all night long with "doubtful ladies ... brought in on Wehrmacht vehicles." He adds, "This behavior found even less understanding as the liquidation of concentration camps in the Samland was spoken about. The prisoners had belonged to a transport of several thousand Jews coming from the Baltic and were being driven on foot toward Elbing."[114] The author then refers to the blending of the prisoners with the general stream of refugees and the subsequent deaths of prisoners whose bodies were left lying unburied at the side of the road.[115] In writing about Danzig being cut off, he describes "the slowly moving wagons on foot: women with children in their arms, old people with hardly any baggage, young people coming across the fields on their bicycles." Then comes a sentence that intrudes shockingly into the depiction of misery, "A group of female concentration camp prisoners appeared on the roadside. Some swung themselves on to the wagons but were unable to hold on for long and vanished again."[116] Unwittingly, the author has depicted the fate of the survivors of Stutthof's sub-camps. Too feeble to hold on to the last prop of survival, they disappeared into the bleak winter landscape of East Prussia.

Figure 1 A Grave and Its Gravestone Bear Witness.

But they must at least be acknowledged—as victims and not as prisoners who suddenly appeared at the side of the road. These women were no sudden apparition but were already the victims of Nazi terror, some for years. This last trek is the final blow inflicted on their emaciated bodies by the Nazis. The bodies of some victims of the marches were later exhumed and given a proper burial. Others have found, in the former "Polish Corridor," a final resting place in recent years, off the main road in the Kashubian village of Będomin, around six miles from the town of Kościerznya and thirty miles from Gdańsk. The gravestone, with a Star of David, indicates that thirty Jewish women are buried there and that they perished in March 1945 on a death march from Stutthof.[117] Local people tend the grave. Gauleiter Forster had boasted about making "the Corridor" free both of Poles and of Jews. We know that he did not succeed in his lifetime; this grave shows that he never will.

Around that time, in the spring of 1945, Günter Grass was taking part in a training session. He writes about this brief exposure to one of the Junker schools during his short-lived tenure with the Waffen SS. During these last weeks of the war, they were training young men who possessed "the proper national and racial consciousness for future positions after the final victory." They wanted to teach these young men "to handle *Lebensraum* issues, to resettle the non-German population, rebuild the cities, manage the economy."[118] Could there be a more striking contrast between these grand designs for a Germandom that had been defeated and the graveyard for Jewish women in Będomin on territory the Germans referred to as "the Polish Corridor?" Where Poles were dispossessed of their homes and identities, driven out in order to provide living space for those described in the Junker schools of Nazi Germany as having "the proper racial consciousness"? Where Jews from the towns of "the Polish Corridor" were driven out of their homes to die in camps like Stutthof or to be sent to Auschwitz or death camps to be annihilated? Będomin is off the beaten track both of history and of geography. May this grave for thirty unnamed Jewish women, cared for by unnamed Poles and Kashubians remain as a commemorative emblem for all the victims of Stutthof and its filial camps after a long hiatus of shame and silence. May they rest in peace.

Figure 2 Tombstone at Będomin.[119]

Epilogue

Stutthof/Sztutowo: *The Silent Zone*

In 1990, Günter Grass referred to "the incomprehensible and indefinable quality of Auschwitz, the open wound, a guilt that will remain."[1] I do not question either his sincerity or the veracity of the statement. Grass's lifelong commitment to exposing the dangers of totalitarian regimes, his engagement with the Third Reich, and the atrocities perpetrated during the Holocaust are a vital part of his legacy. This statement, however, predates two key events in his life—the publication of *Krebsgang/ Crab Walk* in 2002 and his confession in *Beim Häuten der Zwiebel/Peeling the Onion* in 2006 that as a seventeen-year-old he had served in the Waffen SS. His silence had lasted a half century before he could bring himself to speak publicly about his own guilt. Grass was certainly not the only one to suppress a segment of his past, albeit a brief one, but he had meanwhile enjoyed, as few other German writers had, an international reputation for moral correctness and for exposing the hypocrisies of the rest of the world.

In *Sinking Ships*, an article that also predates Grass's confession, historian Robert Moeller correctly points out that it was not Auschwitz that preoccupied Grass in *Crabwalk* but the sinking of the *Wilhelm Gustloff* by a Soviet submarine on January 30, 1945, in which as many as 9,000 passengers, including some 4,000 submarine recruits and 370 naval personnel died. In his novel, Grass placed a by-now familiar fictional character on board the ship—Tulla Pokriefke whom we last saw in *Dog Years* collecting tickets on a tram in Danzig. In Grass's fictional world, she not only survived till 1945 but gave birth during the rescue at sea to a son named Paul, who later became a mediocre journalist in the Federal Republic. Tulla tried to influence Paul to write about the sinking of the *Wilhelm Gustloff* and the loss of so many German refugees fleeing from the Red Army, but it is her grandson who was to take up the challenge, not driven by ambition or artistic talent, but by his internet fixation with a rightwing website devoted to the German tragedy.

Grass's novel coincided with the growing desire in Germany to address German suffering under the Nazis, which, many argued, had been treated as a taboo subject and had languished in postwar silence. For example, a March 25, 2002, headline in *Der Spiegel* noted, it was now time to acknowledge "Germans as Victims."[2] Moeller does not skirt around the issue of German suffering—he refers to the expulsions of twelve million from Eastern Europe and the push to equate their suffering with that of Jewish victims—both of which were perceived as stemming "from a spirit of national and racial hatred."[3] He also notes the opposing views of social scientist Jürgen Habermas, who challenged the notion of "mourning collective fates, without distinguishing between culprits and victims," of historian and camp survivor Eugen Kogon, and of philosopher Karl Jaspers who criticized Germans who were seeking "to mitigate their own culpability for National Socialism by emphasizing their own suffering and who did not recognize the 'blessing of defeat.'"[4] Moeller does not accept that the experiences of expellees were forgotten. On the contrary, he argues, they had been incorporated into the political discourse of the Federal Republic.[5]

But Moeller's focus is much more specific and centers on the representation of history in *Crabwalk*, which, he concludes, is an incomplete one. After asking if it is still possible to include Jews and Germans in the same story, he proposes a solution. And this is where Stutthof enters the discussion. Moeller points out that the port of departure for the *Gustloff* was Gdynia/Gotenhafen, which was not far from Stutthof, site of a German concentration camp from which 37,000 Jews were evacuated in early 1945. Only about 20,000 would survive the "death marches" and attempted evacuations by sea … In telling the tales of war's end, there might be ways to allow the paths of Germans and Jews to cross … But it might be possible to describe January 1945 in East Prussia in ways that also make it possible to hear a Kaddish recited for the victims of the concentration camps that dotted eastern Europe, including the area surrounding Danzig.[6] He continues: "Perhaps it will be possible for writers—of the power, insight, and intelligence of Germany's Nobel laureate- and historians to put these pieces together in a narrative." It may require, he proposes, "walking like a crab," in order to move forward.[7]

I make no claim on any of these qualities nor even on the suggested mode of viewing a segment of history that has engaged scholars for over a half a century. This book has certainly moved forward slowly over several years; its direction and pace have been shaped—if not equally—by both the literary legacy of Grass and the archival work that I have collated from Polish researchers at the Stutthof Museum. I have also included the voices of a diverse group of witnesses and have tried to keep their narratives within the larger frame of the camp and the history of the Third Reich. I trust that my own voice has captured to some degree the dissonance of a camp where so many died on the territory of a former free city, captured in the prose of Grass and within earshot of the nearby Baltic. The first time I visited Stutthof and smelled the pungent fragrance of pines and the salty sea air, I was reminded of the Baltic's haunting cadence as a leitmotif in Thomas Mann's *Tonio Kröger*. I always thought there was nothing lyrical about the sea near Stutthof until I read Ruth Alton's memoir. She wrote:

> Death camp Stutthof.—Most people have never heard of it, since it was not a particularly large camp. However, in terms of dreadful surroundings, it could compete with other death camps. Death camp Stutthof.—Located not too far from the sea. Built on white dunes, surrounded by pine forests. The air was pure and pungent. A strange backdrop for such tragic violence.[8]

In fact, the Baltic acted as a barrier for prisoners who ever thought of escape. Of course, it was there for the SS men to swim in on hot summer days, and later, farther up the coast, it became the burial ground for thousands of prisoners (mostly Jewish women) who perished in its icy waters. Can Germans and Jews then ever be brought together? By bringing Stutthof into the conversation, Moeller implicitly touches on other victims of Nazi terror. No mention of Stutthof would be complete without reference to the suffering of Poles as well as Jews and then to other ethnic groups that made up its population, including Russian POWs. That conversation would lead inexorably to what happened after January 1945 when Soviet soldiers turned on the East Prussian population, pillaged their countryside, and raped with impunity an unprecedented number of women that made the young officer Solzhenitsyn confess to joining them. When the woman begged him in German not to shoot her, he later wrote (in 1950) of that moment of shame: "Have no fear! ... For—Oh!—already/Another's soul is on my soul."[9]

Mercy and Revenge

Few have earned the right to be included in the conversation about reconciliation as has Graf Hans von Lehndorff, who told the story of his lost *Heimat* in the memoir *East Prussian Diary*. It is based on notes he had written during the expulsions, which Count von Lehndorff experienced firsthand during the fall of Königsberg where he worked as a surgeon, tending to the sick and wounded, including women with venereal diseases caused from being raped by Russian soldiers.[10] Two of his brothers had already been killed in action, his cousin had been executed for his participation in the assassination attempt on Hitler, and his mother had been incarcerated for a time by the Nazis for helping Jews and members of the Confessing Church in Berlin. During his flight westward, he learned that the Soviets had killed his mother and remaining brother. All that was left of his ancestral home was for him to view (from afar) the new tenants who had appropriated his family's possessions, and to furtively tend the graves of his ancestors. His diary includes some incidents that are narrated without commentary and gives an ironic view on local response to the prospect of the Soviet invasion. For example, on January 23, 1945, he writes about treating a woman for leg ulcers and advising her to keep on moving before the Soviets arrived. "She said, 'The Fuehrer would never let us fall into the hands of the Russ; he'd gas us first.' I stole a glance at the people around us, but nobody seemed to think there was anything extraordinary about this declaration."[11] He gives firsthand commentary on the naïve notion—at the end of February—of a German victory. A Nazi Public Relations officer gave a "morale-boosting talk at the end of February to the wounded. He declared that hundreds of German tanks had arrived in Pillau with new weapons. They would join a division en route from Breslau. East Prussians should flee westward because everyone could be assured that they would return after Hitler had defeated the Russians ... They were urged to go to see the film 'Kohlberg' which was being shown at the theater."[12]

On April 12, when they were fifteen miles from Königsberg, he describes a night spent in a cow barn that could be read as a parallel text to Solzhenitsyn's *Prussian*

Nights. Women in their group were searched out with lanterns and dragged out to be raped. "'*Davai suda*' 'Come here!' ... has a more horrific sound than all the curses in the world ... It didn't matter to them in the least that they were handling semi-corpses. Eighty-year-old women were no safer from them than unconscious ones."[13] His aunt, Frau von Stein meanwhile had survived. "My aunt had no complaint to make about her treatment by the Poles. They had beaten her once, and that wasn't pleasant; but otherwise all that had happened to her so far has been like a period of convalescence compared with the half year under the Gestapo in Allenstein."[14] Frau von Stein had eventually been accepted in the Polish community and like all the other women, went to work each day and was given flour and a quart of skimmed milk for the day's food ration.[15] Lehndorff was among some 400 Germans who had been allowed to go to the west by the Poles. Rosenberg, the sub-prefect of the area asked him to say a few words about their fair treatment by the Poles, reminding him that the Germans had maltreated the Poles earlier. He complies with the simple statement, "Our people did the same to the Poles earlier on, and unfortunately that is true."[16] In a world of revenge and retribution, his words ring noble and true. They are rare expressions of German responsibility in the immediate postwar period.

There are few depictions of mercy extended to perpetrators or those associated with them in the aftermath of the Nazi defeat that would invite the kind of reconciliation envisaged by Moeller. The last chapter of this book ended with the demise of the Nazi regime and the flight of those who had buttressed it to the end. The prisoners who survived the evacuation marches offer little hope in their narratives, but the exceptions stand out—be it local Kashubians offering food to the starving as they marched—or the one in Helen Lewis's memoir, which is in a different category because it involves an SS man. She had written earlier in her memoir about an SS guard—a teacher in his former life—who had given the women a sandwich on a regular basis while they worked in a sub-camp. He distributed it to different women on the days that he was on duty, and it was a lifesaver to them. During the evacuation marches, he retained his kindness and humanity toward the women under his supervision.

Lewis writes that they found out later that the teacher, during the retreat from the camp and on the march, was in charge of distributing food and medicines and encouraging the prisoners "to keep alive their spirits and their hope of delivery."[17] After the Soviet troops arrived, they were going to, in her words, "make short shrift of the SS man" but the sick prisoners stood up for him and persuaded the liberators that they owed him their lives and they were now responsible for his. Finally, the Russians gave in and let him go. Lewis writes, "where to, nobody knows." She continues, "I have often thought of him, hoping he made his way home to tell his tale and teach again."[18]

Lewis also writes about a later incident when she and other prisoners were recuperating in a hospital under the care of the Soviets. One day a prisoner recognized a former female guard who was now posing as a doctor. The effect was traumatic on the former prisoners who immediately reported her deception to the hospital personnel. She was taken outside and shot.

Liberation was a double-edged sword that brought both revenge by Soviet troops in their path westward and liberation for prisoners trapped in the sub-camps and evacuation centers of Stutthof. Solzhenitsyn remembers the revenge in images of flames and of fire, in the midst of a snow-covered landscape. Military columns are compared to molten lava, sweeping everything away "[w]ith wild cries, whistling, headlights' glare."[19] He identifies local towns: "Klein Koslau, Gross Koslau—Every village—is now a fire"![20]

In other areas, Russians liquidated the German resistance centers one after another. A Soviet officer—Colonel Wladimir Coglin wrote to his mother: "We are walking on corpses, sitting down to rest on corpses, and eating meals among corpses. For the next ten kilometers, there are two dead Fritz's per square meter ... Whole battalions of prisoners of war are being led out with their commanders. I don't understand why we should take them to POW camps. We've got so many of them already and there are fifteen thousand more coming. They walk without an escort, like sheep."[21] Another Red Army officer, L. Labiczew wrote: "Once we got to the banks of the Vistula Bay, the entire beach was littered with German helmets, machine guns, empty food cans, and packs of cigarettes. Along the shore of the sea there were small houses. Wounded Fritzes lay on beds or on the floor. They looked at us in silence. There was no fear or hate in their faces, only dull oblivion, even though they knew that we only had to pick up a gun and shoot them."[22]

But what about local Poles, especially those who welcomed them as "liberators"? This is how Anna Narloch remembers it in Konarzyny, on February 28, 1945:

> The Russians came. We thought they were our friends, our allies, that they had liberated us ....We came out to greet them. They walked all over the neighborhood and were stealing. They took our bicycle, two suits, father's watch and other things. Girls had to hide otherwise they would have been raped. My sister and I hid together. I was 19 and my sister 21 years old. A lot of women were raped in Konarzyny. It was not the kind of liberation we had in mind.[23]

Even former prisoners of the Stutthof camp system, like Cecylia Zabrocka, were not spared harassment:

> I was in Potulice (a sub-camp) from September 1943 till March 1945. Just before the end of the war, we were all told to leave the camp because the camp and its surroundings were being mined and the camp was going to be destroyed. They managed to remove most of the people from the camp, but some of us stayed behind because we were afraid where they would take us next. We hid in the grounds of the camp in a cellar, where we waited three more weeks, until the front moved on. On the day the war ended we found food upstairs in a canteen. The tables were nicely set with plates, and it looked so empty, as if an alarm had gone off and everyone ran out. The gate was open, and in the snow lay the corpses of the worst SS-men, all bundled up in rags so that they wouldn't be recognized. Poles dressed in whatever they could find, put on armbands and stood at the gate. The food supply hall was open, and there was a lot of food—sweet rolls, everything. Beans were in huge pots ready to be cooked for soup, but they didn't have time to make it. My mother and I walked from Potulice on foot, behind the front line. We passed corpses strewn everywhere. We met Russians, and had problems with

them, for sometimes they teased us aggressively, and we had to hide from them for they were chasing women. ... We took quite a few things from the camp, but they were heavy to pull and we tossed them into the ditch on our way home. We even threw away an alarm clock that we had from home. The only thing that mattered was food, and to reach home. ... It was a terrible trek, but we made it home safely—to this place that we call home.[24]

We have already seen in preceding chapters the fate of the SS leaders of Stutthof, but there is one man—Albert Forster—who did not pay for the consequences of his life as a ruthless Gauleiter until well beyond liberation. His presence dominated the first chapter in this book, beginning in the early 1930s when he worked as the active interpreter of Nazi policy in Danzig and then as the man in charge of Danzig-West Prussia. Albert Forster will be forever associated with the implementation of forced Germandom, the expulsion of Jews from Danzig and Pomerania, the annihilation of Polish life, and the murder of *Juden und Pfaffen*. Though he only visited the camp twice—on June 22, 1941, and on April 9, 1943—his influence never receded.[25] Hitler had referred in *Mein Kampf* to the necessity of having fighters to build and win power for a movement. Robert Koehl identified three categories of such fighters in the Nazi movement. In the first two rankings, he places a few of the best known names of the movement. Albert Forster heads up the third ranking, along with four others who "generated the force necessary to unite Germans and drive them forward."[26] What was the fate of this man who, though an outsider to Danzig held the reins for the whole period of the Nazi regime over the whole region? His end was as ignominious as his career was "successful" as a Nazi Gauleiter and Governor/*Staathalter* of Danzig-West Prussia. He had been able to flee from the Soviets, but was finally caught in August 1946 by the British in Warsaw and handed over to Polish authorities. His greatest concern, according to Marek Wąs, was that he would not be allowed to defend himself.[27] Forster is described by Wąs as the consummate politician—astute, skilled, intelligent, and adaptable—a man without moral principles. In 1948, he was ready to collaborate with the Soviets and cravenly offered his political acumen to help their cause, along with his practical experience to track known enemies of the new regime. Interviewed after his trial by a prominent Polish journalist who had been imprisoned in Ravensbrück, he attributed his failures to his inability to speak Polish. He refused to be seen as a victim and did not want to die as a Nazi killer.[28] Unfortunately, for him, this was not the Danzig Senate of the 1930s and his failure to speak Polish was now of no consequence. He was finally hanged on February 28, 1952, and, on March 14, his files were sent to be deposited in Warsaw.

There is equally nothing noble about the public executions following the trials that began in 1946 of those sentenced to death for their crimes in Stutthof and its sub-camps. The only difference with Forster is that they had less time to contemplate their guilt, and he had a lot more. The trial in April 1946 in Gdańsk was followed by a public execution of eleven members of Stutthof's SS men and female guards, presided over by Judge Dr. Józef Tarczewski. According to various sources, between 100,000 and 200,000 people watched it. The proceedings were open to the public, but because of the high interest they had to issue entrance tickets. The final days of the trial were broadcast on the radio. Out of sixteen, eleven were condemned to death—six men and five women. One died during the trial and two received sentences of three to five years in prison. Two were released.

SS man Johann Pauls and kapos Jan Breit, Tadeusz Kopczyński, Wacław Kozłowski, Józef Reiter, and Franciszek Kopczyński each received death sentences, along with the women: Jenny-Wanda Barkman, Elisabeth Becker, Wanda Klaff, Ewa Paradies, and Gerda Steinhoff. Jenny Wanda Barkman, known once as "The Beautiful Apparition," was the only who showed no emotion. After the verdict was read, she said, "Life is truly pleasure-able, and pleasures usually don't last long."[29] The others were crying and begged for mercy. None of the women were older than thirty. All clemency appeals to the Polish President, Bolesław Bierut were rejected. Alojzy Nowicki, Vice-Deputy of Gdańsk prison, was in charge of organizing the executions. He recalls that they had no ropes, so the prisoners had to make their own. He also had to find Catholic and Protestant chaplains willing to minister to the prisoners facing death. He found a Polish Protestant minister who refused on the grounds that he could not be impartial. He said, "I wouldn't be impartial. I wouldn't do it in a true Christian way. Why don't you look for someone else?"[30] On a tip from someone in the Secret Police, Nowicki finally found a German minister who was in hiding in Zoppot. "I went there by car, found him in the attic, still dressed in service garb and with a suitcase. I took him to the car and brought him to the prison so that he could spend some time with the prisoners. He was there for a few days."[31]

Three days before the execution, the Gdańsk media invited people to attend the execution. Many factories gave workers a day off and provided transportation for those who wanted to go to "the event." The city administration was afraid of a mob lynching, so there was a large police and military presence in the background. "It was a sunny day, and beer was sold. Onlookers were packed on house roofs, on trees. When flatbed trucks with the condemned appeared, the crowd started to throw stones at them. The military had to shoot into the air to warn people." Alojzy Nowicki continues his description:

> When those eleven trucks left the prison, on each of them was one of the condemned, next to him a former Stutthof prisoner in striped camp garb, who was the one to put a noose around his neck. The sentenced sat on highchairs on the open truck. The minister climbed up on one flat-bed truck, the priest onto another ... Each of the sentenced was approached by either a priest or a Protestant minister. The crowd yelled, "For our husbands, for our children!" The prosecutor made a sign and the trucks started to move, one after the other. The deaths of those sentenced were cruel, and because the length of the ropes did not match the weight of the convicted, some of them died by asphyxiation and not because their spinal cord was ruptured. According to the doctors, the average dying process was twelve minutes, with one of the guards taking twenty minutes. One of the trucks would not start, so a former prisoner pushed Wanda Klaff from the truck ... When the noose was being placed around her neck, she yelled "Heil Hitler!"[32]

After the executions, the crowd attacked the bodies, cutting off pieces of the rope, which, according to folklore, brought good luck, taking pieces of fabric from their clothes, buttons, etc. It was difficult to impose any kind of order. The bodies of the executed Stutthof personnel were taken to the Medical Academy in Gdańsk and used in anatomy courses. The last public execution took place on July 21, 1946, in Poznań (Posen)—the execution of Warthegau Gauleiter and Governor Arthur Greiser, former president of Gdańsk Senate. The earlier events at the public executions in Gdańsk led to the cessation of public executions.[33]

Other Silences

Grass's relatives from Danzig mourned the loss of Danzig. They lamented—"Our Danzig is no more"—and spoke of all the terrible things they had suffered. Their response to the "reputed crimes" was that they "couldn't have known."[34] "But not a word about the injustices the Poles visited upon us."[35] His mother had never uttered a word about what had gone on or happened to her when the Russian soldiers arrived, "in the empty shop, in the basement ... nothing that might indicate where and how often she had been raped by Russian soldiers. It was not until after she died that I learned—and then only indirectly from my sister—that, to protect her daughter, she had offered herself to them."[36]

And what about Stutthof today? Will it ever be the same kind of village that Grass depicted—a quiet seaside resort, nestled in the pine forests within walking distance of the Baltic and its dunes? The answer is not hard to decipher given the responses by local residents about the presence of the nearby camp. When a local landlady was interviewed about the tourists who come here, she pointed out that it had been hard for a while to attract tourists, but things were changing somewhat. "For many years, this area was a kind of silent zone." She concedes that it is not easy to balance tourist expectations with the history of this place—"Not easy," she repeats. "Even for those who come here, they often don't know that Stutthof is in Sztutowo. As if Sztutowo and Stutthof were detached not only by time but also by distance. People actually think that these are two different towns."[37] A tourist from Kraków admits, "To be honest, I had no idea that this camp existed. I visited Auschwitz, because it is not far from where I live, I visited Majdanek. I know about the camp in Treblinka, but about this Sztutowo, I learned about it in Stegny."[38]

Juden und Pfaffen were bracketed together at the beginning of this history of Stutthof, as targets of a racial hatred that has imposed dark threads on the fabric of its shame. All priests who were sent to Stutthof did not die there. Many were sent to Dachau and assembled in a special barracks where many died. The relatively small community of Jews of Danzig and Pomerania were either killed immediately in Stutthof or sent to other camps. They were not spared. Danuta Drywa is right to insist that Stutthof's relatively small number of Jewish victims within the camp system does not reflect more benign treatment. In fact, she points out that Stutthof was the only camp to murder Jews from the very first days of the war.[39] By the summer of 1944, the destruction of European Jewry was already largely a *fait accompli*.[40] Stutthof's inclusion in "the Final Solution" was thus a later entry, generated by the liquidation of other camps as well as the desperate need for workers for the war effort. Stutthof was conveniently located on the evacuation routes of these liquidated sites, and consequently became a destination. This resulted in a catastrophic loss of Jewish lives in the camp proper, in the sub-camps and especially during the evacuations beginning in January 1945.

The dual identity of Stutthof/Sztutowo is understandably a source of great pain for Catholic priests who today serve churches in this area or who visit it. In a recent publication, sixteen authors reflected on the camp's presence, describing the dual nature of Sztutowo/Stutthof as "somewhere between a beach and a camp." The discussion in one segment focuses on how Polish priests—many of them local—currently view the town and the camp. Author Tadeusz Fułek writes that some priests expressed their struggle with its former history. One priest says he came to get some fresh air, but it would be better if the camp were not there. Another priest complains that his parishioners do not want to talk about the camp, that they avoid the word "obóz" (camp) and use instead the word "muzeum." Each year in September, the Sztutowo parish members retreat to a site on the Vistula to hold mass and to lay wreaths. It is easier, the priest explains, to pray there than in the crematorium. In another interview, a woman remembers that after the camp was closed a complaint had been lodged by Sztutowo citizens about the smell. It was "sweetly pungent and pervasive."[41]

If local residents of Sztutowo struggle today with its past history as a community that once housed a concentration camp, this is hardly the case in Gdańsk, a robust, thriving city that offers a more recent history to tourists who are visiting the shipyards and the sites where local hero Lech Wałęsa gave his speeches during the days of strikes. The Solidarity Movement that challenged Soviet domination seems to be far more relevant as a site of memory in today's Gdańsk than the history of Danzig as a free city in the 1930s. And what about Grass? I suspect that the conferring of the Nobel Peace Prize on Wałęsa in 1983 is more widely known to this generation of Gdańsk citizens than Grass's Nobel Prize for literature in 1999. There is a modest statue of Grass on a playground near where he once lived in Langfuhr (now Wrzeszcz). When I visited several years ago, children were playing in a little park, blissfully unaware that a Nobel Prize winner once lived nearby. There is a plaque on the door of his old house. Grass is gone, along with the city—at least his version of it. No doubt, he still has readers who enjoy stories of old Danzig, but a new generation is reading other stories that are about Gdańsk, written by contemporary Polish writers with narrative skills that have been acknowledged as superb by reviewers in prominent British and international newspapers and journals.[42]

Returning to Moeller's question that I introduced at the beginning of this Epilogue about "telling the tales of war's end?" Might there be "ways to allow the paths of Germans and Jews to cross?"[43] I suggest there is a way, and it is told without rancor in two novels that are set in Gdańsk—*Death in Danzig* by Stefan Chwin and *Castorp* by Paweł Huelle, both of whom were born in Gdańsk. I return to the city that was our *Ausgangspunkt*, not the city depicted by Günter Grass. Both Huelle and Chwin deal with Poland's relationship with Germany, including the Nazi period, and in the case of Chwin with the Jews of Danzig and with the camp Stutthof. Philip Boehm, the translator of Stefan Chwin's novel *Hanemann*, chose (presumably with the approval of the author) to give a title to the original *Hanemann* that is straight from Thomas Mann—*Death in Danzig*. The choice is brilliant and bold, in that it captures not only the essence of Chwin's novel—a lament for a loss that is both personal (the drowning of Hanemann's lover) and a threnody for the community that we know from Grass's *Danziger Trilogy*. Hanemann, a German and former professor of anatomy, has opted to stay in Gdańsk, despite having to live under the scrutiny of the Soviets and their hand-picked, politically compatible Polish residents of Gdańsk, one of the few who had not joined the mass post-1945 migrations to the west. Chwin lingers over the artifacts that remain for the newcomers to utilize—teacups, spoons, monogrammed tablecloths, and other tangible reminders of a life that once was. He is not attempting to reclaim that life, but is cataloguing it with the poetic and clinical precision of an art historian.

Paweł Huelle also draws on a character from Mann's *oeuvre*, the protagonist of *The Magic Mountain*, Hans Castorp. Both men consciously—and very effectively—are playing with revered and cherished icons of German literature, but not with malice or revenge. Like Grass, Huelle mixes fictional and historical characters in his narrative, in fact choosing some characters that Grass himself used—Albert Forster, Arthur Greiser, and Hermann Rauschning. In *The Magic Mountain*, Mann had referred to his hero as having spent four semesters at the Danzig Polytechnic. Huelle not only seizes upon this throw-away line, but assumes the pompous tone of Mann, inserting characters that could easily compete with Mann's during Castorp's prolonged stay at the Swiss sanatorium—the two philosophers with their competing *Weltanschauungen* and an exotic French woman. Later, he sends his hero back home to his uncle in Germany after his year of study in Danzig. The uncle says to him with undisguised delight, "Didn't I say so? Nothing but horrors! It's a good thing you are not going back there again, my dear fellow. The East never does us any good!"[44] The uncle's smug response was triggered by a report he had just read in the German newspaper: Castorp's landlady in Danzig had been convicted, with the help of her Kashubian maid, of poisoning her husband (the uncle had immediately recognized her name). But, the narrator has the last word and directly addresses his protagonist. The German uncle recedes from the text, and Huelle projects on Castorp a future image that places him squarely on the streets of Grass's home turf—Langfuhr—"where hundreds of cars are rushing by from Gdańsk to Wrzeszcz." And he imagines him in the trams where he will only hear Polish and "if anyone still speaks your language here, they are students from the same polytechnic, taking exams in German." He concludes with an unmistakable farewell—"But my dear fellow, please get on your splendid bike."[45] We are thus left in no doubt as to who controls the narrative and the city where it is set.

Stefan Chwin confronts directly in his novel the changes and transformations that have taken place in Gdańsk since the exodus of the Germans and their replacement by Poles from other parts of Poland. His portrait of them is hardly flattering—they are treated with "polite reserve" as outsiders who were not there "when the city was governed by the High Commissioner from the League of Nations." But there is clear sympathy with the old timers, like Mr. J. who had taught earlier at the Polish *gymnasium*. Chwin adds parenthetically, "[W]hich he had paid for with interrogations in the Victoria-Schule and the Stutthof concentration camp."[46] But Chwin's character has been given the ability to view his internment with a measure of gratitude and what he calls "fate:" "Mr. J. felt that fate had been extraordinarily kind to him; after all, he had survived Stutthof, although there had been moments when only a tiny quiver in his heart kept him from throwing himself on the wires. By chance he had survived, and so he was able to spend a lovely May afternoon relaxing in Hanemann's beautiful room at 17 Grottker St., talking about the good old days with his friend like two old school chums."[47] As much as we want to, we cannot contradict Chwin's character by telling him how brave he was to survive. For he would probably remind us of the thousands of courageous men and women who died there of starvation or worse, or who were murdered there. We now know enough about the camp to say that courage may have helped, but Chwin's character is right—it was only a tiny quiver in the heart that kept any of them from the surrounding wires. Chwin has given us a character who survived Stutthof and has placed him on a lovely May day in postwar Danzig—in Gdańsk—to tell his story.

"If it weren't for this camp, Sztutowo would finally come back to life. It would shake off the burden that it is carrying."[48] That's how a local woman summarized the dilemma that the resort faces—the burden of history. A few months before Grass died, I wrote to his secretary, asking her to pass on my letter to him, in which I asked about the burden of the history of Stutthof that he must have carried all his life. Had it cast the longest shadow on his work? I was unaware of his grave condition at the time and did not receive a response. I suggest that the shame of Stutthof weighed on Grass just as deeply as the burden of Auschwitz because, after all, it was close to home. I myself have often retreated to my own home turf to write this book, to the hills near Belfast—a city with its own burden of history, one that Seán Lester, the Irish-born commissioner for the League of Nations in Danzig in the 1930s must have known well. Lester had to leave Danzig with unfinished work. One can understand his disappointment.

As an example of what some may think is unfinished work in this book, I would like to mention the issue of the shoes. More accurately, the issue is the remains of shoes that were found in 2015 by the grandson of a former prisoner of Stutthof. The poet-musician Grzegorz Kwiatkowski stumbled upon them during a walk in the woods near the camp. The shoes were once the personal belongings of Jews who were murdered in Auschwitz. Shoes of all shapes and sizes were sent from Auschwitz to Stutthof to be made into belts and holsters for SS men. When he approached Piotr Tarnowski, the Museum's director, the latter downplayed the discovery and commented that other artifacts had already been absorbed "by nature taking over." Kwiatkowski, however, sees it differently. For him, they are the artifacts of the Holocaust and proof that it happened. I believe that the staff at Stutthof Museum has worked hard and honestly over many years to provide ample proof that Stutthof's history cannot be separated from the Holocaust. Yet, another cannot control how we respond emotionally to the Holocaust. "Wasteland," the haunting song that Kwiatkowski composed after his discovery, expresses the authentic intensity of his response.[49] In order to make the shoes into useful items, Jewish prisoners had to separate the soles from the uppers. It is a fitting metaphor for lives that were ripped apart to serve the needs of the elite of Germandom.[50]

In fact, shoes provoke very strong emotions as artifacts of the Holocaust. I was in a taxi in Belfast when the taxi driver told me he had just returned from Kraków and had visited Auschwitz. I remained silent. Finally, he spoke in a choked voice. "It was the wee shoes," he said. The strong Belfast accent could not mask a visceral response to what he saw at Auschwitz-Birkenau, just like Kwiatkowski's lament about what he discovered in the woods near Stutthof. In July 2017, Prince William and his wife, the Duchess of Cambridge, visited Stutthof, their very first visit to a concentration camp. Photographs of their visit reveal strained, sad expressions. They wrote in the guest book that they were "intensely moved." Whether royal, or a Belfast cab driver or a singer from a Polish "post-punk" band, these voices represent genuine responses that are breaking the silences that have enshrouded the camps, but especially Stutthof. I know there is more to tell, and I hope that other histories will follow. I relate to the cleaning woman in one of the barracks who, when interviewed about her job, said to the visitor, "Come in, please. The barracks is not a Radziwiłł castle, and there are still cobwebs left, even though I clean here all the time."[51]

Notes

Introduction

1. Grass himself called the three novels a "Gesamtkomplex"—a single whole complex which John Reddick described in *The Danzig Trilogy of Günter Grass* as "The Danzig Trilogy," a title by which they have been known ever since (Reddick, *The Danzig Trilogy of Günter Grass*).
2. Throughout this book, I have attempted to provide both the German and Polish names for many of the cities and communities, as the shift in name also brings to light the evolving history that I am narrating.
3. The sentiment was by no means a new one and had been expressed already in 1936 in London's *Evening News* and in the *Daily Mail*—"This country is not concerned in any way with this remote town in the Eastern Baltic ... Nobody here would mind if the Nazis regained it for Germany." Even Australia joined the skepticism: "for neither Britain nor France has or can have the slightest national interest in the Free City. It is a further strange reflection on present-day international affairs that practically the only justifiable claim ever put forward by Hitler against another country should be opposed by the democracies, even to the extent of war" (*Sunday Sun and Guardian*, August 13, 1939, 7).
4. I have put "the Polish Corridor" in quotes to indicate that the term may be offensive to Polish readers. "The Corridor" was a German propaganda term that suggested that the Polish territory of Pomerania was an artificial creation of the Versailles Treaty, whereas the territory belonged to Poland before 1919, and was predominantly ethnically Polish. It is also referred to as "the Danzig Corridor," "the Corridor," and "the Pomeranian Voivodship."
5. Ferguson, "Why Did the Second World War Begin?," 1.
6. See Mawdsley, *World War II*.
7. Cited in Clark, "*Gdańsk, Story of a City*," 74.
8. Koehl, *RKFDV*, 242. In the glossary, Koehl defines *Deutschtum* as "the body of German people, or Germanness, the abstract or essential qualities of the Germans."
9. Uwe Timm's painful struggle with the loss of his brother on the Eastern Front in 1943 is told in *Am Beispiel meines Bruders,* translated as *In My Brother's Shadow* (2005), is one such example.
10. For more on Grass's attachment to Danzig as "'a site of memory'" see Nicole A. Theisz's "Illusions of Return: City and Memory in Günter Grass's Danzig Novels." Drawing on Nora's *Les Lieux de Mémoire,* she points out that "memory attaches itself to sites, whether by having taken place there, or secondarily, when emotional connections to places arise in the process of retrieving and modifying memories" (Theisz, "*Illusions of Return,*" 65).
11. Rushdie, "*On Günter Grass,*" 1.
12. Hunt, "Review of *Hitler's Free City*," 186.
13. Schlant, "Coming to Terms with the Hitler-Past," 54.

14   Stargardt, *The German War*.
15   August 12, 2006, interview with the *Frankfurter Allgemeine Zeitung*, given in advance of the publication of his autobiographical work, *Beim Häuten der Zwiebel/ Peeling the Onion*.
16   An example of this is when Grass denounced Israel in a poem about alleged plans to attack Iran with nuclear warheads. Published in 2012 in the *Süddeutsche Zeitung*, the poem at the same time criticized Germany for providing the means to deliver warheads. His "'poetic rant" did not escape the eye of historian Jeffrey Herf, who pointed out Grass's failure to mention Iran's public statements of hatred toward Israel. Several prominent German journalists also expressed their displeasure. For more, see Herf, "The Odious Musings of Günter Grass."
17   Taberner, *Cambridge Companion to Günter Grass*, 1.
18   Van Gelder, "Gunter Grass replies," 1.
19   Grass, *Peeling the Onion*, 31.
20   Grass, *Peeling the Onion*, 25.
21   Grass, *Peeling the Onion*, 28.
22   Schlant, *The Language of Silence*, 71.
23   Hall, "Günter Grass's 'Danzig Quintet,'" 72.
24   Orski, *Niewolnicza praca więźniów*. This and all subsequent translations from Polish publications are by Dr. Bożena Tieszen.
25   Cited in Wóycicka, *Arrested Mourning*, 182.
26   Wóycicka, *Arrested Mourning*, 184.
27   Wóycicka, *Arrested Mourning*, 174–5.
28   Orski, *Niewolnicza praca więźniów*, 35.
29   Dunin-Wąsowicz's first book was the memoir *Stutthof -Ze wspomnień więźnia obozu koncentracyjnego* (Stutthof—Memoirs of a Concentration Camp Prisoner), written in 1946 and published by PIW (Polski Instytut Wydawniczy), Warsaw. Twenty-five years later, he re-wrote his memoir, amending the shortcomings of the first. I am drawing from this 1970 edition with translations by Tieszen.
30   Before 1970, the following works on Stutthof were published: A short article written by Judge Zdzisław Łukaszkiewicz in the *Bulletin of the Commissioned Search for Nazi Crimes in Poland / Biuletyn Głównej Komisji Badania Zbrodni Hitlerowskich w Polsce*. Warsaw, 1947, Volume III, 61–90. This article was based on stories told by Stutthof prisoners. By the same publisher, in Volume XV, 1965, 66–99—an article written by Maria Jezierska about the sub-camp in Police (Politz) near Szczecin/Stettin.
31   "Operation Reinhard Camps" were named after Reinhard Heydrich, who was assassinated in 1943 by the Czech underground. (More on his role later.)
32   The term "General Government" (also known as Generalgouvernement) refers to the central and southern region of occupied Poland that Nazi Germany claimed as a new province in October 1939, along with other annexed districts in the north and west, including Danzig-West Prussia, the Warthegau, East Prussia, and Upper Silesia. (The region to the east had been annexed in September 1939 by the Soviet Union.) In June 1941, after the Soviet invasion, the General Government was expanded to include the new district of Galicia.
33   On April 10, 2010, ninety-six people, including the Polish president and his wife and other dignitaries, were killed in an air disaster *en route* to a commemoration of the Katyń massacre. The commemoration of Katyń has subsequently taken on an added burden in Poland to keep its memory alive.
34   Drywa, *The Extermination of Jews in Stutthof Concentration Camp, 1939–1945*, 326.

35 Dunin-Wąsowicz, "Broadening the Concept of the Holocaust," 1.
36 For complete text, see Wróbel, *The Devils Playground*.
37 Dunin-Wąsowicz, "Broadening the Concept of the Holocaust," 1.
38 Dunin-Wąsowicz, "Broadening the Concept of the Holocaust," 1.
39 The book by Jan Gross, *Neighbors: The Destruction of the Jewish Community in Jedwabne, Poland* (Princeton University Press, 2001) generated heated discussion and controversy because it challenged the view that only the Nazis committed crimes against humanity in Poland. See also his book *Fear: Anti-Semitism in Poland after Auschwitz*.
40 The Holocaust Speech Law enacted on February 6, 2018, against claims that Poland was complicit in Nazi crimes has since been dropped, although the possibility of a fine remains in place.
41 Michalik, *Sprzątając Zagładę*.
42 Michalik, *Sprzątając Zagładę*, 31.
43 Michalik, *Sprzątając Zagładę*, 31.
44 Borensztein, *Interview 34594*.
45 Grass, *Cat and Mouse*, 37.
46 Grass, *Peeling the Onion*, 110–11.
47 Grass, *Of All That Ends*, 161.

Chapter 1

1   The paramilitary unit of the Nazi party, also known as the Brown Shirts, was organized around 1921 and was a critical instrument of political indoctrination in the early days of Hitler's rise to power. Purged in 1934, it lost its power to the SS. It was disbanded in 1945.
2   Schenk, *Hitlers Mann in Danzig*, 23. All translations are my own.
3   Schenk, *Hitlers Mann in Danzig*, cited on page 32.
4   Levine, *Hitler's Free City*, 14.
5   *Gaue* were first set up in 1926 as Nazi party districts. The term *Reichsgau* refers to those districts that were conquered in 1938 and 1939—Austria and the Sudetenland in 1938 and Memelland in 1939. Danzig was incorporated into the newly formed *Reichsgau* of Danzig-West Prussia on October 8, 1939. The other two *Gaue* in the annexed territories were Warthegau under Arthur Greiser and East Prussia under Erich Koch.
6   For more on the complex diplomatic history of Danzig/Gdańsk see Clark, "Gdańsk, Story of a City."
7   Levine, *Hitler's Free City*, 129.
8   Schenk, *Hitlers Mann in Danzig*, 42.
9   Levine, *Hitler's Free City*, 13.
10 Levine, *Hitler's Free City*, 13.
11 Clark, *The Free City*, 29.
12 Levine, *Hitler's Free City*, 13.
13 Clark, *Gdańsk*, 72.
14 Levine, *Hitler's Free City*, 27.
15 Levine, *Hitler's Free City*, 17.
16 Schenk, *Hitlers Mann in Danzig*, 36.

17 Schenk, *Hitlers Mann in Danzig*, 39.
18 Schenk, *Hitlers Mann in Danzig*, 86.
19 Sodeikat, "Der Nationalismus und die Danziger Opposition," 146 note 15.
20 Sodeikat, "Der Nationalismus und die Danziger Opposition," 144.
21 Sodeikat, "Der Nationalismus und die Danziger Opposition," cited on page 145.
22 Schenk, *Hitlers Mann in Danzig*, 44.
23 Cited by Schenk, *Hitlers Mann in Danzig*, 44.
24 Schenk points out that Rauschning would live to regret this flattery in the years that followed his hasty departure in 1935 from Danzig for Switzerland. In 1948, he emigrated to the USA (Schenk, *Hitlers Mann in Danzig*, 55). He later wrote at length against the perils of National Socialism and about his many personal conversations with Hitler, which have been reduced dramatically in number and questioned (or even worse, ignored as worthless) by leading historians. His purported claim that Hitler said that you can't be a good Nazi and a Christian has been debunked.
25 Wąs, *Gdańsk wojenny i powojenny*, 26. Translated by Tieszen.
26 Steyer and Dwertmann, "Stutthof das Konzentrationslager," 14.
27 Rossino, *Blitzkrieg, Ideology, and Atrocity*, 223.
28 Levine, *Hitler's Free City*, 29.
29 Grass, *Peeling the Onion*, 25.
30 Grass, *Dog Years*, 5.
31 Reddick, *The Danzig Trilogy of Günter Grass*, 266.
32 Reddick, *The Danzig Trilogy of Günter Grass*, 6.
33 The influence of the Greater German Reich encroaching on the free city of Danzig, was noted as early as 1933 by American journalist H.R. Knickerbocker who reported the city elections in May 1933 with the exaggerated claim that the Nazis swept into power: "[A] tornado of Brownshirts that drove fear through the heart of every Pole and Jew in the city and made Europe hold its breath." Cited in Nagorski, *Hitlerland*, 151.
34 Cited in Gageby, *The Last Secretary-General*, 71.
35 Grass, *Dog Years*, 59.
36 Reddick, *The Danzig Trilogy of Günter Grass*, 267.
37 Reddick, *The Danzig Trilogy of Günter Grass*, 269.
38 Reddick, *The Danzig Trilogy of Günter Grass*, 267.
39 Kershaw, *The Hitler Myth*, 90.
40 Lester was so perturbed about the situation in Danzig that he met clandestinely with the spokesperson of the Danzig opposition, Erich Brost, and advised him to start thinking about his personal safety and security, as he (Lester) no longer thought it possible to protect him. Sodeikat comments that the powerlessness of the League of Nations could not be documented more painfully (Sodeikat, "Der Nationalismus und die Danziger Opposition," 165).
41 Levine, *Hitler's Free City*, 75.
42 Wąs, *Gdańsk wojenny i powojenny*, 15.
43 Levine, *Hitler's Free City*, 158.
44 For a comprehensive look at the life of Arthur Greiser, see Epstein, *Model Nazi*.
45 Levine, *Hitler's Free City*, 100.
46 Kershaw, *Hitler Myth*, 82.
47 Levine, *Hitler's Free City*, 121.
48 Levine, *Hitler's Free City*, 143.
49 Levine, *Hitler's Free City*, 102.

50 Wąs, *Gdańsk wojenny*, 19–20.
51 Wąs, *Gdańsk wojenny*, 25.
52 Schenk, *Hitlers Mann in Danzig*, 46.
53 Wąs, *Gdańsk wojenny*, 33–4.
54 Schenk, *Hitlers Mann in Danzig*, 80 and 82.
55 Schenk, *Hitlers Mann in Danzig*, 86.
56 Schenk, *Hitlers Mann in Danzig*, 89.
57 Schenk, *Hitlers Mann in Danzig*, 139.
58 See Doris Bergen's *War and Genocide* for a nuanced view of the supposed "appeasement" assessment that has dogged Chamberlain's reputation as statesman ever since (Bergen, *War and Genocide*, 85).
59 Bergen, *War and Genocide*, 86.
60 Schenk, *Hitlers Mann in Danzig*, 94.
61 Schenk, *Hitlers Mann in Danzig*, 94.
62 Clark, *The Free City*, 32.
63 Bacon, "Danzig Jewry," 33.
64 Lichtenstein, *Die Juden der freien Stadt Danzig*, 76–7. All translations are my own.
65 Cited by Levine, *Hitler's Free City*, 135.
66 Cited in Danuta Drywa, *The Extermination of Jews*, 16.
67 For details on the measures taken against Jews in the Reich, see Epstein, *Confronting the Myths*, 33–5.
68 The history of how they met these challenges in Danzig is told in some detail in *Danzig 1939*, which includes an essay by Günter Grass. "There was resistance to the plan from British Jews—it was illegal, they argued, and the American Joint Committee then provided the funding, based on the purchase of ritual objects belonging to the community that were sent to the Jewish Theological Seminary in New York. The community also sold all its holdings including the Great Synagogue for a fraction of its value." For more on this period, see Bacon, "Danzig Jewry," 25–35.
69 Lichtenstein, *Die Juden der freien Stadt Danzig*, 103.
70 Levine, *Hitler's Free City*, 138.
71 See Gilman, *Jewish Writers in Contemporary Germany*. Gilman points out a linguistic signifier; he has his Jewish character Markus speak in a different way (*mauscheln*) than other characters that mark him as different, as moving across boundaries that are understood as "polluting and polluted" (Gilman, *Jewish Writers in Contemporary Germany*, 220).
72 Grass, *The Tin Drum*, 99.
73 Grass, *The Tin Drum*, 193.
74 Grass, *The Tin Drum*, 192.
75 Grass, *The Tin Drum*, 192.
76 Grass provides some detail that may contradict or amplify that comment: Grass writes that he watched the synagogue in Langfuhr being "plundered, pillaged, and set on fire by a horde of SA men." (Grass, *Peeling the Onion*, 18.)
77 Cited in Von Jörg-Philipp and Kraason, *Von Danzig nach Lübeck*, 13–14.
78 I am following standard practice and translate the word "evangelisch" as "'protestant/ Protestant" and not "evangelical," for which there is a different word.
79 Cited by Gülzow, *Kirchenkampf*, 23 (footnote).
80 Gülzow, *Kirchenkampf in Danzig*, 9.
81 Gülzow, *Kirchenkampf in Danzig*, 15.
82 New York Times, *59 Nazi Leaders*, 1.

83 Gülzow, *Kirchenkampf in Danzig*, 34–5.
84 Gülzow, *Kirchenkampf in Danzig*, 35.
85 Gülzow, *Kirchenkampf in Danzig*, 43.
86 Gülzow, *Kirchenkampf in Danzig*, 42.
87 See Rudolf von Thadden, *Trieglaff*.
88 Cited in Bracher, *The Conscience in Revolt*, 40.
89 Bracher, *The Conscience in Revolt*, 126.
90 Bracher, *The Conscience in Revolt*, 126.
91 Bracher, *The Conscience in Revolt*, 126.
92 Modras, *The Catholic Church and Antisemitism*, 322–33.
93 Bergen, *Twisted Cross*, 68.
94 Bergen, *Twisted Cross*, 132.
95 Railton, *German Free Churches*, 106.
96 Railton, *German Free Churches*, 106.
97 Railton, *German Free Churches*, 121.
98 Railton, *German Free Churches*, 122.
99 Bacon, *Danzig: Treasures*, 31.
100 Reddick, *The Danzig Trilogy*, 223–4.
101 Grass, *Cat and Mouse*, 37.
102 Some writers, like Manfred Durzak have ascribed Grass's characterization of Tulla to the negative image of women as presented by Otto Weiniger in 1903 in his *Geschlecht und Charakter* (Weiniger, *Geschlecht und Charakter*, 150). The book was widely read in the Third Reich and in fact, was in the collection of Amsel's father, reminding the reader of Amsel's own struggle with his Jewish identity. It is recognized as an antisemitic rant without scientific basis that is degrading both to Jews and to women.
103 Grass, *The Tin Drum*, 107.
104 Grass, *Peeling the Onion*, 17.
105 Grass, *Peeling the Onion*, 39.
106 Grass, *Peeling the Onion*, 16.
107 Grass, *Peeling the Onion*, 18.
108 Grass, *Peeling the Onion*, 15.
109 In Keith Miles's analysis of *Dog Years*, he describes the German shepherd dog as a symbol of totalitarianism, the embodiment of evil and the gratuitous violence of National Socialism (Miles, *Günter Grass*, 108).
110 In the official *Guidebook to Stutthof Museum*, a building is listed as the "Doghouse." It was built in 1941, exclusively for guard dogs and their handlers who were Waffen SS soldiers. By May 1943 there were twenty purebred dogs, including German shepherds. The guidebook points out that they weighed more than a starving inmate—twenty-six kilos. The building is now off-limits (Grabowska-Chałka, *Guide*, 3).
111 Hitler did, in fact, visit Zoppot and stayed in the Grand Hotel, as mentioned in the narrative.
112 Grass, *Dog Years*, 30.
113 Grass, *Dog Years*, 29.
114 Grass, *Dog Years*, 48.
115 Grass, *The Tin Drum*, 213.
116 For more information, see Rauschning, *Men of Chaos*.
117 Gageby, *The Last Secretary*, 59.
118 Gageby, *The Last Secretary*, 62–3.

119 Steyer, *Stutthof das KL*, 10.
120 Hitler, *Der Führer spricht*. My trans. of an article found in Leo Baeck Archives, New York City.
121 Hitler, *Der Führer spricht*.
122 Wąs, *Gdańsk wojenny*, 24.
123 Wąs, *Gdańsk wojenny*, 70.
124 Krawczyk, *Pogranicza. Stara Kiszewa*. Translated by Tieszen.
125 Krawczyk, *Pogranicza. Stara Kiszewa*, 98.
126 Krawczyk, *Pogranicza. Stara Kiszewa*, 112.
127 Krawczyk, *Pogranicza. Stara Kiszewa*, 112.
128 Krawczyk, *Pogranicza. Stara Kiszewa*, 112.
129 Krawczyk, *Pogranicza. Stara Kiszewa*, 107.
130 Krawczyk, *Pogranicza. Stara Kiszewa*, 111.
131 Krawczyk, *Pogranicza. Stara Kiszewa*, 112.
132 Krawczyk, *Pogranicza. Stara Kiszewa*, 112.
133 Krawczyk, *Pogranicza. Stara Kiszewa*, 112.
134 Sziling and Wojciechowski, *Neighborhood Dilemmas*, 157.
135 Wąs, *Gdańsk wojenny*, 84–5.
136 Gąsiorowski, *Stutthof das KL*, 16.
137 Epstein, *Confronting the Myths*, 117.
138 Kershaw, *Hitler Myth*, 122–3.
139 Bergen, *War and Genocide*, 94.
140 Clark, *Gdańsk*, 74.
141 Clark, *Gdańsk*, 70.
142 Schenk, *Hitlers Mann in Danzig*, 106.
143 Wąs, *Gdańsk wojenny*, 151.
144 For more, see Badziąg, *Memories of a Boy Scout*, 193.
145 Lichtenstein, *Die Juden der freien Stadt*, 120–1.
146 Lichtenstein, *Die Juden der freien Stadt*, 120–1.
147 Echt, *Die Geschichte der Juden in Danzig*, 229–30. Translations from the German my own.
148 Echt, *Die Geschichte der Juden in Danzig*, 231.
149 Echt, *Die Geschichte der Juden in Danzig*, 229–30, 231.
150 Grabowska-Chałka, *Guide*, 13.
151 Kuhn, *Stutthof: Ein Konzentrationslager*, 10. All translations from the German are my own.
152 Wąs, *Gdańsk wojenny*, 62.
153 von Lang, *Top Nazi*, 143. Jochen von Lang notes that "until September 25, Hitler held court in the old casino hotel on the Baltic Sea resort of Zoppot, where Europe's wealthy came to gamble. Now in this amazing building the winnings were of a different nature" (von Lang, *Top Nazi*, 143).
154 von Ribbentrop had replaced von Neurath in 1938 as Foreign Minister. Several high-ranking officials and military officers had also been dismissed who had earlier voiced objections to Hitler's war plans (Epstein, 117).
155 von Ribbentrop, *Untitled Speech*. The translation of this speech is in British English.
156 von Ribbentrop, *Untitled Speech*, 3.
157 von Ribbentrop, *Untitled Speech*.
158 Cited by Roy, *The Vanished Kingdom*, 242.
159 von Ribbentrop, *Untitled Speech*, 4.

160 von Ribbentrop, *Untitled Speech*, 5.
161 von Ribbentrop, *Untitled Speech*, 6.
162 von Ribbentrop, *Untitled Speech*, 7.
163 von Ribbentrop, *Untitled Speech*, 16.
164 Kershaw, *Hitler Myth*, 4.
165 Kershaw, *Hitler Myth*, 46–7.
166 Kershaw, *Hitler Myth*, 62, 77, and 138.
167 Kershaw, *Hitler Myth*, 139.
168 Kershaw, *Hitler Myth*, 171.
169 Kershaw, *Working towards the Führer*, 113.
170 Grass, *Dog Years*, 270.
171 von Ribbentrop, *Untitled Speech*, 10.
172 A map of the new *Gau* of Danzig-West Prussia can be found in Figure 15.
173 Badziąg, *Es War eine Zeit*, 190–1.

Chapter 2

1 Das Frische Haff was a large body of water that was about seventy kilometers in length and ten kilometers in width. It froze over in the winter, which later became a key factor in the evacuation by ice of refugees fleeing from the Red Army.
2 Grabowska-Chałka, *Guide*, 49.
3 Grabowska-Chałka, *Guide*, 25.
4 For names of victims killed between January 11 and March 22, 1940, see Drywa, *Säuberungsaktion na Pomorzu Gdańskim*, 269–72.
5 Nicole Theisz points out that the central motif of displacement in *Dog Years* involves recurrent images of trains that convey the notion of flight and of fleeing time (Theisz, *Illusions of return*, 73). In this case the train image is one that denotes an end station with no possibility of return.
6 Lendzion was the father of Leon Lendzion who translated *Stutthof: Ein Konzentrationslager vor den Toren Danzigs* into German.
7 Dunin-Wąsowicz, *Obóz Koncentracyjny Sztuthof*, 46.
8 Dunin-Wąsowicz, *Obóz Koncentracyjny Sztuthof*, 68.
9 There is a reference to Jews wearing the Star of David, but since it was not mandated till later (in November) in the occupied territories, this is unlikely.
10 Cited in Sziling and Wojciechowski, *Neighborhood Dilemmas*, 159.
11 Levine, *Hitler's Free City*, 156.
12 Steyer, *Stutthof das KL*, 74.
13 Steyer, *Stutthof das KL*, 75.
14 Grabowska-Chałka, *Guide*, 49.
15 Schenk, *Hitlers Mann in Danzig*, 212.
16 Schenk, *Hitlers Mann in Danzig*, 212.
17 Schenk, *Hitlers Mann in Danzig*, 212.
18 Cited by Schenk, *Hitlers Mann in Danzig*, 147–8.
19 Wąs, *Gdańsk wojenny*, 73.
20 Rossino, *Blitzkrieg, Ideology, and Atrocity*, 227–8.
21 Douglas, *Orderly and Humane*, 45.
22 Douglas, *Orderly and Humane*, 45. Douglas calls it "a convenient ex post facto justification for the onslaught of the Nazis against Poland."

23 Douglas, *Orderly and Humane*, 44.
24 Wachsmann, *KL*, 230.
25 For more on the atrocities committed by the *Selbstschutz* from September–until the end of 1939, see Schenk, *Hitlers Mann in Danzig*, 156–62. The Commander of these units in Danzig-West Prussia was Ludolf von Alvensleben, a favorite of Himmler, who was promoted to the rank of Major General. He was able to elude capture and fled in 1944 to Argentina where he died in 1970. *Die Zentrale Stelle* (The Central Office for the Investigation of Nazi Crimes) established in 1958 in Ludwigsburg, gives the number of Polish fatalities as 5,000.
26 Grass, *Peeling the Onion*, 35–6.
27 Cited in Barnett, *The Soul of the People*, 163.
28 Grabowska-Chałka, *Guide*, 22.
29 Dyke, *Terrifying Story of Hitler's Children*, 1. Around 200,000 Polish children were sent to Germany as part of this program.
30 For more, see Drywa, *Extermination of Jews*, 25–6.
31 For more details see Grabowska-Chałka, *Guide*, 49–62.
32 Orski, *Ort des Terrors*, 565–7.
33 After the war, Mathesius was captured by the Allied forces and hung himself in his cell in May 1947 before his trial.
34 Orski, *Ort des Terrors*, 565–7. My translations from the German.
35 Orski, *Ort des Terrors*, 617.
36 Orski, *Ort des Terrors*, 628.
37 Malak, *Shavelings in Death Camps*, 81. Translated by Bożena J. Tucker and Thomas R. Tucker.
38 Cited by Drywa, *Extermination of Jews*, 25.
39 Orski, *Ort des Terrors*, 584.
40 These statistics and information were taken from Grabowska-Chałka, *Guide*, 67–72.
41 Orksi, *Ort des Terrors*, 716.
42 Orski, *Ort des Terrors*, 664.
43 Orski, *Ort des Terrors*, 664.
44 There was an unsuccessful attempt in March of 1976 in Cologne to convict the former camp leader Molkenthin of Graudenz and other men of murder charges which failed on the grounds of insufficient evidence.
45 Orski, *Ort des Terrors*, 578.
46 Orski, *Ort des Terrors*, 600–1.
47 Orski, *Ort des Terrors*, 602.
48 Orski, *Ort des Terrors*, 623.
49 For more information on the number of filial camps see the article "The Holocaust Just Got More Shocking," *New York Times*, March 1, 2013. Researchers have recently catalogued some 42,500 Nazi ghettos and camps, including forced labor camps. The lead researcher said that, when the research began in the year 2000, they expected to find perhaps 7,000, but the numbers kept climbing. No doubt the dozens of sub-camps of Stutthof are also included—or will be—in that statistic.
50 RG-04-058MI, Reel 238, United States Holocaust Memorial Museum.
51 Koehl, *RKFDV*, 18.
52 Douglas, *Orderly and Humane*, 48.
53 Koehl, *RKFDV*, 100.
54 Malak, *Shavelings*, 70. Malak cites examples of priests who refused to join the list in Stutthof.

55 Schenk, *Hitlers Mann in Danzig*, 205.
56 Only about a half million *Volksdeutsche*, for the 20 million envisaged by the *Generalplan-Ost* were ever placed in new homes (Douglas, 60).
57 For a comprehensive and valuable analysis of the policy in the Warthegau, see the following article—Gerhard Wolf, "*Negotiating Germanness*: Nationalist Socialist Germanization Policy in the Warthegau," *Journal of Genocide Research*, 19:2, 2017, 214–39.
58 Schenk, *Hitlers Mann in Danzig*, 210.
59 Steyer, *Stutthof das KL*, 40.
60 For more see Sziling and Wojciechowski, *Neighborhood Dilemmas*, 173.
61 Mazower, *Hitler and His Empire*, 84–5. See page 196 for table showing the statistics for the four Gaue.
62 Mazower, *Hitler and His Empire*, 196.
63 Mazower, *Hitler and His Empire*, 197.
64 Mazower, *Hitler and His Empire*, 198.
65 Connelly, *Nazis and Slavs*, 9.
66 Connelly, *Nazis and Slavs*, 19.
67 Connelly, *Nazis and Slavs*, 21–2.
68 Connelly, *Nazis and Slavs*, 26.
69 Ceran, *Szmalcówka*, 36. According to Forster, blood of Pommern people was more German than that of Germans living in Baltic lands.
70 Allen, *The Business of Genocide*, 97. He points to a crucial difference in Nazi occupation practices in Eastern Europe and other occupied countries like France. He writes that the occupation of Eastern Europe was different from that of France, Norway, or the Benelux countries in that the Nazis attempted to reconstruct the entire fabric of the conquered lands.
71 Allen, *The Business of Genocide*, 97.
72 Pawlikowski, *Polish Catholics and the Jews*, 107.
73 Pawlikowski, *Polish Catholics and the Jews*, 165.
74 Organisation Todt (OT) was a civil and military engineering organization, founded by Fritz Todt, and was in charge of a large number of engineering projects across Germany and the occupied territories from France to the Soviet Union during the Second World War. Labor was provided by prisoners of war and other forced workers.
75 Steyer, *Stutthof das KL*, 43.
76 Grass, *Tin Drum*, 289.
77 Grass, *Tin Drum*, 82.
78 Grass, *Peeling the Onion*, 180.
79 Berben, *Dachau: The Official History*, 276–7.
80 Malak, *Shavelings in Death Camps*, 58.
81 Malak, *Shavelings in Death Camps*, 64–6.
82 Malak, *Shavelings in Death Camps*, 32.
83 Malak, *Shavelings in Death Camps*, 33.
84 Malak, *Shavelings in Death Camps*, 33–4.
85 Malak, *Shavelings in Death Camps*, 73.
86 I am very grateful to Elżbieta Grot from whose book *Błogosławieni Męczennicy Obozu Stutthof* I have drawn these excerpts.
87 Rogacewski, Komorowski, and Frelichowski were among the 108 priests and clerics who were recognized by Pope John Paul 11 on June 13, 1999, as "Martyrs of World War 11."

88 Grot, *Błogosławieni*, 22. Translated by Tieszen.
89 Danuta Drywa gives the total number of prisoners killed that day as sixty-seven and adds that Jews in the camp had to sort and store the clothing of the dead. *The Extermination of Jews*, 28.
90 Grot, *Błogosławieni*, 24.
91 Grot, *Błogosławieni*, 26.
92 Grot, *Błogosławieni*, 34.
93 Grot, *Błogosławieni*, 45–6.
94 Grot, *Błogosławieni*, 51.
95 In 1942, the KOP united with the home army—Armia Krajowa. Under the authority of the Polish Government in Exile, it had strong military roots with more than 300,000 members intent on defending their country. The Soviets did not view it favorably and in fact, after the failed Warsaw Uprising in which, though supposed allies, they failed to support the Polish defenders, they took reprisals on them (Badziąg, *Es war eine Zeit*, 205).
96 Grabowska-Chałka, *Guide*, 28.
97 Malak, *Shavelings*, 39–40.
98 Malak, *Shavelings*, 40.
99 Grabowska-Chałka, *Guide*, 54.
100 For more, see Grabowska-Chałka, *Guide*, 56–7.
101 Dunin-Wąsowicz, *Stutthof*, 201.
102 Dunin-Wąsowicz, *Stutthof*, 214.
103 Grabowska-Chałka, *Guide*, 28.
104 Orski, *Ort des Terrors, Band 6*, 630.
105 Dunin-Wąsowicz, *Obóz Koncentracyjny Sztuthof*, 84.
106 Later, in 1944, three women—one German, and two Polish women volunteered to work as prostitutes for SS men in Stutthof, who were from occupied territories—Latvia and Ukraine. The women lived separately in a small barracks and received preferential treatment (Dunin-Wąsowicz, *Obóz Koncentracyjny Sztuthof*, 86).
107 Grabowska-Chałka, *Guide*, 52.
108 Grabowska-Chałka, *Guide*, 28.
109 Grabowska-Chałka, *Guide*, 29.
110 Badziąg, *Es war eine Zeit*, 195.
111 Drywa, *The Extermination of the Jews*, 325.
112 Sziling and Wojciechowski, *Neighborhood Dilemmas*, 171.
113 Schenk, *Hitlers Mann in Danzig*, 213.
114 Schenk, *Hitlers Mann in Danzig*, 215.
115 Cited in Schenk, *Hitlers Mann in Danzig*, 214.
116 Splett was arrested by the Soviets after the war and sentenced in 1946 for collaboration with the Nazis to eight years in prison. Released in August 1953, he was sent by Polish authorities to a monastery in Dukla where he stayed until 1956, when he was granted permission to go to West Germany. In 1960, he was awarded the Grand Cross for Distinguished Service (das Große Verdienstkreuz) of the Federal Republic of Germany. He died on March 5, 1964, at age sixty-six (Schenk, *Hitlers Mann in Danzig*, 216).
117 Gülzow, *Kirchenkampf in Danzig*, 29.
118 Gülzow, *Kirchenkampf in Danzig*, 25.
119 Gülzow, *Kirchenkampf in Danzig*, 19.
120 Gülzow, *Kirchenkampf in Danzig*, 20.

121 Gülzow, *Kirchenkampf in Danzig*, 45.
122 Among the leading scholars are Ronald Modras, Dariusz Libionka, Antony Polonski and WilliamW. Hagen. For more information on the Catholic Church in Poland 1914–1939, see Neal Pease's *Rome's Most Faithful Daughter*.
123 Libionka, *Antisemitism, Anti-Judaism*, 237.
124 Libionka, *Antisemitism, Anti-Judaism*, 213.
125 Libionka, *Antisemitism, Anti-Judaism*, 203.
126 Libionka, *Die Kirche in Polen*, 256–7. Translations from German my own.
127 King, *The Nazi State*, 230.
128 King, *The Nazi State*, 232. The Darbyists were active in the rescue of Jews in Occupied France, in the village of Le Chambon, during the period 1942 to 1944. For more see Schwertfeger, *In Transit*, 209–17.
129 Railton, *German Free Churches*, 92.
130 Schenk, *Hitlers Mann in Danzig*, 218.
131 Grass, *Peeling the Onion*, 31.
132 Badziąg, *Es war eine Zeit*, 37.
133 Badziąg, *Es war eine Zeit*, 62.
134 Badziąg, *Es war eine Zeit*, 62–3
135 Badziąg, *Es war eine Zeit*, 65.
136 Koehl, *RKFDV*, 138.
137 Ceran, *Szmalcówka*, 49.
138 Ceran, *Szmalcówka*, 101.
139 Ceran, *Szmalcówka*, 168.
140 Ceran, *Szmalcówka*, 32.
141 Ceran, *Szmalcówka*, 34.
142 Krawczyk, *Pogranicza*, 122.
143 Krawczyk, *Pogranicza*, 124.
144 Common local term for Germans.
145 Zamek Kiszewski, September 1, 1939, in Krawczyk, *Pogranicza*, 121.
146 Krawczyk, *Pogranicza*, 168.
147 Cited in *Szmalcówka*, 35.
148 Dwork and van Pelt, *Auschwitz*, 26.
149 Schenk, *Hitlers Mann in Danzig*, 207.
150 Allen, *The Business of Genocide*, 139–40.
151 Allen, *The Business of Genocide*, 150–1.

Chapter 3

1 The crime could be something as small as "stealing peas." See Figure 8 in the Appendix.
2 Grabowska-Chałka, *Guide*, 29.
3 Wachsmann, *The Dynamics of Destruction*, 30.
4 Wachsmann, *KL*, 83.
5 Montague, *Chełmno*, 13.
6 Montague, *Chełmno*, 39.
7 Friedlander, *Memory, History*, 39.
8 Montague, *Chełmno*, 29–30.

9   Violet triangles designated religious sects, pink triangles designated homosexuals and black ones designated anti-socials, and drunkards. A letter indicated nationality, except for the Germans. Yellow stars were used for the Jews. Second time offenders had three concentric circles painted in vivid colors across the back of the suniform. Apart from the triangles, all heads were shaved in a broad stripe across the top of the head.
10 The main resistance groups and names of their members can be read in *Stutthof Das KL*, 113.
11 For more on this subject see Dieter Pohl, "*The Holocaust and the Concentration Camps*," in *The New Histories*. He also claims that during the second half of 1942, more Jews were confined to these camps than in concentration camps. Most of these forced labor camps in Poland were closed between the end of 1942 and July 1943, following either mass executions or deportation to extermination camps" (Dieter Pohl, *The Holocaust*, 153).
12 See Steyer, *Stutthof das KL*, 115 for more information about 1944.
13 Steyer, *Stutthof das KL*, 117.
14 See Figure 17 in the Appendix for a layout of the subcamps.
15 Megargee, *Encyclopedia of Camps*, 1422.
16 Cited by Orski, *Stutthof das KL*, 147.
17 Dillon, *Dachau and the SS*, 6.
18 Dillon, *Dachau and the SS*, 6.
19 See Wachsmann, *KL*, 401, for information on the transfer of commandants to different camps under the leadership of Oswald Pohl. Max Pauly was sent from Stutthof to Neuengamme. Paul-Werner Hoppe was among five of the newly appointed camp commandants.
20 Cited in Orth, *das KL*, 215–6.
21 Badziąg, *Es war eine Zeit*, 185.
22 Badziąg, *Es war eine Zeit*, 185.
23 Kuhn, *Stutthof*, 68–9.
24 See direct quotation, Wachsmann, *KL*, 552 in an unsourced reference.
25 Sofsky, *Order of Terror*, 108.
26 Sofsky, *Order of Terror*, 109.
27 Sofsky, *Order of Terror*, 110.
28 Sofsky, *Order of Terror*, 101.
29 Wachsmann, *KL*, 193.
30 Wachsmann, *KL*, 104.
31 Yla, *A Priest in Stutthof*, 40.
32 Orski, *Stutthof das KL*, 153.
33 Orski, *Stutthof das KL*, 153.
34 Kuhn, *Stutthof*, 153.
35 Wachsmann, *KL*, 522.
36 Many well-known memoirs speak negatively about the criminal functionaries. A possible reason for it is that the authors observed their criminal superiors in Auschwitz. The SS brought to Auschwitz a band of professional criminals from Sachsenhausen, choosing big, strong, energetic, cruel men who gladly tortured and killed people—in Flossenbürg almost without exception, violent, and cruel. (Dębski, *A Battlefield of Ideas*, 115)
37 Orski, *Stutthof das KL*, 147. Wachsmann refers to the discord among prisoners from the huge territory of the Soviet Union, especially between Russians who remained

38 For more on the fate of the Soviet commissars and Russian POWs, see Wachsmann, *KL*, 259–61. Nine thousand were killed in Sachsenhausen in September and October 1941.
39 Sruoga, *Forest of the Gods*.
40 Sruoga, *Forest of the Gods*, 5.
41 I am not suggesting that there was not violence among regular prisoners. Some became hardened after years of internment and, as we will see later, were severely judged by the postwar tribunals for their acts of violence toward fellow prisoners.
42 Sruoga, *Forest of the Gods*, 214.
43 The Polish version of the proverb is that work is not a hare: it won't run away.
44 Sruoga, *Forest of the Gods*, 216.
45 Sruoga, *Forest of the Gods*, 3.
46 Sruoga, *Forest of the Gods*, 3.
47 Sruoga, *Forest of the Gods*, 12.
48 Cited in Grabowska-Chałka, *Guide*, 56.
49 Wachsmann, *KL*, 258.
50 Cited in Ferenc, *Stutthof das KL*, 106.
51 Grot, *Stutthof das KL*, 195.
52 Cited by Grot, *Stutthof das KL*, 196.
53 Drywa, *Säuberungsaktion*, 41.
54 See Wachsmann, *KL*, 273 for more examples of the role of SS doctors.
55 Dunin-Wąsowicz, *Stutthof*, 90. Wachsmann writes that German doctors were among the most fervent supporters of National Socialism. Half of all male physicians joined the Party and 7 percent the SS (Wachsmann, *KL*, 441).
56 Yla, *A Priest in Stutthof*, 25.
57 Sofsky, *The Order of Terror*, 176.
58 Allen, *The Business of Genocide*, 21.
59 Wachsmann, *KL*, 102.
60 Wachsmann, *KL*, 105–7.
61 Wachsmann, *KL*, 114–15.
62 Her statistics were taken from Alexander Lasik who based his percentage on a total number of 2,000.
63 Cited in an unpublished article by Agnieszka Czerna Chyrek, *Niemcy, obywatele byłego*. Used with permission.
64 Bergen, *Twisted Cross*, 44–5.
65 Evans, *The Third Reich*. See pp. 118–41 for an informed analysis of *Volksgemeinschaft*.
66 For detailed information, see Bergen, *Twisted Cross*, 44–51.
67 Marsh, *Life of Dietrich Bonhoeffer*.
68 Marsh, *Life of Dietrich Bonhoeffer*, 271.
69 According to Agnieszka Chyrek, these SS men belonged to the 36th and 71st units of Gdańsk's *Allgemeine SS, SS-Wachsturmbann,* which had been active in the 1930s and in the assault on Gdańsk/Danzig.
70 Longerich, *Heinrich Himmler*.
71 Longerich, *Heinrich Himmler*, 265.
72 Longerich, *Heinrich Himmler*, 265–6.
73 Allen, *The Business of Genocide*, 114.
74 Longerich, *Heinrich Himmler*, 265–6.

75 Marsh, *Life of Dietrich Bonhoeffer*, 292.
76 Longerich, *Heinrich Himmler*, 743.
77 Wendy Lower gives the case of one SS couple from a mixed denomination where the couple agreed to put aside religious preference and unite as members of an emerging elite. Himmler certified marriages of senior SS men (Lower, *Hitler's Furies*, 69).
78 Marsh, *Life of Dietrich Bonhoeffer*, 160.
79 Van Pelt and Dvorok, in *Holocaust: A History*, 113.
80 Barnett, *For the Soul of the People*, 140.
81 Barnett, *For the Soul of the People*, cited on page 140.
82 The French theologian Aimé Bonifas, deported to Buchenwald in 1943 wrote the following about the great gap between a religious site and religious practice: "The camp was situated directly at the village of Mackenrode. We could recognize all the houses as well as the high tower of a Protestant-Lutheran church. The view of this church was often a mystery to me in the days that followed. I have no way of judging, and I do not know, who are those who assemble there, but how can one speak of heaven so near such injustice?" (Caplan, *The New Histories*, 117).
83 Files of United States Holocaust Memorial Museum, RG-04-058, M.0242.
84 United States Holocaust Memorial Museum, RG-04-058M-0248.
85 Feig, *Hitler's Death Camps*, 192.
86 Wachsmann, *KL*, 272. For more examples see page 273. See also Pohl's after dinner speech, when he encouraged the Auschwitz SS that their work was as vital to the Nazi cause as frontline service in the Death's Head divisions. He was therefore approving the construction of a brothel so that the men could have some diversion. He alluded to the special strains of mass murder "about which no words have to be lost" (Wachsmann *KL*, 360–1).
87 Browning, *Nazi Resettlement Policy*, 310.
88 Browning, *Nazi Resettlement Policy*, 102.
89 Evans draws on research that shows that young people born in Berlin between 1923 and 1928 were disproportionately receptive to National Socialism—62 percent, compared to only 35 percent of those born between 1911 and 1916 (Evans, *The Third Reich in History*, 108).
90 Dębski, *A Battlefield of Ideas*, 18–22.
91 Wachsmann, *KL*, 376.
92 Dębski, *A Battlefield of Ideas*, 184.
93 These First World War veterans had served in "das alte Heer" / "the Old Army." See Figure 13 in the Appendix for the breakdown of the local guards that fit into this category.
94 Orth, *Concentration Camp Personnel*, 49.
95 Gülzow, *Kirchenkampf in Danzig*.
96 Rossino, *Blitzkrieg, Ideology, and Atrocity*, 114.
97 Snyder, *Bloodlands*, 408.
98 Yla, *Shavelings*, 17.
99 Wachsmann, *KL*, 101.
100 As noted in the Introduction, the testimony of Sruoga—and of Dunin—has been validated by historian Orski as credible and accurate. This is high praise considering his memoir *Forest of the Gods* could function as a novel.
101 Sometimes Meyer's name appears as "Theodor Meyer," but I will use the spelling that appears more frequently in the records.
102 Kuhn, *Stutthof*, 186.

103 Meyer's refusal to admit personal guilt is what Religious Studies historian Katharina von Kellenbach calls "the deliberate disassociation of private morality from public agency." She gives as one example the confession of Hermann Schmidt, second-in-command at Buchenwald who told his pastor that he had been "unaware of any cruelty in Buchenwald" (von Kellenbach, *The Mark of Cain*, 73–4).
104 Kuhn, *Stutthof*, 186.
105 Yla, *Priest in Stutthof*, 41.
106 Grabowska-Chałka, *Guide*, 52.
107 Grabowska-Chałka, *Guide*, 57.
108 Dunin-Wąsowicz, *Obóz Koncentracyjny Sztuthof*, 126.
109 Sruoga, *Forest of the Gods*, 40.
110 Sruoga, *Forest of the Gods*, 40–1.
111 Sruoga, *Forest of the Gods*, 43.
112 Sruoga, *Forest of the Gods*, 46.
113 Sruoga, *Forest of the Gods*, 80–1.
114 Sruoga, *Forest of the Gods*, 26.
115 Evans, *The Third Reich in History*, 117.
116 Sruoga, *Forest of the Gods*, 15.
117 Ziegler, *Nazi Germany's New Aristocracy*, 58, note 101.
118 Dębski, *A Battlefield of Ideas*, 184–5.
119 Orski, *The Czechs, Slovaks, and Yugoslavs*, 47.
120 Orski, *The Czechs, Slovaks, and Yugoslavs*, 51.
121 Orski, *The Czechs, Slovaks, and Yugoslavs*, 54.
122 Wachsmann, *KL*, 626.
123 Dillon, *Dachau and the SS*, 248.
124 Allen, *The Business of Genocide*, 13.
125 Allen, *The Business of Genocide*, 32.
126 Allen, *The Business of Genocide*, 43.
127 The Mauthausen Archives kindly sent me a copy of this item, Transport Order –No. 622. See also, Grabowska-Chałka, *Guide*, 99.
128 Grabowska-Chałka, *Guide*, 98.
129 Sruoga, *Forest of the Gods*, 80–2.
130 Grabowska-Chałka, *Guide*, 96.
131 Schenk, *Hitlers Mann in Danzig*, 227. He went into hiding after the war, living under an assumed name. Katzman died in Darmstadt in 1957.
132 Orski, *Stutthof das KL*, 151.
133 Orski, *The Czechs*, 14.
134 Orski, *Stutthof das KL*, 151.
135 Orski, *Stutthof das KL*, 152.
136 Dębski, *A Battlefield of Ideas*, 104.

Chapter 4

1 At least 430,000 Jews were deported beginning in early summer of 1944 from Hungary to Auschwitz and 320,000 of them were declared unfit and murdered (Wachsmann *KL*, 458). The transports to Stutthof would have included hundreds of the survivors of the selections made in Auschwitz.

2   Amt D was the result of consolidation within the IKL. Originally, Glücks was appointed Chief of Staff SS-Gruppenführer of the new IKL by Himmler. By 1940, the IKL came under the control of the WHA under Pohl. In 1942, the IKL became known simply as Amt D (Office D) of the consolidated main office of WVHA.
3   Browning, *Ordinary Men*, xv.
4   Drywa provides details in each of the four chapters of *The Extermination of Jews in Stutthof Concentration Camp, 1939–1945*.
5   *Jews in KL Stutthof*, the catalogue of the 2014 exhibition at the Stutthof Museum, draws on the earlier publication *The Extermination of Jews in Stutthof Concentration Camp 1939–1945* by Danuta Drywa who also supervised the exhibition. The information given here is taken from the exhibition Catalogue, 2014, which has no pagination. Drawn from camp files and the publication cited above, the statistics are the most accurate available to researchers.
6   Drywa, *Catalogue*, n.p.
7   Yla, *Priest in Stutthof*, 178.
8   There is no other documentation in the camp files about the use of gas vans that would corroborate the references in memoirs and oral testimony.
9   Drywa, *Catalogue*, n.p.
10 Buggeln, *Slave Labor*, 60.
11 Buggeln, *Slave Labor*, 60.
12 Buggeln, *Slave Labor*, 60.
13 The statistics given for 1944 by Grabowska-Chałka were a total of 74,000 prisoners, of whom 7,500 arrived by the end of June and the remainder thereafter (Steyer, *Stutthof das KL*, 19). The difference may be the result of Buggeln's numbers referring to new additions over that same time period (Buggeln, *Slave Labor*, 60.)
14 Wachsmann, *KL*, 326.
15 For more see Hoffmann, *History of the German Resistance*, 512–16.
16 Marsh, *Life of Dietrich Bonhoeffer*, 379–80.
17 Kershaw, *Hitler Myth*, 215.
18 Kershaw, *Hitler Myth*, 215.
19 Railton, *German Free Churches*, 129.
20 Grass, *Peeling the Onion*, 90.
21 For a comprehensive look at Sippenhaft see Robert Loeffel's *Family Punishment in Nazi Germany: Sippenhaft, Terror and Myth*.
22 Kuhn, *Stutthof*, 176. All translations my own.
23 Tighe's claim that they were left to starve in bricked-up bunkers (implying they died of suffocation) is not found in any other sources I have consulted (Tighe, *Gdańsk*, 169). He draws this information from a publication in Polish by Pilichowski, Appendix X, Tighe, note 21.
24 Kuhn, *Stutthof*, 178.
25 Kuhn, *Stutthof*, 178.
26 In an article in the *Daily Mail* in 2009, von Hassell, at the time in her early nineties, tells about her experiences in Stutthof, how she became very ill with typhus and how she fell deeply in love with Alexander von Stauffenberg, her fellow-prisoner in Stutthof and who was later to lose his wife, an officer in the *Luftwaffe*, in combat. Von Hassell returned to her own husband, an Italian count and they were finally reunited with their two little sons who had been kept in protective custody in Austria. (Stafford, *Valkyrie Lovers*, 2009).

27   United States Holocaust Memorial Museum Doc. No. 82152985#1, Arolsen Archives. (ITS) Archives. Used by permission. My translation.
28   von Hassell, *Hostage of the Third Reich*, 159.
29   Grabowska-Chałka, *Guide*, 32–3.
30   Kovala, *The Day Soon Dawns*.
31   Kovala, *The Day Soon Dawns*, 86.
32   Kovala, *The Day Soon Dawns*, 95.
33   Lukowski and Zawadzki, *A Concise History of Poland*, 241–2.
34   Dunin-Wąsowicz includes an ironic detail. Prisoners in 1944 were permitted to read the local Nazi paper—the *Vorposten*—and it was from that source that they learned about the Warsaw Uprising.
35   See Grabowska-Chałka, *Guide*, 33 for names of specific resistance organizations that were civilian, military, and political.
36   Grabowska-Chałka, *Guide*, 34.
37   Grabowska-Chałka, *Guide*, 35.
38   Dunin-Wąsowicz, *Stutthof*, 43. Dunin-Wąsowicz himself came to Stutthof with his brother Marek in May 1944.
39   Dunin-Wąsowicz, *Stutthof*, 207.
40   Dunin-Wąsowicz, *Obóz Koncentracyjny Sztuthof*, 148–51.
41   Kwiatkowski, *Interview 43670*.
42   Kwiatkowski, *Interview 43670*.
43   Kwiatkowski, *Interview 43670*.
44   Grabowska-Chałka, *Guide*, 34.
45   For more, see Wachsmann, *KL*, 547–50.
46   Grabowska-Chałka, *Stutthof das KL*, 137.
47   Drywa, *Catalogue*, n.p.
48   Grabowska-Chałka, *Stutthof das KL*, 137.
49   Grabowska-Chałka, *Stutthof das KL*, 137.
50   Grabowska-Chałka, *Stutthof das KL*, 137.
51   Grabowska-Chałka, *Stutthof das KL*, 138.
52   Grabowska-Chałka, *Stutthof das KL*, 139.
53   Cited by Buggeln, *Slave Labor*, note 248, page 61.
54   Grabowska-Chałka, *Guide*, 35.
55   Buggeln, *Slave Labor*, 61.
56   Drywa, *The Extermination of Jews*, 125.
57   Drywa, *The Extermination of Jews*, 126. Arno Chemnitz modeled his work on his earlier experience as a block leader in Buchenwald during the 1941 murders of Soviet commissars (Wachsmann, *KL*, 552).
58   Drywa, *The Extermination of Jews*, 127. Grabowska-Chałka, *Guide*, 88 gives the statistic of at least 2,000—both Jews and non-Jews who died in the *Sonderbehandlung* action.
59   Drywa, *The Extermination of Jews*, cited on page 127.
60   Drywa, *The Extermination of Jews*, 130.
61   Drywa, *The Extermination of Jews*, 30.
62   Drywa, *The Extermination of Jews*, 136. These figures do not include the mortality rates among prisoners who were transported *from* Stutthof to other camps. It is estimated that 25,500 inmates left between 1940 and 1945 for Dachau, Buchenwald, Natzweiler, Neuengamme, Sachsenhausen, Mauthausen, Ravensbrück, Auschwitz, and Gross-Rosen.

63   Dunin-Wąsowicz, *Obóz Koncentracyjny Sztuthof*, 165.
64   Wachsmann, *KL*, 259.
65   Cited by Wachsmann, *KL*, 262.
66   More than 300,000 to 500,000 POWs died each month between October and December 1941. "Soviet commissars" were the target, perceived as the worst element of "Jewish Bolsheviks." Many died in makeshift POW camps, many in the concentration camps. Official sanction had been given—on July 21, 1941, by the head of the Gestapo, Heinrich Mueller who ordered that "selected commissars should be killed inconspicuously in the nearest concentration camp." Nine thousand were killed in Sachsenhausen during a two-month period September–October 1941—more than in other camps (Wachsmann, *KL*, 259–61).
67   Zyklon B—the commercial name for hydrogen cyanide pellets was first used in 1941 as an experiment on Russian POWs. By 1943, 13.4 tons were used in Auschwitz that ultimately killed around a million Jews there. In *The Holocaust Chronicle: A History in Words and Pictures*, (Lincolnwood: Publications International, 2000), 490.
68   Kuhn, *Stutthof*, 122, my translation.
69   Grabowska-Chałka, *Guide*, 82–3.
70   Dunin-Wąsowicz, *Obóz Koncentracyjny Sztuthof*, 117.
71   Sruoga, *Forest of the Gods*, 131.
72   Wachsmann, *KL*, 507. Himmler proposed sending 20,000 Soviet POWs to Stutthof in late 1941. The plans were drawn up in Berlin and sent to Stutthof in March 1942. Himmler was quite ambitious in that he proposed adding 20,000 prisoners at a time when there were 80,000 in the entire system (Wachsmann, *KL*, 280.) The plan never materialized and though there were several thousand Soviet POWs in Stutthof, and they constituted the largest demographic after the Poles, they were sent in the end to other camps in the system (Wachsmann, *KL*, 285.)
73   Buggeln, *Slave Labor*, 11.
74   Buggeln, *Slave Labor*, 11. Buggeln follows recent scholarship (like that of Donald Bloxham) that is concerned with what he calls "the relationship between racist ideology, the desire for territorial expansion, and ad hoc policies dictated by the course of the war." This approach is addressing what he and others consider the overemphasis of interpreting Nazi Germany exclusively as a racial state.
75   Drywa, *The Extermination of Jews in Stutthof*, 173–4.
76   Lower's research indicates that by war's end one tenth of camp personnel were female. At least 3,500 women were trained to be camp guards, mostly at Ravensbrück, and sent to camps, including Stutthof (Lower, *Hitler's Furies*, 142.) The slogan "Der Osten braucht Dich"/"The East needs You" was used to attract women to fill this need for the sake of their country.
77   Orski, *Stutthof das KL*, 230–3.
78   Cited in Drywa, *The Extermination of Jews in Stutthof*, 79.
79   Orski, *Ort des Terrors, Band 6*, 596.
80   Lebensborn was supposedly a home for pregnant, unmarried German women but became a center for ensuring the biological advancement of the German race. SS men were encouraged to father children with women who met racial requirements.
81   Kuhn, *Stutthof*, 56–7.
82   Grabowska-Chałka, *Guide*, 71.
83   Drywa, *The Extermination of Jews in Stutthof*, 177.
84   Orski, *Der Ort des Terrors, Band 6*, 643–4.
85   Wolff, *Sadismus Oder Wahnsinn*, 57.

86 Wolff, *Sadismus Oder Wahnsinn*, 60.
87 Wolff, *Sadismus Oder Wahnsinn*, 50.
88 Wolff, *Sadismus Oder Wahnsinn*, 51.
89 Hedgepeth and Saidel, *Sexual Violence against Jewish Women*.
90 Valk, *Meine Erlebnisse*, 02/234. All translations my own.
91 Valk, *Meine Erlebnisse*, 02/234.
92 In using this adjective, Valk infers a pre-camp meaning and may have forgotten that the camp hospital was the last place that prisoners wanted to go since many who went there did not survive.
93 Valk, *Meine Erlebnisse*, 7.
94 Lewis, *A Time to Speak*.
95 Lewis, *A Time to Speak*, 72.
96 Lewis, *A Time to Speak*, 75.
97 Lewis, *A Time to Speak*, 77.
98 Lewis, *A Time to Speak*, 82–3.
99 Lewis, *A Time to Speak*, 84.
100 Lewis, *A Time to Speak*, 86.
101 Lewis, *A Time to Speak*, 88.
102 Lewis, *A Time to Speak*, 95.
103 Dębski, *Battlefield of Ideas*, 105.
104 Dębski, *Battlefield of Ideas*, cited on page 106.
105 Kuhn, *Stutthof*, 126. My translation.
106 Kuhn, *Stutthof*, 127.
107 I found 1,670 video testimonies about Stutthof in 2014. The number has increased to over 2,100 since that date.
108 Abramowitz, *Interview 12319*.
109 The construction firm Kieferling and Metzger supervised the work. (Orski, *Ort des Terrors, Band 6*, 722). One of the women guards—Emilie Macha—was found guilty by a Polish court on November 16, 1948, and given a twelve-year sentence. She died in prison on February 4, 1949. Berger, the head of the camp, was tried in Cologne on March 14, 1973, for the deaths of prisoners but without an outcome (Orski, *Ort des Terrors*, 724).
110 Abramowitch, *Interview 4627*.
111 Abramowitch, *Interview 4627*.
112 Borensztein, *Interview 34594*.
113 It is estimated that 5,911 Jehovah's Witnesses were arrested between 1933 and 1945—a large percentage considering there were only 6,034 of them. Over 2,000 were executed or died through other acts of violence. See Bracher, *The Conscience in Revolt*, 14. See also Detlaf Garbe's *Between Resistance and Martyrdom: Jehovah's Witnesses in the Third Reich*, trans. Dagmar G. Grimm, (USHMM and University of Wisconsin Press, 2009).
114 Gawior, *Interview 32768*.
115 Sruoga gives more information about the Jehovah's Witnesses who worked with him in the Political Division and according to him, tried very hard to convert other prisoners. For more details, see Chapter 32 of *Forest of the Gods*.
116 Gawior, *Interview 32768*.
117 Kempowski, *Haben Sie davon gewußt?* Translations are my own.
118 The BDM was the female branch of the Hitler Youth. By July 1944, its membership had grown to well over four million girls and young women.

119 Kempowski, *Haben Sie davon gewußt*, 116.
120 She is, of course, wrong in equating the two camps. Struthof was part of the Natzweiler camp in France. The confusion is still (understandably) a common error.
121 Kempowski, *Haben Sie davon gewußt?*, 108.
122 Tighe, *Gdańsk*, 167–70.
123 Wachsmann, *KL*, 507.
124 Kuhn, *Stutthof*, 160, my translation.
125 Kuhn, *Stutthof*, 160.
126 Kuhn, *Stutthof*, 458. By April 1944, camp staff numbered more than 22,000, growing to more than 50,000 by the end of the year (Wachsmann, *KL*, 467). By January 1, 1945, there were around 3,500 female camp guards.
127 For more information, see Distel, *Frauen in Konzentrationslagern*, 204–5.
128 Sheyer, *Bylye Gody*, 74.
129 Sheyer, *Bylye Gody*, 36. Trawniki, located near Lublin, was originally used to house Soviet POWs then expanded into an SS training facility for suitable SS candidates from the occupied territories. In 1942, it became a forced-labor camp for thousands of Jews from the sub-camps around Lublin.
130 For more on the abuse of alcohol and Himmler's attempt to educate the SS leader corps in abstention see Longerich, *Heinrich Himmler*, 32–4.
131 Dunin-Wąsowicz, *Obóz Koncentracyjny Sztuthof*, 30.
132 Grabowska-Chałka, *Guide*, 81.
133 Grabowska-Chałka, *Guide*, 84–5.
134 Dunin-Wąsowicz, *Obóz Koncentracyjny Sztuthof*, 87.
135 Dunin-Wąsowicz, *Obóz Koncentracyjny Sztuthof*, 87.
136 Dunin-Wąsowicz, *Stutthof*, 61–3.
137 Dunin-Wąsowicz, *Stutthof*, 70.
138 Sruoga, *Forest of the Gods*, 185–6.
139 Sruoga, *Forest of the Gods*, 183.
140 Wachsmann, *KL*, 671.
141 Orski, *Niewolnicza praca więźniów*. Translations by Tieszen.
142 Orski, *Niewolnicza praca więźniów*, 139.
143 Orski, *Niewolnicza praca więźniów*, 242, footnote 156.
144 Orski, *Niewolnicza praca więźniów*, 242, footnote 156.
145 Orski, *Niewolnicza praca więźniów*, 242, footnote 156.
146 Orski, *Niewolnicza praca więźniów*, 133.
147 Orski, *Niewolnicza praca więźniów*, 219, footnote 85.
148 I am assuming that Maitre's reference is to Jan Brajt (spelled Breit in his memoir) and not to Jan Breit, a female overseer who, like Jan Brajt, was also executed after the first trial in 1946.
149 Orski, *Niewolnicza praca więźniów*, 37.
150 Yla, *A Priest in Stutthof*, 169.
151 Orth, *Die Konzentrationslager-SS*, 223.
152 Sruoga, *Forest of the Gods*, 169.
153 Sruoga, *Forest of the Gods*, 169.
154 Sruoga, *Forest of the Gods*, 168.
155 Sruoga, *Forest of the Gods*, 168.
156 For more details on Hoppe's trial, see Orth, *Die Konzentrationslager-SS*, 222–5.
157 Segev, *Soldiers of Evil*, 174.
158 Segev, *Soldiers of Evil*, 174.

159 Orth, *Die Konzentrationslager-SS*, 294, my translation.
160 Segev, *Soldiers of Evil*, 7–8.
161 Griesbach, *Ich kann immer noch das Elend spüren*, 94.
162 Wąs, *Gdańsk wojenny*, 108.
163 This may be a flawed memory, as Schenk indicated that the first RAF bombing of Danzig took place in July 1942 when fifty were killed. Schenk, *Hitlers Mann in Danzig*, 220.
164 Wąs, *Gdańsk wojenny*, 67.
165 Wąs, *Gdańsk wojenny*, 111.
166 Wąs, *Gdańsk wojenny*, 109.
167 Wąs, *Gdańsk wojenny*, 108.
168 Sruoga's depictions remind me of those of Arthur Koestler who wrote about his experiences in the French internment camp, Le Vernet in *Abschaum der Erde—Scum of the Earth*. Both men use similar narrative strategies—irony, juxtaposition, poetic, and factual prose-to capture the misery of internment. (Koestler, *Scum of the Earth*).
169 Weilova, *Auschwitz-Häftling Nr. 71978*, "Erinnerungen an Stutthof."
170 Dwork and van Pelt, *Holocaust*, 176.

Chapter 5

1 Kuhn, *Stutthof*, 190.
2 According to Sruoga, items of value, especially money and jewelry were routinely taken from prisoners and stored in bins, after having been entered into the books (Sruoga, *Forest of the Gods*, 80). These stored items that certainly never were returned to their owners may very well have become part of the luggage that also was taken along in the camp evacuation.
3 Orski, *Ort des Terrors, Band 6*, 610.
4 Grabowska-Chałka, *Guide*, 106.
5 Grabowska-Chałka, *Guide*, 105.
6 Grot, *Stutthof das KL*, 284.
7 Dunin-Wąsowicz, *Stutthof*, 224. Dunin-Wąsowicz points out that the *Ehrenhäftlinge* traveled, at least initially, by train. It took the others eleven days to walk 140 kilometers.
8 Grabowska-Chałka, *Guide*, 106.
9 See page 107 of Grabowska-Chałka, *Guide*, for place names.
10 Cited in Grabowska-Chałka, *Guide*, 107.
11 Grabowska-Chałka, *Guide*, 107.
12 Grabowska-Chałka, *Guide*, 108.
13 Grabowska-Chałka, *Guide*, 108.
14 Grabowska-Chałka, *Guide*, 108.
15 Orski, *Ort des Terrors, Band 6*, 607–8.
16 Yla, *A Priest in Stutthof*, 242.
17 Grabowska-Chałka, *Guide*, 109.
18 Grabowska-Chałka, *Guide*, 109.
19 Grabowska-Chałka, *Guide*, 111.
20 Maria Blitz, the last known survivor of the Palmnicken massacre died on June 11, 2016, at age ninety-eight. She had survived the Kraków ghetto, Płaszów, Auschwitz, Stutthof and Palmnicken, *New York Times* obituary, June 14, 2016.

21 There are several histories that give details about this massacre, including Blatman's—see note 24. See also Peter B. Clark's *The Death of East Prussia*, 265–78.
22 Cited in, Grabowska-Chałka, *Guide*, 112.
23 See Daniel Blatman, *The Death Marches* for details of the Palmnicken massacre, 117–25.
24 The camp was still functioning, even the careful documentation of medical procedures. An entry on January 18, 1945, documents the amputation of three fingers (2,3,4) from a prisoner's hand at Elbing: "The shattered fingers we immediately amputated." Iwan Andrejew, Prisoner #812. It was signed by an *Oberscharführer*. United States Holocaust Memorial Museum, RG-04-058MI—Reel 238.
25 Grabowska-Chałka, *Guide*, 113. This report came directly from the Soviet Army's Health Unit.
26 Grabowska-Chałka, *Guide*, 114. A mass grave was exhumed in April 1971 that contained the bodies of 720 people, mostly young women.
27 There is limited evidence of these evacuations.
28 Grabowska-Chałka, *Guide*, 116.
29 Grabowska-Chałka, *Guide*, 116.
30 Grabowska-Chałka, *Guide*, 117.
31 John Toland points out in *The Last Days* that Danzig was both the main port for the evacuation of civilian and military refugees (around one million were now attempting to escape) as well as the last *Festung*/fortress of the Nazi regime. Under the command of Marshal Roskossovsky, Soviet troops had successfully driven a wedge between Danzig and Gotenhafen and had dropped pamphlets from the air, urging German troops to accept defeat. The response from the Führer's headquarters was "Each square meter of the area Danzig-Gotenhafen must be defended to the end." (Toland, *The Last Days*, 303–4).
32 Grabowska-Chałka, *Guide*, 110.
33 Orski, *Der Ort des Terrors, Band 6*, 731. Among those buried in a communal grave in Puck were two prisoners from Lithuania, one an engineer, Antanas Sapalas and the priest Alfons Lipniunas whose remains were exhumed in 1989 and taken home to Lithuania. (Orski, *Ort des Terrors, Band 6*, 732).
34 Grabowska-Chałka, *Guide*, 117.
35 Grabowska-Chałka, *Guide*, 117.
36 Grot, *Stutthof das KL*, 282–3.
37 Cited in Grot, *Stutthof das KL*, 283.
38 For more on the strafing of these ships by the RAF with so many camp prisoners on board see http://www.worldnavalships.com/forums/archive/index.php/t-13395.html.
39 Orski, *The Czechs*, 27.
40 Grabowska-Chałka, *Guide*, 118.
41 Grabowska-Chałka, *Guide*, 119.
42 Drywa, *Ort des Terrors, Band 6*, 516. Egbert Kieser tells how Annemarie Kniep survived her long trek through East Prussia during the Russian offensive, losing all her goods en route but finally reaching Stutthof where she and her fellow refugees "ate warm soup." (Kieser, *Prussian Apocalypse*, 68).
43 Cited in Grabowska-Chałk, *Guide*, 120.
44 Kremer, *Zeugenaussage/Witness Statement* 032040. My translation.
45 Kremer, *Zeugenaussage / Witness Statement* 032040, 10.
46 Kremer, *Zeugenaussage / Witness Statement* 032040, 12.
47 Grot, *Stutthof das KL*, 288.

48 Grabowska-Chałka, *Guide*, 121.
49 Cited by Grot, *Stutthof das KL*, 290–1. See also note 79.
50 Grot, *Stutthof das KL*, 291.
51 Grabowska-Chałka, *Guide*, 123.
52 Grabowska-Chałka, *Guide*, 123.
53 Grabowska-Chałka, *Guide*, 125.
54 Kuhn, *Stutthof*, 162.
55 Kuhn, *Stutthof*, 162.
56 Grabowska-Chałka, *Guide*, 124.
57 Kovala, *The Day Soon Dawns*, 178.
58 Blatman, *The Death Marches*, 159.
59 Blatman, *The Death Marches*, 167.
60 Blatman, *The Death Marches*, 181–2.
61 Yla, *A Priest in Stutthof*, 235.
62 Fern, *Video Testimony RG-50.493.0014*.
63 Abramowitch, *Interview 4627*. Maja Abramowitch was born in 1929 in Dinsk, Latvia.
64 Benadon, *Interview RG-50.146.0001*.
65 Friedrich, *Interview 31653*.
66 Gawior, *Interview 32768*.
67 Griesbach, *Ich kann immer noch das Elend spüren*, 96.
68 Griesbach, *Ich kann immer noch das Elend spüren*, 99.
69 Griesbach, *Ich kann immer noch das Elend spüren*, 106.
70 Griesbach, *Ich kann immer noch das Elend spüren*, 111.
71 The *Volkssturm* was a national militia created in the last months of the war on the orders of Hitler that mobilized German civilians between sixteen and sixty years of age, largely to boost national morale.
72 Griesbach, *Ich kann immer noch das Elend spüren*, 111.
73 Griesbach, *Ich kann immer noch das Elend spüren*, 112.
74 Griesbach, *Ich kann immer noch das Elend spüren*, 112. (See the earlier story of Valk on pp. 125ff).
75 Griesbach, *Ich kann immer noch das Elend spüren*, 126.
76 *The Protocols of the Elders of Zion* was a forged antisemitic publication that originated in 1905 in Russia, and portrayed Jews as conspirators with a secret plan to rule the world. It was widely read and accepted as true, rather than fiction, in the Nazi era.
77 Griesbach, *Ich kann immer noch das Elend spüren*, 130.
78 Griesbach, *Ich kann immer noch das Elend spüren*, 131. On April 20, 1945, the former commandant of Stutthof, Max Pauly vowed that anyone who sullied the SS uniform faced brutal punishment. He had just ordered an officer known for his civility to prisoners over to an SS court. He was executed four days later (Wachsmann, *KL*, 572).
79 Griesbach, *Ich kann immer noch das Elend spüren*, 134.
80 Kieser, *Prussian Apocalypse*, 34.
81 Kieser, *Prussian Apocalypse*, 34.
82 Kieser, *Prussian Apocalypse*, 36.
83 Kieser, *Prussian Apocalypse*, 40.
84 Kieser, *Prussian Apocalypse*, 46.
85 Kieser, *Prussian Apocalypse*, 46.
86 Kieser, *Prussian Apocalypse*, 51.

87   Kieser, *Prussian Apocalypse*, 57.
88   It should be pointed out that *Prussian Apocalypse* (originally published in German in 1978, translated in 2011) is not a chronological, military history, but a series of narratives about the dilemma of East Prussian refugees fleeing from the Soviet advance. It was this aspect that was helpful in telling the story of the Stutthof prisoners, caught up in the struggle to survive.
89   Kieser, *Prussian Apocalypse*, 67.
90   Kieser, *Prussian Apocalypse*, 67.
91   Drywa, *Jews in KL Stutthof*, n.p.
92   Krawczyk, *Pogranicza, (Bożepole)*, 194.
93   Krawczyk, *Pogranicza*, 195.
94   Krawczyk, *Pogranicza*, 195.
95   Krawczyk, *Pogranicza, (Zamek Kiszewski 1945)*, 196.
96   Wąs, *Gdańsk wojenny*, 115. Translated by Tieszen.
97   Wąs, *Gdańsk wojenny*, 116.
98   Wąs, *Gdańsk wojenny*, 117.
99   Wąs, *Gdańsk wojenny*, 133.
100 Wąs, *Gdańsk wojenny*, 133.
101 Katzmann lived under a false identity after the war and died in Darmstadt in 1957 (Schenk, *Hitlers Mann in Danzig*, 227).
102 Blatman, *The Death Marches*, 113–14.
103 Sydnor, *Soldiers of Destruction*, 329.
104 See page 290–1 in Chapter 4 for other information by Segev about Hoppe's final days.
105 Segev, *Soldiers of Evil*, 7.
106 Wąs, *Gdańsk wojenny*, 133.
107 Blatman, *The Death Marches*, 114.
108 Blatman, *The Death Marches*, 115.
109 Blatman, *The Death Marches*, 115.
110 See endnotes in Blatman, *The Death Marches*, 457 for details of testimonies of survivors.
111 Juerman, *Experiences in Riga*, 3.
112 Douglas, *Orderly and Humane*, 62.
113 Douglas, *Orderly and Humane*, 62.
114 Kieser, *Prussian Apocalypse*, 188.
115 Kieser, *Prussian Apocalypse*, 188.
116 Kieser, *Prussian Apocalypse*, 143.
117 Photos used with the permission of Lydia Klein, Kościerzyna.
118 Grass, *Peeling the Onion*, 115.
119 Photos used with the permission of Lydia Klein, Kościerzyna.

Epilogue

1   Cited by Moeller, *Sinking Ships*, 147.
2   March 25, 2002, "*Die Deutschen als Opfer*," headline in *Der Spiegel*.
3   Moeller, *Sinking Ships*, 158–9.
4   Moeller, *Sinking Ships*, 167.
5   Moeller, *Sinking Ships*, 154.

6   Moeller, *Sinking Ships*, 177.
7   Moeller, *Sinking Ships*, 179.
8   Alton, *Deportiert von den Nazis*.
9   Solzhenitsyn, *Prussian Nights*, 105.
10 von Lehndorff, *East Prussian Diary*.
11 von Lehndorff, *East Prussian Diary*, 10.
12 von Lehndorff, *East Prussian Diary*, 32–3.
13 von Lehndorff, *East Prussian Diary*, 68.
14 von Lehndorff, *East Prussian Diary*, 159.
15 von Lehndorff, *East Prussian Diary*, 158.
16 von Lehndorff, *East Prussian Diary*, 251.
17 Lewis, *A Time to Speak*, 97.
18 Lewis, *A Time to Speak*, 97.
19 Solzhenitsyn, *Prussian Nights*, 7.
20 Solzhenitsyn, *Prussian Nights*, 7.
21 Wąs, *Gdańsk wojenny*, 118.
22 Wąs, *Gdańsk wojenny*, 118.
23 Krawczyk, *Pogranicza*, 197.
24 Krawczyk, *Pogranicza*, 198.
25 Schenk, *Hitlers Mann*, 239.
26 Koehl, *RKFDV*, 20.
27 Wąs, *Gdańsk wojenny*, 208.
28 Wąs, *Gdańsk wojenny*, 211.
29 Wąs, *Gdańsk wojenny*, 211.
30 Wąs, *Gdańsk wojenny*, 211.
31 Wąs, *Gdańsk wojenny*, 211.
32 Wąs, *Gdańsk wojenny*, 191.
33 Wąs, *Gdańsk wojenny*, 193.
34 This response reflects what Kershaw claims: "In the first months of 1945, the German people regarded itself as Hitler's main victim" (Kershaw, *Hitler Myth*, 223).
35 Grass, *Peeling the Onion*, 236.
36 Grass, *Peeling the Onion*, 285.
37 Michalik, *Sprzątając Zagładę*, 67.
38 Michalik, *Sprzątając Zagładę*, 67.
39 Drywa, *Extermination of Jews in Stutthof Concentration Camp, 1939–1945*, 325.
40 Browning, *Ordinary Men*, xv. Christopher Browning points out that in mid-March 1942, around 75 percent to 80 percent of all victims of the Holocaust were still alive. By mid-February 1943, the percentages were exactly the reverse.
41 Bloch and Brzezińska, *Sztutowo/Stutthof*.
42 Reviewers refer to Chwin as the "renowned Polish novelist Chwin" (https://www.theguardian.com/books/2004/may/01/featuresreviews.guardianreview31) and "two of Poland's best-known younger writers, Pawel Huelle and Stefan Chwin" (https://www.kirkusreviews.com/book-reviews/stefan-chwin/death-in-danzig/).
43 Moeller, *Sinking Ships*, 177.
44 Huelle, *Castorp*, 232.
45 Chwin, *Death in Danzig*, 233.
46 Chwin, *Death in Danzig*, 130.
47 Chwin, *Death in Danzig*, 138.
48 Zaglade, *Sztutowo*, 64.

49 For the song, see https://www.cbc.ca/radio/ideas/the-invisible-shoes-of-stutthof-concentration-camp-1.5117397
50 Historian and scholar Otto Dov Kulka has written powerfully and poignantly about this subject in his book *Landscapes of the Metropolis of Death*.
51 Zaglade, *Sztutowo*, 31.

Appendix

1 This may be an unfortunate translation issue, as the Polish "niewierzący" (meaning non-believer) has a much different connotation than the German "gottgläubig," which implied some belief in God.

Sources

The archival material that traces the evolution of Stutthof from a relatively minor labor camp to a registered concentration camp under the command of Heinrich Himmler is hardly secondary in volume. A large portion of the camp's documentation is in Polish and, without the help of translators and archivists, I could never have proceeded with a project which has now extended well over eight years. Fortunately—for me—there were also many files in German, and several important secondary works had been translated from Polish into German. Since my approach also embraces literary discourse, the other source for my research is the *Danzig Trilogy* by Günter Grass, as well as his other prose works. These works of fiction and nonfiction have helped support my argument that Stutthof can be better understood by connecting it to Danzig.

With the help of a translator, Dr. Bożena Tieszen, I have been able to draw from the scholarship of Polish historians who write about Stutthof—notably, Danuta Drywa, Marek Orski, Elżbieta Grot, and journalist Marek Wąs. Aleksandra Gluba-Pieprz, doctoral candidate in Jewish Studies at Poznań University, has extended to me invaluable assistance—translating documents, going in person to the Stutthof Museum to locate documents and representing me when I could not be there in person. In the summer of 2019, we visited the state archive—Poznań Archiwum together and consulted files that pertained to Danzig-West Prussia. The United States Holocaust Memorial Museum has been a major source of help and information at every stage of this research. Drawing on its vast resources, I have been able to access directly and in person additional material—including memoirs, both published and unpublished, video testimony and other documents pertaining to Stutthof. In addition to three trips to the Stutthof Museum, I have also visited the US National Archives in Maryland and the Leo Baeck Institute in the Center for Jewish History in New York. An important facet of my research was to explore in person the city of Gdańsk, and to locate the sites of Stutthof's sub-camps, in towns as far apart as Bromberg/Bydgoszcz and Stolp/Słupsk on the Baltic. These trips have given me a much clearer understanding of how scattered the filial camps of Stutthof were, and of the distances that prisoners were forced to walk both to work and during the evacuations.

In tracking the camp's history, I have followed the model set by Polish historians, notably in the German translation of *Stutthof: Das Konzentrationslager (The Concentration Camp)*. The editor of the collected essays, Donald Steyer introduces Stutthof by saying that the camp's history would be incomplete without dealing with the main factors that shaped the German-Polish relationships in Pomerania and Danzig after the Treaty of Versailles. That's where I start. Apart from two on-line histories, there is no comprehensive study on Stutthof in English that I know of. There are several translations from Polish into English and German that are based on archival data, including the official *Guide*, which offers more than the average museum handbook, including detailed information by the late Janina Grabowska-Chałka, which draws directly from archival data on many aspects of the camp's history and resources.

The neglect of Stutthof was noted much earlier in publications that are not viewed as academic, for example, in the popular travel book *The Vanished Kingdom*, about the former East Prussia, in which writer and journalist James Charles Roy has this to say: "I had never heard of Stutthof, nor, do I imagine, have most others from Western Europe or America ... But every Pole, Jew or gentile, knows Stutthof." In a similar vein, the British writer, Carl Tighe pointed out earlier that Stutthof is probably one of the least known of the camps set up by the Nazis. In most of the earlier publications about concentration camps, Stutthof is not mentioned, even by Eugen Kogon. It is also not mentioned in "*Za drutami. Antologia pamięci 1938–45 / Behind the Barbed Wires (Anthology of Remembrance 1939–45)*, published in 1963 in Warsaw. It is briefly mentioned in the French anthology *Tragédie de la déportation 1940–5*, published in Paris in 1955 but is incorrectly described as a sub-camp of Neuengamme.

Why has Stutthof been neglected by English-speaking historians? Marek Orski, a Polish historian actively engaged with the Stutthof files for many years, addressed the general issue of Stutthof's neglect by saying that for a time after the war, all the documents were not in the same place and were widely dispersed; some were held privately, and some were in the Soviet Union. There was no central depository until archivists began to assemble all the documents at the former campsite in the Stutthof Museum. Though established as a museum in 1962, it was not until 1966 that it was placed under the auspices of the Ministry of Culture, the agency from which it continues to receive its support and funding. The history of the Museum's establishment can be attributed in large measure to the tireless efforts of former prisoners and of their family members who in the postwar years could see that the camp had fallen into a derelict state and even had become a target for looters. Those early initiatives have meanwhile been affirmed by the teamwork of archivists and historians (Professor Andrzej Gąsiorowski, to name one) at Stutthof Museum who, working closely with scholars like Professor Grzegorz Berendt at Gdańsk University have published critical information and data about Stutthof. I am indebted to their scholarship for background information.

In the wake of the postwar chaos, including trials that were set up by the Soviets and Poles sympathetic to Soviet ideology, there was also suppression of research, even though camp records of the chaotic evacuation orders of January 25, 1945, survived, and according to Dunin-Wąsowicz, among those records were 826 personnel files of the SS orders. There are also 18,000 files about Polish prisoners (1942–5) and a portion of the transport lists of inmates to and from the camp. Documentation of the Work Division—Wirtschaftsabteilung—is fragmentary but gives information on the role of the sub-camps and the names of local businesses and firms and private individuals who employed the inmates of Stutthof. Camp medical records do not cover the whole period and are confined to the period August 8, 1941, until June 29, 1942, as well as the files of those who were released from the infirmary between March 1942 and January 1945. There is also incomplete documentation of the activities of the DAW. There are about 55,000 prisoner files in Stutthof that include information about nationality, date of birth, religion, date of arrival at Stutthof, sometimes the reason for arrest, as well as characteristic features of a prisoner—height, hair color, special marks, etc. Not all the entries are complete—prisoners often did not write down their real profession, and the majority of them did not know why they had been interned. Regarding credibility, Orski points to the example of Judge Zacharasiewicz who was responsible for collecting the material against the accused between 1945 and 1947, and he endorses two former prisoners, Dunin-Wąsowicz and the Lithuanian writer Balys Sruoga as credible sources. I draw from their testimonies throughout the book.

The Stutthof Museum's own website has been a helpful source of information. It is frequently updated and offers information in several languages on the history of the camp, as well as listing its past and current exhibitions, and its archival offerings for visiting scholars. The Museum has a strong pedagogical mission and attracts many students and young people from local schools and farther afield. I have also consulted *Stutthof Main Camp*, in *Volume 1: Part B, USHMM Encyclopedia of Camps and Ghettos, 1933–45*, edited by Michael McQueen. This monumental work with many volumes is considered as the most comprehensive work on the Nazi concentration camps. Nikolaus Wachsmann's *KL: A History of the Nazi Concentration Camps* has been particularly helpful to me in placing Stutthof within the larger camp system. Other important publications that I consulted include *Der Ort des Terrors: Geschichte der nationalsozialistischen Konzentrationslager, (The Place of Terror: The History of the National Socialist Camps)* edited by Wolfgang Benz and Barbara Distel. I have also drawn from Karin Orth's *Die Konzentrationslager-SS: Sozialstrukturelle Analysen und biographische Studien (Analyses and Biographical Studies of the Social Structures of the Concentration Camps)*. Since the sources used in this book are not all drawn firsthand from archival data and are dependent on translations from Polish historians, many opportunities remain for research by historians with a command of both the Polish and Germans languages.

Bibliography

"59 Nazi Leaders Are Arrested in Danzig; Senate Charges Plotting with Opposition," *New York Times*, December 29, 1936.

Abramowitch, Maja. *Interview 4627. Visual History Archive*. USC Shoah Foundation Institute. Accessed online at the United States Holocaust Memorial Museum, Feb. 2014.

Abramowitz, Rachel. *Interview 12319. Visual History Archive*. USC Shoah Foundation Institute. Accessed online at the United States Holocaust Memorial Museum, Feb. 2014.

Allen, Michael Thad. *The Business of Genocide: The SS, Slave Labor, and the Concentration Camps*. Chapel Hill: The University of North Carolina Press, 2002.

Alton, Ruth. *Deported by the Nazis*. Translated by Vernon Mosheim from Alton, Ruth: *Deportiert von den Nazis*. Accessed online from the Center for Jewish History at https://digipres.cjh.org/delivery/DeliveryManagerServlet?dps_pid=IE8864873.

Aly, Götz. *Why the Germans? Why the Jews? Envy, Race Hatred, and the Prehistory of the Holocaust*. Translated by Jefferson Chase. New York: Metropolitan Books, 2014.

Arad, Yitzhak, Gutman, Yisrael, and Margaliot, Abraham. *Documents on the Holocaust: Selected Sources on the Destruction of the Jews of Germany and Austria, Poland, and the Soviet Union*. Jerusalem: Yad Vashem, 1981.

Arad, Yitzhak. *Belzec, Sobibor, Treblinka: The Operation Reinhard Death Camps*. Bloomington: Indiana University Press, 1987.

Bacon, Gershon. "Danzig Jewry: A Short History." In *Danzig 1939: Treasures of a Destroyed Community*. Edited by Günter Grass, Vivian B. Mann, and Joseph Gutmann. New York and Detroit: Wayne State University Press, 1980.

Badziąg, Kazimierz Anonti. *Es war eine Zeit: Erinerrungen eines Pfadfinders aus Pommerellen*. Translated from the Polish by Peter Chruśielke. Stuttowo: Muzeum Stutthof, 2013.

Barnett, Victoria. *For the Soul of the People: Protestant Protest against Hitler*. New York and Oxford: Oxford University Press, 1992.

Benadon, Maurice. *Interview RG-50.146.0001. Visual History Archive*. The Jeff and Toby Herr Oral History Archive. Accessed online at the United States Holocaust Memorial Museum, Feb. 2014.

Benoit, Jacques. *Mourir pour Danzig?* Paris: la Table Ronde, 1970.

Benz, Wolfgang and Distel, Barbara, eds. *Der Ort des Terrors: Geschichte der nationalsozialistischen Konzentrationslager, Band 6, Die Organisation des Terrors*. München: C.H. Beck, 2007.

Berben, Paul. *Dachau: The Official History 1933–1945*. London: Norfolk Press, 1975.

Berendt, Grzegorz. *Danzig, 1945 & 2005*, in *Danziger Gespräche*. Warsawa: Friedrich-Ebert-Stiftung, 2005.

Bergen, Doris L. *Twisted Cross: The German Christian Movement in the Third Reich*. Chapel Hill and London: University of North Carolina Press, 1996.

Bergen, Doris L. *War & Genocide: A Concise History of the Holocaust*. Lanham: Rowman and Littlefield, 2013.

Blatman, Daniel. *The Death Marches and the Final Phase of Nazi Genocide*. Chapter in *Concentration Camps in Nazi Germany: The New Histories*. Edited by Jane Caplan and Nikolaus Wachsmann. London and New York: Routledge, 2010.

Blatman, Daniel. *The Death Marches: The Final Phase of Nazi Genocide*. Translated from the Hebrew by Chaya Galai. Cambridge: The Belknap Press, 2011.

Blobaum, Robert. *Antisemitism and Its Opponents in Modern Poland*. Ithaca: Cornell University, 2005.

Bloch, Natalia, and Brzezińska, Anna Weronika. *Sztutowo/Stutthof: Gdzieś pomiędzy plażą a obozem*. Warszawa: Wydawnictwo Naukowe Scholar, 2013.

Bömelburg, Hans-Jürgen, Stößinger, Renata, and Traba, Robert, eds. *Vertreibung aus dem Osten: Deutsche und Polen erinnern sich*. Olsztyn: Borussia, 2000.

Borensztein, Paula. *Interview 34594. Visual History Archive*. USC Shoah Foundation Institute. Accessed online at the United States Holocaust Memorial Museum, Feb. 2014.

Bracher, Karl Dietrich, re-ed. *The Conscience in Revolt: Portraits of the German Resistance, 1933–1945*. Revised Edition. Translated by Thomas S. McClymont. Mainz: v. Hase and Kohler, 1994.

Browning, Christopher. "Nazi Resettlement Policy and the Search for a Solution to the Jewish Question, 1939–1941," *German Studies Review*, 9:3 (1986).

Browning, Christopher. *Ordinary Men: Reserve Police Battalion 101 and the Final Solution in Poland*. New York: HarperCollins, 1992.

Browning, Christopher. *Collected Memories: Holocaust History and Postwar Testimony*. Madison: University of Wisconsin Press, 2003.

Browning, Christopher. *Remembering Survival: Inside a Nazi Slave-Labor Camp*. New York: Norton, 2010.

Browning, Christopher. "An American Historian's Perspective," *German Studies Review*, 35:2 (2012).

Buggeln, Marc. *Slave Labor in the Nazi Concentration Camps*. Translated by Paul Cohen. Oxford: Oxford University Press, 2014.

Buggeln, Marc, and Wildt, Michael, eds. *Arbeit im Nationalsozialismus*. Oldenbourg: de Gruyter, 2014.

Caplan, Jane. *Gender and the Concentration Camps*. Chapter in *Concentration Camps in Nazi Germany: The New Histories*. Edited by Jane Caplan and Nikolaus Wachsmann. London and New York: Routledge, 2010.

Carr, Nigel. "Kwiatkowski, Grzegorz. Trupa Trupa Lead Singer Grzegorz Kwiatkowski—The Invisible Shoes of Stutthof Concentration Camp." Last modified May 3, 2019. https://louderthanwar.com/trupa-trupa-lead-singer-grzegorz-kwiatkowski-invisible-shoes-stutthof-concentration-camp/.

Ceran, Tomasz S. *"Szmalcówka": Historia niemieckiego obozu w Toruniu (1940–1943) na tle ideologii nazistowskiej*. Bydgoszcz – Gdańsk: Instytut Pamięci Narodowej, 2011.

Chwin, Stefan. *Death in Danzig*. Translated by Philip Boehm. Orlando: Harcourt Inc., 2004.

Chyrek, Agnieszka. *"Niemcy obywatele byłego Wolnego Miasta Gdańska w załodze obozu Stutthof (1939–1945)"—"German Citizens of the Free City of Danzig in the Stutthof SS-Guard (1939–1945)."* Unpublished article. Muzeum Stutthof w Sztutowie.

Connelly, John, "Nazis and Slavs: From Racial Theory to Racist Practice," *Central European History*, 32:1 (1999).

Clark, Elizabeth. "Gdańsk, Story of a City: When Diplomatic History and Personal Narrative Intersect," *The Polish Review*, 61:1 (2016).

Clark, Elizabeth. "Borderland of the Mind: The Free City of Danzig and the Sovereignty Question," *German Politics and Society*, 35:1 (2017).
"The Danzig Farce." *The Sunday Sun and Guardian*, August 13, 1939. Canberra: National Library of Australia, 2017. Retrieved from https://trove.nla.gov.au/newspaper/article/23141633.
Dębski, Tadeusz. *A Battlefield of Ideas: Nazi Concentration Camps and Their Polish Prisoners*. Boulder: East European Monographs. Distributed by Columbia University Press, New York, 2001.
"Die Deutschen als Opfer," *Der Spiegel*, March 25, 2002. Retrieved from https://www.spiegel.de/spiegel/print/d-21856125.html.
Dillon, Christopher. *Dachau and the SS: A Schooling in Violence*. Oxford: Oxford University Press, 2015.
Distel, Barbara. *Frauen in Konzentrationslagern*. Chapter in *Der Ort des Terrors: Geschichte der nationalsozialistischen Konzentrationslager, Band 1, Die Organisation des Terrors*. Edited by Wolfgang Benz and Barbara Distel. München: C.H. Beck, 2005.
Douglas, R.M. *Orderly and Humane: The Expulsion of the Germans after the Second World War*. New Haven and London: Yale University Press, 2012.
Drywa, Danuta. *The Extermination of Jews in Stutthof Concentration Camp, 1939–1945*. Translated by Tomasz S. Gałązka. Sztutowo: Państwowe Muzeum Stutthof, 2004.
Drywa, Danuta. *Stutthof—Stammlager*. Chapter in *Der Ort des Terrors: Geschichte der nationalsozialistischen Konzentrationslager, Band 6, Natzweiler, Groß-Rosen, Stutthof*. Edited by Wolfgang Benz and Barbara Distel. München: C.H. Beck, 2005.
Drywa, Danuta. *Jews in KL Stuutthof*. Sztutowo: Muzeum Stutthof w Sztutowie, 2013.
Drywa, Danuta. *Polki z Pomorza w KL Ravensbrück*. Chapter in *Zeszyty Muzeum Stutthof. Nr. 3, Band 13*. Sztutowo: Muzeum Stutthof w Sztutowie, 2015.
Drywa, Danuta. *Säuberungsaktion: na Pomorzu Gdańskim w świetle dokumentów KL Stutthof (1939–1942)*. Sztutowo: Muzeum Stutthof w Sztutowie, 2015.
Dunin-Wąsowicz, Krzysztof. *Stutthof: Ze wspomnień obozu koncentracyjnego*. Sztutowo: Muzeum Stutthof w Sztutowie, 1970a.
Dunin-Wąsowicz, Krzysztof. *Obóz Koncentracyjny Sztuthof*. Gdańsk: Wydawnictwo Morskie. 1970.
Dunin-Wąsowicz, Roch. Broadening the Concept of the Holocaust, *London School of Economics and Political Science, International History Blog*, 2015. Retrieved from http://blogs.lse.ac.uk/lseih/2015/05/26/the-last-Nazi-German-concentration-camp-its-legacy/.
Durzak, Manfred, ed. *Der deutsche Roman der Gegenwart*. Stuttgart: Kohlhammer, 1973.
Dwork, Debórah and Van Pelt, and Robert Jan. *Auschwitz: 1270 to the Present*. New York: Norton, 1996.
Dwork, Debórah and Van Pelt, and Robert Jan. *Holocaust: A History*. New York: Norton, 2002.
Dyck, Brent Douglas. *The Terrifying Story of Hitler's Stolen Children*. Warfare History Network, 2016. https://warfarehistorynetwork.com/2016/09/16/hitlers-stolen-children/.
Echt, Samuel. *Die Geschichte der Juden in Danzig*. Leer: Gerhard Rautenberg Verlag, 1972.
Epstein, Catherine. *Confronting the Myths*. Chichester: Wiley Blackwell, 1972.
Epstein, Catherine. *Model Nazi: Arthur Greiser and the Occupation of Western Poland*. Oxford: Oxford University Press, 2010.
Evans, Richard J. *The Third Reich in History and Memory*. Oxford: Oxford University Press, 2015.

Feig, Konnilyn G. *Hitler's Death Camps: The Sanity of Madness.* New York: Holmes and Meier Publishers, 1981.

Ferguson, Niall. "Why Did the Second World War Begin?" *The Guardian*, September 9, 2009. Retrieved from https://www.theguardian.com/world/2009/sep/05/second-world-war-background-causes.

Fern, Lilo. *Interview RG-50.493.0014. Visual History Archive.* The Jeff and Toby Herr Oral History Archive. Accessed online at the United States Holocaust Memorial Museum, Feb. 2014.

Friedrich, Trude. *Interview 31653. Visual History Archive.* USC Shoah Foundation Institute. Accessed online at the United States Holocaust Memorial Museum, Feb. 2014.

Friedlander, Saul. *Memory, History, and the Extermination of the Jews in Europe.* Bloomington: Indiana University Press, 1993.

Gąsiorowski, Andredj. *Chapter 1: Hitlers Vorbereitungen zum Angriff auf Polen und zur Vernichtung der Polen in Pommern und der Freien Stadt Danzig.* Chapter in *Stutthof: Das Konzentrationslager.* From *Stutthof – hilterowski oboz komncentracyjny*, Translated by Rita Malcher. Gdańsk: Marpress, 1996a.

Gageby, Douglas. *The Last Secretary-General: Sean Lester and the League of Nations.* Dublin: Town House, 1999.

Garbe, Detlaf. *Between Resistance and Martyrdom: Jehovah's Witnesses in the Third Reich.* Translated by Dagmar G. Grimm. Madison: University of Wisconsin Press and USHMM. 2009.

Gawior, Cornelia. *Interview 32768. Visual History Archive.* USC Shoah Foundation Institute. Accessed online at the United States Holocaust Memorial Museum, February 2014.

Gilman, Sander. "Jewish Writers in Contemporary Germany: The Dead Author Speaks," *Studies in 20th Century Literature*, 13:2, Article 5. https://doi.org/10.4148/2334-4415.1233.

Goeschel, Christian and Wachsmann, Nikolaus, eds. *The Nazi Concentration Camps 1933–1939.* Translated by Ewald Osers. Lincoln and London: University of Nebraska Press, 2012.

Goldhagen, Daniel Jonah. *Hitler's Willing Executioners: Ordinary Germans and the Holocaust.* New York: Viking Books, 1997.

Grabowska-Chałka, Janina. *Chapter 6: Die Häftlinge.* Chapter in *Stutthof: Das Konzentrationslager.* From *Stutthof – hilterowski oboz komncentracyjny*, Translated by Rita Malcher. Gdańsk: Marpress, 1996a.

Grabowska-Chałka, Janina. *Chapter 12: Die Befreiung.* Chapter in *Stutthof: Das Konzentrationslager.* From *Stutthof – hilterowski oboz komncentracyjny*, Translated by Rita Malcher. Gdańsk: Marpress, 1996a.

Grabowska-Chałka, Janina. *Guide: Historical Information.* Translated by Tomasz S. Gałązka. Gdańsk: Muzeum Stutthof w Sztutowie, 2011.

Grass, Günter. *The Tin Drum.* Translated by Ralph Mannheim. New York: Random House, 1961.

Grass, Günter. *Cat and Mouse.* Translated by Ralph Manheim. New York: Harcourt, 1963.

Grass, Günter. *Dog Years.* Translated by Ralph Manheim. New York: Harcourt, Brace & World, 1965.

Grass, Günter. *What Shall We Tell Our Children?* In *Danzig: Treasures of a Destroyed Community.* New York and Detroit: Wayne State University Press, 1980.

Grass, Günter. "The Jewish Community of Danzig 1930–1939," *Society*, 29:6 (1992). https://doi.org/10.1007/BF02695271.
Grass, Günter. *My Century*. Translated by Michael Henry Heim. New York: Harcourt, 1999.
Grass, Günter. *Peeling the Onion*. Translated by Michael Henry Heim. Orlando: Harcourt, 2006.
Grass, Günter. *Vonne Endlichkeit*. Göttingen: Steidl, 2015.
Grass, Günter. *Of All That Ends*. Translated by Breon Mitchell. New York: Houghton Mifflin Harcourt Publishing, 2016.
Grass, Günter. *From the Diary of a Snail*. Translated by Breon Mitchell. New York: Random House, 2017.
Griesbach, Marga. *… ich kann immer noch das Elend spüren …*, in *Ein jüdisches Kind in Deutschland 1927 bis 1945*. Hannover: Region Hannover, 2008.
Gross, Jan T. *Neighbors: The Destruction of the Jewish Community in Jedwabne, Poland*. Oxford: Penguin Press, 2002.
Gross, Jan T. *Fear: Anti-Semitism in Poland after Auschwitz*. New York: Random House Press, 2006.
Grot, Elżbieta. Chapter 12: *Die letztze Zeit des Lagers*. Chapter in *Stutthof: Das Konzentrationslager*. From *Stutthof – hilterowski oboz komncentracyjny*, Translated by Rita Malcher. Gdańsk: Marpress, 1996a.
Grot, Elżbieta. *Błogosławieni Męczennicy Obozu Stutthof*. Gdańsk: Muzeum Stutthof w Stuttowo, 1999.
Gülzow, Gerhard. *Kirchenkampf in Danzig 1934–1945: Persönliche Erinnerungen*. Leer: Gerhard Rautenberg Verlag, 1968.
Hall, Katharina. *Günter Grass's "Danzig Quintet."* Chapter in *The Cambridge Companion to Günter Grass*. Edited by Stuart Taberner. Cambridge: Cambridge University Press, 2009. doi:10.1017/CCOL9780521876704.006.
Hedgepeth, Sonja and Saidel, Rochelle, eds. *Sexual Violence against Jewish Women during the Holocaust*. Hanover: University Press of New England, 2010.
Herf, Jeffrey. "The Odious Musings of Günter Grass," *The New Republic*, April 4, 2012. Retrieved from https://newrepublic.com/article/102417/grass-poem-anti-semitic-gunter.
Hermand, Jost. *The Hitler Youth in Poland: The Nazi's Program for Evacuating Children during World War II*. Translated by Margot Bettauer Dembo. Evanston: Northwestern University Press, 1993.
Hitler, Adolf. *Der Führer spricht*. München: Bürgerbräukeller, 1939. Accessed through YIVO Library Microfilm collection (2000-Y-1794.5).
Hoffmann, Peter. *History of the German Resistance*. London: MacDonald and Jane's, 1977.
Hollington. Michael. *Günter Grass: The Writer in a Pluralist Society*. London: Marion Boyers, 1980.
"The Holocaust Just Got More Shocking," *New York Times*, March 1, 2013.
Huelle, Paweł. *Castorp*. Translated by Antonia Lloyd-Jones. London: Profile Books, 2007.
Hunt, Richard. "Review of Hitler's Free City," *The Annals of the American Academy of Political and Social Science*, 412:1. https://doi.org/10.1177/000271627441200139.
Jews in KL Stutthof. Exhibition Catalog. Gdańsk: Muzeum Stutthof w Sztutowie, 2013.
Juerman, Esra. "*Experiences in Riga*," Archiwum Muzeum Stutthof. Original from Wiener Library, Nr. 34. Recorded by Midia Kraus, February 23, 1955.
Katz, Joseph. *The One Who Came Back: The Diary of a Jewish Survivor*. Translated by Hilda Reach. New York: Herzl Press and Bergen-Belsen Memorial Press, 1973.

Kempowski, Walter. *Haben Sie davon gewußt? Deutsche Antworten.* Hamburg: Albrecht Verlag, 1979.

Kershaw, Ian. *The "Hitler Myth:" Image and Reality in the Third Reich.* Oxford: Clarendon Press, 1987.

Kershaw, Ian. *The Nazi Dictatorship: Problems and Perspectives of Interpretation,* 4th ed. New York: Oxford University Press, 2000.

Kershaw, Ian. "War and Political Violence in Twentieth-Century Europe," *Contemporary European History*, 14:1 (2005). https://doi.org/10.1017/S0960777304002164.

Kershaw, Ian. "'Working towards the Führer': Reflections on the Nature of the Hitler Dictatorship," *Contemporary European History*, 2:2 (2008). https://doi.org/10.1017/S0960777300000382

Kieser, Egbert. *Prussian Apocalypse: The Fall of Danzig 1945.* Translated by Tony Le Tissier. Barnsley: Pen and Sword Books, 2011.

King, Christine Elizabeth. *The Nazi State and the New Religions: Five Case Studies in Non-Conformity.* New York: Mellen Press, 1982.

Klimowicz, Magdalena, ed. *Difficult Postwar Years: Polish Voices in Debate over Jan T. Gross's Book "Fear."* Translated by Elżbieta Gołębiowska. Warszawa: Polski Instytut Spraw Międzynarodowych/Polish Institute of International Affairs, 2006.

Kłys, Agnieszka. "Niemcy, obywatele byłego Wolnego Miasta Gdańska w załodze obozu Stutthof (1939–1945)" / "Germans, Citizens of the Free City of Danzig in Stutthof SS-Guard (1939–1945)." Unpublished paper in the author's possession.

Klys, Agnieszka and Zahorska, Joanna. *Finowie w KL Stutthof/The Finns in Stutthof Concentration Camp.* Sztutowo: Muzeum Stutthof w Sztutowie, 2016.

Koehl, Robert. *RKFDV: German Resettlement and Population Policy 1939–1945.* Cambridge: Cambridge University Press, 1957.

Koestler, Arthur. *Scum of the Earth.* Revised. London: Eland, 1990.

Kogon, Eugen. *Der SS-Staat: Das System der deutschen Konzentrationslager.* München: Kindler, 1974.

Kovala, Liisa. *The Day Soon Dawns: A Finnish Sailor's True Story of Surviving Stutthof.* North Charleston: Independent Publishing Platform, 2015.

Krawczyk, Maria, ed. *Pogranicza. Stara Kiszewa.* Warszawa: Wydawnictwo Karta, 2013.

Kremer, Jehudith. *Zeugenaussage/Witness Statement 03204.* Sztutowo: Archiwum Muzeum Stutthof.

Kuhn, Hermann, ed. *Stutthof: Ein Konzentrationslager vor den Toren Danzigs.* Translated by Leon Lendzion. Bremen: Temmen, 2004.

Kulka, Otto Dov. *Landscapes of the Metropolis of Death: Reflections on Memory and Imagination.* Translated by Ralph Mandel. Cambridge: Belknap Press, 2013.

Kwiatkowski, Piotr. *Interview 43670. Visual History Archive.* USC Shoah Foundation Institute. Accessed online at the United States Holocaust Memorial Museum, Feb. 2014.

Langer, Lawrence L. *Holocaust Testimonies: The Ruins of Memory.* New Haven: Yale University Press, 1991.

Levine, Herbert. *Hitler's Free City: A History of the Nazi Party in Danzig 1925–1939.* Chicago: Chicago University Press, 1970.

Lewis, Helen. *A Time to Speak.* Belfast: Blackstaff Press, 1992.

Libionka, Dariusz. "Die Kirche in Polen und der Mord an den Juden im Licht der polnischen Publizistik und Historiographie nach 1943," *Zeitschrift für Ostmitteleuropa-Forschung* 51:H2 (2002).

Libionka, Dariusz. *Antisemitism, Anti-Judaism and the Polish Catholic Clergy in the Second World War, 1939–1945.* Chapter in *Antisemitism and Its Opponents in Modern Poland*. Edited by Blobaum, Robert. Ithaca and London: Cornell University Press, 2005.

Lichtenstein, Erwin. *Die Juden der freien Stadt Danzig unter der Herrschaft des Nationalsozialismus*. Tübingen: Mohr, 1973.

Loeffel, Robert. *Family Punishment in Nazi Germany: Sippenhaft, Terror and Myth*. New York: Palgrave Macmillan, 2012.

Longerich, Peter. *Heinrich Himmler*. Translated by Jeremy Noakes and Lesley Sharpe. Oxford: Oxford University Press, 2012.

Lower, Wendy. *Hitler's Furies: German Women in the Nazi Killing Fields*. Boston: Mariner Books, 2014.

Lukowski, Jerzy and Zawadzki, Hubert. *A Concise History of Poland*. Cambridge: Cambridge University Press, 2001.

Malak, Fr. Henryk Maria. *Shavelings in Death Camps: A Polish Priest's Memoir of Imprisonment by the Nazis, 1939-1945*. Translated by Bożena J. Tucker and Thomas R. Tucker by permission of McFarland & Company, Inc. Jefferson: McFarland & Company, 2012.

Marcuse, Harold. *The Afterlife of the Camps*. Chapter in *Concentration Camps in Nazi Germany: The New Histories*. Edited by Jane Caplan and Nikolaus Wachsmann. London and New York: Routledge, 2010.

Marsh, Charles. *Strange Glory: A Life of Dietrich Bonhoeffer*. New York: Knopf, 2014.

Mawdsley, Evan. *World War II*. Cambridge: Cambridge University Press, 2009.

Mazower, Mark. *Hitler and His Empire: How the Nazis Ruled Europe*. New York: Penguin Press, 2008.

McNamara, Paul. *Sean Lester, Poland, and the Nazi Takeover of Danzig*. Dublin: Irish Academic Press, 2009.

Megargee, Geoffrey, ed. *USHMM Encyclopedia of Camps and Ghettos, 1933-1945. Volume 1, Early Camps*. Bloomington: Indiana University Press, 1995.

Michalik, Tomasz. *Sprzątając Zagładę*. Chapter in *Sztutowo/Stutthof: Gdzieś pomiędzy plażą a obozem*. Edited by Bloch, Natalia Bloch and Anna Weronika Brzezińska. Warsaw: Wydawnictwo Naukowe Scholar, 2013.

Miles, Keith. *Günter Grass*. London: Vision Press, 1975.

Modras, Ronald. *The Catholic Church and Antisemitism: Poland 1933-1939*. Chur, Switzerland: Harwood Academic Publishers, 1994.

Moeller, Robert G. "Sinking Ships, the Lost Heimat and Broken Taboos: Günter Grass and the Politics of Memory in Contemporary Germany," *Contemporary European History*, 12, 2003. https://doi.org/10.1017/S0960777303001139.

Montague, Patrick. *Chełmno and the Holocaust: A History of Hitler's First Death Camp*. Chapel Hill: University of North Carolina Press, 2012.

Mosse, George L. *Toward the Final Solution: A History of European Racism*. Madison: University of Wisconsin Press, 1978.

Nagorski, Andrew. *Hitlerland: American Eyewitnesses to the Nazi Rise to Power*. New York: Simon and Schuster, 2012.

Niemeyer, Heinz. *Bibliographie zur Kirchengeschichte von Danzig und Westpresussen*. Leer: Gerhard Rautenberg, 1967.

Orski, Marek. *Des Français au KL Stutthof/Francuzi w KL Stutthof*. Gdańsk: Muzeum Stutthof w Sztutowie, 1995.

Orski, Marek. *Chapter 8: Die Arbeit*. Chapter in *Stutthof: Das Konzentrationslager*. From *Stutthof - hilterowski oboz komncentracyjny*, Translated by Rita Malcher. Gdańsk: Marpress, 1996a.

Orski, Marek. *Czesi, Słowacy I Jugosławianie W KL Stutthof/The Czechs, Slovaks, and Yugoslavs in Stutthof Concentration Camp*. Gdańsk: Muzeum Stutthof w Sztutowie, 1997.

Orski, Marek. *Niewolnicza praca więźniów obozu koncentracyjnego Stutthof w latach 1939–1945*. Gdańsk: Muzeum Stutthof w Sztutowie, 1999.
Orski, Marek. *Filie Obozu Koncentracyjnego Stutthof w Latach 1939–1945*. Gdańsk: Muzeum Stutthof w Sztutowie, 2004.
Orski, Marek. *Band 6, Die Organisation des Terrors*. Chapter in *Der Ort des Terrors: Geschichte der nationalsozialistischen Konzentrationslager*. Edited by Wolfgang Benz and Barbara Distel. München: C.H. Beck, 2007.
Orski, Marek. *Fonowie w KL Stutthof/The Finns in Stutthof Concentration Camp*. Sztutowo: Muzeum Stutthof w Sztutowie, 2016.
Orth, Karin. *Die Konzentrationslager-SS: Sozialstrukturelle Analysen und biographische Studien*. Göttingen: Wallstein Verlag, 2000a.
Orth, Karin. *Die Kommandanten der nationalsozialistischen Konzentrationslager*. Chapter in *Die nationalsozialistischen Konzentrationslager, Vol. 2*. Edited by Herbert Ulrich, Karin Orth and Christoph Dieckmann. Göttingen: Wallstein Verlag, 2000b.
Orth, Karin. *The Concentration Camp Personnel*. Chapter in *Concentration Camps in Nazi Germany: The New Histories*. Edited by Jane Caplan and Nikolaus Wachsmann. London and New York: Routledge, 2010.
Pawlikowski, John T. *Polish Catholics and the Jews during the Holocaust: Heroism, Timidity, and Collaboration*. Chapter in *Contested Memories: Poles and Jews during the Holocaust and Its Aftermath*. Edited by Joshua D. Zimmerman. New Brunswick: Rutgers University Press, 2003.
Pohl, Dieter. *The Holocaust and the Concentration Camps*. Chapter in *Concentration Camps in Nazi Germany: The New Histories*. Edited by Jane Caplan and Nikolaus Wachsmann. London and New York: Routledge, 2010.
Polonsky, Antony, ed. *Studies in Polish Jewry, Vol. 13: Focusing on the Holocaust and Its Aftermath*. Oxford: Littman Library of Jewish Civilizations, 2010.
Railton, Nicholas M. "German Free Churches and the Nazi Regime," *Journal of Ecclesiastical History*, 49:1 (1998). https://doi.org/10.1017/S0022046997005691.
Rauschning, Hermann. *The Revolution of Nihilism*. New York: Alliance Book, 1935.
Rauschning, Hermann. *Men of Chaos*. New York: G. P. Putnam's Sons, 1942.
Reddick, John. *The Danzig Trilogy of Günter Grass: A Study of the Tin Drum, Cat and Mouse, and Dog Years*. London: Secker and Warburg, 1975.
Rossino, Alexander B. *Blitzkrieg, Ideology, and Atrocity: Hitler Strikes Poland*. Lawrence: University of Kansas Press, 2003.
Roy, James Charles. *The Vanished Kingdom: Travels through the History of Prussia*. Boulder: Westview Press, 1999.
Rushdie, Salman. *Introduction to Günter Grass* in *On Writing and Politics*. Translated by Ralph Manheim. San Diego: Harcourt, Brace, Jovanovich, 1985.
Rushdie, Salman. "On Günter Grass." *Granta*. Retrieved from https://granta.com/on-gunter-grass/.
Schenk, Dieter. *Hitlers Mann in Danzig: Albert Foster und die NS-Verbrechen*. Bohn: Dietz, 2000.
Schlant, Ernestine. "Coming to Terms with the Hitler-Past: Reflections on Recent Autobiographical Novels," *Modern Language Studies*, 21:1 (1991). https://doi.org/10.2307/3195118.
Schlant, Ernestine. *The Language of Silence: West German Literature and the Holocaust*. New York: Routledge, 1999.
Schwertfeger, Ruth V. *In Transit: Narratives of German Jews in Exile, Flight, and Internment during "The Dark Years."* Berlin: Franck & Timme, 2012.

Segev, Tom. *Soldiers of Evil: The Commandants of the Nazi Concentration Camps.* Translated by Haim Watzman. New York: Berkley Books, 1991.

Sheyer, Aharon. "Features of Local Murders and Killers," *Bylye Gody*, 5:3 (2012). Retrieved from http://ejournal52.com/en/archive.html?number=2012-09-18-17:49:52&journal=26.

Snyder, Timothy. *Bloodlands: Europe between Hitler and Stalin.* New York: Basic Books, 2010.

Sodeikat, Ernst. "Der Nationalsozialismus und die Danizger Opposition," *Vierteljahrshefte für Zeitgeschichte*, 14:2H (1966).

Sofsky, Wolfgang. *The Order of Terror: The Concentration Camp.* Translated by William Templer. Princeton: Princeton University Press, 1997.

Solzhenitsyn, Alexander, *Prussian Nights: A Poem.* Translated by Robert Conquest. New York: Farrar, Straus and Giroux, 1977.

Sruoga, Balys. *Forest of the Gods.* Translated from the Lithuanian by Ausrine Bayla. Vilnius: Versus Aureus, 2005.

Stafford, David. "The Valkyrie Lovers: How a Passionate Bond between Two Relatives of the Plotters Defied even the Fuhrer's Vengeance." *Daily Mail*, last modified January 13, 2009. https://www.dailymail.co.uk/femail/article-1114668/The-Valkyrie-lovers-How-passionate-bond-relatives-plotters-defied-Fuhrers-vengeance.html.

Stargardt, Nicholas. *The German War: A Nation Under Arms 1939–1945.* London: Vintage, 2016.

Steinman, Louise. *The Crooked Mirror: A Memoir of Polish-Jewish Reconciliation.* Boston: Beacon Press, 2013.

Steyer, Donald and Dwertmann, Franz, eds. *Stutthof: Das Konzentrationslager.* From *Stutthof – hilterowski obóz komncentracyjny*, Translated by Rita Malcher. Gdańsk: Marpress, 1996a.

Sydnor, Charles W. *Soldiers of Destruction: The SS Death's Head Division, 1933 to 1945.* Princeton: Princeton University Press, 1977.

Sziling, Jan and Wojciechowski, Mieczysław, eds. *Neighborhood Dilemmas: The Poles, the Germans and the Jews in Pomerania along the Vistula River in the 19th and 20th Century.* Translated by Katarzyna Mrozowska. Toruń: Uniwersytet Mikołaja Kopernika, 2002.

Taberner, Stuart, ed. *The Cambridge Companion to Günter Grass.* Cambridge: Cambridge University Press, 2009.

Theisz, Nicole. "Illusions of Return: City and Memory in Gunter Grass's Danzig Novels," *Seminar*, 45:1, 2009. https://doi.org/10.1353/smr.0.0055.

Tighe, Carl. *Gdańsk: National Identity in the Polish-German Borderlands.* London: Pluto Press, 1990.

Timm, Uwe. *Am Beispiel meines Bruders/In My Brother's Shadow.* Translation by Anthea Bell. New York: Farrar, Straus, and Giroux, 2005.

Toland, John. *The Last Days.* New York: Random House, 1965.

Valk, Erna. "Meine Erlebnisse in der Zeit vom 10. Dezember 1941 bis 30. Juni 1945." Original manuscript at the Yad Vashem, Jerusalem. Used by permission of Stutthof Museum. Document Number 02/234.

van Gelder, Lawrence. "Günter Grass Replies," *New York Times*, August 15, 2006. Retrieved from https://www.nytimes.com/2006/08/15/arts/arts-briefly.html.

von Lang, Jochen. *Top Nazi, SS General Karl Wolff, the Man between Hitler and Himmler.* Translated by Mary Beth Friedrich. New York: Enigma Books, 2013.

von Hassell, Fay. *Hostage of the Third Reich: The Story of My Imprisonment and Rescue from the SS*. Edited by David Forbes-Watt. New York: Charles Scribner's Sons, 1989.
von Jörg-Philipp, Thomsa and Kraason, Viktoria, eds. *Von Danzig nach Lübeck*. Lübeck: Günter Grass Haus, 2010.
von Kellenbach, Katharina. *The Mark of Cain: Guilt and Denial in the Lives of Post-War Nazi Perpetrators*. New York: Oxford University Press, 2003.
von Lehndorff, Count Hans. *East Prussian Diary: A Journal of Faith 1945–1947*. Translated by Violet M. MacDonald. London: Oswald Wolff, 1963.
von Ribbentrop, Joachim. Untitled Speech, October 24, 1939, Danzig. Recording from the Special Collections, The University of Wisconsin-Milwaukee Archives. Used with permission.
von Thadden, Rudolf. *Trieglaff: Balancing Church and Politics in a Pomeranian World 1807–1943*. Translated by Stephen Barlau. New York: Berghahn Books, 2013.
Wachsmann, Nikolaus. *The Concentration Camp Personnel*. Chapter in *Concentration Camps in Nazi Germany: The New Histories*. Edited by Jane Caplan and Nikolaus Wachsmann. London and New York: Routledge, 2010.
Wachsmann, Nikolaus. *The Dynamics of Destruction*. Chapter in *Concentration Camps in Nazi Germany: The New Histories*. Edited by Jane Caplan and Nikolaus Wachsmann. London and New York: Routledge, 2010.
Wachsmann, Nikolaus. *KL: A History of the Nazi Concentration Camps*. New York: Farrar, Straus and Giroux, 2015.
Wąs, Marek. *Gdańsk wojenny i powojenny*. Warszawa: Bellona, 2013.
Wegner, Bernd. *The Waffen-SS: Organization, Ideology, and Function*. Translated by Ronald Webster. Oxford: Blackwell Press, 1990.
Weilova, Nina. Auschwitz-Häftling Nr. 71978, *Erinnerungen an Stutthof*. Sztutowo: Muzeum Stutthof w Sztutowie.
Weinberg, Gerhard. *A World at Arms: A Global History of World War II*. New York: Cambridge University Press, 1994.
Wolf, Gerhard. "Negotiating Germanness: Nationalist Socialist Germanization Policy in the Warthegau," *Journal of Genocide Research*, 19:2, 2017. https://doi.org/10.1080/14623528.2017.1313519.
Wolff, Jeanette. *Sadismus oder Wahnsinn: Erlebnisse in den deutschen Konzentrationslagern im Osten*. Thüringen: Ernst Bretfeld, 1947.
Wolff, Jeanette. *Mit Bibel und Bebel: Ein Gedenkbuch*. Edited by Hans Lamm, G. David Grossmann, and Nora Walter. Bonn, Bad Godesberg: Verlag Neue Gesellschaft, 1981.
Wormser, Olga, ed. *Tragédie de la Déportation 1940–45*. Paris: Hachette, 1955.
Wóycicka, Zofia. *Arrested Mourning: Memory of the Nazi Camps in Poland, 1944–1950*. Frankfurt-am Main: Peter Lang, 2013.
Wróbel, Piotr. *The Devils Playground: Poland in World War Two*. Montreal, Quebec: The Canadian Foundation for Polish Studies of the Polish Institute of Arts and Sciences, 2000. Retrieved from http://www.warsawuprising.com/paper/wrobel1.htm.
Yla, Stasys. *A Priest in Stutthof: Human Experiences in the World of Subhuman*. Translated by Nola M. Zobarskas. New York: Manyland Books, 1971.
Ziegler, Herbert F. *Nazi Germany's New Aristocracy: The SS Leadership 1925–1939*. Princeton: Princeton University Press, 1989.
Zimmerman, Joshua D., ed. *Contested Memories: Poles and Jews during the Holocaust and Its Aftermath*. New Brunswick: Rutgers University Press, 2003.

Appendix

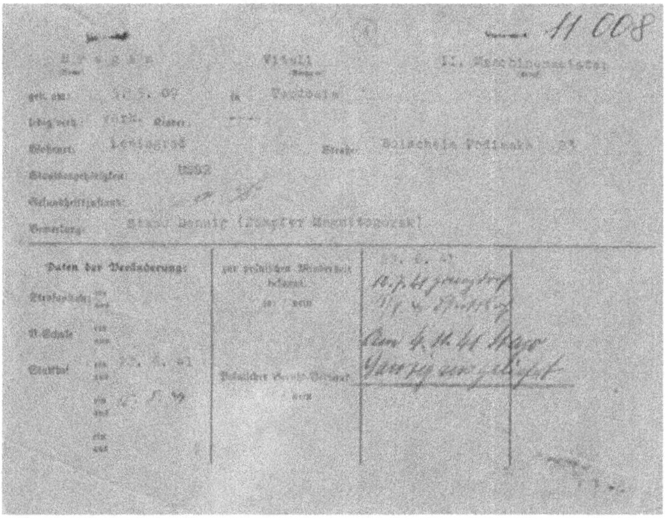

Figure 3 Prisoner Data Collection Card.
Data Collection Card for Vitali Bragin, a Soviet citizen born in Teodosia, who was a sailor on the ship *Magnitogorsk*. Image courtesy of Muzeum Stutthof w Sztutowie, used by permission.

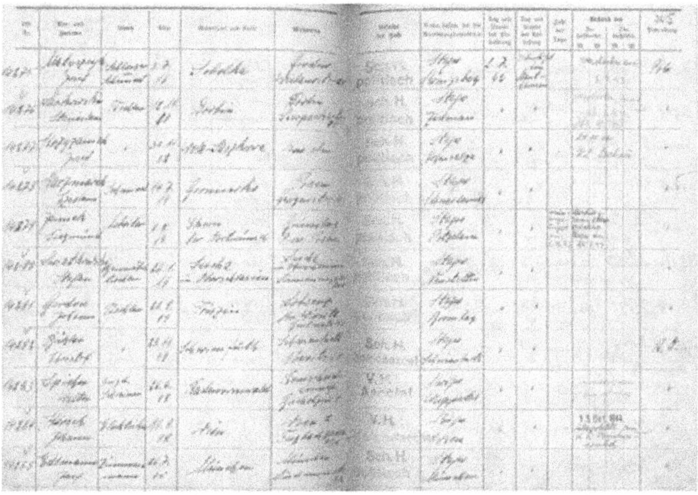

Figure 4 Prisoner list, with reasons for internment.
Sample list of prisoners who were interned for "corrective" purposes, including those identified as homosexual and professional criminals. Image courtesy of Muzeum Stutthof w Sztutowie, used by permission.

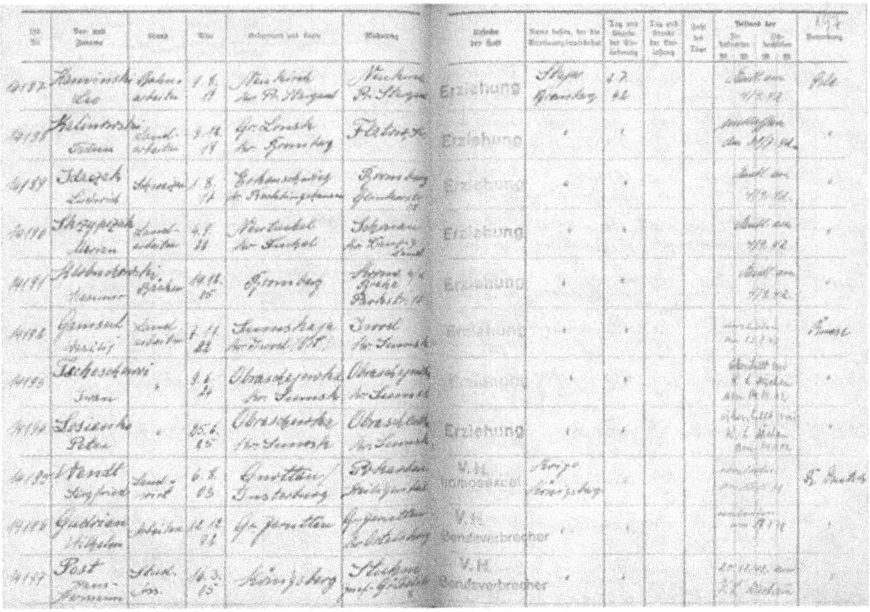

Figure 5 Additional prisoner list.

Additional page of prisoners, listing the reasons they were interned at Stutthof. Image courtesy of Muzeum Stutthof w Sztutowie, used by permission.

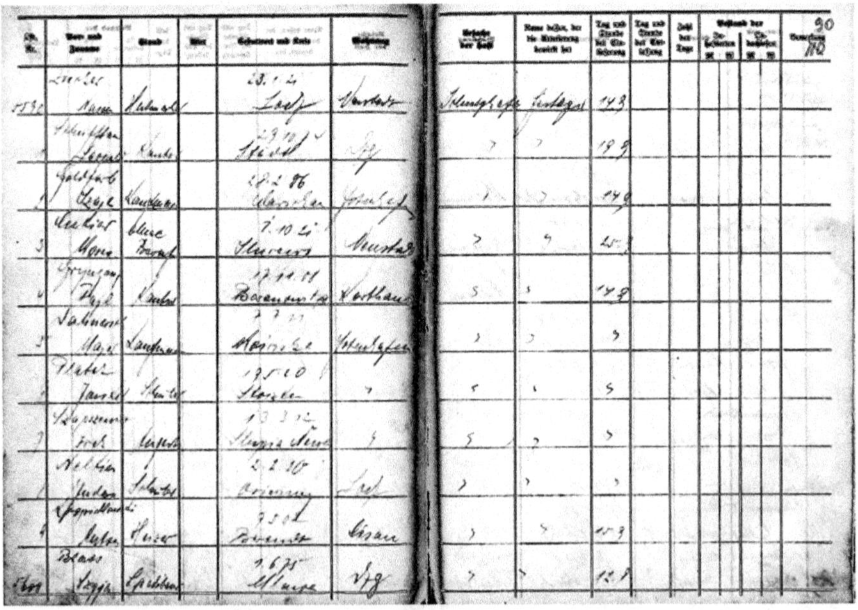

Figure 6 Registration with missing dates of death.

Dates of death were not always recorded for prisoners. Registration book with Leopold Schufftan's enrollment—no 5 591, was murdered in Neufahrwasser (Nowy Port), with no date of death recorded. Image courtesy of Muzeum Stutthof w Sztutowie, used by permission.

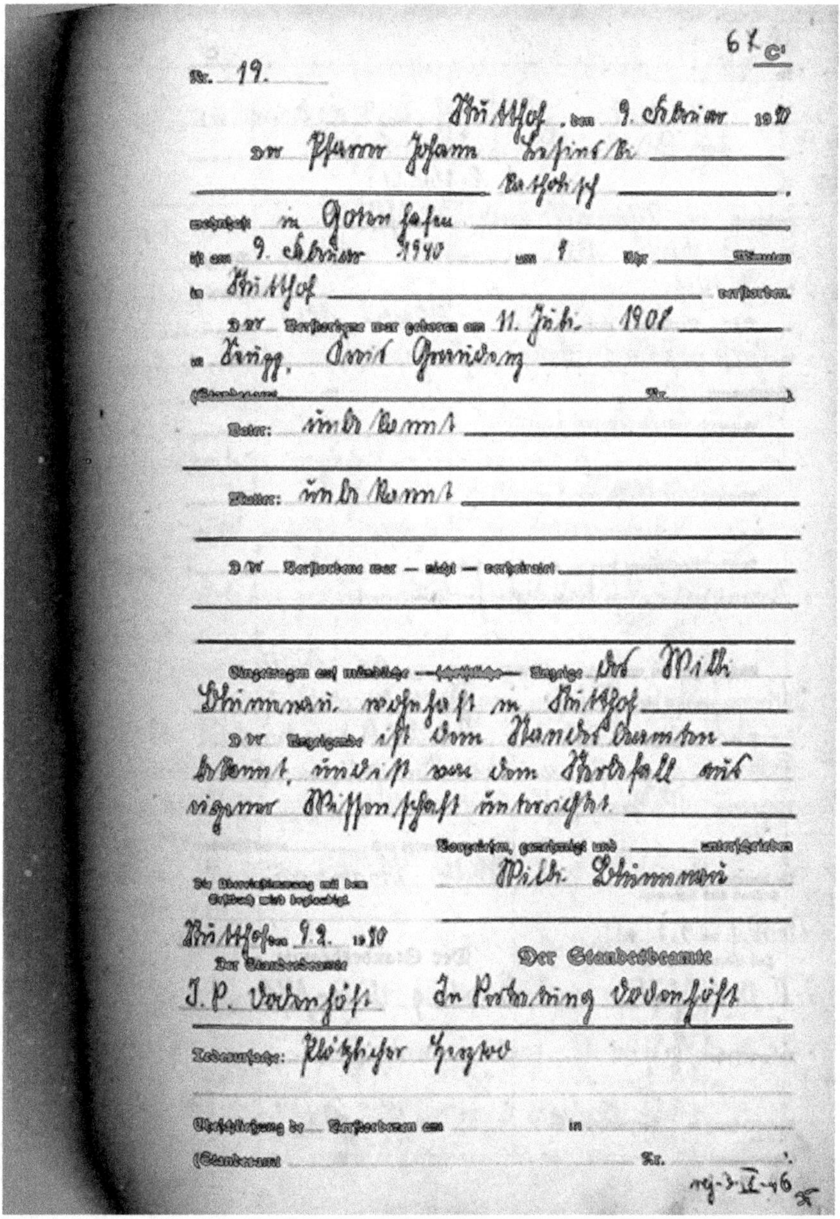

Figure 7 Death Registry page for Jan Lesiński.

Death Registry, from Civil Registry Office, with the name of priest Jan Lesiński, who died suddenly of "heart attack." Image courtesy of Muzeum Stutthof w Sztutowie, used by permission.

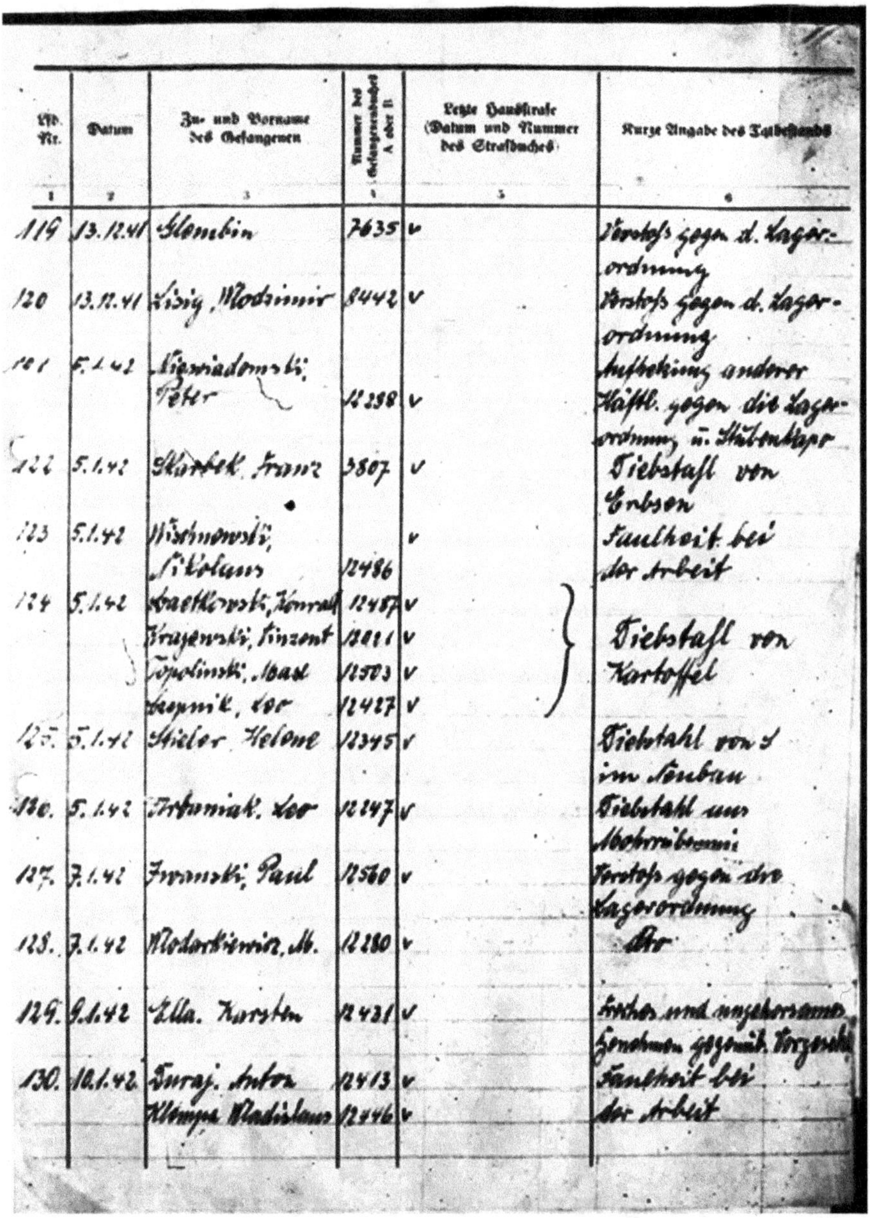

Lfd. Nr.	Datum	Zu- und Vorname des Gefangenen	Nummer des Gefangenenbuches A oder B	Letzte Hausstrafe (Datum und Nummer des Strafbuches)	Kurze Angabe des Tatbestands
1	2	3	4	5	6
119	13.12.41	Glombin	7635	v	Verstoß gegen d. Lagerordnung
120	13.12.41	Lisig, Wladimir	8442	v	Verstoß gegen d. Lagerordnung
121	5.1.42	Niewiadomski; Peter	12238	v	Aufhetzung anderer Häftl. gegen die Lagerordnung u. Stubenklopr
122	5.1.42	Skarbek, Franz	3807	v	Diebstahl von Erbsen
123	5.1.42	Wiśniewski; Nikolaus	12486	v	Faulheit bei der Arbeit
124	5.1.42	Kaetlkowski, Konrad	12457	v	Diebstahl von Kartoffel
		Krajewski, Vinzent	12011	v	
		Topolinski, Josef	12503	v	
		Szopnik, Leo	12427	v	
125	5.1.42	Stieler, Helene	12345	v	Diebstahl von ... im Neubau
126	5.1.42	Artomiak, Leo	12147	v	Diebstahl von Mohrrüben
127	7.1.42	Frankski; Paul	12560	v	Verstoß gegen die Lagerordnung
128	7.1.42	Modarkiewicz, M.	12280	v	Ahr
129	9.1.42	Ella. Karsten	12431	v	Frecher und ungehorsames Benehmen gegenüb. Vorgesetzt.
130	10.1.42	Duraj, Anton	12413	v	Faulheit bei der Arbeit
		Klimzyk Wladislaus	12446	v	

Figure 8 List of Crimes for internment, including "stealing peas."

List of "crimes" including the crime of being caught in the "theft of potatoes" or "stealing peas." Document 1-1-41-1_2947000 from the Arolsen Archives, used with permission.

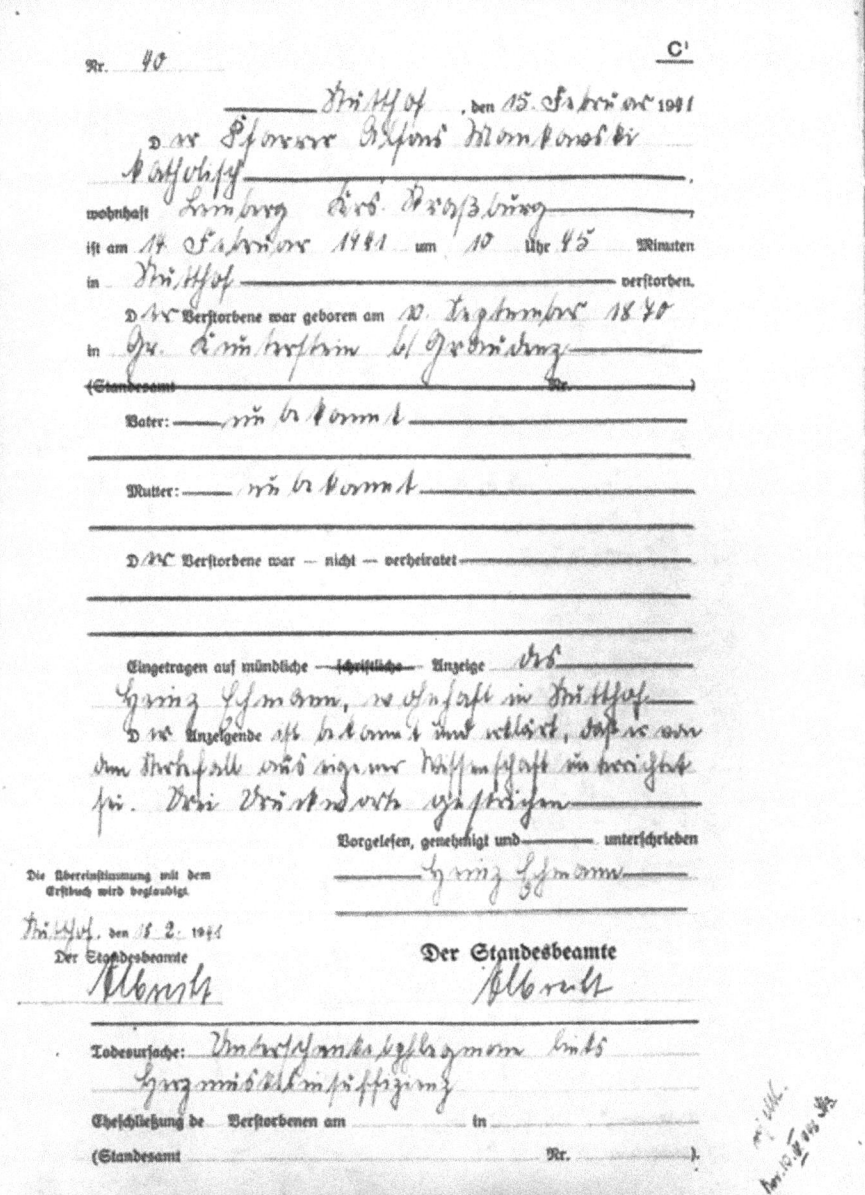

Figure 9 Death Registry entry for Alfons Mańkowski.

Death Registry (from Civil Registry Office) for priest Alfons Mańkowski, who officially died of "left shank phlegmona and heart muscle atrophy." (File Z-V-4-40) Image courtesy Muzeum Stutthof w Sztutowie.

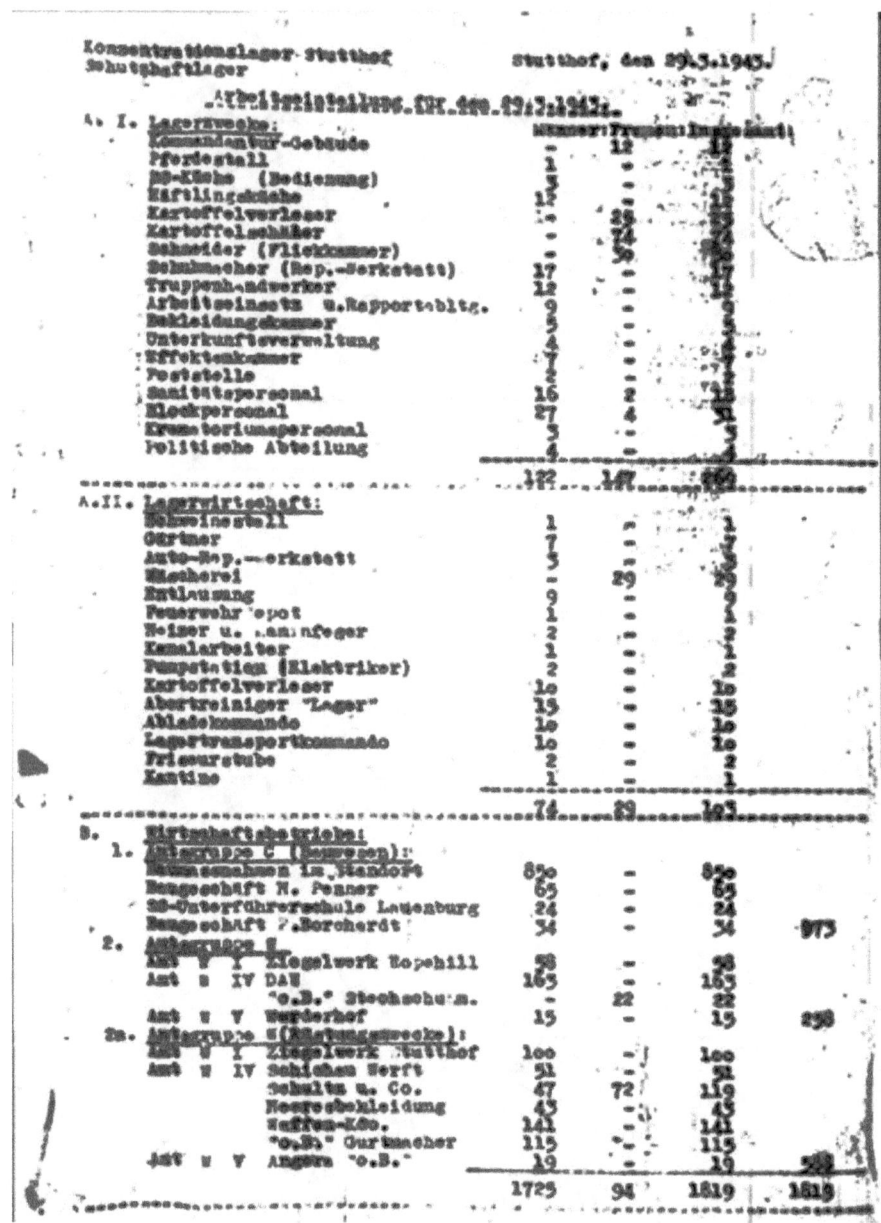

Figure 10 Assignments for work duties.

Assignment for work duties, March 29, 1943. Original image from the Arolsen Archives, #82152966, has been processed for improved readability. Image courtesy Muzeum Stutthof w Sztutowie. Used with permission.

Appendix 229

Figure 11 List of Names, Ranks, and Religious Affiliation of SS Guards with Danzig Connections.

ADRIAN, Paul	Niewierzący/ [Gottgläubig][1]	SS-Rottenführer: 30.01.1942 - 01.09.1943; SS-Unterschaführer: 01.09.1943
AKOLT, Richard	Rzymskokatolickie/ [Römisch-katholisch]	
ALBRECHT, Johannes	Niewierzący/ [Gottgläubig]	SS-Rottenführer: 09.11.1941 - [26.05.1943]
ALLAUT, Andreas	Niewierzący/ [Gottgläubig]	SS-Sturmmann - do: 30.01.1942; SS-Rottenführer: 30.01.1942 - 01.09.1942; SS-Unterscharführer: 01.09.1942
ANKER, Paul	Ewangelickie/ [Evangelisch] - później: Gottgläubig	SS-Schütze: 01.11.1941; SS-Sturmmann - do: 30.01.1942; SS-Rottenführer: 30.01.1942 - 01.02.1944; SS-Unterscharführer: 01.02.1944
ARNOLD, Otto Bruno Arthur		SS-Rottenführer: [12.05.1942]
BANSEMER, Rudolf	Rzymskokatolickie/ [Römisch-katholisch]	SS-Oberscharführer 01.02.1942 - 01.09.1943; SS-Hauptscharführer: 01.09.1943
BASE, Paul	Niewierzący/ [Gottgläubig]	SS-Rottenführer: 30.01.1942 - 01.02.1944; SS-Unterscharführer: 01.02.1944 - [01.09.1944]
BAUMANN, Herbert	Rzymskokatolickie/ [Römisch-katholisch]	
BECK, Willi		SS-Rottenführer: 09.11.1941 - 01.02.1942; SS-Unterscharführer: 01.02.1942 - 01.04.1944; SS-Oberscharführer: 01.04.1944
BECKER, Heinrich	Niewierzący/ [Gottgläubig]	
BECKER, Hermann	Ewangelickie/ [Evangelisch]	SS-Unterscharführer: 01.02.1942 - [01.02.1943]
BEHNKE, Helmut	Ewangelickie/ [Evangelisch]	SS-Rottenführer: 30.01.1942 - [12.03.1943]
BIERNATH, Johann	Rzymskokatolickie/ [Römisch-katholisch]	SS-Rottenführer: 30.01.1942
BLUMENAU, Willi	Niewierzący/ [Gottgläubig]	SS-Unterscharführer: 01.02.1942 - 01.09.1942; SS-Oberscharführer: 01.09.1942
BÖHM, Ernst	Ewangelickie/ [Evangelisch]	SS-Rottenführer: 09.11.1941 - [29.12.1942]
BÖHM, Karl	Niewierzący/ [Gottgläubig]	
BOLHAGEN, Kurt		SS-Rottenführer: 30.01.1942 - [01.08.1942]
BONIN von, Engelbert	Rzymskokatolickie/ [Römisch-katholisch]	SS-Rottenführer: 30.01.1942
BUNTROCK, Karl	Niewierzący/ [Gottgläubig]	SS-Rottenführer: 30.01.1942

BÜRGER, Richard Emil		SS-Rottenführer: 30.01.1942 - [03.11.1944]
BURNELEIT, Willy	Ewangelickie/ [Evangelisch]	SS-Schütze: 30.03.1942 - 16.02.1943; SS-Sturmmann: 16.02.1943 - 01.04.1944; SS-Rottenführer: 01.04.1944 - [04.04.1945]
CHILL, William	Ewangelickie/ [Evangelisch]	SS-Schütze: 01.11.1941 - 01.08.1942; SS-Sturmmann: 01.08.1942 - 01.01.1943; SS-Rottenführer: 01.01.1943; SS-Unterscharführer: 01.01.1943; - [18.01.1945]
CZAJKOWSKI, Alfons	Ewangelickie/ [Evangelisch]	SS-Rottenführer: 30.01.1942 - [16.12.1943]
DAU, Hans	Rzymskokatolickie/ [Römisch-katholisch]	
DIETERT, Hans	Rzymskokatolickie/ [Römisch-katholisch]	
DIETRICH, Kurt		SS-Unterscharführer: 01.02.1942 - 01.10.1942; SS-Oberscharführer: 01.10.1942 - [05.10.1944]
DIRKS, Walter		
DITTMANN, Alfred	Niewierzący/ [Gottgläubig]	SS-Rottenführer: 01.11.1941 - [22.02.1943]
DOBERT, August	Rzymskokatolickie/ [Römisch-katholisch] - później: Gottgläubig	SS-Untersturmführer: 01.11.1941 - 21.06.1942; SS-Obersturmführer: 21.06.1942 - 09.11.1944; SS-Hauptsturmführer: 09.11.1944 - [11.12.1944]
DOERKS, Eberhard		
DOMBERG, Walter	Ewangelickie/ [Evangelisch]	
DUHNKE, Willy	Niewierzący/ [Gottgläubig]	SS-Rottenführer: 30.01.1942 - 01.04.1944; SS-Unterscharführer: 01.04.1944 - [06.07.1944]
EHLE, Paul Rudolf	Niewierzący/ [Gottgläubig]	
EHLING, Hermann	Rzymskokatolickie/ [Römisch-katholisch]	
EICHLER, Andreas	Niewierzący/ [Gottgläubig]	SS-Unterscharführer: 01.02.1942 - [10.03.1943]
EICHLER, August	Ewangelickie/ [Evangelisch]	SS-Rottenführer: 30.01.1942
ELSDORFF, Herbert		SS-Rottenführer: 09.11.1941 - 01.01.1943; SS-Unterscharführer: 01.01.1943
ELTERMANN, Johann	Niewierzący/ [Gottgläubig]	SS-Rottenführer: 09.11.1941 - 01.10.1942; SS-Unterscharführer: 01.10.1942
ENGLER, Fritz	Ewangelickie/ [Evangelisch]	
ENGLER, Herbert		
ENSS, Heinrich	Niewierzący/ [Gottgläubig]	

Appendix 231

FALK, Felix		Niewierzący/ [Gottgläubig]	SS-Untersturmführer: 01.11.1941 - 20.04.1943; SS-Obersturmführer: 20.04.1943 - 21.06.1944; SS-Hauptsturmführer: 21.06.1944
FAST, Wilhelm			
FIGUR, Walter		Ewangelickie/ [Evangelisch]	SS-Rottenführer: 30.01.1942 - 01.04.1944; SS-Unterscharführer: 01.04.1944 - [28.07.1944]
FOTH, Ewald Paul		Rzymskokatolickie/ [Römisch-katholisch] - później: Gottgläubig	SS-Rottenführer: 09.11.1941 - 01.02.1944; SS-Unterscharführer: 01.02.1944
FRIEDLAND, Ernst		Ewangelickie/ [Evangelisch]	
FULLE, Hubert		Niewierzący/ [Gottgläubig]	SS-Sturmmann - do: 30.01.1942; SS-Rottenführer: 30.01.1942
GALLANDT, Walter		Niewierzący/ [Gottgläubig]	SS-Rottenführer: 09.11.1941 - 01.01.1943; SS-Unterscharführer: 01.01.1943 - [01.09.1944]
GISELLA, Josef		Niewierzący/ [Gottgläubig]	SS-Rottenführer: 30.01.1942 - 01.11.1943; SS-Unterscharführer: 01.11.1943 - [31.12.1944]
GLASS, Alfons Richard Friedrich			SS-Unterscharführer - do: 01.09.1943; SS-Oberscharführer: 01.09.1943 - [04.04.1945]
GÖHRT, Ewald		Menonickie/ [Mennonitisch]	SS-Rottenführer: 31.01.1942 - [29.12.1942]
GOIKE, Otto Albert			SS-Rottenführer: 30.01.1942 - [16.10.1942]
GÖRSCH, Martin Johann		Ewangelickie/ [Evangelisch]	SS-Unterscharführer: 01.02.1942 - 01.04.1944; SS-Oberscharführer: 01.04.1944 - 04.04.1945
GÖRTZ, Heinz		Ewangelickie/ [Evangelisch]	SS-Unterscharführer: 01.02.1942 - [20.04.1943]
GÖRTZ, Johannes August		Niewierzący/ [Gottgläubig]	
GOTTSCHAU, Oskar Emil		Niewierzący/ [Gottgläubig]	SS-Rottenführer: 30.01.1942 - [21.05.1943]
GRÄBER, Kurt Walter		Niewierzący/ [Gottgläubig]	SS-Oberscharführer: 01.02.1942 - 01.09.1943; SS-Hauptscharführer: 01.09.1943 - [15.10.1944]
GRABOWSKI, Paul		Ewangelickie/ [Evangelisch]	
GRABOWSKI, Paul Jakob		Niewierzący/ [Gottgläubig]	SS-Rottenführer: 30.01.1942 - 01.09.1943; SS-Unterscharführer: 01.09.1943 - [26.08.1944]
GRÖNING, Bruno		Ewangelickie/ [Evangelisch]	SS-Rottenführer: 22.07.1944 - [31.08.1944]
GROSS, Fritz		Ewangelickie/ [Evangelisch]	SS-Rottenführer: 30.01.1942 - [28.07.1944]
GRÜN, Max		Ewangelickie/ [Evangelisch]	SS-Sturmmann: 18.07.1944 - [20.11.1944]
HANDTKE, Kurt		Ewangelickie/ [Evangelisch]	SS-Schütze: 01.11.1941 - 30.01.1942; SS-Sturmmann: 30.01.1942 - 01.10.1942; SS-Rottenführer: 01.10.1942

HANNEMANN, Edwin	Ewangelickie/ [Evangelisch]	SS-Rottenführer: 09.11.1941 - 01.10.1942; SS-Unterscharführer: 01.10.1942
HANNEMANN, Ernst Walter	Ewangelickie/ [Evangelisch]	SS-Rottenführer: 30.01.1942 - 01.09.1943; SS-Unterscharführer: 01.09.1943 - [10.11.1944]
HAPPKE, Erich Heinrich	Niewierzący/ [Gottgläubig]	SS-Unterscharführer: 01.02.1942 - [11.12.1944]
HASS, Anton	Rzymskokatolickie/ [Römisch-katholisch]	SS-Rottenführer: 15.07.1944
HAUPT, Otto	Niewierzący/ [Gottgläubig]	SS-Sturmmann: 15.10.1943 - [6.06.1944]
HEIN, Albert	Niewierzący/ [Gottgläubig]	SS-Unterscharführer: 01.02.1942 - 01.09.1943; SS-Oberscharführer: 01.09.1943 - [13.09.1944]
HELD, Friedrich	Rzymskokatolickie/ [Römisch-katholisch]	SS-Unterscharführer: 01.02.1942 - 01.04.1944; SS-Oberscharführer: 01.04.1944 - [15.12.1944]
HERRMANN, Friedrich	Rzymskokatolickie/ [Römisch-katholisch]	SS-Schütze: 01.11.1941 - 09.11.1941; SS-Sturmmann: 09.11.1941 - 01.09.1942; SS-Rottenführer: 01.09.1942 - [29.12.1942]
HINTZ, Paul	Ewangelickie/ [Evangelisch]	SS-Schütze: 27.06.1944 - 01.01.1945; SS-Sturmmann: 01.01.1945
HINTZ, Werner	Niewierzący/ [Gottgläubig]	SS-Rottenführer: 31.01.1942
HIRSBRUNNER, Otto-Heinz	Ewangelickie/ [Evangelisch]	
HÖLDTKE, Albert Paul	Ewangelickie/ [Evangelisch]	SS-Rottenführer: 09.11.1941
HÖLDTKE, Wilhelm	Niewierzący/ [Gottgläubig]	SS-Unterscharführer: 01.02.1942 - 01.09.1943; SS-Oberscharführer: 01.09.1943
HOLZ, Herbert	Niewierzący/ [Gottgläubig]	SS-Unterscharführer: 01.02.1942
HORZIG, Franz	Niewierzący/ [Gottgläubig]	SS-Rottenführer: 30.01.1942 - [12.03.1943]
ICHNOWSKI, Eugen	Niewierzący/ [Gottgläubig]	
JÄGER, Helmut	Rzymskokatolickie/ [Römisch-katholisch]	SS-Rottenführer: 30.01.1942
JAHRSEN, Paul		SS-Rottenführer: 30.01.1942 - 01.09.1943; SS-Unterscharführer: 01.09.1943 - [01.02.1944]
JAKUSCH, Bruno	Niewierzący/ [Gottgläubig]	
JANZEN, August	Niewierzący/ [Gottgläubig]	
JANZEN, Kurt	Ewangelickie/ [Evangelisch]	
JASSEN, Erich	Ewangelickie/ [Evangelisch]	

JURTZICK, Hans	Ewangelickie/ [Evangelisch]	
KAMIN, Paul	Niewierzący/ [Gottgläubig]	SS-Rottenführer: 09.11.1941 - 01.09.1942; SS-Unterscharführer: 01.09.1942 - 01.05.1944; SS-Oberscharführer: 01.05.1944 - [11.12.1944]
KARNATH, Walter Gustav	Rzymskokatolickie/ [Römisch-katholisch]	SS-Rottenführer: 30.01.1942 - [30.01.1942]
KEWITSCH, Hans	Niewierzący/ [Gottgläubig]	SS-Oberscharführer: 01.02.1942
KLAFFKE, Adolf Karl	Ewangelickie/ [Evangelisch]	SS-Rottenführer: 09.11.1941 - 01.12.1942; SS-Unterscharführer: 01.12.1942
KLEIN, Erwin	Ewangelickie/ [Evangelisch]	SS-Rottenführer: 30.01.1942
KLEIN, Prosper	Ewangelickie/ [Evangelisch]	SS-Unterscharführer: 01.02.1942 - 01.04.1944; SS-Oberscharführer: 01.04.1944
KLEISS, Hermann		
KNABE, Helmut	Ewangelickie/ [Evangelisch]	SS-Sturmmann: 01.09.1939 - 20.12.1940; SS-Rottenführer: 20.12.1940 - 01.11.1943; SS-Unterscharführer: 01.11.1943 - [15.07.1944]
KNOF, Alfred		SS-Unterscharführer: 01.02.1942 - 01.05.1944; SS-Oberscharführer: 01.05.1944 - [18.12.1944]
KNOTT, Otto		SS-Scharführer: [08.1942]
KNOTT, Willi Friedrich	Ewangelickie/ [Evangelisch]	SS-Unterscharführer: 27.06.1944 - [06.12.1944]
KOHBIETER, Walter	Niewierzący/ [Gottgläubig]	
KÖNIG, Ernst	Niewierzący/ [Gottgläubig]	SS-Schütze: 22.07.1944 - [22.08.1944]
KÖPKE, Horst		SS-Rottenführer: 30.01.1942 - 01.04.1944; SS-Unterscharführer: 01.04.1944 - [15.01.1945]
KÖRBER, Albert Martin	Niewierzący/ [Gottgläubig]	SS-Rottenführer: 30.01.1942 - 01.01.1943; SS-Unterscharführer: 01.01.1943 - [25.03.1943]
KOSSLER, Johann Martin		SS-Rottenführer: 30.01.1942 - [20.09.1942]
KREFT, Siegfried	Niewierzący/ [Gottgläubig]	SS-Rottenführer: 30.01.1942 - 01.09.1943; SS-Unterscharführer: 01.09.1943 - [26.08.1944]
KRÖNKE, Erich	Ewangelickie/ [Evangelisch]	SS-Rottenführer: 09.11.1941 - 01.10.1942; SS-Unterscharführer: 01.10.1942 - [18.11.1943]
KROPP, Alfred		
KROPP, Helmut	Apostolskie/ [Apostolisch]	
KRUMMEREICH, Bruno	Niewierzący/ [Gottgläubig]	SS-Rottenführer: 09.11.1941 - [26.01.1943]

KUHLMANN, Johannes	Niewierzący/ [Gottgläubig]	SS-Rottenführer: 30.01.1942 - [01.02.1943]; SS-Unterscharführer
KUNATH, Edmund	Ewangelickie/ [Evangelisch]	SS-Rottenführer: 22.07.1944 - [08.01.1945]
KUNKEL, Paul Robert	Niewierzący/ [Gottgläubig]	SS-Rottenführer: 30.01.1942 - 01.09.1943; SS-Unterscharführer: 01.09.1943 - [10.11.1943]
KUSCH, Artur	Niewierzący/ [Gottgläubig]	SS-Unterscharführer: 01.02.1942 - [18.10.1944]
KUSCHEL, Erich	Niewierzący/ [Gottgläubig]	
KUSCHEL, Rudolf Georg	Ewangelickie/ [Evangelisch]	SS-Rottenführer: 30.01.1942 - [20.08.1943]
KUTNER, Johannes	Niewierzący/ [Gottgläubig]	SS-Unterscharführer: 01.02.1942 - 04.1945
LANGE, Richard	Niewierzący/ [Gottgläubig]	SS-Rottenführer: 30.01.1942 - [18.07.1943]
LASCHEIT, Emil Fritz	Ewangelickie/ [Evangelisch]	SS-Sturmmann - do: 30.01.1942; SS-Rottenführer: 30.01.1942 - [31.03.1943]
LASNER, Robert	Ewangelickie/ [Evangelisch]	SS-Schütze: 17.09.1944 - 04.10.1944; SS-Sturmmann: 04.10.1944 - [14.11.1944]
LAU, Paul	Niewierzący/ [Gottgläubig]	SS-Rottenführer: 30.01.1942
LEHNAU, Max	Rzymskokatolickie/ [Römisch-katholisch]	
LEHNHOFF, Paul		SS-Rottenführer: 09.11.1941 - 01.09.1942; SS-Unterscharführer: 01.09.1942 - [26.08.1944]
LEISING, Josef	Niewierzący/ [Gottgläubig]	SS-Rottenführer: 09.11.1941 - 01.10.1942; SS-Unterscharführer: 01.10.1942 - [21.05.1943]
LEMKE, Erich		SS-Unterscharführer: [29.05.1942] - 01.09.1943; SS-Oberscharführer: 01.09.1943 - [04.04.1945]
LESSAT, Alfred Franz	Ewangelickie/ [Evangelisch]	SS-Schütze: 15.10.1942 - 01.09.1943; SS-Sturmmann: 01.09.1943 - 01.01.1945; SS-Rottenführer: 01.01.1945
LEWENDEL, Jakob	Niewierzący/ [Gottgläubig]	SS-Rottenführer: 30.01.1942 - 01.11.1943; SS-Unterscharführer: 01.11.1943 - [25.08.1944]
LIESKE, Johann	Niewierzący/ [Gottgläubig]	SS-Rottenführer: 30.01.1942 - [18.11.1943]
LIKERSKI, Franz	Ewangelickie/ [Evangelisch]	
LÖWEN, Heinz Erwin	Ewangelickie/ [Evangelisch]	SS-Rottenführer: 09.11.1941 - [26.01.1943]
LÜDTKE, Bernhard Ferdinand		SS-Rottenführer: 30.01.1942 - [21.09.1942]

LÜDTKE, Rudolf	Niewierzący/ [Gottgläubig]	
LUTZ, Paul	Niewierzący/ [Gottgläubig]	SS-Unterscharführer: 01.02.1942 - [04.04.1945]
MAHLKE, Gustav	Ewangelickie/ [Evangelisch]	SS-Schütze: 15.06.1939 - 15.06.1940; SS-Sturmmann: 15.06.1940 - 01.08.1941; SS-Rottenführer: 01.08.1941 - 01.01.1945; SS-Unterscharführer: 01.01.1945
MAKOWSKI, Willi	Ewangelickie/ [Evangelisch]	SS-Rottenführer: 30.01.1942 - [08.06.1944]
MANKOWSKI, Hugo	Rzymskokatolickie/ [Römisch-katholisch]	SS-Sturmmann: 18.07.1944 - 11.08.1944
MARZAN, Friedrich	Rzymskokatolickie/ [Römisch-katholisch]	
MATHESIUS, Kurt Hermann Eduard		SS-Rottenführer: 30.01.1942 - [05.09.1944]
MEIER, Anton	Ewangelickie/ [Evangelisch]	SS-Schütze: 20.05.1941 - 01.06.1944; SS-Sturmmann: 01.06.1944 - [05.04.1945]
MEIER, Fritz	Niewierzący/ [Gottgläubig]	SS-Unterscharführer: 01.02.1942 - 09.11.1942; SS-Scharführer: 09.11.1942 - 01.09.1943; SS-Oberscharführer: 01.09.1943 - [04.04.1945]
MEINHARDT, Gerhard	Niewierzący/ [Gottgläubig]	SS-Schütze: 01.11.1941 - 01.10.1942; SS-Sturmmann: 01.10.1942 - 20.04.1943; SS-Rottenführer: 20.04.1943 - 01.09.1943; SS-Unterscharführer: 01.09.1943 - [01.05.1944]
MEINHARDT, Paul	Rzymskokatolickie/ [Römisch-katholisch]	SS-Unterscharführer: 01.02.1942 - 01.04.1944; SS-Oberscharführer: 01.04.1944 - [31.12.1944]
MEISSEL, Erich Walter	Ewangelickie/ [Evangelisch]	SS-Unterscharführer: 01.02.1942
MERTENS, Erich Waldemar	Niewierzący/ [Gottgläubig]	SS-Rottenführer: 30.01.1942 - 01.09.1943; SS-Unterscharführer: 01.09.1943 - [15.01.1945]
MERTINS, Fritz	Niewierzący/ [Gottgläubig]	SS-Rottenführer: 30.01.1942 - 01.09.1943; SS-Unterscharführer: 01.09.1943
MICHELSEN, Max	Niewierzący/ [Gottgläubig]	SS-Rottenführer: 30.01.1942 - 01.10.1942; SS-Unterscharführer: 01.10.1942 - [16.11.1944]
MIELENZ, Franz	Ewangelickie - później: Gottgläubig	SS-Untersturmführer: 01.11.1941 - 20.04.1943; SS-Obersturmführer: 20.04.1943
MIELENZ, Johannes	Rzymskokatolickie/ [Römisch-katholisch]	
MIELKE, Erich	Niewierzący/ [Gottgläubig]	
MÖHRKE, Hans	Rzymskokatolickie/ [Römisch-katholisch]	SS-Rottenführer: 31.01.1942 - [01.02.1943]
MOLKENTHIN, Artur	Rzymskokatolickie/ [Römisch-katholisch]	

MÖWE, Johann	Niewierzący/ [Gottgläubig]	SS-Sturmmann: 20.04.1935 - 01.03.1936; SS-Rottenführer: 01.03.1936 - 30.01.1938; SS-Unterscharführer: 30.01.1938 - 01.02.1940; SS-Scharführer: 01.02.1940 - 01.02.1942; SS-Oberscharführer: 01.02.1942 - 01.08.1944; SS-Hauptscharführer: 01.08.1944 - [22.11.1]
MÖWE, Karl	Niewierzący/ [Gottgläubig]	SS-Unterscharführer: 01.02.1942 - 01.09.1943; SS-Oberscharführer: 01.09.1943 - [05.04.1945]
MÜLLER, Bernhard Karl	Ewangelickie/ [Evangelisch]	SS-Rottenführer: 30.01.1942 - 01.04.1944; SS-Unterscharführer: 01.04.1944 - [21.12.1944]
MÜLLER, Leonhard	Ewangelickie/ [Evangelisch]	SS-Unterscharführer: 01.02.1942 - [23.07.1943]
MURNER, Robert Ewald Anton	Ewangelickie/ [Evangelisch]	SS-Rottenführer: 30.01.1942 - [12.03.1943]
NEUBAUER, Paul		SS-Schütze: 01.11.1941 - [18.06.1942]; SS-Rottenführer
ORTMANN, Walter Johannes	Niewierzący/ [Gottgläubig]	SS-Unterscharführer: 01.02.1942 - [20.04.1942]
OTROMKE, Walter	Ewangelickie/ [Evangelisch]	SS-Rottenführer: 30.01.1942 - 01.09.1943; SS-Unterscharführer: 01.09.1943 - [03.09.1944]
OTTO, Gustav	Ewangelickie/ [Evangelisch]	SS-Schütze: 20.05.1941 - 01.12.1941; SS-Sturmmann: 01.12.1941 - 01.02.1943; SS-Rottenführer: 01.02.1943
PATZ, Johannes Anton	Rzymskokatolickie/ [Römisch-katholisch]	SS-Oberscharführer: 28.06.1944
PATZKE, Bernhard	Rzymskokatolickie/ [Römisch-katholisch]	SS-Oberscharführer: 29.06.1944 - [31.08.1944]
PATZKE, Günther	Niewierzący/ [Gottgläubig]	SS-Rottenführer: 09.11.1941 - 01.02.1942; SS-Unterscharführer: 01.02.1942 - 01.09.1943; SS-Oberscharführer: 01.09.1943 - [04.04.1945]
PATZKE, Herbert	Rzymskokatolickie/ [Römisch-katholisch]	SS-Rottenführer: 30.01.1942 - 01.11.1943; SS-Unterscharführer: 01.11.1943 - [14.11.1944]
PAULITZ, Albert	Niewierzący/ [Gottgläubig]	
PAULS, John	Niewierzący/ [Gottgläubig]	SS-Schütze: 01.11.1941 - 01.08.1942; SS-Sturmmann: 01.08.1942 - 01.01.1943; SS-Rottenführer: 01.01.1943
PEIKOWSKI, Paul		SS-Rottenführer: 30.01.1942 - 01.11.1943; SS-Unterscharführer: 01.11.1943
PETERS, Friedrich	Rzymskokatolickie/ [Römisch-katholisch]	SS-Rottenführer: 30.01.1942
PETTKE, Johannes	Niewierzący/ [Gottgläubig]	SS-Unterscharführer: 01.02.1942
PICK, Bruno	Niewierzący/ [Gottgläubig]	

PIENERT, Bruno	Rzymskokatolickie/ [Römisch-katholisch]	SS-Unterscharführer: 01.02.1942 - 01.09.1943; SS-Oberscharführer: 01.09.1943
PLATZ, Arthur	Niewierzący/ [Gottgläubig]	SS-Schütze: 01.11.1941 - [12.03.1943]
PLICHT, Johann	Rzymskokatolickie/ [Römisch-katholisch]	SS-Sturmmann: 17.07.1944
PLUHM, Hermann	Niewierzący/ [Gottgläubig]	SS-Schütze: 01.11.1941 - 30.01.1942; SS-Rottenführer: 30.01.1942 - 01.09.1943; SS-Unterscharführer: 01.09.1943
POCHERT, Otto	Ewangelickie/ [Evangelisch]	
POMMER, Albert		SS-Rottenführer: 09.11.1941 - 01.02.1942; SS-Unterscharführer: 01.02.1942
PREUSS, Leo		SS-Unterscharführer: [20.08.1942 - 05.04.1943]
RAMELOW, Walter	Ewangelickie/ [Evangelisch]	SS-Rottenführer: 09.11.1941 - 01.10.1942; SS-Unterscharführer: 01.10.1942
RAPPEL, Walter		SS-Rottenführer: 30.01.1942
RATHKE, Rudolf	Ewangelickie/ [Evangelisch]	SS-Rottenführer: 30.01.1942
REDDER, Heinrich		SS-Rottenführer: [01.09.1943 - 06.09.1943]
REDDER, Willi Johannes		SS-Rottenführer: 30.01.1942
REDMANN, Klemens		SS-Rottenführer: 30.01.1942
REIMANN, Fritz Gustav	Ewangelickie/ [Evangelisch]	SS-Rottenführer: 30.01.1942
REIMANN, Paul	Niewierzący/ [Gottgläubig]	SS-Rottenführer: 30.01.1942 - [12.03.1943]
REXIN, Otto	Niewierzący/ [Gottgläubig]	SS-Rottenführer: 30.01.1942 - [03.04.1943]
REXIN, Paul	Niewierzący/ [Gottgläubig]	
RINGEL, Paul		SS-Rottenführer: 01.01.1945
ROHDE, Ernst		SS-Rottenführer: [25.01.1943]
ROSENKRANZ, Friedrich Andreas	Niewierzący/ [Gottgläubig]	
RÖSKE, Bernhard		
RUDNICK, Ernst Hermann	Ewangelickie/ [Evangelisch]	SS-Schütze: 22.04.1940 - 01.08.1942; SS-Sturmmann: 01.08.1942 - 01.01.1943; SS-Rottenführer: 01.01.1943 - [11.04.1943]
RUNGE, Johannes	Rzymskokatolickie/ [Römisch-katholisch]	SS-Rottenführer: 30.01.1942 - [29.12.1942]
RUSCH, Herbert	Ewangelickie/ [Evangelisch]	

SALTEN, Paul	Niewierzący/ [Gottgläubig]	SS-Rottenführer: 30.01.1941 - 01.02.1943; SS-Unterscharführer: 01.02.1943
SCHALK, Alfred	Rzymskokatolickie/ [Römisch-katholisch]	
SCHALT, Wilhelm	Niewierzący/ [Gottgläubig]	
SCHARFETTER, Erich Gustav	Ewangelickie/ [Evangelisch]	
SCHEFFKE, Herbert	Niewierzący/ [Gottgläubig]	
SCHILLING, Arthur	Niewierzący/ [Gottgläubig]	
SCHMALZ, Erich Richard	Niewierzący/ [Gottgläubig]	SS-Schütze: 15.04.1942 - 01.10.1942; SS-Sturmmann: 01.10.1942 - 20.04.1943; SS-Rottenführer: 20.04.1943 - 01.09.1943; SS-Unterscharführer: 01.09.1943
SCHMIDT, Gottlieb Karl Max		SS-Unterscharführer: 01.02.1942 - [08.06.1942]
SCHOLL, Benno	Ewangelickie/ [Evangelisch]	SS-Rottenführer: 30.01.1942 - 01.04.1944; SS-Unterscharführer: 01.04.1944
SCHOLL, Max		SS-Rottenführer: 30.01.1942 - [01.10.1943]
SCHÖNFELDT, Ernst Leonhardt	Niewierzący/ [Gottgläubig]	SS-Rottenführer: 30.01.1942 - [21.05.1943]
SCHÖNROCK, Paul	Rzymskokatolickie/ [Römisch-katholisch]	SS-Rottenführer: 30.01.1942 - [24.08.1943]
SCHRAAGE, Alexander	Ewangelickie/ [Evangelisch]	SS-Schütze: 15.01.1941 - 20.04.1943; SS-Sturmmann: 20.04.1943 - 01.09.1943; SS-Rottenführer: 01.09.1943
SCHRÖDER, Bernhard	Niewierzący/ [Gottgläubig]	
SCHRÖDER, Fritz Hans	Niewierzący/ [Gottgläubig]	SS-Rottenführer: 09.11.1941 - [12.03.1943]
SCHRÖDER, Max	Rzymskokatolickie/ [Römisch-katholisch]	
SCHUCH, Richard	Niewierzący/ [Gottgläubig]	SS-Rottenführer: 30.01.1942 - [05.09.1944]
SCHULZ, Albert	Niewierzący/ [Gottgläubig]	SS-Schütze: 01.11.1941 - 30.01.1942; SS-Rottenführer: 30.01.1942 - 01.10.1943; SS-Unterscharführer: 01.10.1943
SCHULZ, Bruno		
SCHULZ, Fritz	Niewierzący/ [Gottgläubig]	
SCHULZ, Johann Albert	Niewierzący/ [Gottgläubig]	SS-Rottenführer: 30.01.1942 - 01.10.1942; SS-Unterscharführer: 01.10.1942 - [02.03.1944]

SCHULZ, Max	Rzymskokatolickie/ [Römisch-katholisch]	SS-Rottenführer: [12.03.1943]
SCHWARZ, Hermann Heinrich	Niewierzący/ [Gottgläubig]	
SEEWE, Max	Niewierzący/ [Gottgläubig]	
SKIERKA-SCHIERER, Leo	Niewierzący/ [Gottgläubig]	
SKROBLIN, Hermann	Ewangelickie/ [Evangelisch]	SS-Schütze: 04.11.1940 - 20.04.1940; SS-Sturmmann: 20.04.1940 - 01.05.1942; SS-Rottenführer: 01.05.1942 - [14.12.1944]
SOIKE, Erich	Rzymskokatolickie/ [Römisch-katholisch] - później: Gottgläubig	SS-Untersturmführer und Kriminal-Sekretär: 20.04.1940 - 04.04.1945
STABENAU, Otto	Niewierzący/ [Gottgläubig]	SS-Sturmmann: 01.02.1944 - 05.04.1945
STOLZ, Paul	Ewangelickie/ [Evangelisch]	SS-Sturmmann: 17.07.1944 - [15.01.1945]
STÜRMER, Emil	Ewangelickie/ [Evangelisch]	
TESSMER, Heinz	Niewierzący/ [Gottgläubig]	
TETZLAFF, John Albert	Niewierzący/ [Gottgläubig]	SS-Rottenführer: 30.01.1942 - [12.03.1943]
THENN, Emil Martin	Ewangelickie/ [Evangelisch]	SS-Schütze: 15.10.1942 - [15.08.1944]
THIEL, Klemens	Niewierzący/ [Gottgläubig]	SS-Unterscharführer: 27.06.1944
THUN, Erich Bruno Robert		SS-Rottenführer: 30.01.1942 - 01.09.1943; SS-Unterscharführer: 01.09.1943
TISSLER, Alfred Friedrich		SS-Rottenführer: [22.09.1942]; SS-Unterscharführer
TOPOLSKI, Friedrich	Rzymskokatolickie/ [Römisch-katholisch]	SS-Rottenführer: 30.01.1942 - [12.06.1944]
TÖPPER, Otto	Ewangelickie - później: Gottgläubig	SS-Oberscharführer: 01.10.1939; SS-Untersturmführer: 30.01.1942 - [22.10.1944]
TREICHLER, Bruno		SS-Schütze: 29.06.1944 - [31.08.1944]
UKLEY, Bruno	Ewangelickie/ [Evangelisch]	SS-Unterscharführer: 01.02.1942
UMLAND, Alfred		SS-Rottenführer: 09.11.1941 - 01.02.1942; SS-Unterscharführer: 01.02.1942 - 01.09.1943; SS-Oberscharführer: 01.09.1943 - [03.1945]
VOLLMANN, Bruno Willi	Rzymskokatolickie/ [Römisch-katholisch]	SS-Unterscharführer: 23.06.1944 - [28.09.1944]

WAGNER, Emil	Ewangelickie/ [Evangelisch]	SS-Rottenführer: 30.01.1942
WALL, Johannes Richard	Niewierzący/ [Gottgläubig]	SS-Rottenführer: 30.01.1942 - 01.09.1943; Unterscharführer: 01.09.1943 - [27.10.1944]
WALLRATH, Johannes	Rzymskokatolickie/ [Römisch-katholisch]	SS-Rottenführer: 30.01.1942 - [31.12.1943]
WALTER, Friedrich		SS-Rottenführer: 30.01.1942 - [02.02.1943]
WANGLER, Walter	Rzymskokatolickie/ [Römisch-katholisch]	SS-Rottenführer: 30.01.1942 - 01.04.1944; SS-Unterscharführer: 01.04.1944 - 04.04.1945
WANNINGER, Leopold	Rzymskokatolickie/ [Römisch-katholisch]	SS-Sturmmann: 01.07.1944 - 01.01.1945; SS-Rottenführer: 01.01.1945
WANSEL, Hans		SS-Rottenführer: 30.01.1942 - 01.10.1942; SS-Unterscharführer: 01.10.1942 - [11.11.1942]
WANSERSKI, Kurt	Ewangelickie/ [Evangelisch]	SS-Sturmmann: 29.06.1944 - [31.08.1944]
WARMBIER, Rudolf	Rzymskokatolickie/ [Römisch-katholisch]	SS-Rottenführer: 30.01.1942 - [23.10.1943]
WARNER, Kurt	Ewangelickie/ [Evangelisch]	SS-Rottenführer: 30.01.1942 - 01.04.1944; SS-Unterscharführer: 01.04.1944 - [11.12.1944]
WEICHBRODT, Otto Albert Ernst		
WEISNER, Andreas	Niewierzący/ [Gottgläubig]	SS-Rottenführer: 30.01.1942; SS-Unterscharführer: [1943]
WEISS, Franz	Niewierzący/ [Gottgläubig]	SS-Rottenführer: 30.01.1942 - 01.09.1943; SS-Unterscharführer: 01.09.1943 - [28.07.1944]
WERNER, Karl	Ewangelickie/ [Evangelisch]	SS-Rottenführer: 30.01.1942 - 01.05.1944; SS-Unterscharführer: 01.05.1944
WESSEL, Horst	Ewangelickie/ [Evangelisch]	SS-Unterscharführer: 06.07.1944 - [21.02.1945]
WIENHOLDT, Gerhard Hermann Otto	Rzymskokatolickie/ [Römisch-katholisch]	SS-Schütze: 01.11.1941 - 20.04.1942; SS-Sturmmann: 20.04.1942 - 01.08.1942; SS-Rottenführer: 01.08.1942 - [01.11.1944]
WIESNER, August Wilhelm	Ewangelickie/ [Evangelisch]	SS-Rottenführer: 30.01.1942; SS-Unterscharführer: [30.10.1942]
WILHELM, Kurt	Niewierzący/ [Gottgläubig]	SS-Unterscharführer: -1.02.1942 - [26.05.1943]
WILLMS, Gustav		SS-Schütze: 22.07.1944 - 01.01.1945; SS-Sturmmann: 01.01.1945
WISNER, Heinz Günter	Ewangelickie/ [Evangelisch]	SS-Sturmmann: 08.07.1944 - 06.04.1945
WITT, Arthur	Niewierzący/ [Gottgläubig]	SS-Schütze: 06.09.1939 - 20.04.1942; SS-Sturmmann: 20.04.1942 - 01.08.1942; SS-Rottenführer: 01.08.1942
WITT, Willi Paul	Niewierzący/ [Gottgläubig]	

WITTE, Erich	Niewierzący/ [Gottgläubig]	SS-Rottenführer: 30.01.1942 - 01.03.1943; SS-Unterscharführer: 01.03.1943 - [06.01.1945]
WOLF, Johann = adres	Ewangelickie/ [Evangelisch]	SS-Schütze: 01.11.1941 - 30.01.1942; SS-Sturmmann: 30.01.1942 - 01.11.1942; SS-Rottenführer: 01.11.1942
WOLFF, Paul Ernst		SS-Rottenführer: 30.01.1942 - [26.01.1943]
WÖLMS, Hermann	Niewierzący/ [Gottgläubig]	SS-Obsturmführer: 01.11.1941 - 30.01.1944; SS-Hauptsturmführer: 30.01.1944 - [23.05.1944]
WÖLMS, Willi		SS-Schütze: [15.08.1942 - 04.08.1941]; SS-Sturmmann: [20.04.1943]; SS-Rottenführer: [15.03.1944]
WORM, Arthur Eduard	Niewierzący/ [Gottgläubig]	SS-Rottenführer: 30.01.1942 - 01.05.1943; SS-Unterscharführer: 01.05.1943 - [08.09.1944]
WROBEL, Johannes Alfons	Ewangelickie/ [Evangelisch]	SS-Rottenführer: 30.01.1942; SS-Unterscharführer: [20.08.1943 - 08.01.1945]
WULF, Ernst	Niewierzący/ [Gottgläubig]	SS-Rottenführer: 30.01.1942
ZIEHM, Hugo Hermann	Niewierzący/ [Gottgläubig]	SS-Unterscharführer: 01.02.1942 - 01.02.1943; SS-Oberscharführer: 01.02.1943
ZIELINSKI, Johann		SS-Rottenführer - do: 01.09.1943; SS-Unterscharführer: 01.09.1943 - [15.08.1944]
ZIEMANN, Bruno		SS-Rottenführer: 30.01.1942 - [21.09.1942]; SS-Unterscharführer
ZIEMENS, Gustav	Ewangelickie/ [Evangelisch]	SS-Unterscharführer - do: 01.05.1944; SS-Oberscharführer: 01.05.1944
ZUBE, Kurt	Rzymskokatolickie/ [Römisch-katholisch]	SS-Sturmmann: 24.10.1944 – [02.12.1944]
ZWINGMANN, Franz	Niewierzący/ [Gottgläubig]	SS-Schütze: 01.11.1941; SS-Rottenführer: 30.01.1942 - 01.10.1943; SS-Unterscharführer: 01.10.1943 – [09.12.1943]

Figure 12 List of Guards with Danzig Connections.

Name	Birthdate	Occupation	Education	Date Joining the NSDAP	Date Joining the Allgemeine SS	Regiment Allgemeine SS
ADRIAN, Paul	1904/07/11	Brygadzista/ malarz pokojowy [Betriebaufseher/Male]	Volksschule	10/03/1933	10/03/1933	036. SS-Standarte III Sturmbann - Danzig
AKOLT, Richard	1901/10/05	Urzędnik kupiecki [Kaufmännischer Angestellter]		01/05/1936		
ALBRECHT, Johannes	1918/08/06	Robotnik rolny [Landarbeiter]		01/05/1936	01/01/1933	071. SS-Standarte 12. Sturm - Zoppot/ Danzig
ALLAUT, Andreas	1906/01/04	Urzędnik [Angestellter]		01/05/1933	20/07/1933	007. Kavallerie 7. SS-Standarte - Hamburg
ANKER, Paul	1906/12/04	Rzeźnik [Fleischer]	4 Klassen Volksschule	01/06/1936		120. SS-Standarte - Kulm
ARNOLD, Otto Bruno Arthur	1914/04/10					
BANSEMER, Rudolf	1896-10-12	Urzędnik biurowy [Büroangestellter]	Volksschule	01/05/1936		001. SS-Reiterstandarte 16. Kavallerie - Insterburg
BASE, Paul	1911/07/09	Zdun [Ofensetzer]		01/05/1938	15/12/1933	036. SS-Standarte 12. Sturm - Danzig
BAUMANN, Herbert	1915/01/17	Robotnik rolny [Landarbeiter]		01/05/1933	01/05/1933	

Name	Birth date	Occupation			Unit
BECK, Willi	1899-09-09				
BECKER, Heinrich	1902/11/12	Magazynier [Lagerist]			036. SS-Standarte - Danzig
BECKER, Hermann	1906/09/22	Stolarz [Zimmerer]	01/05/1936	09/03/1934	001. SS-Reiterstandarte 16. Kavallerie - Insterburg
BEHNKE, Helmut	1912/10/23	Urzędnik rolny [Landwirtschaftlicher Beamter]	20/04/1933	20/04/1933	071. SS-Standarte 6. Sturm - Zoppot/Danzig
BIERNATH, Johann	1909/04/14	Stolarz [Tischler]	01/06/1936	01/01/1934	071. SS-Standarte 1. Sturm - Zoppot/Danzig
BLUMENAU, Willi	1911/04/03	Stolarz [Tischler]	01/05/1936	30/06/1933	001. SS-Reiterstandarte 16. Kavallerie - Insterburg
BÖHM, Ernst	1909/12/19	Malarz pokojowy [Maler]	01/05/1933		071. SS-Standarte 11. Sturm - Zoppot/Danzig
BÖHM, Karl	1908/04/17	Policjant [Polizist]	01/05/1933	12/03/1933	SS-Oberabschnitt "Weichsel" XX: [22.02.1941]
BOLHAGEN, Kurt	1909/02/07				
BONIN von, Engelbert	1906/11/10	Murarz [Maurer]			071. SS-Standarte 11. Sturm - Zoppot/Danzig

Name	Born	Occupation	Education	Date	Unit
BUNTROCK, Karl	1907/08/03	Urzędnik kupiecki [Kaufmännischer Angestellter]		01/02/1933	07/06/1932	071. SS-Standarte 2. Sturm - Zoppot/ Danzig
BÜRGER, Richard Emil	1905/12/12	Pomocnik w kotłowni [Heizungsgehilfe]		01/01/1937	17/03/1935	036. SS-Standarte 5. Sturm - Danzig
CHILL, William	1910/01/06	Urzędnik kupiecki [Kaufmännischer Angestellter]		01/05/1936	15/04/1934	XXVI Abschnitt SS-Sanitätsabteilung - Danzig
CZAJKOWSKI, Alfons	1902/09/18	Robotnik [Fabrikarbeiter]	Volksschule	01/05/1936		036. SS-Standarte 9. Sturm - Danzig
DAU, Hans	1914/11/16			01/12/1939		
DIETERT, Hans	1917/05/18	Robotnik [Arbeiter]			04/07/1937	
DIETRICH, Kurt	1898-09-20					
DIRKS, Walter	1906/10/03	Listonosz [Briefträger]		01/10/1932	01/10/1932	036. SS-Standarte 10. Sturm - Danzig
DITTMANN, Alfred	1901/10/25	Urzędnik kupiecki [Kaufmännischer Angestellter]		01/05/1936	01/07/1934	036. SS-Standarte 1. Reservesturm - Danzig
DOBERT, August	1892-12-13	Kupiec [Kaufmann]	1 Kl. Vsch; 1 Kl. Fachsch; 3 Kl. Höhschule	01/05/1933	08/06/1933	036. SS-Standarte - Danzig: 08.06.1933; 036. SS-Standarte/ Fürsorgereferat: 30.01.1941
DOERKS, Eberhard	1900/10/08	Podmajstrzy murarski [Maurerpolier]		01/03/1933	01/03/1933	XXVI Abschnitt SS-Sanitäts-Staffel - Danzig
DOMBERG, Walter	1912/06/27					
DUHNKE, Willy	1909/03/04	Ślusarz maszynowy [Maschinenschlosser]		01/05/1936		071. SS-Standarte

Name	Birthdate	Occupation	Education	Year Joined Nazi Party	Year Joined SS
EHLE, Paul Rudolf	1909/04/29	Cieśla [Zimmerer]		01/05/1936	01/05/1933	117. SS-Standarte - Konitz
EHLING, Hermann	1922/12/31	Robotnik [Arbeiter]			
EICHLER, Andreas	1906/04/09	Elektryk [Elektriker]		01/05/1936	01/09/1933
EICHLER, August	1906/10/09	Malarz pokojowy [Maler]		01/07/1936	01/06/1933
ELSDORFF, Herbert	1897-06-22				
ELTERMANN, Johann	1905/08/30	Ślusarz [Schlosser]		01/05/1933	15/04/1933
ENGLER, Fritz	1919/11/16				15/02/1938
ENGLER, Herbert	1913/07/27				
ENSS, Heinrich	1915/12/16	Rzeźnik [Fleischer]			
FALK, Felix	1897-10-22	Rolnik [Bauer]	Volksschule		15/03/1933
FAST, Wilhelm	1910/04/26				
FIGUR, Walter	1902/01/28	Dróżnik [Strassenwärter]		01/05/1936	15/07/1933
FOTH, Ewald Paul	1912/07/13	Cieśla [Zimmerer]		01/05/1933	15/07/1933
FRIEDLAND, Ernst	1911/04/12	Zegarmistrz [Uhrmacher]		18/01/1932	18/01/1932
FULLE, Hubert	1907/12/31	Robotnik [Arbeiter]		01/05/1933	01/05/1933
GALLANDT, Walter	1907/10/02	Cieśla [Zimmermann]			
GISELLA, Josef	1906/05/13	Robotnik [Arbeiter]			
GLASS, Alfons Richard Friedrich	1907/03/02				

Includes Names, Birthdate, Occupation, Education, Year Joined the Nazi Party, and Year Joined SS.

Figure 13 Local Guards who had served in the Regular German Army including service in the First World War.

Name	Rank	Previous Service
AKOLT, Richard	SS-Oberscharführer 01.02.1942 - 01.09.1943; SS-Hauptscharführer: 01.09.1943	Altes Heer: 15.09.1915 - 09.11.1918/I wojna światowa
LASCHEIT, Emil Fritz	SS-Schütze: 30.03.1942 - 16.02.1943; SS-Sturmmann: 16.02.1943 - 01.04.1944; SS-Rottenführer: 01.04.1944 - [04.04.1945]	Altes Heer: 1917 – 1919
BONIN von, Engelbert	SS-Untersturmführer: 01.11.1941 - 21.06.1942; SS-Obersturmführer: 21.06.1942 - 09.11.1944; SS-Hauptsturmführer: 09.11.1944 - [11.12.1944]	Altes Heer: 08.08.1914 - 30.09.1919/W tym: Fusilier-Artillerieregiment 17 - Obergefreiter/ Zahlmeisterstellvertreter; Flieger-Abteilung 236/ Unteroffizier - Leiter der Kassenverwaltung: 11.1916 - 05.1917
BUNTROCK, Karl		Altes Heer: 1916 – 1918
GLASS, Alfons Richard Friedrich	SS-Oberscharführer: 01.02.1942 - 01.09.1943; SS-Hauptscharführer: 01.09.1943 - [15.10.1944]	Altes Heer: 15.09.1915 - 03.05.1919 - w tym: - Infanterie-Regiment - Thorn; Dnziger-Infanterie-Regiment 128/Westfeldzug - Gefreiter
SCHÖNROCK, Paul	SS-Rottenführer: 22.07.1944 - [31.08.1944]	Altes Heer: 01.12.1917 - 11.02.1922
GÖRSCH, Martin Johann	SS-Sturmmann: 18.07.1944 - [20.11.1944]	Altes Heer: 02.10.1913 - 15.11.1918/Kavallerie-Dreagonen- und Ulanen - Soldat
KROPP, Helmut	SS-Sturmmann: 15.10.1943 - [6.06.1944]	Altes Heer/Schütze: 04.09.1917 - 31.03.1920
KUNKEL, Paul Robert	SS-Schütze: 27.06.1944 - 01.01.1945; SS-Sturmmann: 01.01.1945	Altes Heer: 05.05.1915 - 01.01.1917
HAUPT, Otto	SS-Oberscharführer: 01.02.1942	Altes Heer: 13.06.1915 - 18.08.1917
ICHNOWSKI, Eugen	SS-Schütze: 22.07.1944 - [22.08.1944]	Altes Heer: 10.09.1914 - 11.1919
KÖRBER, Albert Martin	SS-Schütze: 17.09.1944 - 04.10.1944; SS-Sturmmann: 04.10.1944 - [14.11.1944]	Altes Heer: 1913 - 11.1918
KUSCHEL, Rudolf Georg	SS-Schütze: 15.10.1942 - 01.09.1943; SS-Sturmmann: 01.09.1943 - 01.01.1945; SS-Rottenführer: 01.01.1945	Altes Heer: 17.06.1919 - 31.05.1920 †

MÖWE, Johann	SS-Rottenführer: 30.01.1942 - 01.09.1943; SS-Unterscharführer: 01.09.1943 - [03.09.1944]	Altes Heer: 28.06.1918 - 10.07.1919
MÜLLER, Leonhard	SS-Oberscharführer: 28.06.1944	Altes Heer: 17.01.1915 - 17.12.1918
MÜLLER, Bernhard Karl	SS-Oberscharführer: 29.06.1944 - [31.08.1944]	Altes Heer: 17.01.1915 - 17.12.1918
MURNER, Robert Ewald Anton	SS-Rottenführer: 09.11.1941 - 01.02.1942; SS-Unterscharführer: 01.02.1942 - 01.09.1943; SS-Oberscharführer: 01.09.1943 - [04.04.1945]	Altes Heer: 14.09.1918 - 18.12.1918
ORTMANN, Walter Johannes	SS-Rottenführer: 30.01.1942 - 01.11.1943; SS-Unterscharführer: 01.11.1943 - [14.11.1944]	Altes Heer: 14.09.1918 - 06.12.1918
PLATZ, Arthur	SS-Rottenführer: 09.11.1941 - 01.10.1942; SS-Unterscharführer: 01.10.1942	Altes Heer
ROSENKRANZ, Friedrich Andreas	SS-Rottenführer: 01.01.1945	Altes Heer: 1910 – 1912
STABENAU, Otto	SS-Rottenführer: 30.01.1942 - 01.10.1942; SS-Unterscharführer: 01.10.1942 - [02.03.1944]	Altes Heer: 1918
TETZLAFF, John Albert		Altes Heer: 31.07.1917 - 01.11.1918
THUN, Erich Bruno Robert	SS-Untersturmführer und Kriminal-Sekretär: 20.04.1940 - 04.04.1945	Altes Heer: 10.08.1914 - 29.04.1915/Infanterieregiment 128. und Infanterieregiment 129. - Schütze
TISSLER, Alfred Friedrich	SS-Sturmmann: 01.02.1944 - 05.04.1945	Altes Heer: 15.02.1915 - 13.12.1918
WALTER, Friedrich	SS-Oberscharführer: 01.10.1939; SS-Untersturmführer: 30.01.1942 - [22.10.1944]	Altes Heer: 11.10.1913 - 10.09.1913/Jäger-Bataillon 2 oraz 03.08.1914 - 27.09.1918/ Jäger-Bataillon 2
WERNER, Karl	SS-Sturmmann: 01.07.1944 - 01.01.1945; SS-Rottenführer: 01.01.1945	Altes Heer: 01.08.1914 - 20.12.1918
ZIELINSKI, Johann		Altes Heer: 05.12.1915 – 1917
ZIEMANN, Bruno	SS-Rottenführer: 30.01.1942 - 01.03.1943; SS-Unterscharführer: 01.03.1943 - [06.01.1945]	Altes Heer: 01.04.1915 - 12.1919

† Based on service dates, served in the Wehrmacht, but may not have served in the First World War.

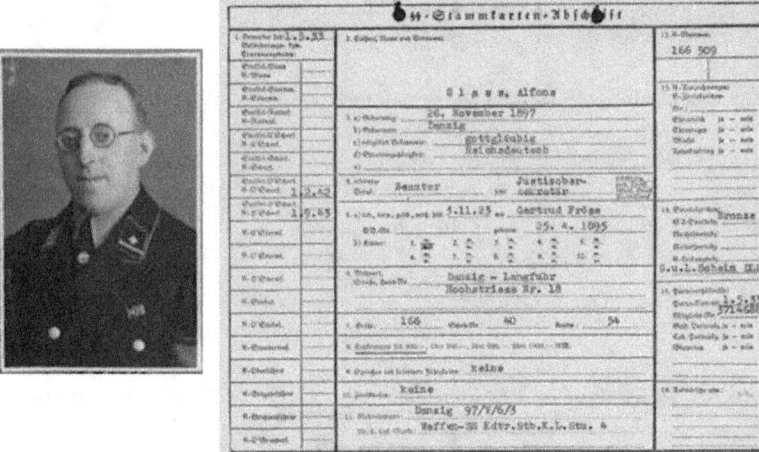
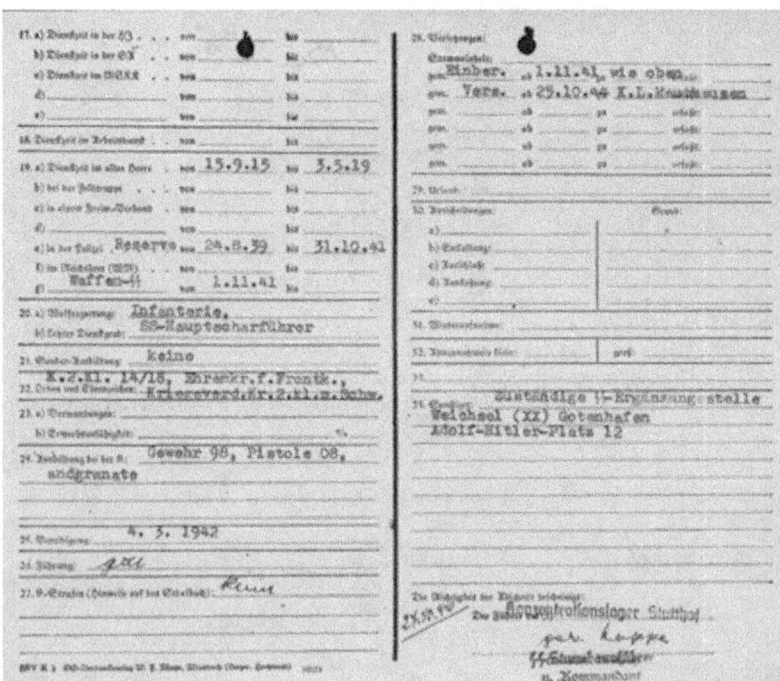

Figure 14 Sample Personnel Card.

Personnel card formats changed over the five year history of Stutthof. This is a sample of the later card format, from a veteran of the First World War. Image courtesy Muzeum Stutthof w Sztutowie.

Figure 15 Map of Occupied Poland, including Danzig-West Prussia.

Areas included in the Danzig West Prussia Gau, 1939–45, including acquisitions
Image courtesy the USHMM. Used by permission.

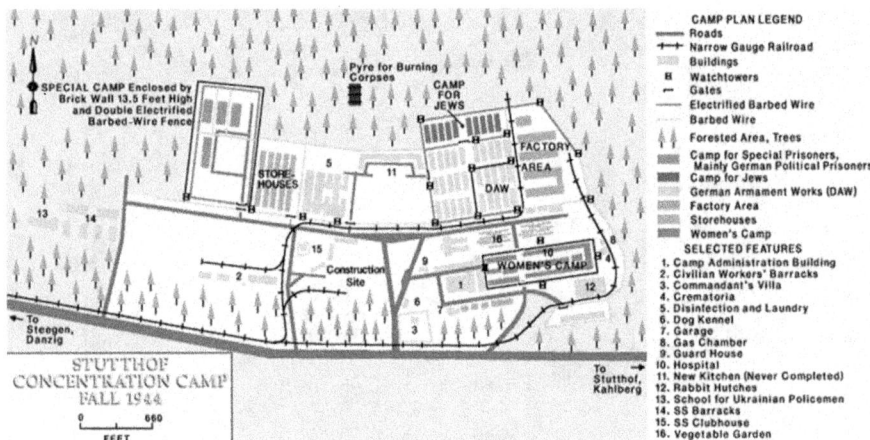

Figure 16 Map of the Stutthof Camp, 1944.

Map of the layout of the camp in 1944.
Image courtesy the USHMM. Used by permission.

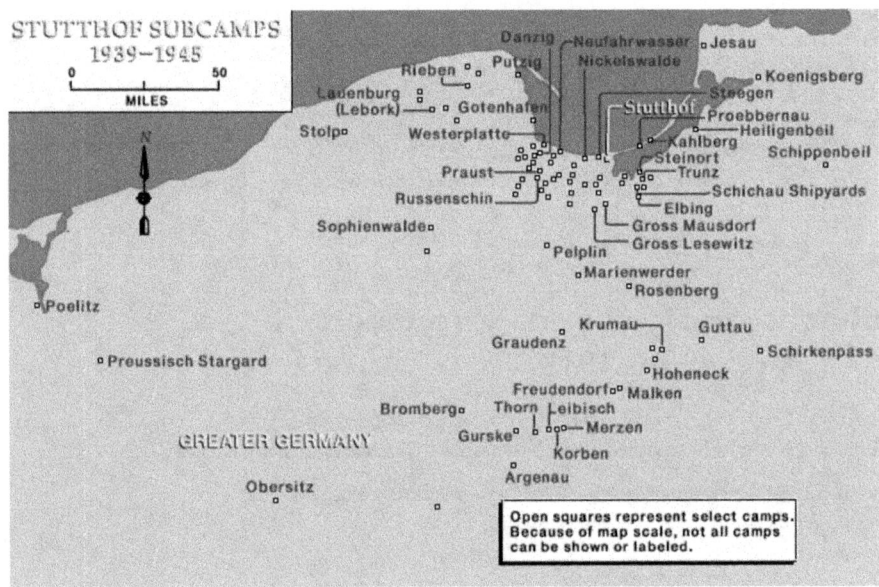

Figure 17 Map of Stutthof Subcamps.

Partial map of Stutthof sub-camps, which may have numbered as many as 210.
Image courtesy of the USHMM. Used by permission.

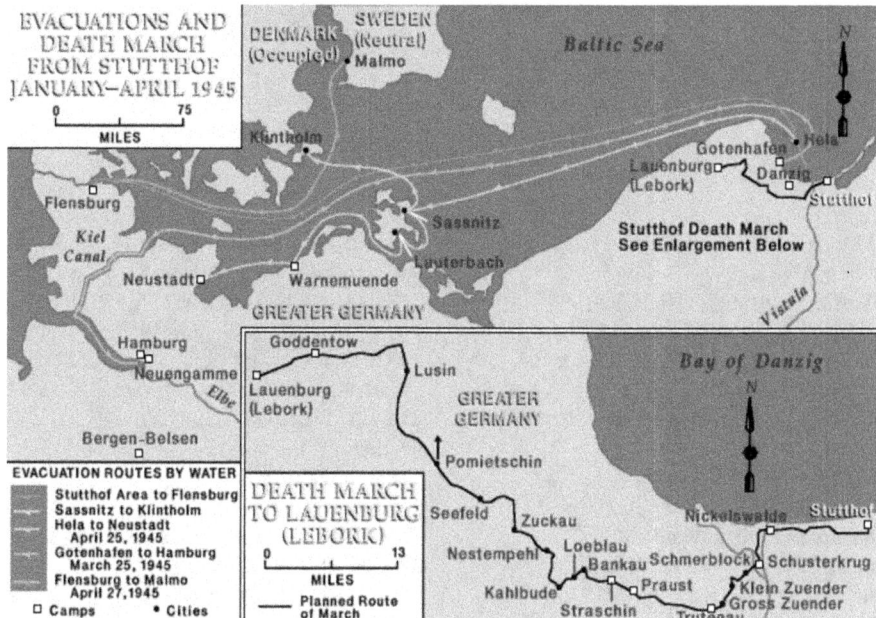

Figure 18 Evacuation routes from the camp, 1945.

Evacuation routes from the Stutthof camp system used between January and April 1945.
Image courtesy of the USHMM. Used by permission.

Index

Aktion T4 *See "Euthanasia Program"*
Allen, Michael 59, 78, 95, 106, 107
Amt D xi, 79, 109, 110, 166, 199
Armia Krajowa (AK) xi, 115, 116, 193
Auschwitz 8, 9, 60, 72, 78, 81, 83, 108, 109, 111, 118, 121, 122, 123, 126, 129, 162, 167, 171, 178, 181

Babi Yar 80
Badziąg, Kazimierz 72, 73, 189
Barkman, Jenny Wanda 177
Bełżec 9
Bergen, Doris 21, 25, 26, 27, 39, 93, 98, 187
Bergen-Belsen 118, 148
Birkenau 110, 118, 126, 182
Blatman, Daniel 157, 167, 207
Bonhoeffer, Dietrich 25, 93, 95
Boy Scouts/Grey Ranks 49, 72, 73
Brown Shirts *See* "Storm Troopers"
Browning, Christopher 97, 109, 197, 199, 211
Buchenwald 2, 76, 82, 84, 86, 97, 114, 201

Central Agency for Relocation (Umwandererzentralstelle) xv, 58, 74
Chełmno/ Kulmhof 50, 69, 71, 80, 81
Church Struggle (der Kirchenkampf) 25, 28
Chwin, Stefan 179, 180, 181
Clark, Elizabeth Morrow 15, 39
Confessing church (die bekennende Kirche) 25, 26, 52, 93, 96, 98, 173
Connelly, John 59
Coradello, Aldo 128, 129

Dachau 2, 18, 56, 60, 61, 62, 83, 89, 92, 100, 121, 130, 178, 201

Danzig-West Prussia 46, 47, 49, 51, 57, 68, 71, 72, 77, 78, 80, 81, 82, 84, 111, 139, 143, 151, 176, 183, 184, 189, 210, 244
DAW xi, 89, 91, 107, 111, 114, 143, 211
Death squads (Einsatzgruppen) 52, 80, 99
Dębski, Tadeusz 98, 108, 128
Demski, Władysław 64
DESt xi, 91, 111
Dora 106
Douglas, R. M. 168, 190, 191, 210
Drywa, Danuta 52, 69, 90, 109, 118, 119, 178, 190, 191, 199
DVL 57, 58, 59, 60, 73, 74, 105, 186
Dwork, Debórah and van Pelt, Robert Jan 77, 96, 141

East Prussia 42, 49, 81, 111, 123, 133, 143, 145, 146, 150, 151, 155, 157, 159, 163, 164, 165, 168, 172, 173, 183, 184, 207, 209, 211
Eicke, Theodor 83, 85, 92, 95, 106
Ethnic German Liaison Office (Volksdeutsche Mittelstelle or VoMi) xv, 57
Ethnic Germans (Volksdeutsche) 57, 105, 161, 191
Euthanasia program 80, 81, 90, 103
Evacuations 10, 104, 129, 143, 144, 145, 147, 148, 149, 150, 151, 153, 155, 156, 157, 158, 159, 164, 165, 166, 167, 172, 174, 179, 210, 211, 247
Evans, Richard, 104, 197

Fall Eva 143
Final solution 109, 110, 137, 138, 167, 178
Flossenbürg 86, 91, 106, 196
Forster, Albert 2, 13, 14, 15, 16, 17, 18, 19, 20, 21, 22, 23, 26, 27, 28, 29, 31, 32, 33, 34, 37, 40, 41, 42, 43, 44, 49,

51, 56, 57, 58, 59, 70, 78, 80, 83, 98, 108, 143, 152, 169, 176, 180
Free church/churches 27, 28, 70, 72, 96, 112
Führer principle (Führerprinzip) 95

Gas chambers 81, 90, 110, 111, 120, 131, 135
Gdynia 9, 15, 16, 38, 40, 49, 52, 56, 57, 58, 149, 150, 154, 156, 172
General Government (Generalgouvernement) xii, 9, 23, 51, 52, 57, 71, 74, 80, 183
German Christians xi, 25, 26, 27, 93, 98, 186
Germandom 1, 3, 4, 5, 13, 15, 16, 17, 21, 22, 23, 27, 31, 37, 44, 46, 47, 49, 50, 52, 55, 58, 68, 69, 71, 73, 75, 77, 78, 79, 80, 81, 94, 95, 98, 106, 107, 112, 113, 114, 141, 169, 176, 181
Gestapo xii, 30, 37, 39, 49, 52, 63, 64, 65, 70, 72, 76, 79, 81, 82, 84, 86, 94, 104, 106, 112, 117, 149, 166, 174, 186, 201
Glücks, Richard 78, 79, 83, 110, 118, 137
Goebbels, Joseph 15, 16, 22, 37, 44
Göring, Hermann 13, 16, 19, 54
Gottgläubig xii, 56, 93, 94, 97, 103, 152
Grabowska-Chałka, Janina 41, 48, 117, 134, 191, 200, 201, 211
Grass, Günter 1, 4, 5, 6, 7, 8, 12, 15, 17, 18, 19, 24, 25, 28, 29, 30, 31, 32, 45, 52, 60, 72, 75, 77, 112, 132, 139, 140, 151, 169, 171, 178, 179, 180, 181
    Crabwalk (Im Krebsgang) 6, 132, 171, 172
    Danzig trilogy 1, 6, 30, 31, 180, 183
        Cat and Mouse (Katz und Maus) 17, 29, 30
        Dog Years (Hundejahre) 6, 7, 8, 12, 17, 18, 19, 29, 30, 31, 48, 171
        The Tin Drum (Die Blechtrommel) 6, 23, 32, 60
    Peeling the Onion (Beim Häuten der Zwiebel) 7, 17, 30, 60, 171, 183, 184, 185, 187
Greiser, Arthur 19, 20, 22, 26, 32, 58, 59, 80, 178, 180

Grot, Elżbieta 63, 64, 84, 144, 149, 153, 154, 192
Güzlow, Gerhard 70
Górecki, Marian 63

Heidl, Otto 90, 103, 110, 119, 120
Heydrich, Reinhard 49, 57, 58, 79, 183
Himmler, Heinrich 2, 13, 19, 33, 37, 42, 49, 52, 57, 58, 59, 68, 78, 79, 81, 82, 84, 86, 92, 93, 94, 95, 97, 98, 99, 100, 105, 109, 113, 137, 141, 152, 210
Hitler, Adolf / Führer 5, 16, 31, 33, 34, 35, 42, 43, 51, 54, 60, 92, 93, 94, 95, 97, 111, 112, 137, 140, 158, 161, 173
Hitler myth 44
Hoppe, Paul-Werner 83, 86, 110, 115, 119, 128, 137, 138, 140, 143, 151, 154, 156, 166, 195
Höss, Rudolf 110, 118
Huelle, Paweł 179, 180

Inspektion der Konzentrationslager (IKL) xii, 69, 78, 79, 92, 151, 199

Jehovah's Witnesses 72, 82, 116, 130, 159, 203
Juden und Pfaffen 4, 46, 49, 60, 61, 72, 108, 178

Kapos 85, 91, 92, 101, 105, 107, 116, 134, 136, 141, 160, 177
Kashubians 1, 23, 25, 28, 31, 34, 37, 51, 58, 60, 67, 76, 102, 157, 164, 174, 180
Katzmann, Fritz 108, 144, 152, 166, 199, 209
Kempowski, Walter 131, 132
Kershaw, Ian 20, 21, 39, 44, 112, 211
Kith and kin 112
Koehl, Robert 3, 57, 73, 82, 176
Komorowski, Bronisław 64
Kristallnacht xiii, 22, 23, 24, 26, 27, 44, 96
Kubista, Stanisław 65
Kwiatkowski, Grzegorz 181
Kwiatkowski, Piotr 116

League of German Girls (Bund Deutscher Mädel) 131
Lebensraum 38, 39, 59, 60, 169
Lester, Seán 19, 29, 33, 181, 185
Lithuanians 3, 11, 37, 38, 85, 86, 102, 105, 108, 117, 122, 124, 141, 146, 150, 207, 212
Longerich, Peter 94, 95
Lower, Wendy 197, 202
Lübeck 13, 143, 150, 151, 154, 162

Majdanek 8, 9, 78, 81, 178
Malak, Henryk Maria 54, 61, 62, 66, 77
Mauthausen 82, 86, 91, 106, 107, 111, 117, 118, 121, 201
Meyer, Teodor 86, 90, 100, 101, 110, 118, 120, 128, 134, 135, 136, 144, 145, 146, 151
Military task forces (Einsatzkommandos) 99
Moeller, Robert 171, 172, 173, 174, 179
Montague, Patrick 81
Muselmänner 89

Neuengamme 91, 100, 103, 118, 143, 149, 150, 154, 156, 195, 201, 211
Nobel Prize 4, 179
NSDAP 13, 15, 16, 17, 20, 187
Nuremberg Laws 18, 20, 23, 27

Operation Barbarossa 80
Operation Reinhard 9, 183
Operation Tannenberg 37
Operation Thunderstorm 111
Orski, Marek 53, 108, 123, 136, 137, 150, 211, 212
Orth, Karin 98, 138, 212

Pauly, Max 38, 48, 53, 56, 68, 74, 83, 95, 138, 209
People's Community (Volksgemeinschaft) 93, 94, 197
Pohl, Oswald 78, 79, 83, 95, 121, 195, 197, 199
Polish Corridor 1, 2, 4, 28, 33, 34, 42, 43, 46, 49, 59, 70, 75, 77, 82, 99, 157, 163, 164, 169, 170, 182
Pomerania 27, 34, 36, 37, 41, 45, 47, 50, 51, 52, 58, 61, 62, 63, 65, 69, 72, 74, 77, 78, 80, 93, 96, 97, 111, 115, 131, 132, 143, 150, 155, 176, 178, 210
Posen/Poznań 49, 58, 63, 99, 141, 178
Post-war trials 2, 51, 58, 96, 100, 105, 110, 133, 136, 137, 211
PZbWP xiv, 8

Rauschning, Hermann 16, 32, 180
Ravensbrück 100, 111, 118, 125, 176, 201
Reich Security Main Office / RSHA (Reichssicherheitshauptamt) 37, 49, 79
Reich's Commission for the Reinforcement of Germandom / RKFDV (Reichskommissariat für die Festigung deutschen Volkstums) xiv, 49
Roma/Sinti 49, 50, 58, 77
Royal Air Force (RAF) 154, 155, 205, 207

SA/Storm Troopers (Sturmabteilung) xiv, 13, 188
Sachsenhausen 60, 61, 63, 64, 65, 97, 111, 118, 120, 131, 162, 196, 201
Scandinavians 107, 114, 144, 149, 152, 153, 156
Schenk, Dieter 21, 39, 58, 72, 185
Segev, Tom 138, 166, 167
Selbstschutz xv, 50, 51, 52, 73, 74, 77, 190
Sicherheitsdienst xv, 37, 58
Snyder, Timothy 99, 100
Sobibor 9
Sofsky, Wolfgang 84, 85
Sruoga, Balys 85, 86, 87, 88, 100, 101, 102, 103, 104, 105, 118, 120, 121, 131, 135, 137, 138, 140, 198, 203, 205, 212
Standardization measures (Gleichschaltung) 20, 95, 98
Stutthof Sub-camps
  Bromberg/Bydgoszcz 49, 50, 52, 65, 82, 86, 122, 123, 125, 148, 160, 161, 210
  Brusy/Bruss 115, 122, 130, 148
  Chojnice/Konitz 73
  Chorab 148
  Dirschau/Tczew 50, 51, 73
  Elbing/Elbląg 49, 56, 57, 91, 94, 103, 122, 123, 125, 143, 147, 148, 162

Gans/Gęś 145, 146
Gdynia/Gotenhafen 56, 57, 58, 149, 150, 154, 156, 172
Grodno/Garten 147
Grudziądz/Graudenz 49, 50, 55
Gutowo/Guttendorf 147, 167
Karthaus/Kartuzy 50, 69
Königsberg 30, 82, 120, 121, 122, 123, 144, 147, 173
Korben 124
Koźliny 50
Neustadt/Wejherowo 50, 146, 153, 158
Pölitz 122
Praust-Kochstedt 122, 123, 129, 148
Putzig/Puck 50, 146, 148, 149
Rusocin/Russoschin 122, 123
Schichau 122
Schöneck/Skarszewy 50
Skurz/Skórcz 50
Stargard/Stargard 50
Stolp/Słupsk 108, 121, 122, 158, 210
Thorn/Toruń 17, 49, 61, 64, 65, 73, 74, 94, 122, 131, 132, 147, 161
Szmalcówka 73, 74

Theresienstadt 72, 109, 126, 129
Todt Organization 60, 122, 123, 161

Treaty of Versailles 1, 3, 13, 14, 15, 22, 28, 38, 42, 44, 77, 95, 183, 210
Treblinka 9
Typhus 48, 83, 90, 111, 113, 114, 119, 123, 125, 135, 139, 140, 145, 146, 148, 150, 152, 153, 154, 156, 158, 160, 167

von Lehndorff, Graf Hans 173, 174
von Ribbentrop, Joachim 39, 42, 43, 44, 189
von Stauffenberg, Count Claus 112, 113

Wachsmann, Nikolaus 84, 85, 86, 98, 99, 106, 132, 136, 195, 196, 197, 212
Waffen SS 5, 6, 7, 12, 24, 169, 171, 188
Wałęsa, Lech 39, 179
Warsaw 9, 56, 65, 84, 108, 176, 183
Warsaw Uprising 115, 220, 228
Wąs, Marek 20, 139, 140, 165, 166, 167, 176
Wehrmacht 41, 58, 60, 69, 107, 124, 129, 145, 146, 151, 155, 168, 242
WVHA xvi, 79, 106, 110, 115, 118, 199

Yla, Stasys 85, 86, 99, 100, 101, 102, 110, 122, 137, 146, 157

Zyklon B 81, 90, 110, 120, 131, 135

www.ingramcontent.com/pod-product-compliance
Lightning Source LLC
Chambersburg PA
CBHW062126300426
44115CB00012BA/1825